Fifth Edition

# Portrait of a Family

## Telecourse Guide

By:

**IN·TELE·COM**
INTELLIGENT TELECOMMUNICATIONS

Authors:
Vicki L. Spandel
Michael D. Hiscox
Interwest Applied Research

with contributions from:
Lynn Darroch
Jeff Kuechle
David Milholland

**Wadsworth**
Thomson Learning™

Australia · Canada · Denmark · Japan · Mexico · New Zealand · Philippines
Puerto Rico · Singapore · South Africa · Spain · United Kingdom · United States

Acknowledgements:

Bulcroft, Kris and O'Conner-Roden, Margaret, "Never Too Late." Copyright © 1986 by *Psychology Today* Magazine. Reprinted by permission. All rights reserved.

Cantor, Marjorie H., Ph.D., "Families: A Basic Source of Long-Term Care for the Elderly." Copyright © 1985 by *Aging* Magazine. Reprinted by permission. All rights reserved.

Horn, Jack C. and Meer, Jeff, "The Vintage Years." Copyright © 1987 by *Psychology Today* Magazine. Reprinted by permission. All rights reserved.

Rice, Berkeley, "Let's Put the PARENT Back in Grandparent." Copyright © 1986 by *50 Plus* Magazine and the author. Reprinted with permission. All rights reserved.

Wadsworth is a division of Thomson Learning.
Thomson Learning is a trademark used herein under license.

Printed in the United States of America
1  2  3  4  5  6  7  03  02  01  00  99

ISBN 0-534-52516-4

# Contents

# About This Telecourse Guide
## Student Guidelines

A telecourse guide is a special kind of document. As its name implies, it literally guides you through a course, helping you to focus your thinking, identifying key ideas, and monitor progress. A telecourse guide that can accomplish these things increases the value of the course; it is much like having a private tutor, but without the expense and logistical difficulties that would involve.

In addition, a telecourse guide must establish a certain context for learning so that the materials which follow will be more effective. Research on learning indicates that students tend to learn more and feel they get more out of a course when their higher level thinking skills are tapped. Without this element, a course can become a tedious and ineffective memorization of data, which is not conducive to long-term educational benefits, nor to the higher purpose of teaching students to think for themselves.

In establishing this context, several options are available. One is to introduce new material in a way that helps you establish a kind of mental network, to make connections with your own experience and with other previous learning. Without this connection, newly introduced material may seem irrelevant, or even incomprehensible. Research has shown that we all learn by integrating new information with our previous experiences. The overview within each telecourse guide lesson is intended to establish a basis for forming this network. It highlights key elements or themes from the text, but does so in a way that shows how the material introduced has relevance for each individual student's life.

Further, we tend to learn material best when we see a purpose to that learning. Part of the function of the overview is to demonstrate why you should care about pursuing the subject any further. A good overview will provide the message that "This is important material. It has implications for your life, for the way you think, for the decisions that will shape the person you are continually becoming."

The function of the objectives is to identify the purpose of *Portrait of a Family* as a course of instruction. Through the objectives, you will see what you're supposed to learn or focus on. However, the deeper purpose of the course is to encourage the same kind of networking and higher thinking that provides a context for the course in the first place. In other words, what we want you to ask is, "How can I apply this to my life or to new experiences? How can I use this information in making intelligent decisions?"

We believe that the *Portrait of a Family* telecourse guide helps you answer these questions through a series of increasingly demanding activities:

❑ The overview sets the stage and heightens interest in the material.

❑ The objectives establish a structure for learning, suggesting what elements of the course require particular attention.

❑ The key terms alert you to the important concepts covered in the lesson.

❑ The assignments section provides reading assignments in the text and shows you how to proceed with learning activities.

❑ The video viewing questions lay out some key questions that will be answered during the video program.

❑ The self-test shows what progress you have made in assimilating the material and beginning to apply it.

❑ The decision questions ask you to apply concepts, integrate ideas, make choices, synthesize, and evaluate.

Once all these activities have been completed, you should be well on your way to integrating the new learning. The test items from the examination bank, while challenging, should also provide some confirmation of learning that has already occurred.

# Family Portraits

## A New Look at a Familiar World

We live in a changing society. That's no surprise. What is surprising, though, is the speed with which changes are occurring. And for many of us, that speed produces a certain amount of tension. We wonder whether we'll change rapidly enough to keep pace with the unfolding world about us; whether, in fact, we ought to be changing at all or clinging to old values and traditions.

With lifestyles, values, and traditions in flux, it is easy to feel out of synch, to question our society and sometimes ourselves. Are we making the right choices—living as we should, according to what society expects or accepts?

Many of us spend a large part of our lives trying to create some balance between what we personally want out of life, and what we believe to be appropriate or acceptable, given the perceived values of our family or society. The questioning of values or traditions that we've been taught are correct or appropriate is difficult at best—sometimes painful.

It might be comforting, therefore, if each of us went through this questioning process just once, and then made the decisions that would govern how the rest of our lives would run. Unfortunately, that is not at all how it works. The questioning of values and goals is a lifelong process.

Even those of us who reach a decision with which we seem momentarily satisfied—the decision to marry, for example—can expect to question that decision, or to ask how things might have been different had we taken another path. Such constant reevaluation is quite natural, even among people who have made careful, well-thought-out choices in their

**Overview**

1

lives. And if the reevaluation seems to point you in another direction, that isn't necessarily because your first decision was a poor one. Quite likely you have changed. Your circumstances and your values have changed. No longer do most of us think that true-for-now means true forever.

Some people see this kind of flux as signaling the disintegration of social structures. How can we hope to have any values, they protest, if we are constantly digging away at the foundations of what few traditions still remain? For others, the prospect of change in any form is stressful. They cling to what is familiar not so much because they value their current lifestyle but because they fear the unknown. What's familiar feels comfortable. And for most of us, what's familiar is whatever we've grown up with—what we've come to know through our own immediate families.

## What is a Family?

Think of your own life growing up. Were most of the families around like your own? If you grew up in, say, the 1950s, perhaps you were part of what might have been considered the typical family of that time: mother, father, and three or four children. But what if you weren't? What if you were an only child, or lived only with one parent, or lived with grandparents, or had twelve brothers and sisters? Chances are that if your lifestyle deviated significantly from that of others within your immediate experience, you felt some sense of alienation. How did you handle it? Did you come to value and appreciate your uniqueness? Or did you seek to make the gap between your lifestyle and that of those around you smaller?

More and more, people are coming to see that the richness of multiple lifestyles existing all around us offers a range of choices. No longer must we model what someone else has done in order to achieve acceptance. We can accept—even admire—the lifestyle chosen by our parents. But we do not have to imitate it, even when it comes to forming our own family group.

What is a family in today's culture? It is any intimate, interpersonal relationship in which people live together with a definite commitment, form an economic unit, care for any young, and gain their identity through being attached to the group. It may include children; it may not. The adult members of the family may be biologically related or not, married or not. The breadwinner may be the father, mother, both, or several adults who share that responsibility. Grandparents or other relatives may be part of the household.

Although the definition of family has broadened significantly if one looks at the way in which the relationships are defined, some things remain relatively unchanged. Families are still characterized by strong, loving bonds that give family members a sense of belonging and a feeling of security. Perhaps we are simply learning as we go that there are many ways to provide that kind of stability.

As we've noted already, the kind of family into which you were born very likely had a lot to do with the way you first defined the concept of family. A child who lives with one divorced parent may have a concept of family very different from that of the child who lives with several unmarried adults that share child-rearing responsibilities—and different still from that of the child who has always lived with biological parents and siblings.

Within a given community, most families may share similarities. But as we move beyond those communities, we soon encounter differences. Typical ranch families in Montana may be very different from typical city families in London. Further, the more we expand the geographic boundaries, the more difficult it becomes to define what's typical or normal. Many customs taken for granted within Western societies may be unusual or even unheard of elsewhere. For example, we may find it usual for one man to marry one woman, or for people to marry because they're in love, or for people to wait until after marriage before having children. In other cultures, it may be common for a man to have several wives, or to have children by several women, or to marry because a mate is of the right status or social class. As we begin to view ourselves as part of a larger world community, therefore, we may find the range of lifestyle patterns widening considerably.

If you're like most of us, you've gained some ideas through your own experience, through reading or through the pictures of family life that's depicted in contemporary films or plays. But are these characterizations accurate?

In their search for the "truth," today's social scientists depend on a wide range of sources for information. The visions of playwrights and film makers may tell part of the story. But a thorough researcher must also rely on firsthand information from surveys, interviews, direct observation, clinical experiments, and long-term studies. Because such information is not readily accessible to most of us on an every-

**Removing Blinders**

day basis, we may find that our own beliefs about what's typical do not always correspond to what is really taking place in our society. Let's look at a few specifics to find out.

❑ *Are you married?* If so, you may be interested in knowing that since the 1950s (when teenage marriage was fairly common), people have been marrying at an increasingly later age—and that trend may well continue, particularly as employment opportunities open up for women. Today, few men marry until their mid-twenties or later. For women the median age for a first marriage is about 24.5 years. If you were married younger than this, your situation might be considered somewhat atypical—according to recent statistics defining what's usual.

❑ *Have you ever been divorced?* Not so long ago, that would have placed you in a small minority. No more. Current projections estimate that only about half of first marriages will last. The number of second marriages is on the rise, but even fewer of those—about 40 percent—are expected to last long-term.

❑ *Do you plan on having a big family?* If so, you'll be in a small group—relatively speaking. The typical American mother today has one or two children. In the 1960s, it was not unusual for a mother in our society to have two or three children; in the 1950s, three to four children was about average. How old are first-time mothers? Increasing numbers are in their thirties.

❑ *Have you been part of a one-parent family—as either the child or the parent?* Consider yourself fairly typical. Predictions suggest that the overwhelming majority of today's two-year-olds will have lived in a single-parent household at some point in their lives before reaching age 18.

❑ *If you are in your late teens or early twenties and you live at home with your parents, is that an unusual situation?* Not in the least. A majority of young men and nearly half the young women of this age are still living with parents or have returned to living with parents. Why? Extended education, difficulties finding employment after high school or college, advantages in sharing living expenses and expanded ideas about what should or could constitute a family are all likely factors contributing to this situation.

❏ *Is premarital sex the exception or the norm?* Statistics indicate that a majority of young men and women have sexual intercourse before marriage.

❏ *Are you finding it difficult to "make ends meet"?* You're not alone. The proportion of the population below the poverty line has risen steadily since the 1970s. Moreover, poverty is unevenly distributed across ethnic groups.

If you're like most of us, you have a built-in curiosity about how your lifestyle compares to that of others. To some extent, knowing who we are means finding out how we fit in. Remember, though, statistics can be misleading. They're often averages, a sort of middle-of-the-road profile that winds up looking like no one in particular. Perhaps our real interest should lie in exploring some of the reasons behind those shifting patterns. And as we look at those reasons, you might be thinking about the choices you have made in your life and those that remain before you. What kinds of information do you need to make a good decision?

## Changing Roles and Relationships

In a very important way, you help shape the norms of modern life. Maybe you think it doesn't make any real difference how you feel about marriage, children, and family relationships. But it does. As you make decisions, you weave the pattern of your own life into the fabric of our culture. That is one of the four themes of this course. The very act of making choices carries a weight of its own. It feeds back into society and somehow changes the social environment.

❏ Personal decisions must be made throughout the life course. Decision-making is a trade-off; once you choose an option, you discard alternatives. Thus, the best way to make choices is knowledgeably.

❏ Cultural beliefs and values influence our attitudes and decisions. And societal or structural conditions can limit or expand our options.

❏ We live in a changing society, characterized by increased economic, ethnic, and family diversity. There is increased emphasis on individualistic values and decreased emphasis on marital and family permanence. This tends to make personal decision-making not only more difficult than in the past, but also more important.

Just as society's definitions of roles and relationships are changing, so will your own. In many ways, the way you view friendship, family, or society is an extension of the way you view yourself.

**Learning Objectives**

On completing your study of this lesson, you should be able to

❏ Identify the four major themes of the *Portrait of a Family* text, *Marriages and Families*, by Lamanna and Riedmann.

❏ Explain, in general terms, where and how social scientists derive the information upon which they base their theories and concepts.

❏ Comment on the ways in which freedom of choice offers new opportunities, yet creates stress.

❏ Discuss the ways in which attitudes and practices relating to marriage and family life have changed over the past several decades.

❏ Define, in general terms, the conflict between family values and individualism.

**Key Terms**

| | |
|---|---|
| Case study | Longitudinal study |
| Family | Naturalistic observation |
| Family values (familism) | Survey |
| Historical data | Togetherness |
| Individualistic (self-fulfillment) values | Values |

**Assignments**

❏ Before viewing the program, be sure you've read through the preceding overview and familiarized yourself with the learning objectives and key terms for this lesson. Then read Chapters 1 and 2, with particular emphasis on pages 4–12 and 20–25 in Chapter 1, "Family Commitments: Making Choices in a Changing Society;" and pages 43–49 in Chapter 2, "Exploring the Family," of *Marriages and Families,* Seventh Edition, by Lamanna and Riedmann.

6

❑ After completing these tasks, read the video viewing questions and watch the video program for Lesson 1, "Family Portraits."

❑ After viewing the program, take time to answer the video viewing questions and evaluate your learning with the self-test. You'll find the correct answers, along with text page references, at the back of this telecourse guide.

**Video Viewing Questions**

1. Carlfred Broderick and Paul Bohannan discuss how the definition of a "family" has changed in recent years. Based on their statements, what is a family today? How does it differ from the television families of the 1950s? Describe a modern American "typical family."

2. While the physical structure of families vary, families are still expected to fulfill certain functions in society and within the home. What do Dick and Barbara consider these functions to be? Can these expectations transcend complicated family structures? According to Ira Reiss, Carlfred Broderick, and Paul Bohannan, what is a "healthy" family?

3. Historians frequently refer to the United States as a "melting pot" of different cultures and ethnicities. Based on the testimony of Dr. Wade Nobles and Kirby Alvy, what effect does a family's cultural heritage have on the function of the family? How do Jess, Peter, and Andrea explain the importance of their individual cultures in their relationships? What would they say about the blending of all cultures the "melting pot" implies?

4. In the past, a traditional lifestyle of marriage with children and mom at home was highly encouraged. Those who did not conform to this model often found negative stigmas attached to their chosen lifestyles. Compare the traditional family model to the highly contrasting views of the Fairfax high school students. How have priorities shifted? What do the shifts suggest about the importance and perception of marriage?

5. What was once "shacking up" or "living in sin" is now a quite common phenomenon. What do Joe and Julie say about the positive and negative connotations associated with an unmarried couple living together? What do they

consider to be beneficial about the arrangement? How does it compare to marriage?

6. What do the statements of Michelle, Glenn, and Donna reveal about the differences between the ideal vision of marriage and the reality of marriage? What expectations were unrealistic?

7. Consider the comments of Chris and Robin, Jennifer, and Mr. and Mrs. Estelle with regard to parent/child relationships. How do these examples demonstrate the stress children may bring to a relationship?

## Self-Test

1. Which of the following probably *best* characterizes how Americans today feel about marriage?
   a. Embittered and ready to abandon marriage as an institution.
   b. Hopeful—yet apprehensive at the same time.
   c. More optimistic than ever before.
   d. Fairly negative, though still willing to maintain the tradition.

2. As in other areas of life, our decisions and attitudes about marriage and family are influenced by our culture and society, but
   a. culture is more influential than is society.
   b. society is more influential than is culture.
   c. individuals can influence culture and society.
   d. we should keep in mind that institutions are a better guide to truth than are individual preferences.

3. Projections indicate that in the future, _____ of all marriages will last a lifetime.
   a. a quarter
   b. a third
   c. half
   d. two-thirds

4. Values that focus on the family as a whole—such as togetherness, stability, and loyalty—are associated with
   a. societal influences.
   b. familism.
   c. individualism.
   d. families in the middle years of the family life cycle.

5. The idea that young persons should select their own marriage partners is

   a. pretty universal.
   b. particular to the United States.
   c. common in many societies, though not universal.
   d. common to only a few societies historically, and diminishing today.

6. To a social scientist, "scientific investigation" generally implies

   a. work done within the confines of a laboratory.
   b. systematic analysis of information gained through surveys.
   c. analysis of data gathered systematically through a variety of sources.
   d. firsthand observation.

7. Paul, a social scientist, has conducted a survey on attitudes toward marriage by the readership of a magazine on American family life. Paul got very good return on his survey (over 80 percent), and the answers are clear-cut and easy to interpret. Would it be all right for Paul to generalize, based on this data, about how Americans as a group feel toward marriage?

   a. Yes, but only because of the high return on the survey forms.
   b. Yes, because clearly Paul has structured his questions in a way that makes results simple to interpret.
   c. Only if he conducts a second survey using the same sample of subscribers and the results turn out about the same.
   d. No, because the readers of this magazine may or may not be representative of Americans as a whole.

8. The *main* reason that social scientists often gather information through a range of sources or methods is that

   a. every method has certain advantages and disadvantages that may influence the accuracy of the data.
   b. it is usually impossible to get more than minimal information from any one source.
   c. tradition encourages use of multiple sources—even though it's often unnecessary.
   d. some methods—like naturalistic observation—are very unreliable, and must be countered by more proven methods, such as laboratory experiments.

9. Probably the *best* definition of family as we know it in America today is

    a. any household in which all members share equally in social and economic responsibilities.
    b. any group in which the members are bound by ties of blood relationship or marriage.
    c. any group in which members, married or not, share child-care responsibilities.
    d. any intimate, interpersonal relationship in which persons form an economic unit and care for young, consider their identity to be significantly attached to the group, and share a strong commitment to maintain the group over time.

10. The *Marriages and Families* text is based on the assumption that people make better decisions if

    a. they have parents who provide good role models to follow.
    b. they place more emphasis on familial values—somewhat less on individual values.
    c. such decisions are based on their own thought-through principles.
    d. other members of the family group share in the decision making process.

## Lesson 2

# The Seasons of Life

## Making Choices and Facing Change

Overview

If you've spent much time around children, and especially if you have children of your own, you know how rapidly they change. Almost every day, if you're observant, you can witness changes in appearance, demeanor, attitudes, abilities, and temperament. Many books on child rearing stress the idea that never again after infancy will changes occur so rapidly or appear so dramatic. But while that point may be well taken, we're increasingly recognizing the fact that people change not only during infancy and childhood, but all through their lives—even into old age. And those changes may be more extensive and far reaching than we had once imagined. So, whether you're now 18 or 25 or 35 or 60, you are still in the process of "becoming." The changes you go through from this time forward in your life may be vast or almost unnoticeable, but change you will.

The nature of change that occurs throughout an adult's life affects not only that individual, but also his or her family and marital relationships. Understanding the factors that precipitate change can help an individual cope better with an evolving identity. The fundamental question "Who am I?" may have many answers.

There are many variables that influence change. The time in which we're born is one of them. If you have parents or grandparents who lived through the Great Depression, for example, you likely know from their recounted tales and adventures how much that experience helped shape their own

Factors that
Influence Change

**11**

identities and value systems. And if you did not share that experience, your own attitudes and values are likely to differ slightly.

We are all products of our own experience. Historical events, including wars, depressions and recessions, or times of economic prosperity, influence not only society as a whole, but the lives of each of its individual members. A soldier who fought in Vietnam, Korea, or the Middle East; a farmer who struggled with dying crops during the drought of the 1930s; a young mother in the 1970s who found she had to seek work because one income would not offer her family the kind of life she wanted for them: all are persons shaped by outside influences over which they have had little or no control. In other words, change sometimes is forced upon us from outside. We change in order to accommodate experience, which we may alter somewhat through our own ingenuity, but which we are often powerless to avoid.

Age influences us as well—in several ways. First, of course, we learn as we become older. Thus, we are the products of not only our immediate environment, but of cumulative experience as well. This means that most of us find ourselves very different persons at, say, 5, 10, 20, 40, and 80 years of age. In addition, we may deliberately modify our behaviors or attitudes according to what we feel is expected or appropriate for certain ages.

Age influences us in other ways as well. Many of us have mental milestones of sorts set up inside our heads. We may tell ourselves that we will be through with school by age 22, married by 25, parents by 30, financially successful by 35, retired by 55, and so on. In creating these milestones—which we often perceive to be consistent with what society or our family expects—we put a sort of time pressure on ourselves that would not otherwise exist. If you have set deadlines like these for yourself, then you already know that once you do so, you may find yourself consistently evaluating your life performance according to these milestones, and measuring your own success and ultimately your own worth by how well you've adhered to the timetable. A heightened awareness of time may encourage some of us to make decisions because the time is right ("It's about time I got married") or because time is running out. ("Why not buy a new car? I'm not getting any younger—may as well enjoy life while I can.")

Without doubt, marriage—which is itself a product of change—also influences other changes in our lives. A married person is no longer simply an individual, but receives a certain amount of his or her identity as part of a couple. We may make some decisions differently because we are married: choosing to live in a place where both persons can find work, for example, or delaying the start of a family because one partner is not ready, or changing occupations because more money is needed to support the household. The list of possible examples is endless. What's important is the fact that suddenly two sets of considerations, views, philosophies, biases, needs, and wants may be influencing the decisions that are made. (The extent to which both partners' needs and wants are considered is a subject for a later chapter.)

Other factors—such as race and ethnicity, religion and culture—may also play a role in the life choices made by an individual. These are all external factors that play upon our lives to a large extent, even when we feel that our choices are deliberate and conscious. What about internal factors? What about our individual identities? Clearly, there is strong influence here, too.

**Making Choices**

People tend to make two kinds of choices. One, which is sometimes called "choice by default," occurs when an individual either doesn't know all the options that are available, or simply takes the path of least resistance. For example, a girl who grows up in a very small town and never travels may marry her high school sweetheart—not so much because he's the best choice for her (he may or may not be), but because he is the person she knows. She isn't aware of other options. In addition, she may find this an easy path to follow. Perhaps it seems too much trouble or too intimidating to move to another town or to travel to unfamiliar places in hopes of meeting someone else. Thus, she makes what might be considered a passive choice.

Some people aren't very happy with the notion that their fate is controlled by chance. They want to take a very active role in plotting their own destiny. Thus, they tend to make what could be considered knowledgeable choices. These are the people who seek to explore available options, whether considering shoes or marriage partners. They want to choose from among alternatives, not just settle for one alternative that satisfies their wants reasonably well.

This doesn't mean that they'll always make the right choices, but they do have certain things on their side. For one thing, knowledgeable choice implies some recognition of what's sometimes called the "gut factor"—that is, paying attention to one's feelings, not simply to what seems logically or rationally correct. Sometimes what feels right, whether in marriage, career choice, or shoes, turns out to be right, even if there's rational evidence to the contrary. A knowledgeable choice implies having knowledge of oneself.

There's more to it than this, however. A knowledgeable choice also implies recognizing the alternatives that are available. A woman whose parents are both teachers may feel teaching is the right career for her because it's what she knows best and sees most. In fact, she might be happier as an attorney, but how will she know without a chance to explore that alternative?

Knowledgeable choices are also based on awareness of potential social pressures. Certain choices may seem appealing because they look more socially acceptable. For example, a man might consciously or subconsciously dismiss a desire to go into nursing if he feels he'll receive more criticism or disapproval for that choice than for, say, opting to be an airline pilot.

And finally, knowledgeable choices demand some ability to foresee the consequences of a decision, rather than impulsively opting for the one that initially seems most attractive. It's often helpful to systematically analyze the pros and cons of a particular choice, especially if it's one that has fairly major impact on one's life: choosing a career, moving, marrying, having children, and so forth. Perhaps a chance to move to New York, for instance, looks very appealing at first glance. But suppose you find you're terrified to drive in traffic, or that you can no longer visit your parents very often because they live in San Francisco. What seems the most appealing option at first may not be so appealing once all the consequences and implications have been analyzed.

No one can predict precisely where a choice will lead. But best guesses based on some thoughtful analysis are generally preferable to relying totally on impulse. It may have occurred to you already that knowledgeable choices also depend heavily on clarification of one's own values. Perhaps this seems obvious. Yet, surprisingly, not everyone is really in tune with his or her personal values and beliefs.

## Personal Choices and Change

Adulthood is considered a time of potential personal development, growth, and change. People go through life constantly evolving and changing, but at different rates. We can all think of people who seem to have changed dramatically over relatively short periods, and others who seem to go through their whole lives upholding the same basic values, engaging in the same sorts of behaviors. They may embrace the same political and religious beliefs all their lives, remain married to one person, pursue one career, and carry the same hobby through from age 10 to age 82. This isn't to say that these people do not change. But for some of us, changes are small and slow to evolve—perhaps because we want it that way. Some of us resist change. For others, change is a way of life. They relish it, revel in it, event flaunt it.

The changes experienced by individuals as they move through the life course are multiplied by two when people are married or form partnerships. A challenge for contemporary relationships is to integrate divergent personal change into the relationship.

For some people transition periods can be turbulent times in which rigorous self-appraisal leads to self-doubt, impatience, and anger. This can be highly disruptive to a family. How can partners make it through such periods and still stay together? Two guidelines may help. The first is for people to take responsibility for their own past choices and decisions rather than blaming previous "mistakes" on their mates. The second is for individuals to be aware that married life is far more complex than is commonly portrayed. A relationship needs to be flexible enough to allow for each partner's individual changes.

## The Course of Family Living

Where does the family fit into this picture? To understand this better, you might start by simply asking yourself in very basic terms who you are. If you had to describe yourself in a series of single words or simple phrases, what would you say? (You might even try this on a piece of scratch paper.) If you're like most people, some of those words and phrases will describe family relationships: father, mother, son, daughter, daughter-in-law, wife, husband, lover, friend, and so on. In other words, as we began to see in the first lesson, the family within which we exist is part of our identity. They're part of who we are and of who we will become.

The *family development theory* is an attempt to look at changes over the course of a lifetime through shifting family relationships and events. Until quite recently, sociologists tended to view the various stages of a family's history largely in terms of the children and their growth and development:

e.g., newly established couples, families with school children, families with young adults, and aging families. But with the new and expanding definitions of family, we're realizing now that these stages have little meaning to some family groups. In fact, what charts the history of a family's life is really the interaction of its various members, and the compilation of the stages through which they individually proceed.

The family development perspective has been an important one in sociology of the family for many years. However, the usefulness of this theory is limited by the implied presumption that families are similar and share a traditional way of life; that everyone marries for a lifetime and divorce does not exist. A number of other theories of family life have been developed by family researchers:

❑ **Family ecology perspective**—explores how families influence and are influenced by their social, political, and physical environment. In addition to offering possibilities and opportunities, society imposes limitations and constraints. Both the opportunities and the limitations influence the behavior of families and family members.

❑ **Structure-functional perspective**—presents a view of the family as a social institution whose values, norms, and activities are directed toward the performance of certain functions for society and its members. The strength of this theory is in the comparative study of societies.

❑ **Interactionist perspective**—looks at internal family dynamics. It explores the interaction of family members, and the "family" that emerges from these interactions and relationships.

❑ **Exchange theory**—has as its focus the impact on family life of men's and women's differential opportunities, resources, and social power.

❑ **Family systems theory**—growing out of psychotherapy, this theoretical framework looks at the family as a whole: the parts of a family make a whole "system" that is more than the sum of the parts. Social scientists have been especially interested in how family systems handle information, deal with problems, respond to crises, and regulate contact with the outside world.

❑ **Feminist perspective**—with a central focus of gender issues, this theory derives from the conflict perspective, exploring the contradictions of the family: the warmest, most intimate group and at the same time one of the most violent and hateful. This theory calls attention to power and explains behavior patterns in terms of the unequal distribution of power.

Among other things, a family provides us with a place to belong, a place where most of us find comfort, security, acceptance—or at the very least, some physical space that is designated the family's own, quite apart from the rest of the world. The family is also a keeper of history. We trace our personal histories through the preservation of pictures and other artifacts that remind us of who we once were and how we came to be the persons we are today.

It's important, however, to remember that individuals need a personal sense of identity that's sometimes apart from the family. Have you ever felt (perhaps during a time of personal crisis or during an especially hectic, stressful holiday) that you really needed to be alone? To just get away somewhere, to a place where even family members couldn't reach you for a little while? If so, then you know the importance of privacy, of having your own individual space within the family boundaries. Even those who value their family relationships highly and who feel very satisfied with family life as a whole experience this need for individual time, space, and freedom. The conflict between family needs and personal needs, as we indicated earlier, is universal, and is a theme we'll continue to explore in the chapters to come.

As you go through this and the following lessons, you might take some time to consider your own identity. To what extent is that identity a function of who you are as an individual? And to what extent do you derive your identity from your place within a family? You might also give some thought to the life choices you have made and will make. To what extent does your role within a family or marriage influence those choices? And how will you change because of them?

## Freedom and Identity within Families

On completing your study of this lesson, you should be able to

❑ Describe the manner in which social influences (including historical events, race, social class, and age expectations) influence personal choices in life.

❑ Compare differences (with examples) in choosing by default and choosing knowledgeably.

## Learning Objectives

**17**

❑ Summarize recent research regarding adult development.

❑ Explain how family development theory has evolved over the past several decades, and describe in general terms how social scientists now tend to view family development.

❑ Explain the importance of achieving harmony between family separateness and togetherness.

❑ Name and describe at least two important functions that families perform in helping individuals develop a sense of their own identity.

## Key Terms

Age expectations
Archival family function
Choosing by default
Choosing knowledgeably
Ethnicity
Exchange theory
Family development theory
Family ecology perspective

Family systems theory
Feminist perspective
Interactionist perspective
Race
Social class
Structure-functional
    perspective
Values clarification

## Assignments

❑ Before viewing the program, be sure you've read through the preceding overview and familiarized yourself with the learning objectives and key terms for this lesson. Then review Chapters 1 and 2, with particular emphasis on pages 12–20 in Chapter 1 and pages 30–43 in Chapter 2 of *Marriages and Families* by Lamanna and Riedmann.

❑ After completing these tasks, read the video viewing questions and watch the video program for Lesson 2, "The Seasons of Life."

❑ After viewing the program, take time to answer the video viewing questions and evaluate your learning with the self-test. You'll find the correct answers, along with text page references, at the back of this telecourse guide.

❑ Read the "What's Your Decision?" scenario at the end of this lesson and answer the questions about the decision you would make based on what you've learned from this lesson. Give these questions some serious thought; they may be used as the basis for class discussion or the development of a more complex essay.

1. How does society often influence the decisions or limit the options of many members of our society? Consider both implicit and explicit limitations and pressures as seen in the comments of Susan, Randy, Linda, and Julia.

2. Both Anita and John wanted to wait to get married. What were each of their reasons for the delay? Is marriage a "rite of passage" to adulthood and how does it apply to Anita and John?

3. Daphne Rose Kingma says a midlife crisis is a developmental phase. How is this reflected in the comments of Warren Farrell?

4. Both Constance and Muriel consider the second half of life to be a positive and exciting transition. Why might this not be true for some people? Give specific reasons and examples in your reply.

5. Carlfred Broderick believes society is now structured to protect the individual; family concerns often take a back seat. Consider this theory in relation to any three of the statements of Bob, Marsha Lasswell, James, Barbara, Jennifer, Reed, or Kimberly. How does Broderick's theory relate to Chris and Robin's "family night"?

1. Social factors influence peoples' personal choices in which of the following ways?

   a. Decisions that run contrary to norms about appropriate social behavior are psychologically and socially difficult.
   b. Social factors limit peoples' options
   c. Both a and b are factors
   d. In the United States, personal choices are never limited by social factors

2. Which of the following is probably the *most accurate* description of how people change through their lives?

   a. Most change occurs during infancy and the preschool years, with very little change occurring after the teens.
   b. All people change throughout their lives, but at various times and to varying degrees.

    c. The most significant changes occur during the early thirties and mid forties, and are part of highly predictable stages.

    d. In truth, some people change dramatically over the course of their lives, while others experience no real change at all.

3. It is sometimes said that "social factors limit people's options." This *most likely* means that

    a. some people have no opportunity to change in their lives.

    b. only a few people have the chance to marry for love.

    c. people who experience war, famine, or other adversity no longer have much control over their lives.

    d. social regulations, such as the supreme court's position on abortion, impact the availability of choices.

4. The growth of immigration in recent decades should increase the impact of ethnicity on family life because

    a. new immigrants retain more of their ethnic culture than do immigrants who have been in the United States longer.

    b. the marriages of recent immigrants seem less egalitarian than do those of couples with similar ethnic background whose families have been in the United States longer.

    c. foreign-born women tend to have more children than do native-born Americans.

    d. *all* of the above increase the impact of ethnicity on family life.

5. In comparing the values and attitudes of white-collar and blue-collar workers, most social scientists would probably agree that

    a. their attitudes and values have become increasingly alike in recent years.

    b. the two groups have almost no attitudes or values in common.

    c. they may or may not be more alike than they once were, but there are still definite differences in their thinking.

    d. the differences have become so minor that it no longer makes good sense to distinguish between the two groups at all.

6. Margery is in her first year at college. She has decided to follow in her mother's footsteps and become an English teacher. About midway through the term, Margery visits a psychology class with a friend and is immediately addicted. "Why didn't I think of taking psychology?" she says later. "It's so much more interesting than my course. If only I'd known sooner." Margery's decision to major in English might be considered an example of

   a. social class influence over personal choice.

   b. midlife transition.

   c. values clarification.

   d. choosing by default.

7. Later, Margery (Question 6) decides that she will change her major to psychology—but only after she has explored some other options as well. She visits a number of classes, talks with her advisor, interviews people within several professions she finds potentially interesting. Margery's strategy at this point is a good example of

   a. values clarification.

   b. transition through the adult life course.

   c. using the "gut factor" to make decisions.

   d. choosing knowledgeably.

8. Which of the following statements is (are) true concerning theories of family study?

   a. Each theory can be thought of as a point of view.

   b. What is significant about families can vary from one theory to the next.

   c. Each theory illuminates our understanding of the family in a different way.

   d. All of the above are true.

9. Which of the following theories of family study focuses on internal family dynamics?

   a. Interactionist perspective

   b. Exchange theory

   c. Structure-functional perspective

   d. Family development theory

10. The central premise of the family development perspective is
    a. the exchange of rewards and costs between participants in a family.
    b. the family life cycle.
    c. a classic interactional perspective on the family.
    d. its view of the family as a social institution.

## What's Your Decision?

Fletcher and Carla have been married almost 25 years. Fletcher makes an excellent living as an insurance salesman (he's head of the regional office), and Carla has never had to work. But now, with her three children grown and off to college or married, she feels bored and restless. She remembers the good times while she was working on her bachelor's degree in psychology, and thinks she'd like to enter a doctoral program and complete her course of study. Fletcher is not really opposed to the idea, though with one child still at school, he's not overjoyed at the idea of more tuition bills.

Still, the money isn't a big problem. What bothers him more is the idea that just when he and Carla would have time to themselves, time to travel or just enjoy each other's company, she'll be off at classes or buried in books. He's used to having her around, and he likes the company. "Anyway," he asks her, "what would you do with a doctorate in psychology, assuming you did stick with it and get all the way through the course?" "Be a child psychologist," she tells him with a shrug, as if the answer were obvious. "It's always been an interest of mine, and now suddenly I've got the time and money to do it. And I know I've got the ability." Fletcher shakes his head. "I'm not doubting your ability. You've always been brainy enough—but remember, you'll be competing against people one-third your age. Have you thought about that? And besides, you can't begin a career in psychology at this time of life. It's ridiculous. Who'd hire you?" Carla isn't discouraged. "If no one else will hire me, I'll work for myself," she maintains. Fletcher sighs. What is the point of arguing with such stubbornness? "Well, give it some thought," he tells her. "If you come to your senses, we'll take a month-long vacation through the Southwest. It'll be relaxing—we'll stop and see the grandkids. Doesn't that sound like a lot more fun than studying?" Carla laughs. She knows bribery when she hears it.

Based on what you know of their situation, do you think Carla should return to school? Or should she just relax and

enjoy life with Fletcher? What are some of the most important factors for her to consider in making this decision? If
Carla does return to school, what are some of the most significant ramifications of that decision?

- ❑ Should Carla return to school?

- ❑ What factors support that view?

- ❑ What factors support the opposite view?

- ❑ What will happen immediately if Carla acts as you suggest?

- ❑ What will their situation probably be five years from
now if Carla acts as you suggest?

- ❑ Are there research studies cited in the text that offer support for your position?

- ❑ If you needed additional research-based information to
support your position, how or where would you get it?

## Lesson 3

# When I Grow Up . . .

## Sex and Gender Identity

It's sometimes said that one of the first things—if not *the* first thing—we tend to notice about another person is whether the person is male or female. And based on that information, we usually have expectations about how that person will act, speak, think, and relate to us in various situations.

Have you ever had the experience of assuming that someone was either male or female—only to discover that you were mistaken? It can be something of a shock. Remember the film *Tootsie*? If you've seen that film—or another in which a man has played the part of a woman, or vice versa—then you know how psychologically jarring it can be to find out that the behavior we attributed to a person of one sex really belonged to another.

Why is that? Well, for one thing, in our society we expect men and women to be different. Not just to look different, but to behave in very different and rather carefully prescribed ways. These expectations are changing somewhat, but they are part of a long-standing tradition in which gender-related differences are pronounced.

Tradition holds that males and females differ on virtually every aspect of personality, character, and behavior. Some behaviors or traits are typically male, some typically female. Think about yourself for a moment. Do you tend to be a warm sensitive person, thoughtful of others, one who can easily imagine how it would feel to be the "other guy"? Are you open in expressing your feelings, always ready to share

25

affection, to show your fondness for another, to be sympathetic, helpful, nurturing? If these things sound like you, then you have what social scientists call *expressive character traits*—and traditionally, these traits are said to be more characteristic of females than of males.

On the other hand, do you tend to be logical in your thinking? To insist on mind over matter, to keep emotions out of your decision making? Are you a competitive person who likes a challenge, who likes the feeling of accomplishing a task others viewed as especially difficult? Are you highly self-confident, a leveler of mountains, as it were? If so, then you possess some *instrumental* characteristics traditionally associated with maleness.

Of course, as social scientists are increasingly discovering, most people are a blend of instrumental and expressive. People are not caricatures—totally emotional or wholly logical. Most of us have a logical, thinking side and an expressive, sensitive side—and this holds true whether we're male or female. Still, the question remains: Is one set of traits more strongly associated with one sex than the other? We are still learning to answer this question—and answering it is what this lesson is all about.

One thing we do know for sure: traditions persist. While most of us are willing to accept the idea of a sensitive, nurturing male who is open about showing emotions, or the idea of a competitive, bright woman who is eager to further her career, few of us are willing to say that there is no relationship whatever between character traits and sex. In other words, we continue to see some behaviors as male, and others as female—even though increasing numbers of men and women are no longer fitting the stereotypic roles. Further, most men and women tend to see themselves as a blend of traditionally masculine and feminine traits.

## Influence of Role Models

What we grow up with has a great deal to do with predicting how we see the world. Think of the roles your parents—or other important adults in your life—filled while you were growing up. Let's say that your father was the primary breadwinner and made most of the major decisions (where to live, which car to buy, how and when to spend money, where to vacation), while your mother fulfilled a very traditional role as a homemaker and caretaker of children (an important role—but certainly less powerful). It would be quite natural for you, in that case, to assume that men are by nature more likely to fulfill leadership roles, that they are "born" decision makers, that they tend to be more logical or organized in their thinking (after all, isn't Dad managing the budget?), and that they're less likely to be governed by emotion (Dad knows how important it is to move to Detroit, even if Mother is distraught at leaving friends and family behind). Similarly, research shows that children from homes where the mother works tend to see women as more competent. We all have a tendency to believe in the roles we've observed firsthand.

Roles are changing, though. Sometimes it's easy to assume that change comes about because it's what we want. In a country where breaking with tradition is a sort of tradition in itself, it may be logical to regard change as something that comes about through deliberate effort. And in some respects, that's true. Women are working hard to achieve better opportunities in the workplace. Many men, in turn, are attempting to be open-minded about sharing homemaking and childcare responsibilities. However, it's only fair to point out that to a large extent, change has simply fallen upon us, like it or not. The nature of modern life itself makes traditional roles increasingly hard to fulfill. The Old West, where "men were men," is a time and place of the past—for the most part.

The shift from an agricultural to an industrial to a serviceoriented society has had important implications for the breadwinner's role. Men today often find themselves in positions where personal achievement is less valued than cooperation with others, where major projects are the result of team effort rather than individual effort. Physical strength and mechanical ability may be of minimal importance—unless the computer's printer breaks down or someone needs it moved from one room to another. A few people, of course—notably farmers and ranchers—continue to find themselves in situations where strength and mechanical skills are critical. But for most of us, the notion of "man against nature" lives on only in books and films.

Further, increased unemployment and underemployment are placing in some jeopardy the self-concept of the man who gains a large portion of his identity through his work. If in your mind "you are what you earn," then you may put yourself under pressure to find a job that affords both money and prestige. But what if you can't?

A man who has no opportunity to fulfill the traditional male role through his work may seek some other outlet: through sports, for instance. He may ride a motorcycle, race cars, break horses, climb mountains—or find any of a number of other ways to challenge himself or his peers. Studies indicate that our overemphasis on the male role can actually be dangerous. Men are more frequently involved in criminal assaults than are women, and are three or four times as likely to be injured or killed in motor vehicle or other serious accidents. Clearly, proving your manhood entails risks—and the risk itself, for some, is part of the myth.

Encouraging males to "give 'em hell" is risky in other, more subtle ways, too. In our society, there may be undue pressure on a sensitive, creative person to act in ways that may seem unnatural. A man may prefer, for instance, to spend his time painting, or reading books, or growing flowers, but may avoid these pursuits for fear they will be perceived as too unmasculine. He may literally spend an entire lifetime finding ways to be male enough to please his parents, family, friends, and society as a whole. And such pursuits, even if not physically dangerous, are not likely to leave him with much sense of personal fulfillment. Few things are more frustrating than not being allowed to be ourselves.

What about women? Are they finding it more difficult these days to fulfill their traditional roles? In many ways, yes. Traditionally, at least since the industrial revolution, the assumption has been that women need to be cared for by men, and that in return for such care, women will provide emotional support and sex, in addition to bearing and raising the man's children. This role might have seemed fairly appropriate a hundred years ago, but today many women are likely to view this tradition with disdain, if not outrage. Even a woman who finds the idea of being cared for by a man appealing would not have such an easy time playing out her traditional role. More than attitudes have changed over the last hundred years.

**Physiological and Biological Theories**

Ethnologists—scientists who study human beings as an evolved animal species—note that male dominance is common among most primates, and suggest that such roles may become genetically established over time. They point to the influence of hormones on behavior. Further, there is some evidence that environmental influences can affect hormone levels, thereby setting up a kind of recurring cycle. Most sociologists tend to discount the view that male dominance is genetic, however, feeling that culture is more significant than genetics.

Perhaps the question is more an issue of perspective. For instance, hermaphrodites, whose sexual identity cannot be clearly determined at birth, seem to accept the role to which they are assigned. In other words, if they are treated like females, they tend to adopt a female role; if treated like males, they tend to adopt a male role.

As we've already indicated, hormones seem to play some role in determining behavior as well. For example, according to a study cited in the text, girls who are exposed to greater amounts of the male sex hormone androgen before birth seem often to be more athletic, more tomboyish. They may decline to play with dolls and may prefer sports. Later in life, they may be more interested in a career—perhaps even a traditionally male-dominated career, such as politics or engineering—than in finding a husband and having children.

How do you find yourself responding to such an attitude? Perhaps you find it admirable. Or, if you're like some people, you may feel somewhat uncomfortable about a woman taking such a strong, decisive and aggressive stand. Our attitudes are likely to be reflected in our behaviors—and thus, to some extent, to influence the behaviors and attitudes of those around us.

**Mixed Influences**

Well, have you come to any conclusions about what determines our sexual destiny? Is it physiology? Biological inheritance? Cultural influence? Most social scientists seem to feel that some combination of biology and culture is responsible for the "selves" we finally become. We are certainly influenced by genetics and hormones, but the biological potential with which each of us is born is undoubtedly further shaped by the cultural environment into which we're placed.

A female, by birth, may have great potential to become a nurturing, expressive, and supportive individual—but if these things are not valued by her society, not encouraged by parents or others who have influence upon her, then they're not as likely to develop. And if she is encouraged to be outgoing and aggressive, she is likely to exhibit related behaviors to some extent, within the bounds of her potential. Perhaps she will not get into fistfights or play football or hunt snakes. But perhaps she will become a very competitive businesswoman. Her behavior is likely, in the final analysis, to be determined by some combination of her own genetic potential and what society is willing to accept and condone.

If you're a female, you may feel that your own aggressive traits have not been encouraged much. You're probably right. Men and women are still encouraged—to some extent—to fulfill traditional roles. Any genetic tendencies toward nurturing are thus encouraged in females, while genetic tendencies toward aggression are encouraged in males.

What we tend to forget is that tendencies do not equal destiny. We may not be able to escape our genetic and cultural influences, but we do not have to be victimized by them either. We can still make some choices about the kinds of roles we wish to play, and the kinds of behaviors we wish to reward (and thereby encourage) in others. And blending some of the traditional male and female traits offers us new possibilities for creating our future selves.

## Learning Objectives

On completing your study of this lesson, you should be able to

❏ Distinguish between instrumental and expressive character traits, and explain how each relates to traditional gender roles.

❏ Explain why social scientists sometimes suggest that the traditional male role in our society can be problematic.

❏ Describe some ways in which both men and women in modern society have difficulty fulfilling traditional roles.

❏ Identify several cultural or social influences (in addition to attitudes) that have had dramatic impact on traditional male and female roles.

❏ Explain what is meant by a male-dominant society, and how accurate this designation is in your region.

❏ Respond to the question: Is anatomy destiny?

❏ Discuss the interaction between heredity and culture in determining our gender identities.

## Key Terms

| | |
|---|---|
| Assignment | Instrumental character traits |
| Ethnologists | Male dominance |
| Expressive character traits | "Separate spheres" ideology |
| Gender | Sex |
| Gender roles | Social learning theory |
| Hermaphrodite | Socialization |
| Hormone | |

❏ Before viewing the program, be sure you've read through the preceding overview and familiarized yourself with the learning objectives and key terms for this lesson. Then read Chapter 3, "Our Gendered Identities," of *Marriages and Families* by Lamanna and Riedmann, with particular emphasis on pages 54–67, 73–75, and 78–81.

❏ After completing these tasks, read the video viewing questions and watch the video program for Lesson 3, "When I Grow Up. . ."

❏ After viewing the program, take time to answer the video viewing questions and evaluate your learning with the self-test. You'll find the correct answers, along with text page references, at the back of this telecourse guide.

❏ Read the "What's Your Decision?" scenario at the end of this lesson and answer the questions about the decision you would make based on what you've learned from this lesson. Give these questions some serious thought; they may be used as the basis for class discussion or the development of a more complex essay.

## Video Viewing Questions

1. What are some of the differences between the roles of men and women described in terms of "gender roles"? How do these roles shape one's self-perception? Note the testimony of the children in your response.

2. Warren Farrell says men have been sexually discriminated against due to the stereotypical image of a "real man" being the "provider." How does this statement relate to the comments of Betty Friedan regarding the masculine mystique? Considering the testimony of the children regarding what their fathers and mothers are supposed to do, has the stereotype been forgotten by this generation?

3. Discuss the domestic frustration of Susan Speer's mother in contrast to Alice Vaviolette's description of the "real woman."

4. Compare the experiences of Mary Leaming, Susan Speers, and the current undergraduates interviewed.

5. The role of women in American society obviously has changed dramatically from the June Cleaver image of the 1950s. But in giving up the structure of the 1950s, new

ideas and new confusionhave emerged regarding what is feminine and what is masculine. Discuss the testimony from Arthur Running Bear, James, and Susan Speers on this subject. Why does Susan Speers find younger men more flexible?

6. Although considerable progress has been made, Americans' self-perception in terms of gender are still riddled with stereotypical expectations and behaviors. What gender-related barriers continue based on the comments of Ira Reiss, Betty Friedan, Carol Sorgenfrei, and Nancy Weber?

7. Daphne Rose Kingma says we are psychologically always 20 to 40 years behind where we are sociologically. What parallels can be drawn between this theory and staggering divorce rates, gender-based job discrimination, and seemingly trivial hostility between couples?

## Self-Test

1. Most social scientists would probably agree that in our society today, gender tends to
   a. play a far less important role in determining self-concept than it once did.
   b. be mostly a matter of choice, rather than genetic or social influence.
   c. affect virtually every aspect of a person's life, including interrelationships.
   d. be the greatest single factor in predicting one's inherent abilities.

2. Which of the following would probably be the *best* example of an expressive character trait?
   a. Intelligence
   b. Warmth
   c. Height
   d. Competitiveness

3. The concept of "gender roles" refers to which of these?
   a. The attitudes and behaviors expected of the two sexes
   b. The masculine and the feminine side of one's personality
   c. Strongly held exaggerations about a category of people
   d. Culturally written and directed "plots" for behavior

4. The term _____ refers to chemical substances secreted into the bloodstream by the endocrine glands, influencing the activities of cells, tissues, and body organs.

   a. alkalydes
   b. pitocins
   c. hormones
   d. pheromones

5. To what extent do individual men and women fit gender stereotypes and scripts?

   a. Differences among men or among women are usually greater than differences between men and women.
   b. Gender traits are opposite and mutually exclusive.
   c. There is considerable overlap in how typical men and women differ, with the exception of the male dominance trait.
   d. Both a and c are true.

6. Which of the following statements provides the *most accurate* summary of what research has taught us about gender differences? Gender differences (i.e., differences between males and females) are most likely

   a. the result of heredity, and very unlikely to be influenced by culture or social context.
   b. a product of cultural influences in which heredity plays virtually no part.
   c. the combined result of cultural influences acting upon biological potential.
   d. a matter of each person's individual choice, with neither biology nor cultural influence playing much of a part.

7. Betty and Fran were talking one day about the role of women in modern society. Betty made this comment: "They say women have equal opportunity, but I have yet to observe it. The truth is, it's still a man's world out there. Men hold the positions of power in most corporations. Men make most of the decisions that influence corporate growth, corporate investment, and employment policy. Given that, what chance does a woman have?" Betty's attitude, as exemplified in this scenario, is

   a. a pretty accurate reflection of reality, given that ours is a male dominated society.
   b. somewhat accurate, though she greatly exaggerates the power that men hold in the marketplace.

c. relatively overstated; following the Women's Movement, equality in the workplace is a given.

d. accurate only for women who lack education; those with advanced education find few barriers to advanced employment or high salaries.

8. Which of these is a topic of biological research that is thought to be linked to innate or inherent differences in male and female behavior?

a. Gonadal distribution theory
b. Ocular perceptive symmetry
c. Neural synapse theory
d. Brain lateralization
e. Y-prime blood differences

9. "Well, after all," Bill told his fishing partners Ed and Tom one day, "it's only natural for men to make most of the decisions. It's more natural for the man to be the head of the household—to earn most of the money—and to decide how it's spent. Males are naturally dominant. You see the same pattern in virtually any primate society." The views that Bill is expressing in this scenario *most closely* match those of

a. anthropologist Margaret Mead.
b. Sigmund Freud.
c. ethnologists.
d. most modern social scientists.

10. Research indicates that the single most crucial factor in determining whether hermaphrodites perceive themselves as male or female tends to be

a. the presence of the hormone testosterone in the mother's body prior to birth.
b. the physical characteristics of the genitalia.
c. whether the mother or father provides a more attractive role model.
d. the sex identity arbitrarily assigned each individual after birth.

## What's Your Decision?

June and Ed have a daughter, Allison, who is eight. Allison is a healthy, active child, very interested in sports. She is bright and does well in school—seems to like it very much. She's particularly adept at science and math, has her own microscope, and raises tropical fish for a hobby. Allison dislikes dolls and seldom plays with other girls—"They're too boring and everything they want to do is dumb." She'd rather spend her time with the boys, climbing trees, riding horses, playing baseball, and catching frogs, snakes, and other animals down at the creek. Ed thinks this is just fine. "She's just a tomboy," he tells June. "She'll grow out of it one of these days and turn into a beautiful young lady." But June isn't at all persuaded that this is the case. "It isn't natural for a little girl to prefer snakes to dolls," she tells her husband. "The neighbors think it's strange. So does my mother. So would any normal person. Look at her—she hardly ever combs her hair. She never wears a dress or anything with frills on it. She might as well be a boy. What sort of mother will she make?" Ed is not convinced that there is anything to worry about, but June feels they should begin insisting that Allison behave "more like a girl." She wants to dress Allison differently, and restrict her playmates—"so that she's with other girls at least some of the time, and has a chance to see how girls act." June also wants to eliminate the baseball. "That's too rough for a girl," she insists.

Based on what you know from this scenario, do you think June and Ed should impose the sorts of changes on Allison's behavior that June is suggesting? What are some of the most important factors for them to consider in making this decision? If they do impose certain rules and restrictions for Allison, what are some of the most significant ramifications of that decision?

❑ Should Ed and June make new rules for Allison?

❑ What factors support that view?

❑ What factors support the opposite view?

❑ What will happen immediately if they act as you suggest?

❑ What will their situation likely be five years from now if they act as you suggest?

❑ Are there research studies cited in the text that offer support for your position?

❑ If you needed additional research-based information to support your position, how and where would you go about getting it?

# Lesson 4

# Adam's Equal or Adam's Rib?

## Gender Roles in Transition

**Overview**

We've all heard the expression "Think for yourself." Some of us may even pride ourselves on our ability to do just that. But what does this expression mean, really? Certainly not to come up with ideas no one has ever heard of before. That's pretty difficult. Usually, when people say this they are encouraging us to sift and evaluate the quality of ideas that bombard us from a wide range of sources.

**Gender Identification**

You may wonder what all this has to do with gender roles. Well, quite a lot, actually. If you were to be abandoned on a desert island shortly after birth, and if you were somehow miraculously to survive, then you would grow up defining for yourself what it meant to be male or female (as well as human) within that context. Of course, that scenario is far from reality. In fact, we grow up in an increasingly busy world, with parents, siblings, other family members, friends, television, radio, books and newspapers, people at school and work, and dozens of other models that provide us with examples of what it means to be male or female. Somewhere around the age of three, we adopt an identity that is either male or female and we tend from that point on to modify our behavior somewhat to suit that identity.

A very young boy, for example, may think it's fun to try on Mom's clothes or wear makeup, but if these things are met with disapproval, he soon comes to recognize that such behaviors—from society's point of view, anyhow—are not suited to the male gender role. And most likely, he'll abandon

37

them fairly quickly. There are always those who insist upon "doing their own thing." But most of us work quite hard to fit in. We wish to be accepted. We wish—without compromising our own sense of integrity or self-worth—to behave in ways that are socially appropriate for our particular gender. And we learn this behavior by observing others and by heeding their responses to our own behavior.

Society has many ways to reinforce our image of male or female. One of the most subtle, yet most powerful, is language. It wasn't so long ago that the pronoun "he" was used to refer to a generic person of either sex. The message seemed to be: assume male unless it's stated otherwise. Lots of women didn't like that message. They wanted equal time, even in the world of pronouns. And so—to the dismay of many copy editors, but the satisfaction of most women—we now tend to say "he or she," or to alternate generic references between "he" and "she."

Most of us know by now that it's considered rather bad form to refer to all unknown persons automatically as "he," but we may engage in other sorts of discrimination—almost subconsciously. For example, suppose you overhear someone commenting on a happy, giggling baby: "Oh, what a husky, sturdy little tyke! Look at those strong legs!" What do you think? Male or female? Suppose you hear this: "Oh, what a precious little bundle! What a sweet smile. Look at those dainty little fingers!" What would you guess? Boy or girl? It's sometimes been said that people have a way of seeing what they want to see. Perhaps the "husky boy" and the "dainty girl" actually don't look very much different at all, but our expectations tend to govern what we think we see.

Those same expectations can predict behaviors, too. For example, research has shown that parents do, in fact, tend to treat male and female infants differently. First, they usually assign a child a name that identifies that child as belonging to one sex or the other. In addition, they tend to roughhouse a bit more with boys—even at a very early age—and to treat girl babies with somewhat more delicacy, and more cuddling.

As you might have guessed, children whose mothers work outside the home have less tendency to be locked into traditional views of gender roles. They may feel it is quite natural for a woman to pursue a career, or for a husband to share in the duties of caring for children and running the home. Social scientists tell us that parents' attitudes about what is appropriate are gradually shifting as well. If you grew up in the 1950s or '60s, the odds are that if you were a boy, you were not expected to dust the house or do laundry, while you probably did help out with such things as washing the car or mowing the lawn. In many homes today, boys and girls are expected to share equally in such chores, with little thought of what is more appropriate for either.

Further, many young girls these days grow up fully expecting to pursue a career—and a high level career, at that. Where once it was common for most girls to imagine themselves as teachers or nurses or secretaries, many more now envision themselves as architects, attorneys, surgeons, engineers or scientists. If this trend in shifting attitudes continues, some social scientists predict that we may be headed toward a far more egalitarian society within the near future. How today's children see themselves, after all, has great implications for what the society of tomorrow will be like.

How do children learn gender roles? We've already touched on some of the general ways in which this happens—examples provided through books and television shows or role models, for instance. Although we really have no definitive explanation, there are several theories about gender socialization:

❑ **Social learning theory** emphasizes the importance of role models combined with the rewards and punishments meted out for conformance or nonconformance, respectively, to these perceived sex-appropriate behaviors.

❑ **Self-identification theory** has children identifying themselves as either male or female by about age three, then adopting the behaviors approriate to their sex as seen in their family, in the media, and elsewhere in society.

❑ **Gender schema theory**, somewhat like the self-identification theory, sees children as developing their own foundation of information about what behavior is typical for boys and for girls. Using this schema, children internalize information relevant to their gender and develop their own roles accordingly.

❑ **Chodorow's theory of gender** takes the position that infants develop a "primary identification" with the person who is their primary caregiver, and must later learn to distinguish themself from this person. Since this primary caregiver is usually a female, boys have a more difficult task of separating than do girls. While girls can identifiy with and model their behavior after this closest and most available role model, boys must learn that they are "not female," making the separation a stressful and emotionally charged one, and leaving the residual affects of disappointment and anger.

## Androgyny

Some social scientists think we might benefit by recasting our definitions of "male" and "female" in more androgynous terms. In other words, we might encourage individuals to think, feel, and behave in both instrumental and expressive ways. Both partners within a relationship would be encouraged to be assertive and self-reliant—yet at the same time, encouraged to depend on the other for emotional support, and to express need for that support openly. It sounds simple and sensible enough. But in a complex society such as ours, concepts like androgyny are easier to describe than to put into practice. There are some important reasons for this.

For one thing, many social scientists have observed that the instrumental-expressive dichotomy is largely a white Anglo middle-class construct. Male-female relationships within other cultures may not so readily conform to the patterns suggested here. In fact, many observers tend to see the women's movement as a white middle-class creation, and to question what relevance it has for, say, black women. Traditionally, black women have worked because they needed to, not because the work has afforded them professional and personal fulfillment. And this pattern has not changed through the last century. For them, there has been no social disapproval of their work outside the home, no struggle to achieve the "right" to be both breadwinner and homemaker. Generally, this dual role has been assumed. And at the same time, their work—often at low-paying jobs—has rarely brought with it greater status, prestige, financial security, or personal reward. Where then do they fit in? And what impact—if any—might a more androgynous society have upon their lives?

While the trend toward a converging of roles is growing, the course has been anything but smooth. In fact, for both sexes, it's a course fraught with ambivalence. On the one hand, a man may ask how he can be successful, and yet be openly expressive and show his emotions? Further, emotional openness often means revealing one's vulnerability—something which, in an achievement-oriented setting, can be the kiss of death. On a more practical level, a man may consider that too much emotion, too much sensitivity, too strong a tendency to empathize with others will simply get in the way. Can he afford to worry about a woman's need to achieve professional and personal fulfillment if he is competing with her for the only available job? After all, there are only so many jobs to go around.

Women also experience ambivalence. Society expects them to be nurturing and supportive—yet, suddenly, to be successful and achievement-oriented as well. These are not easy roles to combine. Further, while it is encouraging women to achieve in the workplace, society is doing very little to offer practical support to those women making the effort. Even today, relatively few companies have progressive childcare programs, or offer realistic compensation to women who want maternity leave. Often, a woman who leaves her job to have a baby risks losing that job forever. A woman may well feel that she is undervalued by a company that forces her to make a choice: child or job. When it comes to issues of both childcare and maternity leave, our society lags far behind some others in finding creative solutions.

Perhaps the ultimate question to ask is whether androgyny can work. And to answer that question best, it may be necessary to bring it right down to the interpersonal level. In other words, to ask whether an egalitarian relationship can work between two human beings in the context of marriage. There is evidence that it can. But contrary to what we might expect, psychologists warn that such a relationship takes more—not less—commitment. If two people truly are equals in terms of their personal characteristics and the roles they play, then many of the traditional reasons for holding the marriage together are simply no longer compelling. For example, the woman is no longer dependent on the man's income; the man no longer looks to the woman as his homemaker and the person who will bear and raise his children. There must be other reasons to maintain the relationship—and these generally relate to personal commitment and the satisfaction two people gain from sharing in each other's lives.

Sociologist William Goode also warns that in a truly egalitarian relationship, both sides must be prepared to accept a certain amount of hurt and anger as the inevitable consequence of shifting roles. True, the man is no longer expected to be the sole breadwinner. And true, the woman is no longer expected to be the sole manager of the household. But where once the performance of these roles might have brought with it a certain admiration and appreciation for the loving sacrifice involved, the attitude of each person may now be, "Well—yes, you've contributed something. But it's no more than would be expected. And as an equal partner, I've contributed just as much." Each may feel that his or her role is no longer valued as much as it once was—and a certain resentment, at least during the transition period, is to be expected.

Further, as Christopher Lasch points out, expectations today tend to be higher. We are less likely to forgive certain kinds of shortcomings as part of the natural trappings that go with belonging to one sex or the other. In situation comedies of the 1950s (remember "I Love Lucy"?), women were often depicted as scheming and flighty, lacking in organizational skill and logic. But they often had an endearing kind of zany creativity, and so were "forgiven" their other shortcomings. Men, on the other hand, were often depicted as hopelessly lacking in insight and intuition, but their skill at sorting things out and making everything okay again prompted "forgiveness" for this "inherent" shortfall. In other words, it was easy to dismiss certain flaws by saying, "Oh, you know how men [or women] are." Once we admit equality, we no longer have the luxury of dismissing things quite so simply. We expect everyone to be logical, orderly, quick-witted, ambitious—and also nurturing, loving, caring, open, intuitive, and sensitive. It's a big order for everybody.

Having considered just how tough the expectations can be, though, we can take some comfort from the fact that—at least for some couples—androgyny is working. And working very well indeed. Linda Haas's 1980 research involving a number of couples living in Madison, Wisconsin reveals that couples can share a wide range of responsibilities, blend roles with virtually no regard to sex, and find great satisfaction in doing so. The couples Haas studied tended to share marital roles equally, and to regard both careers within the family as important. Interestingly, they were not consciously trying to achieve an androgynous model so much as to escape the trap of other models they had viewed as unworkable—the more traditional lifestyles they had witnessed in their parents' marriages or friends' marriages, for example.

**The Benefits of Androgyny**

What are the benefits of androgyny? According to Haas's report, there are many: relief from the stress of feeling solely responsible for any one role (e.g., making all the money, taking care of the children all the time); greater personal fulfillment from doing a wider range of activities and from sharing more activities with a spouse; greater economic and professional security, thanks to a double income and the knowledge that one spouse could stop work for a time to pursue a different career course; better communication and greater intimacy because each has "walked in the other's shoes" and knows what it means to be a breadwinner, parent, homemaker, or whatever; and improved parent-child relationships for a wide range of reasons—more economic security, the father's ability to spend more time with the children, the mother's reduced stress.

The couples in Haas's report are not typical. Not yet, anyway. But they do show that where androgyny is achieved, it can work. Of course, one factor is very important: both partners have to want it. Androgyny as a one-person act has its limitations. As we're discovering, carving out social and gender-related roles for ourselves requires not only fulfillment of personal goals, but a profound, intrinsic awareness of how the roles we write for ourselves fit within a bigger script.

On completing your study of this lesson, you should be able to

❑ Describe the processes of internalization and socialization and their relationship to definition of a personal gender role.

❑ Define gender socialization and explain the various theories explaining the process.

❑ Identify several causes of stress that both males and females experience in the development of a gender role.

❑ Describe, in general terms, some of the ways that gender role may be influenced by race.

❑ Discuss the factors that encourage or inhibit androgyny.

❑ List several potential benefits of egalitarian marriages, and comment on the factors likely to influence the success of such marriages.

## Learning Objectives

Androgyny
Chodorow's theory of gender
Gender schema theory
Intimacy

Internalization
Self-identification theory
Social learning theory
Socialization

## Key Terms

## Assignments

❏ Before viewing the program, be sure you've read through the preceding overview and familiarized yourself with the learning objectives and key terms for this lesson. Then review Chapter 3, "Our Gendered Identities," of *Marriages and Families* by Lamanna and Riedmann, with particular emphasis on pages 67–81.

❏ After completing these tasks, read the video viewing questions and watch the video program for Lesson 4, "Adam's Equal or Adam's Rib?"

❏ After viewing the program, take time to answer the video viewing questions and evaluate your learning with the self-test. You'll find the correct answers, along with text page references, at the back of this telecourse guide.

❏ Read the "What's Your Decision?" scenario at the end of this lesson and answer the questions about the decision you would make based on what you've learned from this lesson. Give these questions some serious thought; they may be used as the basis for class discussion or the development of a more complex essay.

## Video Viewing Questions

1. Describe how boys and girls are treated differently from infancy, including the commentary of Ira Reiss and Lynne Azpeitia in your discussion. How does the testimony of the children fit into your analysis?

2. The importance and impact of role models on children is fundamental to their self-perception and social development. Discuss the commentary of Constance Ahrons, Alma Jacquet, Ray Wells, and Alan Gottfried. With the increasing number of single women raising children, what effect can the absence of a father in the home have on a child's development?

3. How do the toys and activities of children lead to self-perceptions in terms of career opportunities and opportunities in general? Consider the commentary of Irene Cruz in your response.

4. No matter how hard parents try to remove the negative influences of gender roles, little boys playing with dolls on the playground are made fun of by their peers. Discuss the notion of "tomboy" and "sissy." Compare the comments of Constance Ahrons, Lisa, and the children

to that of Paul Bohannan, Bob Pachorek, and Michelle Harway regarding their development of gender orientation.

5. American society and the media are offering more possibilities to both men and women in terms of how each of the genders is portrayed and what is acceptable. Given this, how do you explain Kary's coffee dilemma? Utilize the commentary of Ira Reiss in your response.

6. Describe Jess and Irene's "housefather" situation. Is this a couple simply dealing with the realities of life or a reflection of new freedom? Are the stereotypes realistic expectations for the 1990s?

7. What does Peter and Andrea's cooking situation suggest about cultural tradition and parental influences? Discuss the importance of role models in the home. Consider Carlfred Broderick's emphasis on negotiation between couples.

## Self-Test

1. Which of the following is the *best* example of internalization?

   a. A man passes up an opportunity to steal a car, fearing he'll be caught.
   b. Despite the fact that most families she knows have two or fewer children, a woman decides to become pregnant with her third child.
   c. A young woman who loves baseball decides to give it up in favor of skiing, thinking the latter will be perceived as more feminine.
   d. An attorney torn between two jobs decides to accept the one that is less appealing overall because it promises a better income.

2. Which of the following statements is *most* accurate? In our society, language tends to

   a. strongly accentuate male-female differences, though there are many who actively seek to change this.
   b. accentuate male-female differences only when that discrimination is useful.
   c. minimize male-female differences—almost to the point of creating confusion.
   d. neither accentuate nor minimize differences, but accurately reflect each person's perceptions of reality.

3. According to the text, with whom do *most* infants establish their initial and principal identification?

   a. Father
   b. Mother
   c. Mother for girls, father for boys
   d. Whoever provides them with the most affection

4. According to Chodorow's theory of gender, _____ is more difficult for a boy than for a girl.

   a. embracing the economic role
   b. developing a sense of self
   c. establishing an early sense of identity with one's mother
   d. the task of separation

5. Gender socialization studies show *all but one* of the following to be true.

   a. Gender stereotypes are stronger among blacks than among whites.
   b. Parents handle infant sons more roughly than daughters.
   c. Girls toys tend to encourage social skills, while boys develop spatial ability and creative construction.
   d. Typical girls play offers little experience in group leadership, decision making, or applying and enforcing rules.

6. Social scientists point out that men sometimes experience great stress in trying to cope with traditional gender expectations. Probably the *main* reason for this is that

   a. they feel pressured by the overemphasis on productivity and achievement.
   b. most men, whether they admit it or not, are more given to expressive than instrumental kinds of behavior.
   c. following the relative success of the women's movement, men have had to compete with women for jobs and money.
   d. unlike women, men lack the physical and emotional stamina to thrive in a competitive society.

7. Which of the following probably *best* summarizes the way black feminists tend to view the women's movement?

   a. They strongly oppose it since the movement takes attention away from the more important issues of civil rights.

b. They view it as their best hope of attaining equal rights in the workplace.

c. They are generally supportive, but question the real relevance of the movement to the black woman's experience.

d. They are totally neutral, viewing the movement as neither harmful nor beneficial to black women.

8. In talking with a friend one day, Sam made the following comments: "Seems to me men and women should be more alike in the sharing of roles. What's the difference who brings home the income or who takes care of the kids? People make too much of that. What's important, really, is loving each other and making a team effort." Based on these comments, which of the following *best* sums up the relationship between Sam's attitude and that of society as a whole?

a. Sam's attitude, which would have been unheard of in the 1950s, is fairly unusual even in today's society.

b. Most people today would disagree with Sam unconditionally.

c. Sam's attitude pretty well typifies the way most people feel today.

d. A growing majority of people today would probably agree with Sam, although some ambivalence to changing roles is still very common.

9. Which of the following is the *best* example of ambivalence?

a. At one point, Joe had a strong fear of women as potential intellectual equals, but now hopes to marry a woman who is intellectually as capable as or more capable than himself.

b. George, who has a successful and growing career as an attorney, often wishes he could share with his wife the emotional toll that the struggle for success is taking on him.

c. Bill, a dentist, is highly resentful of the fact that his wife, Phyllis, seems to feel that her career as a medical secretary should have the same status as his.

d. Larry, a steelworker, encourages his two sons to obtain more education than he had so that they can "build a career that's satisfying and that brings in some real money."

10. Persons who evidence the positive qualities traditionally associated with both masculine and feminine roles are known as

   a. hermaphrodites.
   b. androgynous.
   c. gendered.
   d. feminists.

## What's Your Decision?

For the past ten years, Allen has been a highly successful businessman, the manager of a small publishing firm. A weakened local economy has brought some hard times, however, and it isn't so easy to make ends meet with a wife and two children to support. The future of the publishing firm does not look promising; no new contracts have come in for some time, and those Allen is working on now are near completion. Allen's wife, Noreen, is a very talented commercial artist. She has worked for Allen off and on for several years, though he's never offered her a serious position, believing that it was important for her to spend the majority of her time at home with the children. Noreen has recently been offered an excellent position with a firm in a nearby city. The job pays well—about $10,000 per year more than Allen is making right now. It would mean a move for them, however, and it might mean that Allen would be out of work for a time. He would need to help out at home, getting settled in a new house, caring for the children, establishing a routine of getting them to school each day, and so forth. In time, Noreen says, they could probably hire a housekeeper, given her increased income. But for Allen, it will mean a serious interruption to his career—and he may even have to look for a job outside his field, or be content to stay at home for a time. Allen feels the move signifies he's giving up. "Let's face it," he tells Noreen. "I've failed. If I'd made a better living, we wouldn't be faced with this decision." But Noreen looks at it differently. "You made the major income for years—now it's my turn. What's wrong with a little role reversal? So long as we get the job done, what difference does it make who does which parts?"

Based on what you know of their relationship and their situation, do you think Noreen should take the job? What are some of the most important factors for Allen and Noreen to consider in making this decision? If Noreen does take the new job, what are some of the most significant ramifications of that decision?

❑ Should Noreen take the new job?

❑ What factors support that view?

❑ What factors support the opposite view?

❑ What will happen immediately if Allen and Noreen act as you suggest?

❑ What will their situation likely be five years from now if they act as you suggest?

❑ Are there research studies cited in the text that offer support for your position?

❑ If you needed additional research-based information to support your position, where or how would you go about getting it?

## Lesson 5

# Learning to Love

## Personal Bonds in an Impersonal World

Turn on the radio any time of the day, and many of the songs you'll hear revolve around one central theme: love. A number of the books we read and write (as well as poems, plays, short stories, film scripts, and other works) also deal with love in some fashion—even those that just take a sidelong glance at human relationships. Almost no other subject consumes so much of our conscious (and perhaps subconscious) thought.

Why is this so? The reasons are numerous and complex, but two of the most important are that (1) most of us spend a good deal of our lives struggling to define love in some personally satisfying way, and (2) all of us share a profound need for love in some form—it's a part of what makes us human.

**Expressing Love**

If you're like most people, you may feel from time to time that this is a rather impersonal world. Cold, even. Ironically, a society in which sexual mores seem fairly relaxed does very little to encourage spontaneous expressions of warmth and affection. For the most part, we tend to keep those with whom we relate on a day-to-day basis at a comfortable distance. Even close friends meeting each other on the street tend to be somewhat restrained in displaying affection.

Of course, if you do not feel genuine affection for the other person, then going beyond simple niceties may seem inappropriate. But even if you do, you may be reluctant to express your true feelings. Friends often know each other a very long time before they will say "I love you . . . I'm glad you're part of my life." Some may never say it.

Very often, we allow what we consider appropriate or businesslike behavior to govern our actions. How many of us would allow a strong bond of friendship—even a marital relationship—to disrupt an extraordinary business or career opportunity? Some would, no doubt. Others might consider that bad judgment. Part of growing up in our society means coming to terms with the fact that love isn't always practical or wise.

On the other hand, this is also a society which seems to encourage expressions of sexual feeling through films, music, advertisements, and literature. Being sexually desirable is seen as a highly positive characteristic. Some of us may even confuse being lovable with being sexually desirable. This can place feelings of self-worth in grave jeopardy, particularly if we believe we are not thin enough, young enough, or beautiful enough to be sexually appealing—and therefore, lovable. In some ways, then, we receive rather conflicting messages about what it means to be lovable, and how we ought to behave in order to be worthy of others' love.

Social psychologists who've made a study of love have defined several sorts of behavior that approximate love, and that may feel like love to us at some point, but that do not have the characteristics of true love—as defined in this lesson. Two such forms of simulated love are *martyring* and *manipulating*. Martyrs maintain relationships by giving others more than they receive in return. While it sounds selfless and noble, there's a catch to martyring. Aware that they're not receiving as much as they're giving, martyrs become angry, even though they seldom express it directly. This and the imbalance of the relationship has negative consequences.

Manipulators do not feel they're lovable either, and so test their partners' love constantly—sometimes in very demanding ways. Have you ever had someone give you this sort of ultimatum: "If you really loved me, you would. . ."? How did it make you feel? Perhaps you felt rather torn, wanting to make the person feel loved on the one hand, yet resenting the need to prove your love on the other. The truly frustrating part of this situation is that the manipulator's need to have love demonstrated is generally insatiable. You can never pass the test once and for all, but must—like heroes of old—complete ever more daring and impossible feats to demonstrate the intensity of your love.

In the relationship of the martyr and manipulator, we see bits of ourselves reflected—even if we have not fully acted out these roles. All of us, whether we see ourselves as worthy or not, have a real psychological and physical need to be loved. In fact, love is closely related to self-worth in several ways. Those of us who have the strongest feelings of self-worth seem to be the most capable of loving others. In addition, feeling loved is important to building and maintaining strong feelings of self-worth. However, the feelings of self-worth must come first. Overdependence on being loved by some- one else can be dangerous.

If you've ever been in love, then you know something of the physical and emotional intensity of passionate love—the rapid heartbeat, a general feeling of supreme well being that some people describe as a kind of floating sensation (notice how often, in poems and songs, lovers' feet never touch the ground), that breathless can't-wait-to-see-you-again sensation. Passion is one form of love, but it's far from the only form.

**Styles of Love**

Other kinds of love include an affectionate or companionate style of loving characterized by deepening commitment, respect, and friendship over time. There is the very practical, almost rational, kind of love that is based on satisfaction of mutual needs. You may know couples who remain together because of emotional or economic security. And then there are also altruistic, playful, and obsessive forms of love. In real life a relationship is never entirely one style. In fact, the same relationship can be characterized at different times by features of several styles.

One thing we can say for certain about love, regardless of the form it takes, is that it is a deep and vital emotion that satisfies personal needs. It involves caring for and accepting our partners, and committing ourselves to sharing love and intimacy.

According to psychologists, high self-esteem is a prerequisite for loving others. Those who feel good about themselves can empathize with their loved ones and affirm their potential.

**A Prerequisite to Loving**

Self-esteem is quite different from selfishness or narcissism. People with strong self-esteem do not tend to extoll their own virtues to any willing listener. Yet, they generally like themselves.

If you're a person with a high level of self-esteem, you probably have some definite values and convictions you will defend, whatever the circumstances. You generally trust your own judgment, and although you will listen to others, you feel no qualms about following your own path without guilt, even if others are critical.

Do you remember the last time you received a heartfelt compliment? Did you respond graciously, or were you uncomfortable—a little embarrassed even? If your self-confidence is strong, you find it easy to believe that others will like and admire you. Yet at the same time, you're likely to appraise yourself as the equal of others, neither inferior nor superior.

What if your feelings of self-esteem are not very strong? Can you do anything about it? According to most psychologists you can, and should, if you want to be capable of giving and receiving love within a healthy relationship. This lesson offers a few specific suggestions to counter feelings of inadequacy, such as building upon your existing talents rather than lamenting shortcomings.

As your self-confidence grows, you will find yourself feeling more lovable, and therefore more capable of believing that someone else could and should love you. You won't be as likely to interpret your loved one's independent activities as signs of declining devotion. If, for example, your partner decides to spend a night bowling with friends, you won't characterize that as desertion. If he or she meets an old friend at the library, you won't be consumed with jealousy, fearing that you no longer come first.

Emotional strength is vital to any loving relationship. The strongest bonds are between partners who are interdependent. They have a strong sense of their own identities, yet they need each other as well, and recognize that need. Neither total dependence nor total independence builds so strong a bond. If one partner in a dependent relationship leaves, the other is devastated—sometimes forever. If one partner in an independent relationship leaves, the other may scarcely notice the change. Neither situation produces the kind of healthy, lasting love that most of us associate with happiness and satisfaction.

## Discovering Love

Love, some people say, is a cyclical process—a kind of emotional unfolding that may go on for the full duration of the relationship. Human beings are enormously complex creatures. The ability to appreciate that complexity, and to know and reveal ourselves a little at a time, seems to have a great bearing on the duration and intensity of the love we feel.

Most of us are aware of the importance of revelation early in a relationship. On a first date, for instance, we may spend a large portion of the time just getting to know one another—asking questions, telling anecdotes that show who and what we are. But once we've made a more lasting commitment, is there any reason to prolong this process of mutual self-disclosure? According to those who study relationships, spending time together, and gradually revealing ourselves by shedding the outer layers that hide and protect our innermost selves promotes a strong, lasting bond.

Don't get the idea, though, that as people reveal more and more of themselves, love just moves along in its steady course. It's quite normal to experience periods of relative disenchantment, during which you may notice that your loved one is sometimes grouchy, has no sense of color coordination, snores, or dislikes animals (including your dog). It hurts to lose a fantasy, even if you suspected the euphoria of first love was too good to be true. Some couples break up at this point, others stay together, and still others try to get one another to change. Disappointment can ultimately give way to a period of acceptance in which we look at each other with both eyes open—disheveled hair, big feet, and all—and love anyway.

What we may have learned is that love doesn't survive just because it's grand and wonderful. The truth is, love is hard work. Perhaps the old saying, "Love conquers all," should be revised: Lovers can conquer all—given enough grit, patience, and humor. And through the hard work, they may learn a great deal not only about love, but about themselves as well.

On completing your study of this lesson, you should be able to

**Learning Objectives**

❑ Discuss some of the ways in which life in an impersonal society takes an emotional toll upon its members.

❑ Describe the concepts of romanticizing, martyring, and manipulating, and explain why each is different from true love.

❑ Explain, in general terms, the cyclical development of love.

❑ Identify and define several contemporary love styles (e.g., eros, storge, pragma, agape, ludus), and explain how these variations relate to real-life examples of loving relationships.

❑ Distinguish between legitimate and illegitimate needs, and describe the influence of love in fulfilling each.

❑ Discuss the importance of a strong self-concept in giving or receiving love.

❑ Discuss the concept of love as a process of discovery, and comment on the importance of maintaining this process in a loving relationship.

**Key Terms**

| | |
|---|---|
| A-frame relationship | Ludus |
| Agape | Mania |
| Dependence | Manipulating |
| Eros | Martyring |
| H-frame relationship | M-frame relationship |
| Illegitimate needs | Narcissism |
| Independence | Pragma |
| Interdependence | Self-disclosure |
| Legitimate needs | Self-esteem |
| Love | Storge |
| Love styles | Wheel of love |

**Assignments**

❑ Before viewing the program, be sure you've read through the preceding overview and familiarized yourself with the learning objectives and key terms for this lesson. Then read Chapter 4, "Loving Ourselves and Others," of *Marriages and Families* by Lamanna and Riedmann.

❑ After completing these tasks, read the video viewing questions and watch the video program for Lesson 5, "Learning to Love."

❑ After viewing the program, take time to answer the video viewing questions and evaluate your learning with the self-test. You'll find the correct answers, along with text page references, at the back of this telecourse guide.

❑ Read the "What's Your Decision?" scenario at the end of this lesson and answer the questions about the decision you would make based on what you've learned from this lesson. Give these questions some serious thought; they may be used as the basis for class discussion or the development of a more complex essay.

1. Love has been described in a variety of ways. It represents anything from a warm fuzzy feeling inside to a loss of appetite. What does love mean to you? What common themes exist between love as described by experts and guests on the program and your definition? Is there a difference between loving and being in love?

2. One's definition of love begins to be formulated at a very early age. Young children between the ages of 5 and 6 months begin to form and express emotional attachments to those around them. How do children formulate conceptions of love? What factors help to determine how they will love in the future?

3. How does "first love," usually experienced by adolescents and young adults, differ from more mature love? Describe the roles of self-esteem and self-awareness in "first love" and in all relationships.

4. Anita, John, and Candy believe falling in love has a great deal to do with timing. However, timing involves much more than being at the right place at the right time. What do they mean by timing? Be detailed in your answer.

5. Most relationships involve strong initial physical attraction. How do Jess and Irene, Rob and Carrie, Peter and Andrea, and Chris and Robin describe the development of intimacy and love from this initial attraction?

6. What do Daphne Rose Kingma and David Viscott say about the ability of one's partner to fulfill the expectations frequently brought to a relationship? What do Anita, Donna, and Carlfred Broderick each think is a fundamental element to any relationship in order to make love last?

# Video Viewing Questions

1. Probably the *main* reason that people feel modern society is so impersonal is that
   a. love is no longer as highly valued in this society as it once was.
   b. we are often encouraged to think and act in ways that deny our emotions.
   c. most people in this society marry for practical or financial reasons.
   d. because of our emphasis on individualism, an every-man-for-himself philosophy naturally prevails.

# Self-Test

2. Imagine that an individual lives and works in an environment where isolation is the norm, and expression of love or affection is strongly discouraged. *Most* psychologists would likely agree that such a situation would be

   a. potentially very detrimental, both emotionally and physically.
   b. somewhat detrimental emotionally, but not physically.
   c. lonely—but not really detrimental, even over a long period.
   d. neither nurturing nor detrimental for most people—though in fact, certain people seem to thrive on isolation.

3. Sylvia has been married for over 30 years to the same man—George. She has moved with him whenever he received a promotion, often against her own unexpressed wishes. They vacation when and where George wants to go, though he isn't aware that Sylvia has other desires. They don't argue often; in fact, Sylvia rarely protests directly or expresses her disappointment and hurt. The behavior that Sylvia exhibits in this scenario is an example of

   a. martyring.
   b. manipulating.
   c. mania.
   d. ludus.

4. If the relationship between George and Sylvia (Question 3) continues in its present manner, which of the following emotions is *most likely* to characterize the way Sylvia will feel?

   a. Extremely content and satisfied
   b. Deeply in love, though not necessarily caring or loving
   c. Very guilty
   d. Angry

5. Suppose that Sylvia (Questions 3 and 4) decides to let George know how she feels and what she wants. No longer is it fair for George to decide the vacation plans or automatically accept transfers to other cities. Which of the following is *most likely* to occur in their relationship?

   a. It will become far more stable and lasting.

b. It will become somewhat more stable over time, but the change will take a very long while and will be slow.

c. Ironically, the relationship will become less stable—and may even dissolve altogether.

d. At this point, after 30-some years of marriage, such a small change is not likely to have much effect at all.

6. Ted and Elaine complement one another. He knows nothing about the domestic arts; she knows nothing about fixing the car or the plumbing. She gets a thrill out of gardening; he doesn't know a lily from a tomato plant. She enjoys completing the income tax forms; he can't stand anything having to do with completing government paperwork. She is in charge of the checkbook; he couldn't care less about the exact amount in the checking account as long as the checks don't "bounce." They agree that they love one another. Which of the following applies?

a. storge
b. pragma
c. ludus
d. agape

7. Which of the following is *most true* of the various love styles (eros, storge, pragma, agape, etc.)?

a. They are stages of emotional development through which any loving relationship almost always passes.

b. They are distinctive ways of expressing love or love-like emotions—any or all of which may characterize a given relationship at various times.

c. They are various ways of imitating or mocking true love, though none of them is really a form of genuine love.

d. These love styles were common to previous times and cultures, and were forerunners of the more contemporary forms of love we know today.

8. According to the text, men in our society have great difficulty in

a. bridging the gap between liking and loving.
b. falling in love with women of their own social class.
c. establishing relationships between their lovers and their own parents.
d. communicating about love verbally.
e. being "just friends" with women.

9. John is a person who often finds himself strongly influenced by the expressed opinions of others. As he listens, he often concludes that he has not thought through issues as clearly as he might. He's a conscientious worker, though admits he makes more than his share of mistakes and that he needs to improve. He knows his boss has been generous to tolerate his longer than usual "breaking in" period. Despite his lack of confidence, John is delighted to learn that the office gang has accepted him enough to invite him to their holiday get-together. Based on what you know of John from this scenario, what would you predict about his ability to give and receive love?

   a. It would be extraordinarily high; John demonstrates great sensitivity to others' needs and feelings.

   b. It would be moderately high since John is obviously a thoughtful person, but somewhat decreased by his over-attention to work-related issues.

   c. It would probably be rather low, due primarily to the fact that John is distinctly lacking in self-esteem.

   d. There is simply no way to tell without seeing John's behavior in a more personal situation.

10. If John (Question 9) were to engage in a loving relationship, which of the following models do you think would *most likely* depict the structure of that relationship?

   a. A-frame

   b. H-frame

   c. M-frame

   d. John would be equally at home in any of the three types of relationships

## What's Your Decision?

Mick and Sadie have been married for 36 years—most of them reasonably peaceful. Each feels the other is a little stubborn from time to time, but then, that's life, isn't it? In reality, Sadie has a tendency to get her own way, though it can't honestly be said Mick objects. "Oh, heck—life's too short to be fighting it out all the time," he rationalizes. "What's the point? Most things just aren't that important, if you want to know the truth." For her part, Sadie takes a slightly different view: "When people love each other, it's no big deal to make concessions. That's just Mick's way of showing he cares about my feelings."

There's one point now, however, that they can't seem to come to terms on. Sadie wants to sell their 40-acre farm and move into a comfortable condo in the city. "We'll be closer to hospitals, closer to the theater and stores, closer to our grandchildren," she argues. "Life will be easier, and a whole lot more interesting. I get tired of looking out at these same empty fields day after day. With the kids gone, country life is plain lonesome." But Mick doesn't agree at all. "This is our home you're talking about," he counters. "Our kids grew up in this house. It's packed with memories. You want some stranger wandering around in here, making new memories that we're not part of?" Sadie shrugs. "It's just a house, Mick. I'd like some comfort in my later years. The life out here is too hard anymore. It's sapping the juice right out of us. You're just too stubborn to admit you're getting older, but I'll tell you the truth—I don't feel like chasing chickens and mending fences anymore. Anyway, if you loved me, you'd see it my way. You'd take me where I can be happy." Mick shakes his head. He hates the thought of disappointing Sadie, but leaving the old place is just about more than he can bear.

Based on what you know of their situation, do you think Mick and Sadie should move? What are some of the most important factors for them to consider in making this decision? If they do move, what are some of the most significant ramifications of that decision?

❑ Should Mick and Sadie move?

❑ What factors support that view?

❑ What factors support the opposite view?

❑ What will happen immediately if Mick and Sadie act as you suggest?

❑ What will their situation probably be five years from now if they act as you suggest?

❑ Are there research studies cited in the text that offer support for your position?

❑ If you needed additional research-based information to support your position, how or where would you go about getting it?

# Lesson 6

# The Pleasure Bond

## Sexuality and Relationships

Many of us tend to associate the onset of sexuality with adolescence. This is most likely because we think of sex as a strong biological drive to share physical intimacy with another human being—the kind of intimacy most of us experience for the first time somewhere between puberty and early adulthood. But physical intimacy is only part of sexuality. In fact, experts contend that humans are sexual beings from infancy to old age. Obviously, then, sexuality is more broadly defined than we may have first imagined.

**Overview**

How do we develop our first definitions of sexuality? As with anything else, our earliest ideas tend to come from experience, and from the kind of home environment in which we grow up. Think of your own experience as a young child, of the behaviors and attitudes that were most common in your surroundings. Were your parents open in discussing sexual matters? Did they answer your questions about sexuality frankly and honestly? Did you feel comfortable asking such questions? The attitudes and behaviors of your parents or other important adults in your life are likely to have significant influence on the way you view sexuality today.

**Developing Sexual Concepts**

While families and individuals obviously differ tremendously in their attitudes and behaviors, a certain modesty about sexual matters is fairly common within the American culture. In most homes, for example, children do not see their parents engage in sexual intercourse; in other cultures, this might be quite common. Nudity is often frowned upon—

some parents even feel inhibited talking freely about male and female anatomy.

Such attitudes and behaviors in themselves are not inherently good or bad. But they may have a profound influence on the attitudes children develop regarding sexuality, and how they obtain their information about sex. If your parents felt embarrassed, inhibited, or just not sufficiently informed to teach you about sexual matters, then you probably found yourself looking elsewhere for information: books, films, friends—or your own experience. And sometimes, you may have found the answers more than a little puzzling.

Our culture tends to provide extraordinarily mixed messages about sex. On one hand, its importance is exaggerated. The *commercialization* of sex would have us believe that sex plays a vital role in virtually everyone's life, that frequent and satisfying sexual encounters with highly desirable partners are the norm, and that life without sex is dull and meaningless. On the other hand, as a counter to liberation of societal views on sex, we may still hear other messages that suggest sex is dangerous, or even immoral, and that suppression of sexual desires is virtuous and admirable. Dealing with these seemingly irreconcilable points of view can lead to great frustration and considerable confusion. While it is well beyond the scope of this course to establish moral standards, perhaps we can be of help in sorting through and evaluating some of the messages.

One of the major themes of this lesson is the notion that sex is a holistic concept. First, sex is not just something two people do in bed together. It affects all aspects of their lives. Virtually all activities *can* have either a sexual component or an impact on the development of a sexual relationship between two people who value each other.

In another sense, sex is holistic in that it involves a total body response. In part, this is because all five senses may be involved in sexual stimulation. Think of your own version of a romantic evening, and you'll likely recognize that sex is more than touch. It is also the look of your surroundings or of a special someone you find attractive. It's what you hear—a voice, the rain on the roof, music, the crackle of the fire. It's what you smell, what you taste—and what you think about. For some persons, one kind of stimulation is more important than another, but virtually everyone is capable of sexual response through all five senses. Let's take a closer look at what happens physically during the various stages of sexual response.

Sexual response, according to psychologists and sexual therapists, proceeds through four distinct phases. In the first phase, known as the *excitement phase*, all the senses are alert—drinking in whatever stimuli are present. During the early part of sexual arousal, the pulse and heartbeat quicken, breathing becomes more rapid, muscles tense, and genital blood vessels become congested. Some women experience a sexual flush. In anticipation of intercourse, a man will often experience an erection; a woman, lubrication of the vaginal walls. All this may come to a sudden halt if the phone rings or the baby cries. But once the stimuli return, the excitement phase will resume.

The second phase, known as the *plateau phase*, is primarily an intensification of the early excitement. During the plateau phase, a man may experience the beginning of a sexual flush, the woman a more intense flush—one sign that orgasm is imminent. The plateau phase, which both partners may find highly pleasurable, can be deliberately prolonged if the stimuli are intermittently withdrawn and then resumed. However, if the stimuli are withdrawn and not resumed, the resultant winding down can be slow and painful.

The third phase, known as the *orgasmic phase*, is a veritable explosion which releases the built up sexual tension in the body. During this phase, heart and pulse rates peak, breathing is very deep and fast, and the senses—which previously were so alert—are now diminished, as if everything were turned inward. The muscles contract strongly—not only the genital muscles, but those of the arms and legs, and even the hands and feet. Men usually experience just one orgasm, generally accompanied by ejaculation of sperm. Women, however, may experience multiple orgasms—though research indicates that only about 15 percent of the women in our culture report being multiorgasmic.

During the fourth, or *resolution phase*, the partners' bodies gradually return to a normal state. Women may remain aroused during this period, however, and with renewed stimulation, may experience orgasm again.

We've talked a little about how individuals become sexually aroused. While no two persons are probably exactly alike, we can make some generalizations. First, as we've already mentioned, all five senses are important in arousal. For some of us, the scent of a familiar cologne or after-shave lotion, or the strains of a special song may have sexual power. There is no

**The Stages of Sexual Response**

**Forms of Sexual Expression**

**65**

doubt, though, that the sense of touch is especially significant for virtually everyone. We are particularly vulnerable to the stimulation of what are called the *erogenous zones* of the body—those areas especially sensitive to physical touch. The genitals and the surrounding area, the lips, and the tongue are erogenous zones for virtually all people. But, as many psychologists and sex therapists point out, any part of the body can become an erogenous zone through association. For example, if a man regularly massages his wife's back prior to sex, she may come to find sexual pleasure in the massage itself.

*Masturbation* is also a common form of sexual expression—more common than many of us may realize. Despite religious taboos, research indicates that nearly all persons learn to masturbate at an early age, and a large percentage of married men and women regularly engage in masturbation. Sociologists view it as a natural practice, one which persons in all cultures learn early in life, and generally continue unless social or religious prohibitions make them feel guilty about it.

Some people may question whether masturbation—moral considerations aside—is a particularly desirable activity for those who are trying to establish a strong sexual relationship with another person. But counselors and therapists suggest that it may be a helpful way of exploring and understanding one's own sexual needs and desires. Of course, this implies that once you understand your own needs better, you'll be willing to share what you feel with a partner—an issue we'll address in just a bit.

Such activities as kissing, fondling, and cuddling can be a particularly satisfying, as well as an arousing form of sexual expression. Often, men and women have a strong desire simply to be close, to feel loved, to feel cared for. They may find it very appealing to sleep together without sex, just to be close. But fearing that their desires may not be understood by their partners or anyone else, they may engage in sexual intercourse even though all they wanted was to be held. Many therapists suggest that such activities as holding hands, hugging, or just lying together in bed may be considered sex in the broadest sense. Recognizing and appreciating a partner's need for this kind of closeness—with or without intercourse—can promote a stronger, more open sexual relationship.

*Sexual intercourse* is also a significant form of sexual expression—though it's important to keep in mind that it is not the *only* form of sexual expression. As with all forms of sexual intimacy, there is wide variation in what people view as acceptable, and also in what they do themselves. Despite the fact that we're generally becoming more experimental as a society, for many people intercourse is still performed in a fairly traditional manner. That is, the two partners lie face to face, the woman on the bottom, the man on top. But as therapists are quick to point out, there is nothing inherently right or natural about this position, and whatever partners feel comfortable with is right for them.

Many people, including social scientists, have attempted to determine what influences *sexual orientation* within our society. That is, why some people are heterosexual, some homosexual. As yet, we have no definitive answers.

Homosexuals do not appear to be distinct in their early family relationships and structures. Furthermore, homosexuals who become parents are likely to have heterosexual children. These conclusions obviously cast some doubt on causal theories related to heredity and environmental determinants.

Freud (and some modern-day psychologists) have suggested that people are born with both heterosexual and homosexual tendencies, and that society tends to reinforce one and suppress the other. While this theory cannot be directly disproved, the percentage of homosexual persons within the general population tends to stay about the same (around 10 percent) from culture to culture, regardless of whether the culture holds a very tolerant or intolerant view of homosexuality. This fact would seem to point to some biological basis for homosexuality; but again, further research is needed before any definite conclusions can be drawn.

Often, we tend to think of heterosexuality or homosexuality as a definite dichotomy. That is, we imagine that a person is one or the other. This may not be at all the case. Some researchers suggest it is far more accurate to say that homosexuality and heterosexuality exist along a continuum, with some people holding a very strong orientation one way or the other, others a less well-defined preference, and still others some tendency both ways.

Defining sexuality on the basis of experience can also be misleading. Many men and women have had some homosexual encounters during adolescence. But there is little relationship between this practice and later sexual orientation. In fact, many people who consider themselves homosexual or heterosexual can report an isolated incidence of what is for them nontypical sexual behavior. Thus, the definition of ho-

## Homosexuality

mo- or heterosexuality would appear to be more strongly linked to attitude and orientation than to behavior per se.

**Sex and Society**

We've already indicated the importance of early experience in establishing sexual attitudes. In addition to what we learn from parents, friends, siblings, and others, much of how we feel about sex is a result of socialization. And, as we've also indicated, we're likely to receive some rather mixed messages. The cultural messages have changed over time and can generally be identified in the United States by historical periods.

*Patriarchal sexuality* is characterized by beliefs, values, attitudes, and behaviors developed to protect the male line of descent. This attitude is found in the patriarchal society of early America. According to this scenario, the man "owns" a woman and her sexuality. She is quite literally his, and by implication, the children she bears are his children. In addition, this perspective looks on sex as a purely biological function, the purpose of which is to produce children. You can see what implications this might have for premarital sex, homosexuality, anal and oral sexual activities, contraception, sex between older persons, and so forth.

Patriarchal sexuality assumes that while men have an urgent sex drive, women are naturally passive with respect to sex—though they can be aroused if a man is persistent enough. For the most part, it's accepted that a man is somewhat harder to satisfy, and in fact, he may need to look outside of marriage to obtain total sexual satisfaction. Such behavior (while not overtly encouraged) is covertly tolerated—for men. It would not, however, be tolerated for women. In fact, according to this message, it is the woman's role to keep her man happy, meaning that she tries to satisfy him sexually, with little or no thought of personal fulfillment. And of course, if needs are minimal to begin with—as the message suggests—then fulfillment is simpler.

With the twentieth century came the emergence of *expressive sexuality*. According to this scenario, sexual fulfillment is basic to the humanness of both men and women. Sex, in other words, is part of what makes us who we are. All people, then, need to express themselves sexually, and the needs of men and women are equal in this regard. Further, sexuality is not just a biological drive to enhance reproduction. Rather, it is an important means of sharing intimacy with another person. Sexual pleasure, then, is a legitimate pursuit in its own right, an open communication vital to the establishment of a strong "pleasure bond" between partners.

Okay, you may ask, what happens if two potentially compatible partners received different messages? Well, it can cause conflict, ambivalence, even loss of confidence. For example, a man who comes from a fairly traditional background may have some difficulty adjusting to a very expressive wife who feels comfortable initiating sex or honestly stating her needs and wishes. He may feel that she's too demanding, and may accuse her of being rather unfeminine in an effort to conceal his own anxieties. If you've experienced similar conflicts within your own life, don't feel that you're alone. In a time of shifting attitudes and behaviors, such reactions are quite common.

Although the expressive sexuality point of view still predominates today, the message that sex is a legitimate means to individual pleasure, relationships aside, emerged in the 1920s and came to characterize the sexual revolution of the 1960s.

Perhaps the most significant change in sexuality among heterosexuals since the 1960s has been in marital sex. Many couples are incorporating more of the expressive sexuality message into their sexual relationships, and learning to communicate more openly as a result. Surveys indicate that a growing number of men regard love (not sex) as the most important thing in life, and that many believe love makes sex better. There also seems to be a growing tendency for men to listen to their partners, to share thoughts and confidences, and to disclose feelings.

Still, open communication doesn't come automatically. What makes it happen? Researchers Masters and Johnson suggest that a relationship based on equality is key. They encourage each partner to assume responsibility for his or her own sexual pleasure. In other words, they caution against blaming the other person for one's own sexual frustrations or dissatisfaction . . . and encourage spontaneity and mutual cooperation.

Sexual pleasure is derived, in part, from doing what *we* want to do—not what parents or others have said was O.K., or what society approves of, or what we've seen others do. Sexuality is a highly personal form of creative self-expression. It takes a certain selfconfidence—or self-esteem—to be willing to express one's sexuality honestly and without fear

**Making the Transition**

of rejection or ridicule. Those with the courage to be themselves stand the greatest chance of gaining real satisfaction through a sexual relationship.

Sexual therapist Carmen Kerr advises women to be very open about what they want in a relationship: Say what you want, she suggests—be explicit and be thorough in your requests. She also advises rehearsing ahead of time in order to feel more comfortable. Those who are shy with a partner may gain confidence by practicing in front of a mirror or with a response group. Other therapists recommend getting rid of gender stereotypes that can get in the way. A man who is forever trying to be cool and tough may have difficulty responding to the warm, tender advances of a nurturing partner. Similarly, a woman who thinks that making the first move is unfeminine may be reluctant to show a man how she truly feels.

## Sexual Activity and the Phases of Life

Early on we mentioned that sexuality is a part of life from infancy onward. The nature of a sexual relationship may change, however, as partners age.

Most couples today begin their sexual relationship before marriage. Studies that have attempted to determine the impact of this practice on sexual adjustment in marriage are contradictory. One thing we do know, however, is that premarital patterns of sex may not be very good predictors of how a sexual relationship will be after marriage.

For most couples, sexual activity is more frequent during the early years—and particularly the very first year—of marriage. There are many probable reasons for this—reasons linked to biological, social, and lifestyle factors. In general, young married partners often experience less stress (from crying children, intruding relatives, unpaid bills, etc.) than do older married couples. Also, a general expectation that sex *ought* to be part of a good marriage may encourage a younger couple to make additional effort to set aside time for sex, to plan for it. Older couples may be more likely to let outside activities interfere.

Does sex get better over time? Some people think so. Though it may not be so frequent during the middle years of marriage, it may still be very satisfying. During this period of their lives, many people find they feel less inhibited than they once did. Women may be more confident, more assertive. Also, following menopause, they may feel a new spark of freedom since they no longer have to worry about pregnancy.

What about sex in later years? Here, sociologists seem to hold rather divided views. Historian Thomas Cole warns against an overly optimistic point of view. People do get old, he reminds us, and there is as yet no way to stop the biological clock, however much we might like to romanticize. On the other hand, research indicates that for some, a strong sexual bond (and sexual activity) may persist into old age. And in fact, it is quite true that some men never become impotent. And some couples continue to have intercourse even into their nineties. But it is necessary to point out that a positive attitude, while important, is not likely to be the only significant factor in determining the longevity of one's sex life. General health and physical condition are important too. And, social scientists add, the general pattern of sex established early in life is likely to persist. In other words, couples who don't engage in sex much during the middle years of life aren't likely to take it up in their sixties, nor are those who do likely to abandon it.

When satisfaction with sex declines, that situation may well reflect the condition of a marriage as a whole. Remember, we indicated earlier that sex is a holistic concept. It is more than physical intimacy. It seems also to be a pervasive bond, a closeness between two people who share themselves on many levels, through many forms of expression. And while it may be unrealistic, at any age, to expect bells and banjos with every sexual encounter, it may be quite realistic to expect a deep level of satisfaction through what is probably the most intimate form of communication human beings can have.

On completing your study of this lesson, you should be able to

❏ Define the concept of human sexuality in broad terms.

❏ Explain why sociologists look on humans as sexual beings from infancy through old age.

❏ List and describe the four primary phases of the human sexual response.

❏ Describe several different ways in which human beings become sexually aroused and express their sexuality.

❏ Describe several ways in which sex-related attitudes and behaviors are changing in our society.

# Learning Objectives

❏ Compare and contrast the patriarchal sexuality and expressive sexuality messages, and describe the influence each is likely to have on behavior.

❏ Explain the relationship between sexual pleasure and self-esteem.

❏ Discuss the importance of open communication in establishing a satisfying and rewarding sexual relationship with a partner.

❏ Trace the probable course of sexual activity as partners age.

❏ Discuss and relate various theories regarding the development of sexual orientation.

## Key Terms

Ejaculation
Excitement phase
Expressive sexuality
Heterosexual
Homosexual
Holistic view of sex
Multiorgasmic
Orgasm
Orgasmic phase
Patriarchal sexuality

Plateau phase
Pleasure bond
Pleasuring
Refractory period
Resolution phase
Sensuality
Sexual arousal
Sexual intercourse
Sexual orientation
Spectatoring

## Assignments

❏ Before viewing the program, be sure you've read through the preceding overview and familiarized yourself with the learning objectives and key terms for this lesson. Then read pages 108–130 in Chapter 5, "Our Sexual Selves;" and Appendix B, pages 561–562, of *Marriages and Families* by Lamanna and Riedmann.

❏ After completing these tasks, read the video viewing questions and watch the video program for Lesson 6, "The Pleasure Bond."

❏ After viewing the program, take time to answer the video viewing questions and evaluate your learning with the self-test. You'll find the correct answers, along with text page references, at the back of this telecourse guide.

❑ Read the "What's Your Decision?" scenario at the end of this lesson and answer the questions about the decision you would make based on what you've learned from this lesson. Give these questions some serious thought; they may be used as the basis for class discussion or the development of a more complex essay.

## Video Viewing Questions

1. The media and advertising industry pushes the forbidden fruit of sex on children every day through television. Consider how Paula Abdul sells Diet Coke and Revlon sells perfume. For the most part, these images are completely removed from most people's daily experience and run contrary to the way parents try to socialize their children. What happens when the media clashes with mom? What did the teenagers interviewed say about sex? Is there any relationship between this and a skyrocketing teen pregnancy rate?

2. Discuss the comments of David Viscott, Michelle Margules, and Alma Jacquet regarding their view of sex growing up in the 1950s tradition. What can be the result of being scared into not having sex?

3. The 1960s produced an environment encouraging sexual experimentation and multiple partners. People with a variety of sexual preferences were free to express their sexuality. What is "coming out of the closet"? Based on the numerous testimony of homosexuals and lesbians in the video, is this a traumatic experience? Why? What did the 1960s do for the homosexual community? Consider that it was not until 1973 that being gay was no longer listed as a psychological disorder.

4. Why does Margo Kaufman believe the sexual revolution killed romance? Discuss the commentary of David Viscott, Carlfred Broderick, and Reed about the real cost of free love. What does Constance Ahrons say about AIDS and sex in the 1990s?

5. How does sex change in a relationship over time? Discuss the experiences of Tom and Candy, Joe and Julie, Glenn and Donna, and Barbara and Dick.

## Self-Test

1. A social scientist would probably agree with which of the following statements? In general, humans are sexual beings

   a. from infancy through old age.
   b. from puberty through old age.
   c. from puberty through midlife.
   d. primarily during the teenage years.

2. The term "sexual orientation" is defined as

   a. the existence of sexuality as basic to the humanness of both men and women.
   b. whether one prefers sex partners of the same sex or the opposite sex.
   c. the "sexual messages" men and women receive from society.
   d. the way in which people act out their sexual feelings.

3. During this phase of sexual arousal, which lasts only a few seconds, heart and pulse rates peak. Breathing becomes much deeper and faster, and individuals may experience a lack of oxygen. Senses of smell, taste, hearing, and sight are diminished, and muscles throughout the body may contract strongly. This phase is known as the

   a. excitement phase.
   b. plateau phase.
   c. orgasmic phase.
   d. resolution phase.

4. *Most* counselors and sex therapists would probably agree that masturbation is

   a. a deviant, sexually immoral act.
   b. neither moral nor immoral, but fairly abnormal.
   c. normal behavior, but a real threat to establishment of a good sexual relationship.
   d. helpful to sexual development.

5. Erogenous zones are

   a. topics of conversation that sexually excite some people.
   b. taboo topics that repress rather than increase a desire for sexual expression.
   c. areas of the body that are sensitive to sexual arousal through touch.
   d. parts of the world where public nudity is common.

6. Most social scientists would likely agree with which of the following? According to the best research we now have, sexual orientation is *most likely* to be determined by
   a. the kind of home environment in which an individual grows up.
   b. heredity, since homosexual parents tend to have homosexual children.
   c. social influence; the more permissive the society, the higher the rate of homosexuality.
   d. none of the above answers is correct; as yet, we know very little about how an individual's sexual preference develops.

7. Bill is 36, has been married for 14 years, and has three children. While Bill was in high school, he had a homosexual relationship with another high school friend. It lasted only a brief period of time, and was his only homosexual encounter. Bill now prefers to have sex with women, and with one exception (a woman), has been totally faithful to his wife. They generally have sex once or twice a week, and Bill considers their relationship "pretty good—better than most, and enough to keep me happy." According to this scenario, Bill would most likely be classified by most social scientists as
   a. heterosexual.
   b. homosexual.
   c. bisexual.
   d. bisexual with strong homosexual tendencies.

8. Patriarchal sexuality incorporates all but one of the following beliefs. Which is *not* part of the message?
   a. Orgasm is necessary for males, but not for females.
   b. The only true value of sex lies in its procreative potential.
   c. Women, if aroused, have as much capacity for sexual excitement and orgasm as men.
   d. A sexually passive woman can be aroused if the man is persistent and skillful enough.

9. Most psychologists and sex therapists today would probably agree that making the transition from patriarchal to expressive sexuality is
   a. desirable and fairly simple, given that our society supports openness in matters of sex.

b.  desirable, but far from simple since society tends to give us mixed messages about sex.

c.  both difficult and undesirable in the long run, since studies show most people are happier in more traditional roles.

d.  inevitable following the women's movement, but highly undesirable.

10. Which of the following factors is likely to be most important in establishing a good sexual relationship with a partner?

a.  Heterosexual preference

b.  Age

c.  Self-esteem

d.  Previous sexual experience

## What's Your Decision?

Sheila and Homer have been married for 12 years, and until recently have had what Homer describes as "a fairly peaceful, normal sex life." By this, Homer means that they generally have sex on Saturday nights—"when everybody has had time to catch their breath, you know"—and on a rare occasion, perhaps one other time during the week. Homer regularly initiates any sexual activity, and assumes that Sheila will either be in the mood or will get in the mood, given enough coaxing. Sex lasts a predictable half hour or so, following which, Homer usually has enough energy left to watch the late show or read the paper.

Lately, though, things have been a little different. Sheila has taken on a new role—a role Homer finds rather demanding. "She's like a different woman," he confides to a friend over coffee one morning. "All of a sudden, she's telling me what she likes and doesn't like. It's nerve-wracking, let me tell you. I don't know what to expect from one week to the next. She's always been this mild, meek little woman. Now she's saying our sex life can get better if we try new things. I didn't see anything much wrong with it before. I don't see any reason to change at this point in our lives. It's like she's gone crazy." Sheila is aware of Homer's anxiety and wonders if she's gone too far. Still, she feels it would be wonderful to have a relationship in which she could really enjoy sex too. "For 12 years," she tells her friend Elaine, "I've pretty much just done things the way Homer felt comfortable. When is it my turn? Don't I have just as much right to my feelings as Homer has to his?"

What's your decision? Based on what you know of their relationship, do you think Sheila should persist in trying to be more open with Homer and in getting him to change his behavior somewhat? What are some of the most important factors Sheila should consider in making this decision? If she does persist in trying to establish more open communication, what are some of the most significant ramifications of that decision?

❏ Should Sheila persist in trying to be more open with Homer?

❏ What factors support that view?

❏ What factors support the opposite view?

❏ What will happen immediately if she acts as you suggest?

❏ What will their situation be five years from now if she acts as you suggest?

❏ Are there research studies cited within the text that support your position?

❏ If you needed additional research-based information to support your position, where or how would you obtain it?

## Lesson 7

# Epidemic Proportions

## Sexually Transmitted Diseases

**Overview**

Most of us tend to associate sexuality with pleasure. As social scientist Nelson Foote has observed, the fact that we are less inclined these days to view sex merely as a means of producing children has given sexuality a certain recreational connotation. In some ways, it has become a form of adult play. But we must use some caution in taking this viewpoint too lightly. For while a sexual relationship may be one of the most pleasurable and rewarding experiences two human beings can share, it also demands a heightened sense of responsibility. The sexual choices we make, the sexual activities in which we choose to engage, may have profound consequences for our own lives, and those of our partners—or children.

**Sex and Personal Choice**

Not so very long ago, one of the primary fears associated with sexual activity—both in and out of marriage—was fear of unwanted pregnancy. These days, with widespread availability of contraceptives and better education about their use, that fear is greatly diminished. Women now tend to feel that they have choices about whether or when to become pregnant.

One might suppose that with the issue of unwanted pregnancy more under control, we would experience newfound freedom with regard to sexual expression. In some ways, this is true. We are certainly freer than we were, even a few years ago, to look upon sex as either a recreational activity or as a means of establishing a loving bond with another person. But other fears, other worries, persist.

How do you feel about your own sexuality? Do you feel it's strictly your own business, and that no one else should have the right to tell you how to think or how to behave? If so, a number of people would agree with you, but some, including a few people with political power, would not. In 1986, for example, the U.S. Supreme Court upheld a Georgia sodomy law, ruling that consenting adults have no right to private homosexual conduct. Depending on how one defines the act of sodomy, this law may also have implications for the behavior of consenting heterosexual adults as well. And that is far from the only instance in which sex and politics have mixed.

No one can listen to the news very long these days without hearing arguments over the rights of a woman to have an abortion, or the rights of gay persons to be equal and full participants in community life. School district battles over sex education are common in our society. While some people take the stand that it is best for young people to be as informed as possible about sexual issues, others argue that it's not the school's place to provide such information. They further contend that sex education itself may encourage sexual activity or permissiveness among young people.

Is ignorance equivalent to innocence? That's far too broad a question for this course to answer. But it is one you may need to answer in your own life. This lesson may offer some information that will be helpful to you in doing that.

## The AIDS Issue

Of all the sex-related issues that have helped polarize political and religious camps within the past few years, perhaps none has captured such universal attention as that relating to sexually transmitted diseases, particularly AIDS. It's important to recognize from the outset that AIDS—or any STD (sexually transmitted disease)—is more than a medical problem. To appreciate the difference, contrast AIDS with, say, the common cold.

Like AIDS, the common cold is—at this point in time—incurable. Unlike AIDS, of course, colds are rarely fatal, and tend to run their course within a short time. For this reason, and many others, our attitudes about people with colds are different from our attitudes about people with AIDS. For one thing, most of us don't live in great fear of colds. We don't worry about whether people with colds are teaching our children or holding down jobs in our communities or serving us in the restaurants we patronize. We don't generally look on the common cold as retribution from God for a sinful life. And while we may not have come up with a cure for the common cold, we are certainly supportive of research and medication to relieve its symptoms.

Our attitude toward AIDS and toward those inflicted with AIDS tends to be altogether different. First, those who view homosexual behavior or sexual permissiveness in general as sinful are likely to see AIDS as a sign of God's wrath—and thus to view it as something a sinful society has brought upon itself. (Think of the implications this has for research, among other issues.) To further complicate the situation, AIDS, along with other STDs, happens to strike members of lower socioeconomic groups with greater frequency than members of the middle and upper class groups. This means, among other things, that there has generally been less financial support and political clout favoring research and education related to AIDS. Those most afflicted simply lack the wherewithal to combat the problem. And until recently, some would say that those less affected have not cared enough. It seemed for quite a while to be somebody else's problem.

This nonchalant attitude is changing rapidly as AIDS spreads through both the homosexual and heterosexual communities, and as we've learned that AIDS can be spread in ways other than homosexual or heterosexual contact.

This lesson takes the position that while these mounting fears are very real and in many respects quite justifiable, it also makes sense to look on the problem as objectively as possible and to take an informed approach. Even now, new research is proceeding more rapidly than in the recent past and providing updated information about the spread and control of AIDS and other STDs. Therefore, personal research is encouraged, using the information offered here as a viable starting point. That having been said, let's take a closer look at some of the most pressing issues relating to sexually transmittable diseases.

**AIDS—What Is It?**

What is AIDS? While we don't yet have the information needed to answer this question as completely as we might like, we do know that it is a viral disease that destroys the body's immune system. Hence its name: Acquired Immune Deficiency Syndrome. Persons afflicted with AIDS become highly susceptible to other diseases—diseases that might not strike others or might not have such devastating effects.

Thus, in the case of a person with AIDS, the immediate cause of death might actually be a form of pneumonia or cancer.

The primary risk groups in the U.S. are homosexual and bisexual men (who together account for about 55 percent of cases) and all intravenous drug users (about 25 percent of cases), who acquire AIDS by sharing needles with infected persons.

A smaller number of people contracted AIDS from blood transfusions that occurred before the blood supply was routinely screened (beginning in 1985), and through organ transplants. AIDS can also be spread through heterosexual contact, though it is more likely to be spread from men to women than from women to men because of anatomical differences. Infants can be infected from mothers before or during birth—and possibly through breast milk.

One of the most frightening issues related to this disease is the fact that a carrier of the virus may be unaware of its presence for as long as nine or more years, and during that time may infect others if no precautions are taken. Further, not everyone infected with HIV (Human Immunodeficiency Virus) will ever develop full-blown AIDS—though such persons may still infect others. Experts believe that susceptibility may have something to do with hereditary resistance to disease in general, as well as overall health. But these are hypotheses yet to be completely confirmed.

Of course, one of the reasons for the fear—aside from the fact that AIDS is virtually always fatal, even with current medical treatment—is that until a few years ago, most of us had never heard of AIDS. Suddenly, people around us were dying of it. The geometric increase in reported cases of AIDS, while not as high as some sources projected, has been sufficient to set most of us on edge.

**The "At Risk" Population**

The most recent research suggests that if you are actively engaged in homosexual or bisexual activities, you are at risk—especially if you have had more than one partner over the past five or six years. If you are heterosexual, but your partner may have had relations with an infected person—either hetero- or homosexual—you could also be at risk. Intravenous drug users are also at risk if they are sharing needles. Those who had blood transfusions before 1985 (when routine screening began) may also be at risk. Voluntary testing for such persons is probably advisable.

What about everyday contact? If you work or live with someone infected with the AIDS virus, what are the chances of your becoming infected as well? Barring sexual contact or the sharing of intravenous needles, the risk is very small, according to research. Most experts state flatly that AIDS is hard to get. Studies indicate that even use of common towels, toothbrushes, and bathing facilities will not spread AIDS. Nor will kissing. Health personnel who care for AIDS patients can be protected from infection by wearing rubber gloves. Experts do not agree on how rapidly AIDS is likely to spread through the heterosexual community, though the prevailing opinion, as expressed by the chief AIDS epidemiologist at the U.S. Center for Disease Control, suggests that the spread will be slow and gradual—particularly if educational efforts continue and those at risk use sensible precautions.

The general fear and concern over AIDS, as well as its entry into the heterosexual community, have had one benefit: increased media attention on the disease, and resulting increase in support for research to control the spread of AIDS. But that's the medical side. What about the social and political implications?

As Americans, we are constitutionally guaranteed certain rights of privacy. Yet, so great is the fear over the spread of AIDS, that those very rights are being threatened on some fronts. There are those, for example, who strongly favor mandatory blood testing for certain groups of people: hospital patients, persons applying for marriage licenses, and public employees, for example. In some contexts, blood testing is already routine—the military has had mandatory testing since 1985, and federal prisons will soon initiate such a program.

Not everyone likes the idea of mandatory testing. Aside from the threat to liberty issues, there are logistical problems. Big ones. First, high-risk individuals may simply choose to avoid testing situations, and as a result may also avoid the very educational programs that might help them. Second, given that there is no cure to offer victims, one must question the morality of simply presenting the bad news and then leaving such persons with little or no social or financial support with which to combat the problem. Third, initial screening tests are unreliable, requiring expensive follow-up tests. Consequently, massive testing is simply prohibitive in cost. Many persons argue that the money would be far better spent on an improved education program that could reach more persons in the long run and probably have more impact in controlling spread of the disease. And finally, some persons argue that proposed testing programs are more likely to reach low-risk than high-risk persons, thus making the overall impact highly questionable.

## Social Implications of AIDS

What of the social implications? Because of society's fears, AIDS victims not only suffer physically, but are also likely to suffer rejection in a variety of forms. They stand to lose their jobs, their friends, their place in society. Increasing numbers of gays report being victims of physical assault because of the association of AIDS with the gay community.

Recent legislation suggests that in the future, those who knowingly expose others to possible infection with AIDS virus may be charged with criminal assault. Further, AIDS care is very expensive. Who will pay these costs? So far, that is still a matter to be decided. But the odds that either the government or private insurance companies will assume a major portion of such costs appear slim. Almost inevitably, families with AIDS victims stand the chance of being left financially devastated, quite aside from their personal loss.

There are other, less immediately apparent, implications. Some social psychologists, for example, worry that emphasis on the dangers of AIDS and other STDs will have a serious negative effect on the ability of young persons to establish warm and loving sexual relationships. There is even some indication that in the future, sex may be limited to serious relationships—and many people would view that as a plus. But there is also the concern that constant bombardment with sex-negative messages may have a debilitating effect on what many psychologists would see as a healthy view of sex as a natural form of self-expression.

Further, concern over infection with AIDS may reduce the already diminished sex ratio of men to women. As researchers point out, most gay men would not be considered candidates for marriage, but other infected men might be. Women are likely to be even more cautious in the future about selecting partners. And relationships in which one partner may have been exposed to infection could be threatened—particularly in a case where a partner has not been honest about sexual preference or other sexual relationships. The very trust on which solid relationships depend is severely jeopardized when partners become fearful of being honest with each other—or have reason to doubt a partner's honesty.

Also, pressures to expand and improve sex education programs within schools are likely to increase—and to meet with some resistance among those who fear there is too much emphasis on sex already. But without openly explicit discussions of such topics as homosexuality, drug use, anal and oral intercourse, and use of condoms, experts fear that there is little hope of having any real influence on behavior. Even now, despite the widespread publicity regarding the dangers of AIDS, surveys indicate that a large percentage of college students take few precautions against AIDS.

So-called safe sex, usually meaning the use of condoms, may not be practiced because persons are not informed about the use of condoms, or because they fear using condoms will reduce the physical pleasure of sex, or because they may see any form of artificial birth control as an intrusion on the romance or spontaneity of a relationship. Of course, as some experts point out, condoms—though certainly effective as a precautionary device—are not a guarantee against infection. If the condom is broken during intercourse, infection can still result. Their use is generally promoted nonetheless on the theory that most persons are not going to give up sex entirely, and further, it is very difficult to know that one's partner is totally safe.

Along with the general fear surrounding the AIDS phenomenon has come a growing sadness associated with witnessing such a high proportion of early deaths. In our culture, which increasingly emphasizes the benefits and possibilities of remaining youthful into our forties, fifties, and beyond, it is sad to be burying so many persons in their forties, thirties, twenties—and much younger. The loss of friends and family, especially when such loss may occur in a context of social isolation or even hostility, can be emotionally debilitating and demoralizing. Support groups may offer some assistance, but the general tenor of fear so pervasive within our society leaves families and friends of AIDS victims with few places to turn. Educational programs do not purport to offer real comfort to those whose lives have been touched by AIDS, or to the rest of us, for that matter. But they can offer suggestions on minimizing risk, together with some confirmation about who is not likely to be at risk.

According to a report from the Surgeon General, you should feel fairly safe from infection if you are celibate, or have been in a long-term, securely monogamous relationship of at least five years' standing, and if you have not used intravenously injected illegal drugs during that period. If these conditions do not reflect your situation, then the concepts of social and

**Precautions Against AIDS Infection**

sexual responsibility imply that you need to make some careful choices about your sexual behavior.

For one thing, you may wish to consider the value of limiting sexual relationships to "persons who are worth the risk." This may mean establishing a close, otherwise significant relationship before having sex. It also suggests that openness with the partner must be an important element of the relationship. Social psychologists stress the importance of being honest about other sexual relationships, and of asking one's partner to do the same. This is not an age, they warn, in which one can afford to be inhibited or shy about asking for information. Too much is at risk. Those contemplating childbirth, for example, have a social and personal obligation to ensure that an unborn child is free of risk from infection—and that is an obligation two partners must undertake together.

Not all of us are likely to feel comfortable with the new levels of honesty being required here. Suddenly, topics we didn't feel very much at home with before are becoming required conversation. Consider, however, the costs of being reticent or silent on these issues. If we do not demand to know whether sexual partners are safe, or ask others to do the same, we are increasing the health risks to ourselves, our families, our unborn children. Perhaps more than any time in our history, our choices about sexual activity have profound social and moral consequences—not only for ourselves personally, but for everyone whose lives we touch.

These are choices we cannot escape, comfortable or not. As health care experts point out, simply going on with life as usual is only one way of making a choice—and it could be a very dangerous way. Perhaps once we have had a chance to sort through all of the fear and apprehension, we will begin to sense how very much the choices made by each individual affect all of us. And out of those choices, we will create a new level of social responsibility. What form it takes depends, in part, upon you.

**Learning Objectives**

On completing your study of this lesson, you should be able to

❏ Describe ways in which outside pressures (e.g., religious, political) influence sexual attitudes and behaviors.

❏ Explain why issues relating to sexually transmitted diseases go beyond medical considerations to affect us socially, personally, and psychologically.

❑ Define the concept of "sexual responsibility" as it relates to the threat of sexually transmitted diseases.

❑ Define, in general terms, the disease known as AIDS.

❑ List several means by which AIDS is likely to be transmitted, according to current research.

❑ List several means by which AIDS is *not* likely to be transmitted, according to current research.

❑ Identify those subgroups within the population thought to be at greatest risk from AIDS.

❑ Explain why some persons think the existence of STDs (especially AIDS) poses a real threat to civil liberties.

❑ Describe, in general terms, the impact AIDS has had on the sexual patterns and behaviors of gay persons and the public as a whole.

❑ List at least five precautionary steps which those who study AIDS recommend following as a protective measure.

| | |
|---|---|
| AIDS | Primary risk group |
| Condom | Safer sex |
| Gonorrhea | Sexually transmitted diseases |
| Herpes simplex virus | Syphilis |
| HIV virus | |

## Key Terms

## Assignments

❑ Before viewing the program, be sure you've read through the preceding overview and familiarized yourself with the learning objectives and key terms for this lesson. Then read pages 130–140 in Chapter 5, "Our Sexual Selves," of *Marriages and Families* by Lamanna and Riedmann.

❑ After completing these tasks, read the video viewing questions and watch the video program for Lesson 7, "Epidemic Proportions."

❑ After viewing the program, take time to answer the video viewing questions and evaluate your learning with the self-test. You'll find the correct answers, along with text page references, at the back of this telecourse guide.

❏ Read the "What's Your Decision?" scenario at the end of this lesson and answer the questions about the decision you would make based on what you've learned from this lesson. Give these questions some serious thought; they may be used as the basis for class discussion or the development of a more complex essay.

## Video Viewing Questions

1. The AIDS epidemic has had a tremendous impact on Americans and their sexual relations. Saying the word condom is no longer a taboo. The compelling testimony of the AIDS patients demonstrates the magnitude of human loss the virus has caused. This has motivated some sectors of society to get involved in fighting the virus and treating its victims. Discuss the comments of Randy Shilts regarding why AIDS has become a huge epidemic. Compare the initial response of the Federal Government to AIDS versus that of the Tylenol/cyanide scare of 1982.

2. Discrimination against "high risk" people in America has soared along with the number of AIDS-related deaths. Discrimination comes in many forms. Discuss the variety of ways these people are being treated unfairly and consider the reasons for it. Consider the testimony of Greg Day, Keith, Slater, and Dr. Schramm. Is the fear justified?

3. AIDS is far from just a homosexual/IV drug user problem. AIDS education has been introduced in many high schools, some of which are handing out free condoms. MTV runs AIDS awareness public service announcements all day. Consider the testimony of Kary, Greg Day, Dr. Schramm, and the high schools kids in the video.

4. Testing for the HIV virus is now fairly simple and more easily available than in the past. For those who want to know if they are positive, taking the test is their decision and they live with the results. What do you think about the idea of forced testing for AIDS? Consider the earlier discussion on AIDS discrimination in your reply. Include the commentary of Dr. Schramm and Randy Shilts as well.

5. How has AIDS brought the gay community together? In many areas of the country, AIDS has mobilized non-gay Americans in the fight against the virus. Why did Ruth

and Bonnie decide to get involved? According to Keith and Jerry, what are the rewards?

6. Randy Shilts believes independent support systems are simply not enough. Why? Why does Dr. Schramm believe America has to stop politicizing AIDS in order to fight effectively?

**Self-Test**

1. In our society, matters regarding personal sexual behavior and attitudes are

   a. left strictly to each individual.
   b. pretty much regulated by the government.
   c. primarily controlled by religious institutions.
   d. considered personal, yet greatly influenced by political and religious groups.

2. Which of the following *best* depicts the way in which Americans today tend to look upon STDs (sexually transmitted diseases)?

   a. Virtually everyone considers STDs to be primarily a medical problem.
   b. Most persons believe that STDs represent evidence of God's judgment against an increasingly sinful society.
   c. There is a real mixture of attitudes—some regarding STDs as a moral issue, others seeing it as a medical problem.
   d. Most people view STDs as merely another pandemic (worldwide epidemic), which has neither moral overtones nor any real relevance to modern medical practice.

3. Many persons believe that the *main* reason there was a more rapid commitment of effort to finding a cure for herpes than to finding a cure for AIDS was that

   a. herpes was seen as largely a middle class condition, while AIDS was seen as tending to affect primarily lower socioeconomic groups and persons disfavored by society.
   b. herpes was just a simpler thing to cure—most people recognized that finding a cure for AIDS was just too difficult to tackle.
   c. herpes received relatively more significant media attention than did AIDS.

d. *none* of the above; they are grossly misinformed; in fact, commitment to treating and curing herpes was extremely minimal in comparison to the initial commitment to finding a cure for AIDS.

4. Eunice and Frank have been dating for about two months, and though they have not had a sexual relationship, Eunice knows that this is what Frank wants. She is nervous about it, however, having had an affair with a man she believes may have been exposed to AIDS. She has no reason to believe that the other man is in fact infected with AIDS. But she's afraid that if she says anything to Frank, it will threaten their relationship. According to this lesson, the *best* thing for Eunice to do at this point would be to

a. say nothing, but simply refuse all sexual advances from Frank.
b. talk to Frank about the situation so that he will be fully informed.
c. go ahead and have sex if that is what Frank wants—after all, Bob probably will never develop AIDS.
d. assume that Bob will develop AIDS and stop dating Frank or anyone else until she has all the facts.

5. AIDS acquires its name from the fact that it attacks the body's

a. vital organs.
b. ability to respond sexually.
c. immune system.
d. general muscle tone.

6. According to information cited in the text, the number of Americans who currently have HIV but are not yet suffering symptoms of AIDS is

a. 218,301.
b. 800,000 to 1 million.
c. 9 to 11 million.
d. none of the above; current information is so limited that no one knows how many cases of HIV exist.

7. The use of condoms as a means of achieving safer sex is

a. effective for homosexual partners but not heterosexual partners.
b. useful for genital sex but not oral sex.
c. not entirely accurate because condoms can break or be used improperly.

    d. no longer true because of recent mutations in the AIDS virus itself.

8. Burt is a drug addict. He takes drugs intravenously, and sometimes shares needles with friends—some of whom are homosexual. Is Burt likely to be at high risk for developing AIDS?

    a. No—as long as he does not have sexual relations with his homosexual friends.

    b. Yes, definitely; the sharing of intravenous needles is one of the primary ways by which AIDS is thought to be transferred.

    c. No, because even though AIDS can be transferred by needles, there is no reason to believe that any of Burt's friends has AIDS.

    d. Only if Burt's general health has been weakened by his addiction; otherwise, he's probably at no real risk.

9. Under the 1992 Americans with Disabilities Act,

    a. the federal government provides financial assistance to AIDS patients.

    b. it is illegal for most companies to fire an employee solely because he or she is HIV positive.

    c. insurance companies cannot refuse health insurance to an HIV-infected individual

    d. both b and c are provided under this legislation.

10. Racial and ethnic minority populations have been disproportionatley affected by HIV/AIDS, with the highest rates among

    a. non-Hispanic blacks.

    b. Hispanics.

    c. non-Hispanic whites.

    d. Native Americans

## What's Your Decision?

David and Louise are parents of three young children, all of whom attend the local elementary school. Theirs is a very conservative neighborhood, with a strong religious influence. Traditionally, the neighborhood has opposed a sex education class within the public school, feeling that it is the prerogative of the church or of each family to provide sex education to children in a manner that makes them comfortable. Now, however, with the rising attention to AIDS, some members of the community once again have suggested that a modern sex education program, with open discussion of heterosexual and homosexual relationships and the means by which AIDS can or cannot be transmitted, would be advisable. If there is sufficient community support, the school will provide such a program. Therefore, all parents must be involved in the decision, and each person's vote is significant. The decision will be resolved through a series of community meetings, held at the school. David and Louise are unsure of their position, and are having difficulty coming to terms with their feelings. Their oldest child is in sixth grade; the others are in fourth and third. They have provided minimal sex education in their home up to this point. Both are fairly shy, introverted persons who feel somewhat uncomfortable discussing sexual matters openly. Neither has ever spoken to any of the children about sexual intercourse or about birth control. Both are concerned that a school-based program will ignore fundamental moral issues that would more likely be stressed in a church-based program. Yet—both are also worried about the very real threat of AIDS.

What's your decision? Based on what you know of their situation, do you think David and Louise should support the local sex education program? What are some of the most important factors for them to consider in making this decision? If they do support the program, what are some of the most significant ramifications of that decision?

❏ Should David and Louise support the school sex education program?

❏ What factors support that view?

❏ What factors support the opposite view?

❏ What will happen immediately if they act as you suggest (and if their vote determines whether the program is or is not put into place)?

❏ What will their situation probably be five years from now if they act as you suggest?

❏ Are there research studies cited in the text that offer support for your position?

❏ If you needed additional research-based information to support your position, where or how would you go about getting it?

## Lesson 8

# Going it Alone

## Being Single

If you're old enough to have been watching television in the 1950s (or if you're a fan of syndicated reruns), you may recall programs such as "Leave It to Beaver" or "The Adventures of Ozzie and Harriet." Such shows tended to portray what was at that time considered to be typical American family life: two people who had married for love and their adoring children—of whom there must be at least two. Family bonds were strong; no one stormed off into the night without other family members having a very good idea where they were going and for what purpose. Problems were solved within a single 30-minute episode, money was available for those who worked hard, and there was never any serious threat to the family unit. Divorce? An extreme, not very widely approved measure, and one not likely to be seriously entertained within the tranquil refuge of the happy 1950s family (at least not the Hollywood version)—even during the family's most turbulent or trying moments; divorce was not a viable option.

What about the single life? Again, that was likely to be viewed as something out of the ordinary. We had to wait awhile until the 1970s to see television series that focused on what it meant to be single. (Remember "The Mary Tyler Moore Show"?) During the 1950s, those celebrating (or enduring) the single life didn't generally have their own series. When they happened to appear on someone else's series, they often became the victims of elaborate schemes to "cure" their singleness through matchmaking. It wasn't that the single lif-

**Overview**

**Marriage as the Norm**

estyle was viewed as deviant or immoral—though it could be portrayed that way—just highly undesirable.

For many of us who were part of the baby boom generation, the happy milk-and-cookies family of the 1950s represented the accepted norm. It is only now, in retrospect—and with the benefit of historical research—that we're coming to realize that, in fact, the early marriage and family emphasis of the 1950s was something of an anomaly—a deviation from other, more common patterns.

Early in this century, it was not unusual for men and women to delay marriage until well into their twenties or even beyond. Nor was it particularly unusual for them to remain single, either through lack of options or as a matter of choice. Gradually, however, there was a trend toward marrying at an earlier and earlier age—a trend which peaked during the 1950s and 1960s. Many sociologists now feel that those who suffered the lean years of the Great Depression came to place an extraordinarily high value on marriage and other family ties, having experienced the enormous stress of a downside economy that rocked family stability to its foundations. Marriage came to be increasingly viewed as both appropriate and desirable.

If you're between 25 and 50 years of age, chances are very good that you grew up assuming (or, at least, having your parents assume) that one day you would be married. Probably you spent some time thinking about what married life would be like, what sort of person you'd like to marry, and how your life would change as a married person. Chances are also good that you spent some time answering questions about your marital status—questions from friends or family: "When are you planning to marry?" "Are you dating someone seriously?" "Are you still living at home?" "Have you thought about starting a family?" Even those of us who learned to field these questions with grace and humor understood the implicit, underlying assumptions: being married is good. It's valued in our society. And what's more, it's expected; "When are you going to *settle down* and become part of things?"

## A Change in Views

Today, our views are somewhat different. The trend toward more marriages and earlier marriages has reversed itself. We are again seeing patterns that were more common at the turn of the century: later marriages, and fewer marriages. Of course, there are some differences. Divorce is far more common than ever before in our social history; and it's also more acceptable. If you were an adult during the 1950s, you can probably recall a time when you had few if any friends who were divorced. Now, virtually all of us have friends, acquaintances, and business associates who are divorced (some more than once)—and we ourselves are increasingly likely to go through divorce at some point in our lives.

Attitudes toward the single life are shifting as well. No longer is it necessarily assumed that everyone will—or should—marry. This is not to say that marriage is no longer seen as desirable. Despite its many pitfalls and heartaches, most of us have a fairly high regard for marriage; and most of us will attempt it at least once. Nevertheless, we're coming to see it as one alternative lifestyle—not the *only* desirable lifestyle. We're also developing a healthy respect for the single life, and learning to recognize that while it may have a number of drawbacks, it affords some real advantages and benefits, particularly when singles are no longer harassed by the negative attitudes of society.

How do you view single life? Do you imagine a lonely widow stroking her cat, gazing out the window at a cloud-filled sky and dreaming of how things used to be? Or do you imagine a swinger, coming home to an urban condo after a fast-paced day at an executive office suite for a quick change of clothes before heading out for a night of fun and romance? Actually, both these scenarios are fairly common, but they're only two out of thousands of possible singles stories.

**A Typical Single Person?**

There is no typical single. As we shall see in this lesson, singles lead lives as complex and diverse as any of us. They're both male and female, young and old, rich and poor. They live in all types of environments, hold down all sorts of jobs, and vary in degrees of personal acceptance and appreciation for the lifestyles they follow. Some are expressly happy and content; others are miserable and lonely. They do have one thing in common, however: virtually all face certain predictable challenges and difficulties.

For a long time, researchers tended to see singlehood as a temporary state, a viewpoint based on the assumption that everyone wanted, ultimately, to be married. Today, researchers are much more likely to see singlehood as a lifetime alternative to marriage, not just a temporary state. Not all agree on why this shift has occurred. Some have pointed to growing disenchantment with the institution of marriage itself. Most research, however, does not seem to support this assumption; other factors seem to play a bigger role.

During the 1970s, for example, when educational and occupational opportunities were really opening up for women, many women delayed marriage because they thought it would interfere with their prospective career. It was hard enough, they reasoned, to juggle a job and university coursework without having a husband (and possibly children) to worry about. Some of these women had every intention of marrying later. Sometimes, however, that didn't work out quite as planned.

The pool of eligible men, it seemed, was dwindling, and was no longer sufficient to satisfy the number of better educated women—many of whom were looking for someone with an education equal to or surpassing their own. And with the passing of time, researchers note, opportunities to marry tend to consistently decrease. Women who do not marry by their mid-thirties face the statistical reality that with every passing year, the odds of finding a suitable marriage partner decrease. Not a cheerful thought for those who really want to marry, perhaps. But, as we've said, that's not everybody.

Increasing numbers of people, however, are *choosing* to remain single. And we're increasingly adopting the viewpoint, as a society, that whether you remain married to one person for 50 years, or marry and divorce, or remain single all your life, is your own business. None of these choices has much to do with whether you're a worthwhile person, a valued friend, or a good prospect as an employee.

Despite growing acceptance of the single lifestyle, many singles may still be viewed as selfish, concerned only with their own happiness. Or, they may be envied their freedom, their opportunity for a fun, freewheeling life, unencumbered by responsibility. Even with our expanding awareness of what it means to be single, there are still those who hold on to the old myths.

At the same time, it probably is accurate to say that singles, if not exactly selfish, do have more individualistic values. They may tend to place more importance on friendships and on personal growth opportunities than do married persons, and somewhat less importance on family values, love, or having children.

## Single Lifestyles

Do singles live differently? Sometimes—for a variety of reasons. For one thing, despite our lip service about accepting singles, many of us continue to feel that they just do not fit in. For most of us, three is still a crowd. We may hesitate to invite single friends to a party unless we can pair them up with possible partners. Single or married, we tend to want our friends to come in pairs.

But of course, singles aren't dependent on the invitations of married friends for a good time. Many spend a large portion of their time (more than most married people) in social activities. They have more leisure time, for one thing, and they may also find it more enticing to spend an evening away from home. A married person whose life is crowded with work and family activities may treasure the hours at home. To a single person, by contrast, home may be the place where he or she is most alone. Therefore, an active social life may be a way of relieving loneliness. Singles may also be more inclined to engage in community volunteer work—as a way of filling hours they'd otherwise be spending alone, and as a way of meeting people. Single people tend to be busy people, one way or another.

Remember that swinging single returning to the condo at the end of the work day? While that particular scenario might not be what we could call typical, it's still fair to say that large portions of singles are drawn to the city life. They may move from a small town to a mid-sized city, or from a small city to a larger city in search of two things singles tend to value: (1) anonymity, and (2) more social opportunities. Small town environments, for the most part, are not conducive to an active social life for singles.

But it's also true that the single life, no matter how active, can also be a life of real loneliness. Let's clarify something, though. Aloneness and loneliness are not at all the same thing. Just as it's possible to be lonely in a crowd, so also is it possible to be lonely in the midst of a family. A large family may guarantee that we'll not be alone. (Indeed, many of us find ourselves yearning for moments of privacy.) But it's no guarantee that we won't feel isolated, separated, and different from those who surround us.

True loneliness—a desolate or empty feeling that comes from not having someone with whom to communicate or share experiences—affects everyone in every social circumstance. It is more common to singles than to married people, however, simply because they do spend such large portions of time alone. Further, the single person who's actively seeking someone to marry may be all too keenly aware of isolation from others, and may feel very different from the rest of the world if most friends are married. Such feelings can be heightened by the pressures of well-meaning friends and family who urge marriage as a way of alleviating the lonely feelings.

## Different Types of Singles

In coming to terms with the single lifestyle, singles adopt somewhat different patterns. Researcher Robert Staples identifies five singles types.

The *free floating* single—as the label suggests—is a person who dates openly and is not especially interested in establishing a long-term relationship with anyone. Most of us have known at least one such free spirit in our lives—and often we imagine that beneath the free and easy facade, these people are really unhappy and searching for true love—but are they?

The second type, according to Staples' definition, is the person in an *open-coupled relationship*, one who has a relatively steady partner but who is free to date others. Sometimes, Staples points out, such a relationship is open-coupled only in a unilateral sense. That is, one partner is free to date others, while the other is expected to remain faithful.

In the *closed-couple relationship*, partners look only to each other for romantic and sexual needs. They tend to feel that an openly sex- ual relationship is alright if there is true affection and commitment (though not necessarily marital commitment) between partners. Members of a closed-couple relationship remain faithful to each other until the relationship is dissolved through mutual agreement.

*Committed singles* not only share a relationship; they share a household as well. Their commitment is deeper and is often seen as a first step toward marriage—or at least engagement. They have either agreed to maintain a permanent relationship, or are at least entertaining the possibility.

The *accommodationist*, in contrast to people in the other singles categories, is one who either temporarily or permanently lives a solitary life. This person does not date. She or he may have numerous friends, however, and may lead an active social life with members of both sexes. But the focus in this person's social life is on friendship or the value of an activity for its own sake, not as a way of establishing a relationship.

Staples also points out that within any of these categories, singlehood may be viewed as either temporary or stable (that is, accepted as permanent). To that categorization, social researcher Peter Stein adds the concept of voluntary versus involuntary singlehood. For example, a 24-year-old woman who still lives with her parents but is hoping to marry would be considered an *involuntary temporary single*. A nun would be considered a *voluntary stable single*.

Of course, conditions can change. The nun may discover she's made the wrong choice. She may determine as she approaches 30 that it's more important to her to have a husband and children than she'd once believed, and therefore may leave her religious order. The woman living with her parents may decide to pursue a medical career and find it occupies so much of her life and energy that she no longer has the interest in marriage she once had.

Consider your own life situation. Do you hold the same attitudes about the importance of marriage in your own life that you once held? Even if your answer is yes, the odds are very good that somewhere along the line, even if you do not make a significant change in your lifestyle, you will feel somewhat differently about the relative importance of being married or being single.

## Satisfaction with Life

If you want to start a lively discussion at a social gathering, ask who's happier—the married man or the bachelor, the single woman or the married woman. The married man supposedly envies the bachelor his freedom, his opportunity to engage in sex just for fun, his leisure time, and his ability to head for the beach at a moment's notice, without concern for what the wife or children might want to do. The bachelor, meanwhile, may envy the married man his sense of security, his social acceptance and status, and the loving closeness that comes with long-term relationships in which people grow to know and accept one another over time.

So who is really happier? While we cannot offer any across-the-board generalizations that apply to everyone, recent polls indicate that the proportion of singles who said they were "very happy" increased sharply from 1972 to 1986, while the percentage of marrieds who said they were "very happy" declined.

Some researchers also believe that marriage is more psychologically (and perhaps physically) stressful for women—that women may be more likely to feel resentment, may feel less power within the relationship, may make more accommodations to her family, and may be subject to more depression and worry than married men. Think of the married couples you have known. Would you agree with these findings? Some researchers do not. In fact, recent findings indicate that married women tend to feel more satisfied with their lives in general than never-married singles, although the percentage is declining. As a woman ages, and the pressure to marry mounts, the level of satisfaction and happiness a single woman who has never married experiences is directly related to how much she enjoys her job and whether or not she is single by choice.

Regardless of whether married or single life is ultimately more beneficial or fulfilling, we've come a long way in accepting the single life as a legitimate lifestyle choice. But what about for ourselves? How will we make the right choices? Taking a realistic look at what it means to be single, and what it's likely to mean for the future, can make for better (if not necessarily easier) decisions. That's what this lesson is all about.

## Learning Objectives

On completing your study of this lesson, you should be able to

❑ List several reasons behind the increasing number of singles in today's society.

❑ Discuss ways in which attitudes toward marriage have changed since the turn of the century.

❑ Discuss ways in which attitudes toward being single have changed since the turn of the century.

❑ Explain how and why the phrase "the typical single" has no real meaning in modern American society.

❑ Contrast temporary vs. stable, and voluntary vs. involuntary, singles.

❑ Differentiate between "aloneness" and "loneliness," and explain how this contrast applies to singles.

❑ Compare, in general terms, the happiness and health of those who are single and those who are married, and indicate how the statistics are changing.

## Key Terms

| | |
|---|---|
| Accommodationist | Involuntary temporary singles |
| Closed-couple relationship | Open-coupled relationship |
| Committed singles | Single |
| Free-floating relationship | Voluntary stable singles |
| Involuntary stable singles | Voluntary temporary singles |

❏ Before viewing the program, be sure you've read through the preceding overview and familiarized yourself with the learning objectives and key terms for this lesson. Then read Chapter 6, "Being Single: Alone and with Others," of *Marriages and Families* by Lamanna and Riedmann.

❏ After completing these tasks, read the video viewing questions and watch the video program for Lesson 8, "Going it Alone."

❏ After viewing the program, take time to answer the video viewing questions and evaluate your learning with the self-test. You'll find the correct answers, along with text page references, at the back of this telecourse guide.

❏ Read the "What's Your Decision?" scenario at the end of this lesson and answer the questions about the decision you would make based on what you've learned from this lesson. Give these questions some serious thought; they may be used as the basis for class discussion or the development of a more complex essay.

## Assignments

## Video Viewing Questions

1. Ira Reiss believes marriage is still a goal for most people, but it has become less important than it was in the past. Discuss this idea in the context of the statements given by two or more of thefollowing: Alma, Michelle Margules, Michelle Burnelle, Kimberly, Laura, or John. Does this explain why people seem to be waiting longer to get married? Justify your answer.

2. Why do single people often worry about money? What does Nancy Weber reveal about the difficulties of meshing a highly rewarding career and a long-term relationship?

3. Note the comments of Dr. Wade Nobels, Julia and Nathan Hare, Sonyia, and Rosalind. Describe the predicament black women face as each of them sees it. Who's opinion do you agree with the most? Why?

4. Why are more and more single women becoming involved with married men? What might be appealing about this type of relationship? What does Susan Speers say on the subject? Do you agree? Why or why not?

5. Single life grants an individual a great deal of freedom. It also, however, brings with it a degree of loneliness. How do Carol, Sonyia, John, and Rosalind deal with loneliness?

6. Despite the stereotypical swinging single image, many singles find it difficult to meet new people. Review the frustrations felt by Nancy Weber, Sonyia, Margo, and Carol Sorgenfrei. Why do they find the singles scene unpleasant or unsatisfying?

7. Being single by no means implies only people who have never been married. A huge range of single lifestyles exists along with a host of different needs and expectations. Compare andcontrast the statements of Rosalind, Ray Wells, Carol Sorgenfrei, Susan, and Sam, noting the variety of expectations. List the pros and cons of being single. What do you envision for your life?

## Self-Test

1. Which of the following best describes the trend we've witnessed in the American adult population since the 1960s?

   a. More adults are marrying, but divorce is also on the rise.
   b. Increasing numbers of adults—whether divorced, separated, widowed, or never married—are single.
   c. The trend toward marriage is increasing very slowly, while the divorce rate has stabilized, and may even be on a decline.
   d. The number of adults who are divorced, separated, or widowed is on the rise, but the number of never-marrieds is declining rapidly.

2. Which of the following best categorizes the prevalent attitude toward singleness in our society today?

   a. Singlehood is becoming accepted as a more common lifestyle choice.
   b. Singlehood is tolerated for the widowed or divorced, but is not widely accepted as a chosen lifestyle.
   c. The single way of life is definitely viewed as atypical and undesirable, though singles are rarely characterized as deviant or immoral these days.
   d. Despite lip service to the contrary, most Americans cling to a traditional view that the single life is usually somewhat deviant and immoral.

3. According to the best definition you can construct from reading this chapter, which of the following persons would be considered single?

    a. *All* of the following.

    b. A nun who has chosen to remain single for life, and who has never been married.

    c. A man who has been widowed twice but who has not been married for the past five years.

    d. A divorced mother with three children.

4. Ed was born in 1934, and married his high school sweetheart in 1953. During the mid-1950s, Ed and his wife had three children, whom Ed worked hard to support. His wife did not work outside the home. Based on what you know from this scenario, which of the following attitudes toward marriage and family do you believe Ed is most likely to hold?

    a. Based on trends we've witnessed since the 1950s and 1960s, Ed is likely to place a low value on marriage and family life, and will probably divorce once all three children are financially independent.

    b. As a product of the Depression Era, Ed is likely to place an extremely high value on marriage and family life—as was characteristic among 1950s families.

    c. Despite the strong influence of the family-oriented 1950s, Ed—like most of us—will be most influenced by the liberalizing attitudes of the 1980s, and will likely remain married but have several affairs.

    d. There is no way to tell from the information given; the time in which one is born or married has little to do with predicting attitudes.

5. Which of the following is true of the changing profile of the singles population?

    a. More singles are moving to the suburbs.

    b. Cohabitation patterns, which peaked in the 1970s, have dropped off dramatically in recent years with the emergence of the New Christian Right.

    c. The number of singles living with one or both parents is on the rise.

    d. Both a and c are true.

6. Emily is a school nurse who enjoys her job very much. She has never been married, lives at home with her parents, and has never thought too much about marriage un-

til recently. She is 34. "It's hard sometimes being with those little kids all day. Often, I wish one or two of them were mine. I know time is running out for me, but I don't want to marry just anyone for the sake of being married. It has to be the right person—but yes, sure, I wish it would happen. And soon." The attitudes and feelings Emily expresses in this scenario are

a. relatively unusual among singles today, few of whom actually value or seek marriage.
b. uncommon for singles in general, but very common among singles who live with parents and face constant pressure to marry.
c. typical of most singles, who tend to be depressed, lonely people longing for marriage and family.
d. neither uncommon nor typical. While many singles share Emily's views and goals regarding marriage and family, others do not.

7. Research consistently finds married individuals physically and psychologically healthier and happier than singles. Are there any alternatives to marriage that could provide the elements required for mental and physical well-being?

a. Yes. Living with another adult could serve as a functional alternative.
b. Yes. Singles with high income levels can provide for themselves all the security and comfort required for health and happiness.
c. No. Although a high percentage of men who are single by choice report being "very happy."
d. No. There is no substitute for traditional marriage.

8. Robert Staples, who specializes in research on African-American families, notes that the proportion of married African-Americans has declined sharply—mostly because

a. there are more black women than men.
b. the rate of homosexuality among black men exceeds the rate among black women.
c. more black men than black women have married partners of other races.
d. all of the above.

9. Martha is a 41-year-old biology teacher just completing her doctorate. When Martha first left college, she had no

thought of marrying, and dated in fairly open relationships for a number of years. She has had prolonged and intimate affairs, but has never been engaged and never seriously thought of marrying—till recently. Now, she feels the time is right for her to settle down and find someone to be a permanent companion—". . . another biology teacher, I hope!" According to this scenario, Martha could best be categorized as a

a. temporary voluntary single.
b. stable voluntary single.
c. temporary involuntary single.
d. stable involuntary single.

10. Singles are often characterized as more lonely than married people. Probably the main reason for this is that

a. the research up till now has simply been too limited to recognize the fact that most singles, far from being lonely, have an active and fulfilling social life.
b. despite research findings to the contrary, married people have a built-in psychological need to see single people as lonely.
c. singles usually prefer to live alone, and therefore almost never establish close friendships or even strong sex-based relationships if they can avoid it.
d. singles often are lonely because, outside of marriage, it is often difficult to establish the kind of primary relationship that offers stability and personal security.

## What's Your Decision?

Miriam is a woman in her late thirties who lives in her own small house in the suburbs a few miles from her parents' condominium in the city. Miriam has two older sisters, both married with children, who also live in the city. She has a good job as an administrative assistant; the salary is only moderate, but it's enough to keep Miriam comfortable, and she enjoys the work. Chance for promotion within her small company is poor, but on the other hand, job security is outstanding; she's an integral part of the company, and she knows that as long as it's around she'll have a job.

Miriam's parents have long been urging her to marry, and lately they've really been putting the pressure on—to the point that Miriam is beginning to go out of her way to avoid family get-togethers. She has a boyfriend—a free-lance court reporter named Jake—who makes an excellent living and would be more than willing to get married. He makes no secret of the fact that he's crazy about Miriam, and that he would like her to marry him and come and live in his spacious country home on ten acres. Though theirs could hardly be classed as a torrid love affair, they do have sex on occasion, usually during weekends at Jake's house.

Although Miriam is fond of Jake, she doesn't really feel she loves him or wants to make any permanent commitment. Further, she believes sex really belongs in marriage, for which she is simply not ready. In fact, she tells her parents, she isn't sure she'll ever be married. "I just have different goals, I guess," she explains to their seemingly deaf ears. "What's wrong with that? Look, I'm very happy here in my own house, with my own job, no one to depend on and no one to answer to—except my cat. That's the way I like it. Stop feeling sorry for me." Miriam has built up quite a bit of vacation leave and plans to take three weeks of it this coming summer to tour Europe. Jake wants to go along, and suggests, none too subtly, that it would make a perfect honeymoon trip. He's even willing to pay all the expenses if Miriam will marry him. "It isn't as if we're strangers," he reasons. "We've been dating for six years anyway, and if you're not passionately in love with me now, well, maybe that will come with time. Meanwhile, I want to make you happy—and comfortable." Miriam's parents think the idea sounds perfect. What do you think?

Based on what you know of the situation, do you think Miriam should marry Jake? What are some of the most important factors for her to consider in making this decision? If Miriam does marry Jake, what are some of the most significant ramifications of that decision?

❑ Should Miriam marry Jake?

❑ What factors support that view?

❑ What factors support the opposite view?

❑ What will happen immediately if Miriam acts as you suggest?

❑ What will her situation probably be five years from now if she acts as you suggest?

❑ Are there research studies cited in the text that offer support for your position?

❑ If you needed additional research-based information to support your position, how or where would you go about getting it?

# Lesson 9

# The Marriage Market

## Getting Together

Most of us grow up believing that we'll marry one day. And when we do, we suppose that it will be for love—or at least, that love will play an important part in the decision. The love we fantasize about prior to marriage tends toward the romantic: hearts and flowers, candlelight and wine, holding hands under the moonlight—that sort of thing. We tend not to daydream so much about holding down two jobs so that the beloved can finish college, or taking care of him or her during an illness, or learning to overlook the other person's little faults (never filling the car with gas, leaving socks on the floor). But love can take many forms and make many demands. Furthermore, the real reasons that people marry turn out to be fairly complex. This is not to say that love doesn't play an important part. On the contrary, love is a key ingredient in establishing and maintaining most relationships, both in and out of marriage. But other factors push people toward marriage as well—emotional needs, a desire to spend time with someone who shares common goals and values, the hope that two really *can* live as cheaply as one, or the desire to have and raise children with someone we admire or like. And if we can find someone to love who meets all or most of these other needs, so much the better.

How about you? What do you think is important to look for in a marriage partner? Character? Social conscience? Strong religious convictions? Sense of humor? Money? Status? Intelligence? Education? Compassion? Keep your priorities in mind

**Overview**

**Choosing a Marriage Partner**

**107**

as you work through this lesson. At the end, you might ask yourself whether your priorities shifted at all, or whether you became aware of priorities you didn't even realize you had.

We tend to take it for granted that romantic love leads to marriage. In films, we cheer for the hero to win the girl. And filmmakers, well aware of our bias, tend to play to it—most of the time. Hence, films in which the hero dies in the end, or the girl abandons her true love (the ne'er-do-well but nevertheless dashing and handsome musician) in favor of the more sensible choice (the ordinary but nonetheless more affluent, better educated businessman) tend to be in the minority. We like love to conquer all. We believe in its power, even when things haven't gone that way in our own lives.

This romantic tradition is very American—and rather modern. Historically, marriages were based on more practical considerations: income, social status, comparability of backgrounds, the desirability of pooling (and thereby protecting) resources so they would not be squandered on the "unworthy." In many cultures, marriages were, and sometimes still are, arranged by parents or other respected elder members of a family who presumably knew how to bargain for the best possible match.

Were these marriages happy? Who can say? Most of us would probably feel quite uncomfortable having our lives so arranged for us. Yet, in all fairness, these practical pre-arranged marriages had some things going for them: family approval of the union, a known source of income, social compatibility, and so on. These and similar factors, no doubt, worked in favor of most pre-arranged marriages. But what about love? Can it evolve out of a relationship that is in other ways correct or appropriate? Perhaps. Nearly everyone, after all, has some lovable qualities. But what if the love did not happen—ever? What then? No matter how right a relationship may seem from a practical, rational standpoint, if it is without love, the partners can be very lonely. What seems to make most marriages work, then, is some mixture of the practical and the romantic. But as anyone who's ever been in love with the "wrong" partner, or out of love with the "right" one will tell you, finding this balance isn't as simple as one might hope.

Was it just good old American individuality that killed off the pre-arranged marriage tradition? That may have played some part. Most of us do like the notion of "doing our own thing," at least in theory. A larger factor, however, has been the movement away from family-centered rural lifestyles to urban-centered, independent lifestyles, in which children often grow up, move away from home and shift for themselves, not only financially but socially and emotionally as well. Even if we wanted someone to work out our marriage plans for us, many of us might not find anyone with the time or inclination to take on the task.

This doesn't mean that the choices we make are free from outside influences. Most of us are aware of certain social expectations regarding the selection of marriage partners. And as those of us who have families know, even when family members are not directly involved in the decision making, they feel they have a right to comment on whether they feel we've made a good choice. Lack of social approval, family approval, or both, can result in severe stress—even for partners who truly believe that love will conquer all.

It seems logical to assume that once people started selecting their own mates, the old notions of choosing a marriage partner on the basis of wealth, property, and social prestige would die out. In fact, most of us approach marriage very much as our ancestors once did. We bring to the exchange the best we feel we have to offer, and we scrutinize very carefully the resources offered us in return.

Now, of course, two young people don't usually sit down at a bargaining table and spell out in direct, frank language how each might benefit the other in a marital arrangement. This bargaining process, which we call courtship, usually takes weeks or months, or even years. During the process, the two prospective partners take time to know each other. Each may discover qualities, internally or within the other person, that make the bargaining more interesting. Further, courtship provides a context within which love can evolve and flourish. It's a time for looking at another human being in many situations, many moods. But realistically, it's also a time for assessing the potential value of another person as a marriage partner, and that assessment usually begins with the very first meeting.

Think back, if you can, to the first time you dated someone you felt you might be serious about. Do you remember how you made conversation, how you asked or answered questions to create a favorable impression of yourself and to get information you wanted about the other person: Where did you go to school? What kind of work do you do, or plan to do? Where do your parents live? What did your father do?

**Beginning the Bargaining Process**

Where do you plan to live? What do you like to do in your spare time?

Do any of these questions sound familiar? Notice that as we ask and answer these questions, we're not just getting to know someone; we're also finding out, indirectly, about his or her background, education, status, and ambitions. We're beginning the assessment process, however subtly. And as the courtship progresses, we endeavor to learn more. The questions may become more personal, more direct: How do you feel about having children? Do you think people should live together before marriage? Would you consider changing your religion?

Of course, dating someone isn't quite like holding job interviews, where we may have just two weeks to find someone suitable. Usually, we feel we can take our time in making this important decision. And, unless you're a believer in whirlwind courtship, you're likely to spend a great deal of time just observing someone's behavior. Perhaps you'll also talk to that person's family and friends. You may even decide it would be wise to live with the person for a time. But regardless of your information-gathering methods, somewhere in the back of your mind you're likely to ask yourself whether the rewards of the relationship will offset the costs.

We can all understand the basics of economic bargaining, and the importance of tradeoffs, even in a very personal arrangement like marriage. But in love and marriage, as in economics, not everyone looks for the same things. An economic bargain may be reached because one person needs cash rather than land, while the other party is looking for acreage to farm. When these two people meet, both feel they benefit from the exchange.

Good marriages are based on the same kinds of mutually satisfactory arrangements. At face value, a man who is young, good looking, well educated, and bound for a promising career as an attorney may seem to have a great deal to bargain with. A woman interested in marriage may consider him a good catch. After all, his earning potential should afford her some degree of social status and prestige; he will probably be well accepted by her family and friends; and since he's relatively well-read and educated, he will offer her some stimulating companionship.

**Bargaining in Bad Faith**

Let's suppose, however, that our hypothetical attorney—call him Mel—also has a vicious temper, dislikes children and

110

small dogs, is adamant about living in the heart of the city where he can best pursue his career (regardless of how his wife may view that option), and wants a wife who will keep herself busy with domestic chores, rather than work outside the home. These characteristics—which might limit his appeal considerably with some women—are not likely to be immediately visible.

During courtship, most of us tend to do a good deal of what social scientists call imaging—that is, we try very hard to make ourselves appealing and attractive to others, not only physically but psychologically and socially as well. We try to be personable and congenial, even if that is a far cry from our true selves. It's ironic that during this courtship period of discovery, many of us do a great deal of covering up—in order, of course, to drive a better bargain.

Getting back to Mel, then. . . . In assessing his marriageability, we must ask two questions: (1) Will his true nature surface during the courtship period? (2) Will a prospective partner consider his earning power and status sufficiently desirable assets to offset the liabilities of a generally unpleasant disposition? As you can see, a lot depends on what a prospective partner is looking for—and on what she is willing to give up.

Not only do people differ in their needs and values, but what's rated by society as most desirable is also subject to change over time. Not so very long ago, most men might have been attracted to women who could cook well; keep an immaculate house; raise healthy, polite children; and perform other, assorted domestic chores. Now, a man may look for a professional woman who will share his career or at least help provide household income. With their double income, they may invest in a housekeeper, eat out four or five times a week, and take their clothes to a dry cleaner's. Neither may want children, and if they do have children, they may spend another portion of their income on daycare so that they can both work.

At one time, a man might have considered marrying in order to legitimize a sexual relationship. These days, a woman is likely to derive little bargaining power from withholding sex until after marriage. Other women will be willing to engage in a sexual relationship even if she is not. On the other hand, other women may not be as kind and loving, as humorous, as skilled at public speaking, or as capable of holding down a professional position with a high-level income. Today, we're learning to look beyond cliches in identifying what is important to us.

## Marrying Our Own Kind

Sometimes, we also need to look beyond what society condones or advocates. Social pressures strongly demand that we marry persons like ourselves. If you've married or even dated someone outside your own race, religion, social class, or even geographic area, then you know from experience just how strong familial or social pressures can be to stick with your own kind. As much as the individuality within us may rebel against this kind of conforming, there are some logical reasons behind pressures that encourage *homogamy*.

There's a general feeling that people with similar backgrounds and experiences are likely to share similar interests and values. (Notice, we said "likely." It doesn't always happen that way.) Two 27-year-old black Catholics who have grown up in the same neighborhood in Boston and who both hold doctorates in psychology are likely—*likely*—to have considerably more in common than one of them will have with a 55-year-old white Protestant rancher from Arizona who barely graduated from high school.

Age, race, religion, culture, and social class establish boundaries that society (as well as parents and friends) urge us not to cross. But increasing numbers of people are crossing them. And although some problems are incurred, the results aren't always negative. In fact, we're learning some interesting things about love, marriage, and values in the process.

For one thing, while statistics do indicate that marriages among people with like characteristics seem more stable over time, we also know that differences in race, religion, or other characteristics certainly do not doom a marriage to failure. Many cross-over marriages not only endure, but flourish, in part because common values are ultimately more significant than more superficial likenesses—such as race or ethnic background. Thus, an interracial marriage in which partners must overcome major differences in value systems is not likely to remain stable over time. However, one in which the partners share common values is likely to be more stable than a marriage between two people who are racially and culturally identical, but who look at the world very differently. In addition, those who do cross boundary lines with open eyes, understanding, and tolerance may find the experience enriching rather than stressful.

As a society, it's probably fair to say that we're a long way from advocating or wholly approving marriages between dissimilar partners. But we're not so intolerant as we once were. We've adopted a somewhat more open-minded attitude, becoming increasingly willing to give less traditional forms of marriage a chance.

In the same vein, we're becoming somewhat more open about the way we define sex roles within a marriage. At one time, it was expected that the husband would be the primary breadwinner, as well as being taller, stronger, better educated, and a bit older. Those expectations are softening, however, particularly as more women are working in professional positions and as more men are recognizing the need for two partners to share in the responsibilities of running a household. Some sociologists even predict that it may not be unusual in the future for an aggressive, professionally successful woman to marry a less aggressive, nurturing man who will take on most of the domestic responsibilities of the marriage (including, perhaps, primary responsibility for raising the children), while she provides most of the outside income.

When we cease to have role expectations based on sex, men and women will be more free to base their selection of a marriage partner on personal needs—the desire for love, companionship, sexual compatibility, and emotional nurturing—rather than financial security or social status. As you may have concluded yourself, such a shift in thinking could place men and women on a more equal footing within the marriage marketplace, with neither expected to play a particular role, but both expected to contribute significantly to the emotional stability of the marriage.

## Love in Marriage

Which brings us back to the primary focus of our discussion—the importance of love within marriage. Maybe you are thinking that with all this talk of finances, social status, and common background there is little room for love in the marriage marketplace. To the contrary. It's still around. It's just that we've come to realize that it isn't always so simple to make things go right. On the other hand, very few counselors would advocate basing a marriage solely on practical considerations (e.g., income, convenience) with no concern for establishing a loving relationship.

All of us need love. The danger lies in hoping that if the magic is strong enough, then differences will go away, problems will dissolve. Love is powerful, to be sure. But in order for it to thrive, it needs support. Married partners—worn from the stress of working out philosophical or religious differences, pacifying unhappy parents, fielding the probing questions of intolerant friends, combining meager incomes to pay the rent or feed a baby they weren't ready for—may have little energy left for snuggling by the fire. The point is not that love is unimportant. The point is, rather, that love seems more likely to flourish in an environment where certain basics of the relationship have already been worked out—or where, at the very least, the partners have some plan for dealing with their difficulties. Some people say that love is strengthened through adversity. That may be true, provided that some point of resolution is reachable. Too many obstacles may strain energies and tolerance levels past the breaking point.

**Making the Choice**

How will you determine whether a marriage partner is right for you? Maybe you're thinking we're about to suggest the use of a questionnaire. Actually, that's not such a bad idea on one level. Oh, we're not advocating the paper-and-pencil sort of questionnaire that you fill out at the kitchen table. Nothing that formal or empirical. But it isn't a bad idea to spend some time asking yourself—and your prospective partner—questions about values, needs, goals. You might do this as a part of courtship, getting to know each other as you date. You might just do it mentally, as you observe one another over a period of time. You might even decide, as anthropologist Margaret Mead advocated at one point, that it would be a good idea to approach marriage in stages, perhaps cohabiting for a period of time to see whether talking about how it will be to live together is the same thing as doing it. Chances are that the person you've known primarily as a dinner date, tennis opponent, or sexual partner will take on new dimensions when he or she shares your rent, takes up closet and bathroom space, doubles the amount of laundry and dishes, and complicates your social calendar.

As you learn to know each other (through the sharing of both the good times and bad), you may decide that the costs of a relationship outweigh the rewards—for you, or for you and your partner. Painful as breakup can be, it's usually less painful prior to marriage than after. Perhaps that's why we're becoming, as a society, somewhat more tolerant of cohabitation.

The implicit sexual freedom associated with cohabitation still makes some people uncomfortable. But on the positive side, people who live together seem to learn a great deal—

about themselves, their partners, and the give-and-take nature of marriage itself. Imaging—the construction of a human "happy face"—is pretty easy to pull off on a three-hour date once a week. It's more difficult for people who are together all the time, and who sooner or later will see each other's real faces. Some of those people will decide that the reality looks okay—pretty good, even—and will formalize their commitment through marriage. It's still a matter of trade. But, the trading is undoubtedly more fair when both sides have a clear idea of what they're getting.

On completing your study of this lesson, you should be able to

❏ Describe, in general terms, how and why the modern idea of marrying for love evolved over time.

❏ Explain how the economically based concepts of "marriage market" and "exchange theory" apply to modern-day courtship.

❏ Explain why women are at some disadvantage today in the traditional exchange.

❏ List some potential advantages and disadvantages of homogamy (choosing partners like ourselves).

❏ Describe the complex interrelationship among heterogamy (marriage between unlike partners), marital stability, and values clarification.

❏ Explain how courtship can, paradoxically, work both for and against the development of intimacy between partners.

❏ Discuss relative advantages and disadvantages of cohabitation.

❏ List and describe several guidelines that potential partners can use in determining their readiness for marriage.

**Learning Objectives**

| | |
|---|---|
| Cohabitation | Exogamy |
| Courtly love | Heterogamy |
| Date rape | Homogamy |
| Dating | Hypergamy |
| Dowry | Imaging |
| Endogamy | Pool of eligibles |
| Exchange theory | Two-stage marriage |

**Key Terms**

## Assignments

❏ Before viewing the program, be sure you've read through the preceding overview and familiarized yourself with the learning objectives and key terms for this lesson. Then read Chapter 7, "Committing to Each Other," of *Marriages and Families* by Lamanna and Riedmann.

❏ After completing these tasks, read the video viewing questions and watch the video program for Lesson 9, "The Marriage Market."

❏ After viewing the program, take time to answer the video viewing questions and evaluate your learning with the self-test. You'll find the correct answers, along with text page references, at the back of this telecourse guide.

❏ Read the "What's Your Decision?" scenario at the end of this lesson and answer the questions about the decision you would make based on what you've learned from this lesson. Give these questions some serious thought; they may be used as the basis for class discussion or the development of a more complex essay.

## Video Viewing Questions

1. Consider the comments of Warren Farrell and Marsha Lasswell regarding what qualities men and women look for in a mate. Why does Farrell believe women prefer the Alan Alda type? Explore what Lasswell means by people "on our level."

2. David Viscott, Daphne Rose Kingma, Joe and Julie, and Glenn and Donna each emphasize love and emotion as highly important factors in a relationship. Consider the status of wealth, social class, looks, and other factors that inevitably come into the picture. How can these factors enhance or draw away from purely emotional attraction? Discuss the possibility of love conquering all.

3. Discuss the positive and negative effects of couples with different religious backgrounds. What are Kathy Wexler, Glenn, and Donna's thoughts on the subject? How can dissimilar backgrounds be a highly enriching experience for both partners?

4. Consider the problems interracial couples face, both between one another and from friends and family. Note the observations of Kris, Glenn, and Barbara Rover in your discussion. Is accepting prejudice a healthy attitude?

5. Remembering Emily, Roger, Toby, Kristen, Kimberly, John, and Deanne's comments, describe and explain how perception and dating goals change with age and why.

6. Kary Vail, Alma Jacquet, John, and Margo all discuss problems and complications with dating, especially in terms of money and sex. Who should pay? What should the rules be, if any? Why do these factors frequently lead to problems, especially with more women than ever living financially independent lives?

7. In the United States, relationships and dating are given a great deal of attention, from the Oprah Winfrey show to scientific studies. What has changed to make this issue so seemingly important? Warren Farrell believes men and women need to first walk in each other's shoes to begin to understand the opposite sex. Why is this important? Do you think it is important for men and women to try to understand each other? Justify your answer.

8. Discuss the differences between a couple living together and getting married. What are the benefits and drawbacks of each? Consider Richard Varnes's comments and the experiences of Glenn and Donna, Joe and Julie.

## Self-Test

1. Which of the following probably *best* sums up the relationship between love and marital success?
   a. In comparison to such practical concerns as similar background and education, love is relatively unimportant in predicting marital success.
   b. Despite what most Americans think, love is really a negative factor that can actually jeopardize marital success by making partners focus too much on emotions.
   c. Love is the one factor vital to the success of any marriage; other factors are relatively incidental in comparison.
   d. Love is one of several criteria—including maturity, sound reasoning, and the sharing of common goals and interests—which are equally important for marital success.

2. The idea of combining the practical and economic elements of marriage with developing intimacy and love is
   a. a new goal, historically.

b. a throwback to the Middle Ages, when courtly love preceded most marriages.

c. gradually falling into disfavor, as more people accept the value of approaching marriage rationally.

d. common to many cultures, though it has never gained much favor in our society.

3. The process of seeking and finding a suitable marriage partner is often analogously compared by social scientists to shopping in a marketplace. Which of the following probably *best* reflects the value of this analogy?

a. It's a sound one in that people do bring to a marriage certain personal and financial resources which they hope to trade for other resources.

b. It makes sense in terms of choosing from among alternatives, but beyond that the analogy is stretched considerably.

c. Actually, it makes little sense since economic considerations are not—or should not be—a part of looking for a mate.

d. Though it's an excellent analogy in a culture where brides are sold or where women are expected to provide a dowry, it doesn't hold up in our culture.

4. The basic idea behind the exchange theory is that whether or not a relationship continues depends *primarily* on

a. how the partners evaluate the relative rewards and costs of continuing that relationship.

b. whether each partner believes he or she is giving and receiving equal amounts of love.

c. each partner's ability to share equally in all marriage-related responsibilities, regardless of traditional sex-determined roles.

d. whether partners view each other as equal in terms of intellect, education, financial resources, and other factors.

5. Rita is an attorney working for a prestigious firm. Rita also holds a doctorate in business psychology, and has written a number of books that have sold well. Her husband, Bob, has a bachelor's degree in psychology and occasionally teaches a night class at the local university, but they're primarily dependent on Rita's income. They have three small children, for whom Bob takes primary responsibility. He also keeps house and does most of the cooking. Based on what you know from this scenario,

which of the following do you think is the *most important* factor in predicting the success of this marriage?

a. Bob's ability—eventually—to obtain a job with a higher income than Rita's.

b. Bob and Rita's personal satisfaction with their nontraditional arrangement.

c. Society's willingness to accept people in such nontraditional roles—which right now is not very great.

d. The financial and emotional dependence of the children. Once the children are grown, Bob and Rita will likely go their separate ways.

6. Which of the following is the *best* example of a homogamous marriage?

a. Marriage between two high school sweethearts, one of whom is Chinese.

b. Marriage between a 32-year-old black high school graduate, and a 31-year-old black college teacher.

c. Marriage between two Jewish college professors, one of whom is fifteen years older than the other.

d. none of these is a good example of a homogamous marriage.

7. John is a man of average looks and intelligence. He's a college graduate with a four-year degree and comes from a lower middle class family. According to the exchange theory, John is *most likely* to marry a woman who is

a. better looking and more intelligent, though similar in background and education.

b. similar to him in looks and intelligence, though possibly less well educated and from an equivalent or lower social class.

c. better looking, but less intelligent, less well educated, and below John in social class.

d. about the same as himself with respect to all the factors mentioned.

8. George is a black social worker and a devout Catholic. His wife, Mina, is a Jewish school teacher, seven years older than George. They have been married for ten years and have one child. According to most social scientists,

the marriage between George and Mina will probably succeed only *if*

    a. they have additional children.

    b. Mina converts to Catholicism.

    c. despite their differences, they share a common set of values.

    d. none of the above. They are simply so different that regardless of how hard they try, George and Mina's marriage is doomed.

9. Which of the following *best* sums up the importance of physical attractiveness in establishing a relationship?

    a. It is especially important early in a relationship, but tends to become less important with time.

    b. It is critical throughout the duration of a relationship.

    c. For most people, it is never very important; most of us tend to notice other things about a person first.

    d. Men tend to notice physical attractiveness throughout a relationship; for most women, though, it's relatively unimportant at any point.

10. In analyzing the potential benefits of cohabitation, *most* social scientists would probably say that

    a. while it's usually not a negative experience, it offers few, if any, benefits to people serious about establishing a good marital relationship later.

    b. it *can* be a valuable learning experience for people who need to know more about each other and the nature of marriage.

    c. while it has practical benefits—financial, for instance—it offers virtually no emotional or psychological benefits.

    d. for most people, it is an emotionally and psychologically damaging experience that threatens the probability they'll have a stable marriage later.

## What's Your Decision?

Bob and Erika have been dating for nearly four years. They cannot decide whether to marry. Bob is a 38-year-old attorney from a white middle class family. He has been married once before, and has a child from that previous marriage; the child lives with Bob's former wife, Elaine. Bob is a Catholic, but no longer attends church regularly since the divorce. Erika is black, from a Protestant, lower middle class family. Her mother never worked outside the home; her father was a blue-collar worker who supported her mother and eight children, of whom Erika is the youngest. She is 23, and the first member of her family to graduate from college. She has never been married, though she has cohabited (briefly) with two men, both black, both older than herself. Erika likes outdoor sports and an active life. Bob is a homebody, who enjoys sitting by the fire, reading or talking. They have some friends in common. Bob's father (his mother is deceased) supports the marriage and likes Erika very much. Erika's parents are generally negative; the rest of her family tends to be divided.

Based on what you know of their situation, do you think Bob and Erika should marry? What are some of the most important factors for them to consider in making this decision? If they do marry, what are some of the most significant ramifications of that decision?

❑ Should they marry?

❑ What factors support that view?

❑ What factors support the opposite view?

❑ What will happen immediately if they act as you suggest?

❑ What will their situation probably be five years from now if they act as you suggest?

❑ Are there research studies cited in the text that offer support for your position?

❑ If you needed additional research-based information to support your position, how or where would you go about getting it?

# Lesson 10

# Variations on a Theme

## The Family Defined

What sort of family did you grow up in? Did you live with both parents? Brothers or sisters? Were your parents married? Was your father the primary breadwinner, your mother the primary homemaker? Did you tend to think of your father as the head of the family, the main decision maker, the one to whom others deferred? To the extent that you answered yes to these questions, you can consider your family to have been of the traditional nuclear variety: two monogamous, heterosexual parents and their children (biological or adopted), all fulfilling pretty well-understood roles. To the extent that you answered no to these questions, your family probably deviated somewhat from the usual pattern—what some people would even call the natural pattern.

This concept of the nuclear family evolved from a long-standing Judeo-Christian tradition. It gained widespread legal and social support, and has been a dominant institution in Western culture. But it is far from the only form the family has taken.

During the past two decades or so, other family forms have gained enough prominence to suggest that it's time to rethink the way we define family. Alternative family forms often entail some serious problems, both social and legal. On the other hand, they also offer some benefits worth considering. If nothing else, by exploring these alternatives we may come to hold less rigid expectations about the various roles family members are expected to play.

**Overview**

**The Changing Family**

Today's American family is changing in two very important ways. First, we are moving from a traditional patriarchal structure toward a more egalitarian or democratic structure. Where once the father determined whether and how the family would spend money, how they would spend their time, and where they would live, such decisions now tend to be more a matter of mutual agreement.

There are certainly exceptions. You may know of a family in which the father has changed jobs or gotten a promotion and simply announced that everyone would be moving—like it or not. At one time, such a decision would have been taken for granted. Now, we are likely to question the value of a lifestyle in which only one member of a group has the power to make decisions that dramatically affect others.

The second change is a movement toward diversity. That is to say, families are not all alike. You may ask if they ever were. Weren't there always differences? Certainly. It's just that until a few years ago, the nuclear family we talked about earlier was considered the norm. Not only was it the most common family structure, but it was the one that received the most attention. Families depicted in books, in films, and on television tended to reflect the traditional structure for the most part. Looking back to your childhood years, you may not recall many polygamous or homosexual families, or families who were members of communes. Even single-parent families and step-families tended to be the exception.

If you still don't know many polygamous or homosexual families, don't feel that you're hopelessly conservative or that the new mainstream America somehow skipped right past you. These alternatives are still relatively rare. The point is that family structure is becoming more diverse all the time. About half the families in our society, for example, have no children under age 18. About a fourth of those with children have only one parent. And that trend toward diversity is likely to continue.

More of us are looking at alternatives in a more positive way. During the 1950s, alternative family structures—with the exception of the extended family, in which grandparents shared the home—were often considered deviant. The prevalent opinion was that the nuclear family was somehow natural, and by implication, other forms were considered unnatural. What do you think? Do you regard diversity as healthy? Do you find some alternatives more acceptable than others?

This lesson attempts to take an objective look at a number of alternatives, providing an opportunity for evaluation of the pros and cons of each. Keep in mind that each alternative structure has evolved to meet some human need, and that while these alternatives tend to solve some problems, they can create others. As usual, making choices requires balancing the rewards against the costs.

In considering what sort of family structure makes the most sense for each of us, it helps to think first about what it is the family provides. Or to put it another way, what functions does the family perform? Tradition is only one force that keeps families together. If there were no other advantages, most of us would probably retire to individual cubbyholes at the end of the day. And there are those among us who do prefer solitude. Most of us, however, find family life rewarding for several reasons.

**Functions of the Family**

Let's say you want to have children. You don't have to get married or be part of an existing family to do this. But there are advantages to both. For one thing, despite growing open-mindedness, people who choose to have children outside of marriage and a family structure can still expect to bump up against a big wall of disapproval. Perhaps this strikes you as moralistic and unyielding. In some respects, you may be right. But there are important social reasons for this attitude.

The family has traditionally been accorded responsibility for the socialization of its children. That is, the family is not only responsible for feeding and clothing children, but for seeing to it that they learn to behave in socially acceptable ways, and that they are educated to a level that enables them to be productive members of the society. One person alone can take on these responsibilities, but—as you'll probably agree if you've ever been a single parent—it isn't easy. Raising children requires time and energy. It's easier if there are two people to share the task, and easier yet if there are grandparents, aunts, uncles, or others to help out. When it comes to child rearing, families make good sense.

Reluctance to condone out-of-wedlock childbirth is, in some ways, society's way of saying that for each child born, there should be some support network in place to ensure proper upbringing. In our culture, we tend to think that such upbringing is the family's—not society's—responsibility.

Families also provide economic support. Few of us today live the way rural families of the 1800s did, building our own log houses and eating the food we've grown or raised ourselves. Not many of us butcher our own beef or spin our own wool. But in many ways, the lifestyle of the homestead family foreshadowed many of the cooperative patterns we see today.

Pooling earning power within a two-income family means a better lifestyle for everyone. There's also a certain security in pooled resources. Suppose you lose your job. If you're living alone, with only yourself to depend upon, you could be in real financial trouble. As a member of a family unit, you might have enough of an economic cushion to tolerate unemployment for a time. Perhaps you'd even have the luxury of looking for work that would enable you to advance your career rather than being forced to take the first available job. And as you gain stability in your new job, you in turn would provide the same kind of support to others in the family whose jobs may be threatened. In an economy plagued by relatively high levels of unemployment and recurring periods of recession or inflation, such security is no small matter. Financial considerations alone make the prospect of single living less than appealing to many people.

Finally, families provide emotional security. There was a time when a certain degree of emotional satisfaction was provided by the community. And for some people, no doubt, this is still the case. If you've ever lived in a small town, for instance, you know something of the closeness, the family-like feeling that can evolve in a small community of people.

But for most of us living in urban environments, or moving from place to place, that closeness just doesn't exist. The world can seem a rather impersonal place. We commute to work on crowded buses or hectic freeways, rarely seeing the same people twice. There may be a certain camaraderie in the workplace, but unless you work with close friends or family members or within a very small company, you're likely to feel some distance there, too.

The family is the place where you're most likely to feel at home, to feel accepted, to feel that you can show your true self—good and bad—and still be loved and cared for. Families provide acceptance and support in times of crisis. If you break your leg, lose your job, or wreck the car, chances are you'll turn to your family for support, understanding, and help.

Wait a minute, you may say. What if your family isn't made up of warm, loving, supportive people? Suppose they're critical, argumentative, and generally selfish? Let's first acknowledge that family life isn't always wonderful for anybody. There are inevitable conflicts, problems, hard times.

But it's important to balance rewards against costs. If the costs become too high, you may decide to look for alternatives—a new family, or a different kind of family.

As we'll see in this lesson, people do not usually remain within one family structure throughout their lives. They tend to move from structure to structure. In addition, people deal with family conflict in a variety of ways, some more effective than others. But that's a topic for future discussion. For now, let's return to our concept of changing structures, and look at some of the different forms modern families can take.

Even within fairly traditional nuclear families, roles are changing. As few as 25 years ago, it was widely accepted that the father would have primary responsibility for earning and managing the family income; the mother would have primary responsibility for managing the household and raising the children. Today, the majority of married men and women agree that child-rearing and moneymanagement responsibilities should be shared.

**Changes in Family Structures**

There's still considerable controversy over who should have primary responsibility for earning income or doing housework—or whether these duties should also be shared. Perhaps surprisingly, researchers tend to find that both men and women, while willing to share, are somewhat reluctant to totally forego their traditional territories. In other words, while some men like the idea of having their wives work, they continue to feel that the man should have primary responsibility for bringing home a paycheck. And while some women like the idea of having help with the housework, they also like the sense that they're a bit more skilled than their spouses at household tasks. Still, the trend is toward a softening of traditional roles, toward more sharing. A husband who stays at home with three children, shops, makes dinner, and handles social and school related responsibilities while his wife goes to the office and attends business lunches would still be in the minority—but he probably wouldn't make headlines or raise eyebrows anymore.

And while the nuclear family is busily reshaping itself, other family structures are gaining attention. Because so many families today are in an economic crunch, and because more households than ever before are headed by women (who still, on average, have lower incomes than men), increasing numbers of households are opting for an extended family structure. Grandparents, married sisters and brothers, aunts and uncles, cousins or other family members (even friends who are looked on as family members) may be part of the household, pooling financial resources and sharing in the responsibilities of keeping the household running.

Some sociologists predict a recurring trend toward "vertical" family structures—several generations living under one roof with the primary bond to the family—versus a more "horizontal" structure, in which the primary bond is to the marriage partner. The extended family network has been common in other societies, and within some American subcultures—the black and Asian communities, for instance. But for most white middle class Americans, it's a rather new way of looking at things.

Single-parent families are becoming more common as well. If you were born in the 1960s or later, chances are you grew up with a number of friends whose parents were divorced or separated. Had you been born one or two decades earlier, however, you would probably have had few if any friends from single-parent families.

The increase in divorce is one primary factor in the growing number of single-parent households. Adoption by single persons has also become increasingly common. Single women who become pregnant are no longer quite so likely to put a baby up for adoption—even if the pregnancy was unplanned. Many of these women are keeping their children, a decision that is more socially acceptable than it once was. Further, it is no longer unusual for a woman to make a deliberate choice to become pregnant and to have a child out of wedlock. By choosing to have a child, but not to marry, she is defining family structure in her own way. Admittedly, this is an option that would not have been so readily open to her a few years ago.

Several family lifestyles continue to exist in the minority, but their numbers are growing. These lifestyles include communal living, polygamous marriages, and homosexual families. Most of us have some fairly definite expectations regarding each of these lifestyles, but often the reality doesn't match the myth.

For example, some of us may think of a commune as a rural community, characterized by a laid-back or religiously-controlled lifestyle and open sex. Actually, communes exist in a wide variety of settings. They may be work-oriented, may allow members to own their own land, and may encourage small family units within the larger community. Childcare responsibilities may be shared among all members, or may be left to the smaller family units. And sex may be open, or as restrictive as in the larger society, especially—as in the Israeli kibbutz—where strict moral and religious codes are observed.

Not many of us have a great deal of experience with polygamy, either firsthand or through observation. And one of the primary reasons is that, for now at least, it's illegal in this country. This doesn't mean it isn't practiced. But it's generally practiced covertly.

Some people practice polygamy because it is sanctioned by their religion. There are numerous examples of polygamous unions in the Old Testament, for instance, and the practice at one time was sanctioned by the Mormon church. For other people, polygamy may be more a matter of practicality. In some black communities, for instance, if there are not enough marriageable men to go around, one eligible man may find himself dividing his time between two households.

Researchers who have investigated black polygamous families remain divided regarding the relative benefits of this structure to the black community, and to the women who participate. Do they enter the arrangement with full awareness? Do they approve of the situation, condone it, or merely accept it? Are they resigned to this lifestyle because they feel they have no other alternatives? More research is needed before we can answer these questions.

It might have occurred to you to ask another intriguing question: just how common would polygamy be in our society if it were legal? While no one can really answer that question directly, it's probably worth pointing out that what's viewed as anomalous or unnatural is often simply the result of adapting, or making the best of limited alternatives. In other words, those who practice polygamy may do it not so much because it's an appealing alternative in itself, but because it offers a means of establishing family closeness and security when other means are not available.

Some homosexual families, in which members of the same sex live together and share sexual and emotional commitment, consider themselves married. They may even go through a ceremony that formalizes their union, though such rituals are not legally recognized in our society. Homosexual unions tend to have a shorter lifespan than heterosexual marriages, but some go on for many years, and some homosexual partners seek to adopt children.

Homosexual families—like communal and polygamous families—can generally expect to incur social disfavor. If you lived next door to a homosexual family or to a polygamous family, would you notice? Would you mind? If you wouldn't, it's pretty safe to say that you're somewhat more accepting of differences than the American public in general.

## Meeting Needs Through the Family

When we think of what keeps a nuclear family together, we tend to think first of such things as emotional and financial security, including the inherent need all of us have for a place to be loved and accepted. We may also think of the family as a logical and nurturing structure for the raising of children. But we tend to place relatively little emphasis on the sexual aspect of the relationship between husband and wife. By contrast, homosexual and polygamous unions may seem to us to have a strong sexual emphasis—even to the point where we overlook or underplay other motives for establishing these families. That viewpoint may lead to some misconceptions.

Regardless of sexual preference or socioeconomic background, all people seem to share a common need for establishing the warm, caring bonds that characterize family life. For some people, the traditional nuclear family structure may provide a familiar and easily-achievable outlet for these needs. For others, nontraditional forms may be more attainable, or may simply meet personal needs better.

For example, a homosexual male may feel very frustrated in a traditional nuclear family, married to a heterosexual female. A single woman who wants to be part of a family structure but who cannot find a suitable marriage partner may settle—at least temporarily—for a polygamous structure, even if that arrangement would not be her first choice. The point is, there are some needs that are difficult to meet outside of the family environment. Therefore, regardless of age, race, religion, or socioeconomic background, the drive to be part of a family seems very strong.

What is the future likely to hold? Will we continue to think of the nuclear family as the natural and proper family structure? Or will we become even more tolerant of other family lifestyles? While no one can make definite predictions, we can say that many forces are at work that favor greater flexibility. Changing roles for women, for example. The increasing mobility of our society. Relaxation of some legal restrictions, such as allowing single parents to adopt children. These and other factors are encouraging us to refine our thinking about family life and how the concept of family is defined.

How about you? Think of the place where you feel most at home, where you feel the strongest sense of emotional and financial security. Chances are, this setting forms the basis for the way you personally define the concept of family. And if you think back over the course of your life, you may see that your definition of family has changed through the years. Perhaps at one time the family to whom you felt the closest bond included one or both parents, some brothers or sisters. Now it may include a husband or wife, lover, children of your own. As you go through this lesson, take time to think about how your personal definition of family compares to the alternative lifestyles presented. Looking at those alternatives may cause you to refine or expand your own definition of what a family can be.

## Learning Objectives

On completing your study of this lesson, you should be able to

❑ Explain the difference between the traditional nuclear family and the concept of family as we're coming to define it today.

❑ Identify and describe three major functions that families perform within our society.

❑ Describe at least two ways in which family structure in America is changing.

❑ Contrast patriarchal traditionalism with more egalitarian approaches as these terms apply to family structure.

❑ List and describe at least five alternative family forms.

❑ Identify at least one major reason for the evolution of each alternative family form.

❑ Describe several ways in which roles are changing even within fairly traditional nuclear families.

❑ Describe at least two situations in which legal restrictions or developments have had an impact on family structure.

## Key Terms

Child-free family
Dual-career marriage
Dual-earner family
Economic interdependence
Egalitarian marriage
Group marriage
Head of household
Homosexual family
Patriarchy
Polygamy
Single-parent family
Social institution
Socialization
Step-family
Traditional society
Vertical family

## Assignments

❏ Before viewing the program, be sure you've read through the preceding overview and familiarized yourself with the learning objectives and key terms for this lesson. Then read the following sections in *Marriages and Families* by Lamanna and Riedmann:

— Chapter 1: "Defining the Family," pages 4–10, including Box 1.2 on pages 7–9.
— Chapter 2: "The Structure-Functional Perspective," pages 32–39 including Box 2.1 on pages 36–37, and Focusing on Children 2.1 on pages 37–39.
— Chapter 5: "Constructing Gay Male and Lesbian Identities Amid Homophobia," pages 114–116; "Comparing Gay Male and Lesbian Sexual Behaviors," page 116; and Box 5.1, "Lesbian 'Sex'," pages 118–119.
— Chapter 6: "Income and Residential Patterns of Singles" and "Domestic Arrangements of Singles," pages 157–171.
— Chapter 11: "Remaining Child-Free," pages 333–334.
— Chapter 15: "Remarried Families: A Normless Norm," pages 506–511.
— Chapter 16: "An Extended Family," page 548.

❏ After completing these tasks, read the video viewing questions and watch the video program for Lesson 10, "Variations on a Theme."

❏ After viewing the program, take time to answer the video viewing questions and evaluate your learning with the self-test. You'll find the correct answers, along with text page references, at the back of this telecourse guide.

❏ Read the "What's Your Decision?" scenario at the end of this lesson and answer the questions about the decision you would make based on what you've learned from this lesson. Give these questions some serious thought; they may be used as the basis for class discussion or the development of a more complex essay.

## Video Viewing Questions

1. Based on the comments of Steve Bohannan, Wade Nobles, Marsha Lasswell, Constance Ahrons, and Anita Allen, what societal pressures have changed or influenced the modern family? How have these pressures changed the family itself? Consider Rob and Carrie's comments in your response.

2. Describe Rob and Carrie's household. Does it look at all like the traditional "Cleavers"? In what way?

3. Discuss the problems and benefits of extended families. Cite the commentary of Glenn, Barbra and Linda, Barbara and Dick, and Paul Bohannan.

4. Discuss the particular emphasis placed on the family in the black community as seen through the statements of Wade Nobles and Dr. Nathan Hare.

5. Discuss the problems of single parenting and maintaining a sense of family. Note the experiences of Jackie Louis and Judy Sullivan. What can be the effects of remarriage? Explore this complicated issue from the perspective of both the testimony in the video and personal observation.

6. Does the communal family described fulfill the same obligations and needs as a traditional family? Should it? In what ways does it fail? Discuss the benefits and drawbacks to Felicia and Walter's situation. In a society as complex as ours, does simply meeting the needs of family members override legal and societal prejudice?

## Self-Test

1. Which of the following *best* sums up the functions provided by most modern families, regardless of structure? Today's families tend to provide

   a. both financial and emotional support to all members.
   b. strong emotional support, but relatively little financial support.
   c. some financial support, but almost no emotional support.
   d. neither financial nor emotional support, though the concept of family is still respected as an enduring tradition.

2. In looking at the evolution of family structure over the past several decades, most researchers would probably agree that today's family is

   a. remarkably unchanged as an institution, considering the enormous social pressures it has survived.
   b. far more liberally defined than in the past.
   c. moving increasingly toward a basic nuclear structure, characterized by strong marital ties.
   d. really without structure, since family tends to be defined by residence, rather than personal relationships.

3. The concept of "responsible reproduction" suggests that

   a. couples should have no more than two children, one to replace each of the parents.
   b. pregnancy should be planned, not accidental.
   c. families should be economically self-sufficient before making the decision to have children.
   d. children should be born within a family setting.

4. Traditionally in U.S. society, the husband or father has been recognized as head of household. Today, this tradition

   a. is more strongly entrenched than ever.
   b. still influences attitudes and practices, but the trend is toward more equality in marriages and families.
   c. is legally upheld in virtually all states, despite recurring attempts to undermine it.
   d. has no real influence upon family life or structure.

5. Marla is a widow with two small children. She lives with her father, Bill, and her two sisters, Arlene and Helen, neither of whom is married. Bill is retired. Marla and Arlene, who are both employed, share household expenses; and Helen, who does not work outside the home, has primary responsibility for the care of Marla's children. This arrangement could *best* be described as

   a. a nuclear family with some nontraditional roles.
   b. a commune.
   c. an extended family.
   d. a step-family.

6. In an egalitarian marriage, which of the following would be *most* likely?

   a. The husband would make most decisions concerning work or money, while the wife would make most decisions relating to homemaking or childcare.
   b. The husband would share in housework and childcare responsibilities, but retain control over money management and would be the primary breadwinner.
   c. The husband and wife would share most responsibilities and would share equally in decision making, regardless of the nature of the decision.
   d. In a departure from traditional roles, the husband would make most decisions regarding the home or childcare, while the wife would handle decisions relating to money matters.

7. Which of the following statements is *not* true of homosexual relationships?

   a. Homosexual relationships tend to be more egalitarian
      than heterosexual relationships.
   b. Gays are less likely to be in stable relationships than
      are lesbians.
   c. By law, homosexual marriage is not legal in the U.S.
   d. All of the above are true of homosexual relationships.

8. Which of the following is an example of a single-parent
   family?

   a. *All* of the following (b, c, and d) are valid examples of
      single-parent families.
   b. Bill, a widowed father, is raising his two children—
      though they stay with Bill's mother during the day
      when Bill is working.
   c. Barbara is a 36-year-old never-married woman who
      became pregnant by choice two years ago and is now
      raising her child.
   d. Eileen is a divorced mother of two adopted children.

9. Studies show that intimate homosexual relationships
   tend to be very like heterosexual relationships in that

   a. one person tends to adopt a primarily female role,
      while the other assumes a primarily male role.
   b. both members of the relationship struggle to balance
      personal, individual needs against the needs and
      goals the two partners share.
   c. without a strong sense of sexual bonding, there is lit-
      tle to keep the relationship going.
   d. after a period of conflict, one person eventually
      emerges as the primary decision maker.

10. Probably the *main* reason for shifting family structures
    over the last few years has been

    a. our previous inability to define what we really meant
       by family.
    b. a general tightening of laws governing family struc-
       ture and behavior within that structure.
    c. a parallel shift in needs and expectations that really
       demanded more flexibility in lifestyles.
    d. declining commitment to the whole concept of family,
       with increasing emphasis on individuality and "doing
       your own thing."

## What's Your Decision?

Phil and Ann have been married only five months. They're happy, but they're finding marriage entails lots of struggles. Phil is studying to be an architect. He hasn't much more schooling left before getting his degree, but it's going slower now. He has to work during the day in a grocery store to make ends meet, and is attending night school. Finding time to study is difficult. Ann is pregnant with their first child, and will soon have to give up her job as a nurse, at least temporarily. She'd like a year at home with the baby.

Phil's mother and sister Eileen (who has a brand new baby) live together in a large house owned by Phil's mother, who is widowed. They are willing to have Phil and Ann come to live with them for a time, and Phil thinks it's a great idea. "We won't have so many bills. I won't have to work so many hours, and you can stay home with the baby for a while. You and Eileen will get along great—both being new mothers."

Ann hates the idea. She has been waiting a long time to get Phil to herself, away from family influence and the constant intrusion on their time. "I don't mind doing without a few things," she tells him. "It means more to me to have a place of our own—just you and me and the baby. I don't feel like being part of a giant family sprawling out in all directions."

Based on what you know of their situation, do you think Phil and Ann should move in with Phil's mother and sister? What are some of the most important factors for them to consider in making this decision? If they do move in with them, what are some of the most significant ramifications of that decision?

❏ Should Phil and Ann move in with Phil's mother and sister and become part of a larger, extended family?

❏ What factors support that view?

❏ What factors support the opposite view?

❏ What will happen immediately if they act as you suggest?

❏ What will their situation probably be five years from now if they act as you suggest?

❏ Are there research studies cited in the text that offer support for your position?

❏ If you needed additional research-based information to support your position, how or where would you go about getting it?

## Lesson 11

# Great Expectations

## The Marriage Bond

Think of the range of married people you know—some old, some young, people of different religious and political views, perhaps of different cultures or races, some of them quiet and stoical, some dynamic. Now imagine that you could put yourself in each person's shoes for a short time to look at their married life from the inside out, the way they see it, with all the hopes, good times, frustrations, and heartaches intact. How might your own way of looking at marriage change? Such an opportunity might bring home the point that marriages, like the people who shape them, are all different. Each has its own personality, its own style. Yet among these differences are woven some common threads that we can trace to help us understand the nature of marriage itself, one of the most complex of all contractual commitments, and a relationship like no other.

**Overview**

Most of us probably took our early conceptualizations of marriage from what we observed as children, the marriage of our parents or others whom we knew well. If those marriages were essentially stable and uneventful, we may have grown up with the notion that people really do live happily ever after. Not jubilantly, perhaps, but happily enough. If those relationships were characterized by stormy encounters, mistrust, verbal or physical abuse, lack of rapport, or just a general feeling of detachment, then we might view marriage as a trap, society's way of smothering personal needs and feelings, rather than fulfilling them.

**Our Beliefs about Marriage**

Sometimes, those of us who grow up observing less-than-happy marriages vow that our lives will be different, that we will not fall victim to the same patterns, making ourselves and others around us miserable. But just how will we go about making things different? Rather than imagining ourselves working through problems, toughing it out, we may be tempted to think that we'll just bypass the problems in the first place by marrying the right person. If the match is a good one, or if there's enough love, somehow everything will be okay; or so we think. The problem with this theory is that love—as an extension of ourselves—is subject to change over time. After all, people are not static. They tend to need and want different things at ages 25, 40, 60, and 75. As they change, their ways of giving or receiving love change, too.

## Changing for a Successful Marriage

What are the implications of this change for successful marriage? Well, for one thing, it's unlikely that one way of relating to another person will do for all time. Marriages must evolve to stay healthy. The process isn't automatic, however. We have to work at it—all the time. In addition, being in tune with our own needs and wants provides somewhat better assurance that we'll marry for the right reasons in the first place. And those reasons are not the same for everyone.

For many people, romantic love is considered the ideal precursor to marriage. But—perhaps surprisingly—not everyone feels like that. The upper middle class son of well-to-do parents might think that all that hearts and flowers stuff is just fine for those who have time to indulge, but that more practical, down-to-earth considerations should prompt marriage. He is looking for a wife who is socially suitable, who will feel comfortable entertaining 20 business associates and their spouses at a moment's notice, and who will stress the same social and educational values he holds in raising their children. Hearts and flowers in this case are secondary considerations to social and educational compatibility.

The point is, we do not all marry for the same reasons. Nor do we value the same things within marriage. One person's notion of a peaceful, tranquil marriage might be another's idea of a crashing bore. Marriages tend to take on different patterns, and within most of these patterns we can find couples who are eminently satisfied and others who long for something different.

Where do you fit in? Part of the answer, as we've suggested, lies with knowing yourself and what you want before you marry. And part lies with recognizing that marriage isn't something that happens to you, like rain. You can shape it, change it, and mold it to suit yourself and your partner.

Our Expectations of Marriage

You may be thinking to yourself that despite all these differences, there are certain fundamental things that people tend to look for in marriage. You're right. What social scientists sometimes call the *marriage premise* comprises a set of expectations revolving around two primary ideas: (1) that marriage will be permanent; and (2) that each spouse will be the most important person in the other's life. Let's consider each of these separately.

The idea that marriage should be viewed as permanent (or even close to it) may strike you as rather ludicrous in this age of rising divorce rates and multiple remarriages. But we tend to be a romantically resilient lot, reluctant to let go of the notion that marriage—whatever the divorce statistics might indicate—is for keeps. Most of us who marry take a vow to love the other person 'til death do us part, or for as long as we both shall live. And on an emotional level, at least, we mean it. Further, research indicates that we tend to enter marriage filled with hope that the initial feelings of warmth and affection will not only last, but even grow with time.

At the same time, most of us aren't marching through life with earplugs and blinders; we know that separation and divorce are realities. So we live with a certain cultural conflict: the desire to view marriage as permanent, and the knowledge that very often it's anything but. Our success in dealing with this conflict has a great deal to do with whether we view marriage passively—as something that happens to us—or whether we believe we have something to do with how our own marriage eventually develops. In other words, do we believe we're in control of our own marital destinies? If so, then we can make marriage last forever, if that's what we want.

Psychologists warn, however, that in order for a marital relationship to be satisfying long-term, couples must give up the notion that theirs will be the world's first conflict-free, total-bliss marriage. Conflict, they warn, is inevitable. During periods of a marriage, we may feel resentment, anger, even hatred toward a spouse. That doesn't mean that love won't survive. Sure, the early glow may pass. But if, through conflict, we establish a closer intimacy, love may grow stronger.

What about expectations of primariness? Most of us marry with the assumption that we'll be the single most important person in the other's life, taking first place over friends, former lovers, parents. For some people, primariness implies sexual exclusivity as well. Other people take a more open view, feeling that sex outside marriage is all right (even, sometimes, desirable) provided that the primary emotional bond remains with the spouse.

If there's truth to the old saying that actions speak louder than words, then we can assume that most of us do not value strict monogamy quite so much as we say we do. In practice, millions of married men and women have at least one extramarital affair. And contrary to what we're often conditioned to think, these affairs are not always prompted by disillusionment with the spouse or with the marriage as a whole. Some people simply want variety. Some are looking for more emotional fulfillment. Others are out to prove that they're still young and desirable—to more than one person.

The reasons for extramarital affairs, researchers tell us, are exceedingly complex and difficult to sort out; few people who have sex outside marriage are motivated by just one thing. What seems more important than analyzing various motives (which we may never totally understand, even within ourselves) is realizing that sexual infidelity is not necessarily the same thing as marital infidelity, as some people define it. In other words, for many people, primariness is a powerful emotional bond that is much more encompassing than sexual compatibility, which they tend to view as only one expression of affection.

Extramarital affairs do not necessarily spell the end of a marriage. For one thing, the spouse sometimes knows of or even approves of such affairs. So-called open marriages that encourage sex with other partners are far from the norm, but they're probably a good deal more common than many of us realize. And even when the partner does not know about or approve of the affair, the stability of a marriage tends to be determined by the degree of trust between the two partners. If their marriage is highly rewarding in other ways, and if the trust is strong, the odds are against one affair shattering the relationship. On the other hand, marriage *can* be fragile. Let's consider some of the different kinds of marriages to get a better idea about what sort of glue holds them together.

## Intrinsic and Utilitarian Marriage Relationships

Remember our executive? The one who married the wife who could entertain 20 business associates without biting her nails? Keep that fellow—call him Erik—in mind, and contrast his motivation with that of Keith, also a college graduate, also from an upper middle class family. Let's say that Keith spends most of his college life dating Molly, a girl whose background is much like his own. Molly doesn't plan to work outside the home once she and Keith marry; she plans to spend her energies supporting him in the fulfillment of his career. They plan to have two, possibly three children. Their relationship is pleasant, harmonious, satisfying—but not exactly electric. Keith has the feeling something is missing, but what? Molly is such a fine person, and they seem so well suited. She gets along well with his family; in fact, they assume the two will marry as soon as Molly (sensibly) completes her education and Keith is firmly established in his profession.

Enter Rita. Rita and Keith meet at an after-ski party, and are drawn to each other despite a number of differences. They have different religious affiliations, different political views. Rita is from a lower middle class family. She has worked her way through college and is older than Keith. She tends to be far more liberal, and plans to spend her life as a social worker. She wants to travel and write books, and tends to see homemaking not as a career or source of fulfillment, but as something to get out of the way so they can move on to what's really important in life.

Rita and Keith's relationship has deep emotional and sexual overtones from the first. They talk seriously about life, about values, about giving of oneself, about the importance of enjoying work and not just doing it for the money. For the first time, Keith feels he has a "soul mate, someone who really understands me, and someone who values me for myself." Very soon, Keith finds he does not want to spend time away from Rita. Not only are they romantically and sexually compatible, but they're becoming close friends as well. Gradually, to his parents' (and some friends') dismay, the relationship with Molly disintegrates. Keith finds he cannot abandon his feelings just for the sake of being practical.

The kind of relationship Keith and Rita are establishing within this scenario is what social scientists term *intrinsic*. It is a relationship based on deep personal feelings, emotional fulfillment, strong sense of rapport, and concern for the other person's welfare. The kind of relationship that Erik (our first executive) was looking for was of the *utilitarian* variety—a relationship based on such practical considerations as social and financial appropriateness, or the partner's ability to perform certain important functions: homemaking, child rearing, income providing, and so forth. Neither of these broad types of marriages is necessarily better than the other; what really matters is what is right for the individual. Some people are more satisfied in one sort of relationship, some in another.

In real life, of course, the division between intrinsic and utilitarian marriage isn't quite so cut and dried as we've presented it here. Most marriages are a combination of the two. That is, we may marry primarily for love, but also stop to consider that the person whom we're marrying is capable of providing the practical things we want: good parenting, ability to earn a living, witty companionship, or whatever. Or, we may marry for very practical reasons and find more enchantment than we'd hoped for.

Within each of these major divisions, marriages tend to take on a variety of patterns. That is, not all practical marriages are precisely alike, nor are all intrinsic marriages necessarily alike. Some utilitarian marriages are almost like business arrangements, in which each spouse fulfills the other's expectations in an almost formal way, but each tends to stay out of the other's life. Husband and wife may each have their own friends and social life and interests, getting the job done as a marriage partner, but not looking to that marriage as a source of real fulfillment. Other utilitarian marriages are more companionable. Spouses may participate together in a wide range of activities—community service, school related activities, sports—and enjoy each other's company much as casual friends who share a deep mutual respect.

Similarly, intrinsic marriages can simply imply a strong emotional closeness. Or they may take the form of a total marriage in which partners share virtually every aspect of each other's lives (often including work), and seem to grow ever closer through the experience. For these fortunate (and seemingly rare) people, familiarity breeds love, not contempt.

Okay, you may ask, do we have any real control over the sort of pattern a marriage takes? After all, aren't we to some extent victims of circumstance, our needs and wants determined by the environment in which we grow up? To some extent, that's probably true. But that's no reason to be swept along in the tide like so many ships adrift, hoping to land in a safe harbor somewhere. Let's get back to Keith for a moment. In initiating his relationship with Rita, Keith learned some important things about his own needs. He learned, for instance, that having rapport with his partner was more important to him than marrying someone whom others might consider more socially acceptable. And he used that information to make a deliberate choice about the kind of married life he would have. So can you.

One way social scientists recommend making this happen is through establishment of a marriage agreement. To some people, that sounds like a pretty cold, businesslike approach to an institution that's supposed to be at least a little romantic (no matter how much we talk about being practical). But in fact, a written agreement is only an expression of what we're thinking and feeling inside anyway. Used properly, it can be a means of establishing better understanding, of sharing feelings that might otherwise be suppressed till it was too late.

## The Marriage Agreement

Look at it this way: If you were going to apply for a job with Company X, would you just present yourself on their doorstep one day and say, "Give me anything. I'm sure you'll find the job that's right for me."? Not likely. Even if they complied, the chances of making a good match would be remote at best. You wouldn't be happy, probably—and soon, neither would Company X. When we're looking for work, most of us are fairly direct about making our needs and expectations known in advance—before commitments are made. For some reason, though, we're more reluctant to negotiate about this very personal but even more important contract: marriage. And this may be very unwise.

The chances for a marriage to develop as we'd like it to are enhanced if both people understand clearly what the other expects and hopes to get out of a relationship. If one partner is hoping for heart-to-hearts by the fire, while the other only wants company on the golf course, neither is likely to find the relationship satisfying, and conflict is inevitable.

Well, you may say, isn't courtship the time to iron all that out, get things into the open? Sure, if you can bring that off. Lots of people don't, however—for whatever reason. They tend to avoid potentially inflammatory subjects during courtship, valuing peace more than conflict resolution. Or, they may not be in touch with their own feelings and needs as well as they should be prior to marriage. Or, they may make assumptions about the other person that are unwarranted.

Behavioral clues are important during courtship, but don't assume you can judge everything about a person by the way he or she acts. A woman who loves children doesn't necessarily want any of her own. A man who's spent most of his life on a horse ranch may decide that it's the city life with its cultural advantages he really favors. A woman who's spent several years completing law school may feel she'd really like to take some time off and travel or take up oil painting before beginning to practice law. Often, psychologists warn, we don't know our potential mates as well as we might think. Often, we don't even know ourselves as well as we might.

A personal, written agreement provides a chance for both persons to clarify values and expectations, and to gain some new insights about what the other person wants. What sort of information should you include in such a document? Anything that's important to you, the social scientists say. Take nothing for granted. Do you expect your partner to be sexually faithful to you? Put that down. Do you expect him or her to do most of the housework, including repairs? Say so. Do you want to wait five years before having children? Do you plan to practice birth control in the meantime? Whose responsibility will the birth control be? Better spell these things out.

How about relatives? Do you plan to spend time with his family during the holidays? Will members of her family live with you? State your feelings in advance, and avoid misunderstanding later. Would you consider separate vacations? Do you need a night or so each week just to be alone with your own thoughts? Go bowling with friends? Just read a book uninterrupted? Say so now and you are less likely to be accused of being antisocial or introverted later.

Don't think that designing a personal marriage agreement is like filling out a job application form. Certain standardized information is part of every job application, but a marriage agreement offers you a chance to be creative, to plan a marriage design that you feel is right for you. Further, realize that your needs and goals—and those of your spouse—will change many times during the course of your marriage. So agreements should be renegotiated from time to time.

A marriage agreement is simply a way of getting feelings out in the open and clarifying expectations, *not* a means of holding someone to a specified set of rules. And don't worry that you'll reveal too much. No matter how detailed your agreement, there will be plenty of room for discovering each other through the course of a marriage. However, marriage has a tendency to be stressful enough without the constant discovery of basic information that both should have had from the outset: he wants three adopted children; she wants a baby of her own.

Written agreements are gaining some popularity these days among couples who look at the contract as a reasonable, effective way of improving their chances for successful marriage. Not everyone likes this approach, of course, and you may not. What's important is not the agreement itself, but the goal that it tries to achieve—some real sharing of ideas prior to marriage . . . and even more, some creative thinking about what marital relationships can or should be.

Many of us may have thought at some point that we would like our marriage to be somewhat different from that of our parents, relatives, or friends. Yet often, our plans to be different are really just an attempt to polish the old tarnished model. Designing a marriage that responds to our needs, and is truly creative, is a fairly new concept for most of us. But after all, we're all unique, aren't we? If we paint a picture, it will be different from all other pictures in the world. You can, if you choose, "paint" your marriage in the same way.

On completing your study of this lesson, you should be able to

❑ Explain the marriage premise, including the concepts of permanence and primariness.

❑ Describe how expectations regarding permanence and primariness have changed over the past few decades.

❑ Discuss, in general terms, some of the reasons why people engage in extramarital affairs, and the impact of such affairs on the stability of a marriage.

❑ Contrast utilitarian and intrinsic marriages.

❑ Identify five marriage relationships, and state whether each is utilitarian, intrinsic, or some combination of the two.

❑ Explain why working-class marriages often cannot be defined as either utilitarian or intrinsic.

❑ Distinguish between static and flexible marriages.

❑ List at least three reasons for writing your own personal marriage agreement.

**Learning Objectives**

## Key Terms

Conflict-habituated marriage     Primariness

Devitalized marriage     Sexual exclusivity

Flexible marriage     Static (closed) marriage

Intrinsic marriage     Strict monogamy

Marriage premise     Total marriage

Passive-congenial marriage     Utilitarian marriage

Personal marriage contract     Vital marriage

## Assignments

❏ Before viewing the program, be sure you've read through the preceding overview and familiarized yourself with the learning objectives and key terms for this lesson. Then read Chapter 8, "Marriage: A Unique Relationship," of *Marriages and Families* by Lamanna and Riedmann.

❏ After completing these tasks, read the video viewing questions and watch the video program for Lesson 11, "Great Expectations."

❏ After viewing the program, take time to answer the video viewing questions and evaluate your learning with the self-test. You'll find the correct answers, along with text page references, at the back of this telecourse guide.

❏ Read the "What's Your Decision?" scenario at the end of this lesson and answer the questions about the decision you would make based on what you've learned from this lesson. Give these questions some serious thought; they may be used as the basis for class discussion or the development of a more complex essay.

## Video Viewing Questions

1. Dr. Carlfred Broderick compares the relative success of marriages that begin when partners are teenagers, in their mid-to-late twenties, and older. Marriage at which of the three age groups tends to be more stable? How do the experiences of Tom, and Glenn and Estelle fit into this pattern?

2. David Viscott and Tad Goguen Frantz suggest wrong and right reasons for marrying. Based on your reading and experience, what would you consider the five most important reasons for marrying someone?

3. According to Kathy Wexler it's not enough to just understand the person you are planning to marry. What does she consider just as important?

4. Living with someone may be one way to find out what married life with that person may be like. What difference did the marriage ceremony seem to make to David Viscott and his wife, to Michael and Roberta, and to Bob and Carol? How do their experiences mesh with the Arond and Parker survey reported in your text?

5. Those who indulge in sexual encounters outside their marriage do so for a variety of reasons, according to Ira Reiss and Kathy Wexler. Does an extramarital affair reflect the end of the marriage? What do Alma and Tom Seibt have to say?

6. What influences the kinds of marriage relationships couples build? Note the comments of Constance Ahrons; Joe and Julie.

7. Tom Seibt and Marsha Lasswell talk about the early years of marriage, and the basic stages through which couples move. What factors contribute to early happiness?

8. Imagine that you have an opportunity to respond to the comments of either David Viscott, Constance Ahrons, Kathy Wexler, or Tad Goguen Frantz regarding intrinsic and utilitarian marriages. Whether you choose to agree or disagree with the comments that are made, or choose to present an objective analysis of one of their points of view, be sure to document your comments with research cited in the text or other authoritative sources.

9. Think about the comments of Marsha Lasswell and Tad Goguen Frantz regarding long-term marriages, and apply it to your parents or others you know who seem to have successful relationships. From your observations, how did the changes they experienced as individuals affect their relationship?

## Self-Test

1. Two colleagues, Mike and Steve, were discussing marriage one day, following the conclusion of a psychology class. "Well, if you ask me," Mike commented, "marriage is marriage. Beyond superficial differences—like who does the vacuuming or who has the bigger paycheck—marriage is pretty much the same experience for every-

body." *Most* social scientists would probably say that Mike's comment in this scenario is

a. slightly exaggerated, but basically accurate.
b. if anything, an understatement; the truth is, once the honeymoon is over, marriages tend to follow almost identical patterns.
c. true with respect to working-class marriages, but dramatic differences are seen among upper middle-class marriages.
d. a real distortion of the truth since virtually every marriage has unique characteristics.

2. The marriage premise entails which of the following important expectations?

a. Ultimately, about half of all marriages will likely end in divorce.
b. Cohabiting provides a sound beginning for a successful marriage.
c. Each spouse will regard the other as the most important person in his or her life.
d. A well-thought-out, written marriage agreement provides the best basis for a successful marriage.

3. The expectation of sexual exclusivity in marriage is

a. a relatively new idea in our culture, and one that seems unlikely to catch on.
b. a strong, long-standing tradition in American culture—though our real-life behavior might suggest otherwise.
c. common among most other cultures of the world, though little respected in our own.
d. one which Americans almost universally hold, and condone both in marriage vows and in behavior.

4. Research shows that most people who have extramarital affairs tend to do so

a. for a variety of reasons that may be neither very clearcut nor very easy to explain.
b. for revenge, following the revelation that the spouse is having (or has had) an affair.
c. strictly for variety—to break the monotony of being married to one person.
d. in an effort to deal with midlife crisis and to prove that they're still sexually desirable.

5. Bernie returned from a bowling tournament one night to find his wife, Marie, nervously pacing the floor and watching for him out the window. "Where have you been?" she demanded (even though they both knew she knew very well). A long discussion ensued, in which Bernie (again) defended his rights to a night out, while Marie protested that they had less and less time together. "I never see you," she exclaimed. "You might as well be married to your bowling ball—it gets out more than I do!" The feelings Marie is expressing in this scenario can *best* be described as an example of

   a. a joint-conjugal relationship.
   b. passive conjugal marriage.
   c. flexible monogamy.
   d. jealousy.

6. Fred describes his 15-year marriage to Edith this way: "You couldn't ask for a better housekeeper or cook. Everything just so, all the time. She's an excellent mother to the kids. They're always clean, well-behaved. She takes them to piano lessons, gymnastics, all over—I never have to worry over those details. And she's organized—keeps my calendar better than I do. You can have that hearts and flowers stuff. Listen, give me a woman who's a good business manager, and I'll show you just how happy a marriage can be!" Based on Fred's description, we can conclude that his marriage to Edith is *most likely* to be

   a. utilitarian.
   b. vital.
   c. total.
   d. intrinsic.

7. Probably the *primary* feature defining an intrinsic marriage is the

   a. amount of time the two spouses spend together.
   b. mutual respect each has for the other's abilities and talents.
   c. extent to which each is able to achieve independence outside the marriage.
   d. intensity of feelings each has for the other.

8. Martha and John have been married for 18 years, and neither can remember a totally peaceful day during that time. Both can find a dozen reasons at any given time for nagging or harassing the other. "I'll get on her about her

cooking or driving," John says, "but the funny part is, it's rarely the thing at hand that's really bugging me—it's a build-up of feelings." Martha admits to the same thing: "It's sort of a habit with us, I suppose. Some days I get tired and think it would be nice to just get along, but then he'll start in, and soon we're off and rolling." Based on what you know from this scenario, which of the following would you say is *most likely* to be true?

a. Their marriage will end in divorce—probably within the year.

b. If they continue their pattern of fighting, and do not suppress their feelings, most of the conflicts will eventually be resolved.

c. Appearances to the contrary, both John and Martha probably derive some sense of satisfaction from their relationship.

d. Both John and Martha recognize that the tension and stress within their marriage is abnormal—though they are powerless to do much about it.

9. Louise and Ted have been married for 41 years. They live on a small cattle ranch and share all the work associated with the ranch. "We'll never retire," Ted laughs. "We enjoy our work too much, and enjoy the fact we're together. It's hard to separate the two. Most people would say 41 years is a long time to be married. To us, it seems more like 41 days. I barely have to look at her to figure out what she's thinking [winks at Louise, who starts to laugh]. See what I mean? I've been reading her mind like that for 39 of the 41 years and she's starting to like it." Louise and Ted's marriage could *best* be described as

a. utilitarian.

b. total.

c. vital.

d. passive-congenial.

10. *Most* psychologists and marriage counselors would probably recommend that a marriage agreement *not* touch on which of the following issues?

a. Sex.

b. Possible reasons for divorce.

c. Money.

d. None of the above; most would agree that any subject on the minds of prospective marriage partners be covered in a written marriage agreement.

Claire has been dating two men during the past year, and both are interested in marriage. She finds both attractive but in very different ways. Sam is somewhat older than Claire and a practicing physician. He's been married once before, has a child from that marriage (whom Claire is very fond of), and has a substantial income that would make Claire financially comfortable. He's willing to have more children if Claire wants them, though he freely admits that isn't a priority for him, and that he will gladly turn all childcare over to Claire (or provide her with a housekeeper or governess, if she wants). Sam tells Claire openly that he has been lonely living by himself and would like a companion—especially when he travels, as he frequently does, to seminars and other meetings. Life with Sam promises to be financially and socially rewarding, and very busy.

Jim is quite different from Sam. He's younger—a year younger than Claire, in fact. He's passionately in love with Claire and they have an actively sexual relationship. They also spend a great deal of time hiking, canoeing, riding horses, playing tennis, and pursuing other interests they hold in common. Jim shares Claire's interest in children and would like several of their own. He is employed as a game warden and makes only a modest income—without great hopes of it ever increasing dramatically. Chances are, he tells Claire, she will have to work for at least part of their marriage, but he promises that they'll have such a great time on the weekends, that will make up for it. When Claire is with Jim, she feels totally at home. She wishes he had a bit more income—but you can't have everything.

Based on what you know about Claire and her relationships with Sam and Jim, who would you suggest that Claire choose to marry? What are some of the most important factors for Claire to keep in mind in making her decision? Which relationship do you think will result in the most lasting happiness? Why?

❏ Should Claire marry Sam or Jim?

❏ What factors support that view?

❏ What factors support the opposite view?

❏ What will happen immediately if she chooses as you suggest?

❏ What will her situation be five years from now if she chooses as you suggest?

# What's Your Decision?

❑ Are there research studies cited in the text that offer support for your position?

❑ If you needed additional research-based information to support your position, how or where would you go about getting it?

# Lesson 12

# Intimate Connections

## Communicating in Relationships

We learn most of what we know about relating to other human beings long before we enter marriage. Most of us learn it within the context of a family, both by interacting with others, and by watching other family members do the same. It's been suggested that the family is, in fact, the single most powerful environmental influence in our lives. From our families, we may gain a sense of support, of being accepted or loved—or we may experience profound and emotionally damaging rejection or hurt.

For most of us, family life is a mixture of ups and downs. On some days, we may feel secure and loved; on other days, it may seem that no one really understands us at all. Sound familiar? As you were swinging back and forth—between loved and misunderstood—did you ever wonder what was going on inside you?

In 1902, Charles Horton Cooley coined the term *looking-glass self* to describe the concept by which people come to accept the evaluations they get from other persons, and especially from family members. Psychologists sometimes term family members (and even close friends) *significant others*, meaning that these are persons whose opinions we value, and whose messages to us may shape our attitudes and behaviors in important ways.

Do you recall hearing a parent (or brother or sister) at some time offer a personal evaluation of you? "Oh, John's always so thoughtful," "Martha's never been on time in her

**Overview**

**The Family and Self-Concept**

life," "Sally never has known the value of money," "Ralph thinks only of himself," "What an artist that Sheila is!" In their comments and evaluations—no matter how casual—family members hold up a looking glass for us, and when we peer inside, we generally find what they have conditioned us to expect.

Clearly, the looking glass self-concept has important implications for the development of self-concept. Children who hear mostly warm, loving, complimentary comments, tend to gain a picture of themselves as valuable human beings. Children who hear mostly criticisms and negative remarks may feel that they are not valued—that they are failures.

The interaction we have with family members produces not only an overall positive or negative self-concept, but also a personal association with specific traits. Mother tells little Billy that he never pays attention when someone is talking. Soon Billy sees himself as someone who cannot listen—and his behavior in school exemplifies his definition of himself as a nonlistener. The teacher's response is likely to reinforce this image—further confirming his lack of listening skills. Later in life, when his wife accuses him of paying no attention, he may counter that he's simply never been very good at listening. How could he think otherwise?

How do you tend to think of yourself? As kind? Inventive? Emotional? Logical? Precise? Sloppy? Artistic? Intelligent? Slow? Humorless? Sarcastic? Compassionate? Chances are that if you think back, you can recall comments, attitudes—perhaps even specific anecdotes—that reinforced this image of you, both in your own mind and in the minds of others.

So powerful is the influence of the family over its members that psychoanalyst R. D. Laing compares it to hypnotism. It isn't just that we act in the way that other family members want or unconsciously program for us; we actually become a certain kind of individual through that influence—at least in our own minds. Our mental evaluation of ourselves can be so powerful, so pervasive, that we may believe it even if it flies in the face of reason and reality. The man who is told repeatedly that he has a mechanical flair may feel quite confident taking it upon himself to repair the family car—whether he really knows what he's doing or not. The man who's told he couldn't change a lightbulb without extensive assistance is not likely to take on the leaky faucet, even if realistically he might be quite capable of handling the repairs. In many ways, we become what we're told we are. But as powerful as family influence may be, it isn't the only influence. Most of us, at some point, venture out into the world—where we encounter other reactions, other responses.

This widening of one's personal audience, so to speak, can have various consequences. For one thing, it enlarges the scope of influence over our behavior. A child whose personality has been shaped primarily by mother and father (or other adult caretakers) and by siblings may now be influenced by teachers, friends, and associates at school; a Little League coach, priest, or minister; and a host of other influential persons. If a child's behavior strongly manifests acceptance of a particular trait ("Oh, Kelly is so shy!"), that trait may be reinforced by others who take note of the behavior and comment on it ("I wish Kelly would raise her hand in class—I know she knows the answer, but she's just too shy to volunteer"). On the other hand, broadening the audience also raises the possibility that outsiders will note behaviors others have missed or passed over. Sometimes, this can have a positive influence. For example, a teenager who's often been told he is selfish may hear from a teacher or other influential person that he is in fact rather thoughtful and considerate. The contradiction may give him the courage to protest the image that's been cultured within his immediate family.

Families influence our thinking not only about ourselves, but about the world around us. How often have you felt your own convictions about some political, religious, or moral principle deepening when you heard it confirmed by friends or family? If you've had this experience, then you know how *consensual validation* works. It's the experience of reaffirming a shared truth about the world. It feels good to know others think as we do. (We must be right then, mustn't we?) Indeed, some psychologists suggest that one reason marital break-up can be so devastating is that without the partner, we lose that sense of validation.

## The Drive for Family Cohesion

Recognizing the importance of the family within our lives prompts many of us to seek ways of keeping family members together, of creating a strong bond. Psychologists and sociologists refer to this as a drive for family cohesion. In an effort to discover what particular behaviors created strong family cohesion, social scientist Nick Stinnett studied 130 strong families and identified six important characteristics.

First, according to Stinnett's studies, cohesive families are open about expressing appreciation. They say what it is they like about each other, and work hard at building each other up psychologically. Second, they arrange personal schedules so that they have time together. They truly seem to like being with each other, and while they may have individual pursuits, they also place some priority on family time. Third, they work on communication. They take time to talk to each other. And they listen. Contrary to what we might expect, they do fight. But their arguments tend to focus on the source of the conflict, and finding a way to resolve it, rather than on the personalities (or previous behaviors) of the persons involved. Fourth, they share a genuine commitment to each other's welfare, and to the welfare and security of the family as a whole. Fifth, they seem to have a strong spiritual orientation—meaning not so much a formal religious affiliation, but simply a sense that some greater power or source of comfort exists. And finally, they tend to deal with crises in a positive way, to find something good even in the worst of times. Stinnett's work shows beyond doubt that good family relationships do not just happen. Family members have to work at it—and it's a full-time job that demands the cooperative effort of all family members.

Like larger families, couples have to work on building their relationships as well. Studies indicate that among the most important things couples can do in keeping their relationship strong is to build in time for intimacy. In our society, the work ethic tends to be so deeply ingrained that many of us neglect the personal side of our lives. Yet, special time without interruptions from children, pets, relatives, work, telephone, or whatever, is very important to maintaining a strong, affectionate bond. Most therapists suggest that couples need to plan time for intimacy on a regular basis. This doesn't mean they need to have sex. They may walk along the beach or just sit by the fire and talk. What's important is making a time commitment that says to another person, "For this time, you are so important that I will not allow anything else to interfere with our relationship."

We've already noted that families wield a powerful influence within our lives. Sometimes that influence works in highly constructive ways—sometimes in destructive ways. Researchers Bach and Wyden, for example, note a behavior they term *gaslighting*, in which one partner works on eroding the other's sense of self-esteem or sense of reality. This can happen in a number of different ways. The partner may use humor or sarcasm, for example, to point out the other's flaws—sometimes in front of other people. The attempt to undermine self-confidence in this way is sometimes deliberate, but probably just as often it's quite unintentional. Either way, the results can be damaging. The victim of gaslighting may question a partner's intentions, and be told that he or she is crazy, since no harm was meant. A related behavior, *scapegoating*, involves a tendency to consistently blame one person for whatever goes wrong: "If *you* were just different, life would be wonderful . . ."

One antidote to such destructive behaviors is for the victim to begin thinking more independently, and to challenge these negative messages. People do this more readily when they have built supportive relationships outside the family. A second strategy is to begin to develop an atmosphere of encouragement rather than criticism within the family.

On completing your study of this lesson, you should be able to

❏ Describe how a family serves as a powerful environment in influencing individual growth and behavior.

❏ Explain the influence of significant others within the context of the interactionist perspective.

❏ Name and describe at least five ways in which strong families work to build cohesion.

❏ Describe the concept of negative family power, and list several specific negative behaviors which can damage relationships within a family.

**Learning Objectives**

Attribution
Conflict taboo
Consensual validation
Family cohesion
Gaslighting

Interaction
Looking-glass self
Scapegoating
Significant others

**Key Terms**

❏ Before viewing the program, be sure you've read through the preceding overview and familiarized yourself with the learning objectives and key terms for this lesson. Then read pages 258–260 and 279–282 from Chapter 9, "Communication and Conflict Resolution in Marriages

**Assignments**

and Families," of *Marriages and Families* by Lamanna and Riedmann.

❏ After completing these tasks, read the video viewing questions and watch the video program for Lesson 12, "Intimate Connections."

❏ After viewing the program, take time to answer the video viewing questions and evaluate your learning with the self-test. You'll find the correct answers, along with text page references, at the back of this telecourse guide.

❏ Read the "What's Your Decision?" scenario at the end of this lesson and answer the questions about the decision you would make based on what you've learned from this lesson. Give these questions some serious thought; they may be used as the basis for class discussion or the development of a more complex essay.

## Video Viewing Questions

1. Lynne Azpeitia and Rene Kipnis argue that couples need to develop listening and communication skills to work through disagreements that will invariably arise. Does Michelle Margules' relationship with her husband reflect this contention?

2. Michelle Harway says that one's own family environment while growing up strongly influences subsequent behavior in relationships. What skills may Glenn have obtained from his family that perhaps Joshua did not?

3. In a marriage, individuals undoubtedly bring their own needs, goals, and expectations, which they hope will be fulfilled, to the relationship. Note the statements of Margo Kaufman, Kathy Wexler, Lynne Azpeitia, and David Viscott. How do they suggest we avoid bringing unrealistic expectations to a relationship?

4. How are each of Jess and Irene's communication skills and original family's behavioral patterns reflected in their statements regarding how they handle disagreements?

5. Tad Goguen Frantz, Paul Bohannan, and David Viscott all stress the importance of communication in working through differences. Why? What do they suggest may result if a couple fails to communicate?

6. Another common area of contention between couples is the desire to change one's spouse in some way. How did Joe and Julie handle each other's idiosyncrasies differently from the experiences of Kathy Wexler, Dick, and Janet? Based on your conclusions, what would you recommend Kathy Wexler do to alleviate this humorous but real problem? Should she just learn to live with his shirts, or is there another solution?

7. Note the examples of bonded families in the presentation. What methods or activities do they use to promote familial closeness? What role does communication play in the cohesiveness of these families? Give specific examples.

8. Double income households, long working hours, and children often leave modern couples little time for themselves. Document how Candy and Tom, Glenn and Donna, and Barbara and her husband each keep their relationships strong through the use of communication.

**Self-Test**

1. Which of the following *best* sums up the extent to which the family environment influences self-concept?
   a. It is probably the single greatest influence for virtually everyone.
   b. It is a strong influence, though later environments (such as school or work) can sometimes be even more influential for a significant minority.
   c. For most people, the family provides just one of many influential environments.
   d. It is rather minimal for most of us—though there are some exceptions.

2. Rodney is 6 years old. He is just learning to read. Often, when he reads aloud to his family, someone will get up and begin a new activity. His father usually continues to read the paper while "listening with one ear," though he sometimes nods to Rodney or comments, "Good for you son. Keep reading." Which of the following do you think is the *most probable* way Rodney will respond?
   a. He will feel driven to improve his reading skills so that he can hold everyone's attention.
   b. Because of his father's encouraging comments, he will likely begin to think of himself as a skillful reader and a good person.

    c. He will begin to doubt his abilities, and may even lose his confidence in reading to others.

    d. He'll come to realize that he's valued for himself—not for external factors like reading ability.

3. Alice perceived her mother as a meek, unimaginative woman who held few strong opinions of her own. She vowed she would not be the same kind of wife if she ever married. Alice's ability to keep that vow, to create her own individual version of what a wife should be, will depend *mostly* on

    a. whether she's able to physically distance herself from her mother so that she is rarely exposed to that negative model.

    b. the strength of her own self-concept, and the way she's been taught by others to perceive herself.

    c. her husband's willingness to tolerate someone with opinions and ideas of her own.

    d. none of the above; studies indicate that none of us is able to really spring free from role models provided by parents.

4. Fred wishes that his daughter, Lee Anne, would act more responsibly. She seems always to be forgetting things, neglecting her household chores, forgetting her lunch money, losing books—and on and on. The *best* approach Fred could use in changing Lee Anne's behavior, according to the text, would probably be to

    a. explain very carefully and systematically the benefits of leading a responsible life.

    b. just tell Lee Anne outright to begin acting more responsibly.

    c. be very open about showing his anger and frustration, and point out specifically why her behavior is so irritating.

    d. tell Lee Anne that she is a very responsible person and that she acts in a responsible fashion.

5. Which of the following is the best example of consensual validation?

    a. A man comments that his wife always becomes flustered before guests arrive—and sure enough, at the next dinner party, she gets so nervous she drops the hors d'oeuvres tray.

    b. A father insists that family members begin spending more time together, even if that means cancelling some personal plans to make more family time.

    c. Every time something goes wrong in the family, virtually everyone tends to blame Leslie—after all, she's the one with the ornery disposition.

    d. After hearing her husband echo her views on tax reform, Phyllis is glad she voted as she did—even though her friend Millicent disagrees.

6. The term "family cohesion" is defined as

    a. the emotional bonding of family members.

    b. the absence of anger and conflict among family members.

    c. the reliance of family members on each other to help affirm their definitions of the world around them.

    d. a negative tendency for members of especially close families to develop an "us against the world" attitude.

7. Which of the following would probably be the *most important* thing a family could do to help members develop a strong sense of family cohesion?

    a. Ensure that only one parent works outside the home.

    b. Take time to openly express appreciation for one another.

    c. Have all family members pursue the same hobbies or recreational activities.

    d. Enforce a strong taboo against arguments within the family.

8. The process whereby the qualities ascribed to us by other people become part of the way we see ourselves is

    a. attribution.

    b. socialization.

    c. amelioration.

    d. self-realization.

9. Irene and Hank have been married for 10 years, and get along reasonably well most of the time. Often at parties, however, Irene surprises Hank by making a sarcastic remark—to which he's reluctant to respond in front of others. Later, when he brings it up, Irene denies the whole thing or says that Hank is misinterpreting her. "Honestly," she asks him, "don't you have any sense of humor any more? You must know by now that I'd never hurt

you." Which of the following *best* describes Irene's behavior as depicted in this scenario?

a. Consensual validation

b. Gaslighting

c. Scapegoating

d. Passive aggression

10. Emily is 3 years old and likes to sing. She has a real talent for it, though a music teacher would probably hesitate to call her "gifted." Her parents encourage her to sing at church and at parties, and Emily usually responds enthusiastically because she gets a lot of applause, praise, and hugs from all the relatives who enjoy seeing her show off. According to the interactionist perspective, as Emily grows up, she will probably have which of the following attitudes?

a. She'll continue to see herself as a talented singer.

b. She'll become distrustful, recognizing that given her limited talents, people she trusted were probably not telling the truth about their feelings.

c. Emily will probably not develop any strong opinions about her own talents till she can obtain the objective evaluation of a music professional.

d. Thanks to a loving environment, Emily will have a strong self-concept, but she'll probably never really think of herself as a singer.

## What's Your Decision?

"How many times do I have to tell you not to interrupt me when I'm on the phone! Just wait until your . . ." What started as the nineteenth reprimand of the day was aborted mid-sentence when Steve's mother, Janice, caught sight of the fuzzy caterpiller in Steve's outstretched hand. Her dislike of creatures of any variety became an overwhelming force and she propelled his small body toward his room.

"I'm afraid I'm going to loose control with Steve one of these days," confides Janice to her husband George later that evening. "He's like a pesky mosquito buzzing around your head when you're trying to get to sleep, only he buzzes around me every waking moment. It's driving me crazy! And he's getting worse. Maybe he needs to see a doctor. Maybe he's hyperactive. They have medication for that, you know."

George considers what Janice has said and quietly broaches an old and sensitive subject. "Maybe he just needs more of your attention. . . "

"Oh, no! Not that again," bemoans Janice.

"Wait a minute," responds George. "Before you get defensive, hear me out. I've been doing some reading and what I'm finding out is that a child who isn't getting the attention he needs will keep going after it any way he can. If he can't get a positive response, he'll settle for a negative one, trying to make himself feel important the only way he knows how. Any response is better than being ignored. I'm not saying that you mean to ignore the child, " he hastens to add, "but you must admit that you're always involved in a project—if it's not gardening or sewing then it's reading or painting or something. I get busy, too, the few hours I'm home. He's always on the outside looking in."

"Now, I know that a 7-year-old is not the most stimulating conversationalist in the world, but if we both made an effort to listen to him—*really* listen to him—if he felt we were interested in his caterpillar discovery, maybe he'd be satisfied to go about his business again and leave us to ours. We've got to find a way to break this cycle."

As they talked, they came up with a plan—simple but concrete, just three basic objectives: (1) to look for opportunities to give Steve *positive feedback; (2) to remember to listen*; and (3) to *devote some time* just to Steve, going to the zoo, playing a favorite game, or maybe just talking. They agreed to police each other—to give each other a nudge when they forgot.

Based on what you know about their situation, should Janice and George give the plan a try? What are some of the most important factors for them to consider in making this decision? If they do implement this approach, what sort of results can they expect?

❑ Should the plan George and Janice developed be implemented?

❑ What factors support that view?

❑ What factors support the opposite view?

❑ What will happen immediately if they act as you suggest?

❑ What will their situation probably be five years from now if they act as you suggest?

❑ Are their research studies cited in the text that offer support for your position?

❑ If you needed additional research-based information to support your position, how or where would you go about getting it?

# For Better or Worse

## Constructive Conflict

What do you suppose is the best predictor of success in a marriage? Social compatibility? Comparable education? Similarity in age? Common values? All those things may be important—and they're the sorts of things social scientists and marriage counselors have tended to stress for years. However, a factor that may be more important than any of these is a couple's skills in relating to one another: communicating, understanding, disclosing their personal selves. An important part of communication for married couples is fighting. And while fighting may be a natural activity for most of us, fighting *well* isn't. It has to be learned.

Hold on a moment, you may be saying to yourself. Doesn't everyone know how to fight? After all, put two toddlers together with one toy truck, and a fight is likely to ensue. The kind of fighting we're talking about in this lesson is different, however. It doesn't involve a struggle for survival (unless we're talking about survival of the relationship). Nor is it a selfish process. Nor is there any winner in the usual sense of the term. This kind of fighting is a productive, useful process, sometimes called *bonding* fighting. Its purpose is not just to promote the viewpoint or well-being of one individual over another, but rather to improve communications, solve problems, and build each partner's self-concept (instead of tearing it down)—all at the same time. If you think that sounds difficult to accomplish, you're right. Learning to fight well can take years—even a lifetime. It begins with acknowledging that conflict is part of healthy relationships.

**Overview**

165

As Americans we tend to nurture the notion that the family is the center of harmony, a peaceful refuge in an otherwise troubled world. A refuge it may be. But realistically, is there any such thing as a conflict-free family? Psychologists say not. In fact, they suggest that too little conflict, like too much, may actually be a warning that something is wrong.

The reluctance to express anger leads to what psychologists term *anger insteads*—ways of releasing aggression that may seem to us more socially acceptable than the anger itself. Thus, instead of saying "I hate the way you're making me feel today," a husband may overeat, act bored, come down with a headache, withdraw into silence, or gossip about someone else. Such behaviors can be self-destructive, and can also undermine the relationship, since they're inherently dishonest—an attempt to mask true feelings.

These anger insteads are one form of *passive aggression*. Chronic criticism, nagging, and sarcasm—all are indirect ways of expressing anger—anger which is, remember, very real. The problem with these methods of releasing anger is that they only work on a very temporary basis. The wife who hurls a sarcastic comment at her husband may feel a few seconds' worth of relief from her pent-up anger, but since she has avoided dealing with the real issues, nothing is resolved and her anger quickly returns.

So widespread is the cultural taboo against anger, that we've found any number of alternatives to saying what it is we really feel. The wife who is angry about the amount of time her husband spends at his job may neglect to deliver an important phone message and later say she forgot—a form of what psychologists call *sabotage*. A related behavior, called *displacement*, involves directing the anger one feels at someone or something else rather than at the person who is the real cause. Often, this way of dealing with anger can take some rather bizarre, irrational forms. For example, a husband who is angry because his wife is attending night classes instead of spending time with him may accidentally spill coffee on her research paper.

Sometimes anger takes a very passive form. In a devitalized marriage, the partners might not look angry at all, just bored. They may go through routine duty interrogations relating to each other's day at the office: "How are you? Fine—and you? Oh, fine. What happened today? Not much—how about you? Uh, what? Oh, same old thing—you know . . ." Then each may retire into a private world of reading, work, television, telephone calls, or other means of escaping the other's presence.

If we were to create a list of unhealthy ways to handle our anger, overt violence (both physical and verbal) would obviously head that list. But psychologists point to some other don'ts as well. Evading anger and conflict is one of these. Leaving the house until things quiet down, retreating in sullen silence to the basement or bedroom, announcing that you simply can't take it, or striving to have the last word (then hanging up the phone before your partner can respond) are all behaviors to be avoided.

Another "don't" is the behavior known as *gunnysacking*—storing up memories of small infractions which you appear to overlook at the time, but which you may bring up later, when the moment is wrong. A related behavior—*kitchen sink fighting*—is equally inappropriate. This behavior, as its name suggests, involves reaching into your gunnysack for ammunition, then throwing everything but the kitchen sink at your unsuspecting partner. In other words, you deal with anything but the issue at hand—her mother, his dirty socks, her spending habits, his laziness, etc. Kitchen sink fighting not only fails to deal with the issue at hand, but for obvious reasons, is likely to leave you with a whole new collection of issues to stuff back into that bulging gunnysack.

As we mentioned before, learning to fight well can take years—even a lifetime. It doesn't just happen. You have to work at it. And there are specific tactics that can help you learn the process. Let's look at a few of them.

The first tactic is called *leveling*—and it means just what its name implies: being totally honest and forthright. Think of the last time you were involved in a disagreement. Were you candid about your feelings? Or did you hold something back, try to make the other person guess how you felt? Good fighting demands honest revelation of one's feelings, even when that is difficult. Of course, it doesn't mean being tactless. It's perfectly all right to couch your remarks in civil—even neutral—language. But it isn't all right to leave things out for fear of hurting someone (yourself included), or to gain some psychological advantage by not revealing too much of yourself.

The second tactic involves using what are called *"I" statements*. Many of us, when involved in a fight, tend to become accusatory: "How could *you* do this to me? It's *your* fault. If *you* had listened—or been on time, or done what I'd asked, etc.—this would never have happened." Psychologists suggest that it's more productive, and also helpful in diffusing anger, if instead of accusing another person, we focus on our own feelings and reactions: "*I* worry when you're late. *I* feel hurt—or angry, or confused, or left out when you do that. *I* understood you to mean something else." This practice is often useful in clarifying misunderstandings, and it also lets a partner know how his or her behavior affects you. Of course, it takes a certain amount of self-esteem to be able to do this, but without the sharing of feelings, developing a truly intimate, rewarding relationship is difficult.

A third tactic calls for *giving feedback*. There are various ways to do this. Some people find it useful to verbalize what they've understood a partner to say. It is a way of not only clarifying problems, but also saying to a partner, "I understand, I'm listening, what you have to say is important to me." Good feedback takes some attention to body language as well. Research indicates that during any conflict, people are much more likely to respond to such things as facial expression, gestures, body posture, and tone of voice than to what's being said per se. It doesn't help to shout "I love you" if your facial expression and posture are drowning out your words with a message of their own: "You annoy the heck out of me—I can hardly bear the sight of you." Good feedback, like using the "I" statements, takes strong self-concept. It means really thinking about another's thoughts and feelings, and not becoming defensive—even when we hear how we've fallen short in another person's view.

Tactic four: *check it out*. Maybe you think you know another person really well. So well, in fact, you can almost predict what that person is going to do or say—how he or she will react in a particular situation. Research indicates that when people are honest and open about their feelings, most of us who think we know others well will be in for a few surprises. Good communication requires us to be open to those surprises, to acknowledge the fact that perhaps we don't know it all, and to allow the other person to be the final authority on his or her own feelings. Again, ego only gets in the way.

The fifth tactic calls for *choosing your time and place*. Very few of us are accustomed to doing this—at least not in marriage. If you have a serious issue to discuss with your employer, chances are you'll schedule a formal appointment. Both of you will have time to think over the issues, prepare some remarks and questions, and generally come to feel ready for the encounter. Few of us, however, engage in such formal preparations prior to a discussion with a spouse. Something triggers a response, and wham, we spring into action, right then and there. Social psychologists suggest, however, that when major issues are at stake, it would be wise to take our time, plan ahead, schedule a particular time for the encounter, and think through our presentation in advance. This may sound a little too premeditated if you haven't tried it before, but it has some advantages. For one thing, it gives the message that fighting is an important means of resolving conflicts. Scheduling a discussion with a partner says to that partner, "I'm prepared to listen to your side of things. This is too important to leave to chance. We need to make special time for it." It also helps guarantee that the timing will be right, that you won't spring an unexpected argument on your partner just as she's leaving for work, or about to go to bed, or as you're on your way out the door to attend a seminar in St. Louis. Fair fighting means allowing plenty of time for both sides to be heard.

Tactics six and seven are closely related. First, it's important to focus on the issue at hand. The question is this: Are you really interested in resolving the problem—or do you just want to make the other person feel guilty, angry, hurt, or whatever? If it's the former, then you will tend to focus on the problem to be solved, rather than on what happened yesterday or last month or last year or before you got married. And second, it's important to know what the fight is about before you get into it. You need some mutual understanding that sets the stage and sets the tone. Otherwise, some unsuspected last straw may cause you to just plunge in before you're ready, and before you know what's happening you're in over your head, trying to keep afloat in a sea of emotional issues that threaten to overwhelm you. So—keep it focused, keep it limited, deal with one thing at a time, and know the territory in advance.

Eighth, be open to compromise. It's a good idea, psychologists say, to go into any argument armed with at least one potential solution to the problem at hand. Anybody can register a complaint. Finding solutions is harder. If you go into an argument with the idea that complaining is your job and solving things is your partner's job, you're likely to meet a big wall of resistance and resentment—rightly so. An attitude that says "Here's what we might do . . ." suggests that you're willing to make things better, and that you think making things better is at least partly your responsibility.

Are you willing to change? Well, that's tactic number nine. Too many of us may be tempted to say, "I'm too old . . . too stubborn . . . too set in my ways . . . too whatever . . ." We may also subscribe to the myth that true love never demands change. ("If she really loved me, she'd accept me as I am.") Remember, though, that true love has three focal points: the self, the partner, and the relationship. Sometimes, change is desirable for the good of the relationship. And desire for change does not necessarily indicate lack of love; just the opposite could be true.

The tenth tactic: abandon the "fight to win" approach. We live in a very competitive society. Virtually everything, from education to work to recreation has a competitive side. And—sometimes, unfortunately—we may tend to carry that competitive component into areas where it really doesn't belong: onto the highway, for example, or into a marriage. In productive, useful marital fighting, there's no room for competition. The process, in fact, only works if it's a team effort. There cannot be a winner and loser in the usual sense. Marital arguments are not won; they're resolved. Or, to look at it another way, if the fighting process proceeds as it should, both persons will be winners because both will emerge with a stronger self-concept than before.

### Ending a Fight

So much for tactics. Let's explore some other aspects of marital fighting. If there's no winner and no loser, how does anyone know when the fight's over? Psychologists suggest that a fight ends when both sides feel they've had a fair chance to be heard. A solution to the problem may be reached at this point, or there may simply be a commitment to finding a solution. Some problems are harder to resolve than others, and the fight itself need not continue till resolution is reached.

Sometimes, it's necessary to postpone a fight for a time if one or both partners becomes too angry, tired, frightened, or otherwise emotionally distraught. Research indicates that a woman may show she's reached her emotional limits by crying. A man, who is culturally conditioned not to cry, will usually show he's reached his limits in some other way—perhaps with an outburst of temper or sudden retreat into silence. When either side suspects that the other has had enough, the best strategy is often to say, "Shall we just suspend this for awhile and pick it up later?" Little is to be gained by pushing one partner or the other past an emotional breaking point.

Well, now that you've considered a few tactics for fair fighting, and have had a chance to see what it's generally about, do you feel ready to approach your own marital disagreements in this way? Don't be surprised if you feel hesitant or unsure. Remember we said earlier that constructive fighting is not a natural process; it takes time to learn to do it well. Further, most of us are influenced strongly by our early experience.

Think of your own parents (or other adults with whom you lived as a child). If your experience is like that of most American children, then many of the fights you witnessed or overheard were probably a radical departure from the processes we've described here. It's important to be conscious of the kinds of behaviors that have been modeled for you, because they're what you are likely to emulate—unless you make a conscious effort to change. Building new habits isn't easy.

It starts, in part, with the acceptance of new attitudes. Many of us—even those who live in a relatively hostile environment—grow up with the idea that fighting is wrong, something to be avoided. Psychologists tell us, however, that fighting is natural and even healthy in the most intimate of relationships.

Another attitude many of us cling to is the idea that children should never witness a marital fight. But to look at it another way, how will they learn to deal with their own conflicts if they never see a positive model of how it can be done? Again, if the fighting is constructive and healthy, there is little reason to keep children sheltered from it.

Let's suppose that you've changed your attitudes about fighting, and you've modified your fight tactics to match this new you. How will you know when you've gotten good at the game? Are there some signs? Yes, there are. First, partners who have become adept at fair marital fighting find that they're able to maintain high levels of self-esteem, both within themselves and within a partner. They do not emerge from disagreements feeling drained, unappreciated, wholly depressed, desperate. Instead, they may feel a renewed sense of commitment to the other person and to the relationship—together with new insight regarding their own behavior.

Second, good fighters gain an increased sense of intimacy, even through the fighting. They feel comfortable sharing their personal, innermost feelings, and through that mutual sharing come to feel even closer to the other person. Thus, they may feel that the fight was worth it because something

**Building a Habit of Fair Fighting**

**The Techniques of Fair Fighting**

important was gained. Third, fair fighters are often able to carry on a fight in a normal tone of voice. They may even inject some humor. Their fights may not even look like fights at all, according to our usual definition. They don't make faces, throw things, shout invectives, bang the walls. They discuss issues openly and honestly—but often quietly.

And finally, good fighters are often able to reach resolution very quickly. They get to the heart of it, solve the problem, and move on. Research indicates that couples who practice fair fighting get better at it over time. They may get so good, in fact, that casual observers may scarcely be aware of it when a couple moves from conversation into argument and back again.

It's only fair to point out that nobody's perfect. Even couples who have taken courses, read books, gone through therapy, and practiced fair fighting strategies aren't going to practice what they've learned all the time. No strategies or tactics or new attitudes are going to take all the bite, all the hurt out of fighting. People are still going to be unfair—at least some of the time. They're still going to say and do things they don't mean once in a while. Research indicates, in fact, that marital partners who are happy and well adjusted tend not to read too much into comments made during fighting.

While we're being realistic, we might also acknowledge that there are times when being open to a new way of doing things isn't enough. Both partners have to want to make fighting fair. If a new approach to fighting doesn't feel right, one partner may revert to the old way of doing things, and that's going to make any real progress hard to come by.

## Marital Communication

Couples differ in their expectations of closeness or distance, and in their attitudes about conflict. Mary Anne Fitzpatrick, a prominent marital communication researcher, has identified four marital types based on different ideologies of marriage:

❏ Traditionals are very interdependent, favoring sharing and disclosure. They avoid conflict except on important issues, which they do not hesitate to address.

❏ Separates avoid both conflict and more positive modes of engagement with each other. These couples are not very interdependent at all.

❏ Independents value autonomy and change; they favor nontraditional sex roles and are open in engaging in conflict. These couples are moderately interdependent.

❏ Mixed couples do not share the same ideology.

When looking at marital communication, an important element is the match between a couples' ideology and their communication behavior. The more the partners communication matches their ideology of marriage, the more satisfied the couple is with their marriage.

On completing your study of this lesson, you should be able to

❏ Explain how the myth of conflict-free love may sometimes encourage forms of passive aggression, and provide several examples of how it might be expressed within a family.

❏ Define the concept of alienating fight tactics, and provide several examples of such tactics.

❏ List and describe at least six specific tactics partners can use to make fighting a more positive process.

❏ Discuss the various difficulties inherent in learning to change fighting habits.

❏ Discuss the myth of conflict-free conflict, and its implications for the outcome of learning to fight productively.

❏ Describe the various roles a marriage counselor might play in helping a couple learn to fight fairly.

**Learning Objectives**

Anger insteads
Bonding fighting
Checking it out
Conflict-free conflict
Conjoint marital counseling
Displacement
Feedback

Gunnysacking
"I" statements
Kitchen-sink fighting
Leveling
Mixed (or double) messages
Passive-aggression
Sabotage

**Key Terms**

❏ Before viewing the program, be sure you've read through the preceding overview and familiarized yourself with the learning objectives and key terms for this lesson. Then read pages 260–279 from Chapter 9, "Communication and Conflict Resolution in Marriages and Families;"

**Assignments**

and Appendix H, pages 591–592, of *Marriages and Families* by Lamanna and Riedmann.

❏ After completing these tasks, read the video viewing questions and watch the video program for Lesson 13, "For Better or Worse."

❏ After viewing the program, take time to answer the video viewing questions and evaluate your learning with the self-test. You'll find the correct answers, along with text page references, at the back of this telecourse guide.

❏ Read the "What's Your Decision?" scenario at the end of this lesson and answer the questions about the decision you would make based on what you've learned from this lesson. Give these questions some serious thought; they may be used as the basis for class discussion or the development of a more complex essay.

## Video Viewing Questions

1. Anger is a natural part of any relationship. Different people have different styles of anger. What influences the way people deal with conflict? Are there good and bad expressions of anger, and if so, what criteria determines the classification?

2. Often partners have enormously different ways of dealing with conflict. Note the examples of Muriel, Peter and Andrea, and Anita. How do each of them confront their partner's different fighting style? Why is it important to recognize these differences?

3. Why does Michelle Harway stress the importance of confronting problems immediately when, or soon after, they arise? How do Barbara and Dick confront problems and how does this effect their relationship generally?

4. When anger is not expressed at the time it occurs, it often surfaces later in the form of anger substitutes. How do the comments and examples of Marsha Lasswell, Alice and Dave specifically recognize the dangers of anger substitutes?

5. All couples fight and, as with anger, the styles vary. Based on the comments of Lynne Azpeitia, Alice Laviolette, Glenn and Donna, David Viscott, and Barbara, what are the most important aspects of fighting fairly? What can be gained or maintained through fighting fairly

that might not be achieved with other tactics? Can a fair fight be won? Explain your answer.

6. Why do some couples and experts recommend "scheduling" a fight? Why is this break important for some people to keep fights fair? Use testimony from two or more of the following for your response: Michelle Harway, Alice Laviolette, Tom, Jess and Irene, and Margo.

7. Saying "I'm sorry" is extremely difficult for many people. However, simply saying the words may not solve anything. How do both Peter and Andrea, and Barbara and Dick end fights? Do you agree with both or one of the methods? If so, what is the most important aspect of each of the examples? If not, why?

**Self-Test**

1. The main goal of bonding fighting is to
   a. find a solution to the problem at hand in as short a time as possible.
   b. build up each partner's self-esteem, thereby bringing the partners closer together.
   c. determine which partner will emerge the winner.
   d. determine which partner (if either) is the cause of the problem at hand.

2. Jane has a habit of not finishing her food at meals. She just pushes it around on her plate. Jack doesn't like to watch her do this, and finds himself growing angrier every time they eat together. He feels this is rather petty on his part, though. Jane is a bright, considerate person—a fine wife and mother. He feels guilty being angry over such a small thing. One day they have an argument about balancing the checkbook, and Jack finds he is more angry than the occasion would seem to warrant. Jane doesn't understand why Jack is so upset. Most social psychologists would probably advise Jack to
   a. just admit that it's really Jane's eating habits that are making him so angry.
   b. avoid all arguments with Jane till he can come to terms with his immature response to her behavior.
   c. focus on the problem with the checkbook; even if it isn't the real issue, it's a more reasonable thing to be angry about.

d. simply let Jane know how very angry he feels and leave it to her to figure out the reason behind it.

3. Brad has been waiting two hours, through a rainstorm, for Verna to show up for a dinner engagement. He's been alternately angry and worried for most of that time. Finally, she steps out of a taxi and runs in from the rain, smiling, flustered, apologetic for being late. A number of possible opening remarks flash through Brad's mind. Which of the following statements would probably be most productive?

a. Well, I see you're late again.

b. Why can't you ever be on time?

c. You never seem to think of calling me.

d. I worry when you're late.

4. Alex and Whitney have been fighting for over an hour. Both are tired, physically and mentally. They seem to be getting nowhere. Whitney is sitting on the couch, looking at Alex, who stands over her, fists clenched, face flushed, eyes glaring. His muscles are tense. "If I didn't love you so much," he says through his teeth, "you wouldn't make me so angry." Which of the following messages is Whitney most likely to get from this encounter?

a. Alex really loves her deeply, despite everything.

b. Alex simply isn't sure of his feelings—he's an ambivalent person.

c. Whitney is a good person, worthy of love—even if Alex doesn't always know how to show it.

d. Alex's primary response right now is anger—even if he is trying to mask it with a declaration of love.

5. Walt and Tania feel themselves about to enter a serious discussion. There are angry feelings on both sides, and a lot of misunderstandings to straighten out. Walt suggests that they both collect their thoughts and sit down at 7:00 p.m. that night to hash things out. According to information presented in the text, is this likely to be a good idea?

a. Not at all; the time to work out a disagreement is right when it first arises.

b. It will probably give Walt an edge, and that's why he's doing it; once Tania has cooled down, she may not be able to argue her side effectively.

    c. Probably not, since making an appointment to fight is the height of phoniness.

    d. In fact, making an appointment for a fight has real advantages—time to organize thoughts and to prepare oneself for facing some criticism.

6. Which of the following is a good tactic to follow in constructive fighting?

    a. Offer some generalizations (e.g., you tend to be thoughtless, selfish) that help the other person see what his or her behavior is really like.

    b. Try to go beyond the issue at hand to focus on the larger problem of helping the other person amend his or her behavior.

    c. Avoid bringing up any issues or offering any comments that are likely to result in hurt feelings.

    d. Enter the argument prepared to propose at least one solution to the problem at hand.

7. Lester and Amy are trying to come to terms over whether to move in with Lester's parents. It's an emotional discussion, and they're nowhere close to resolution. After three hours of heated debate, Amy finds herself breaking into tears. At this point, the best thing for Lester to do is probably to

    a. give in—no issue is worth causing another person that much pain.

    b. conclude that he has won the fight, and draw the discussion to a close as gracefully as possible.

    c. suggest to Amy that they continue the discussion another time when both have had time to recover.

    d. ignore her crying; it is just a manipulative tactic that's counterproductive to the philosophy of fair fighting.

8. Gary tends to view fighting as a way of life. He grew up in a home where his parents fought frequently, and he can remember the fights reaching a certain pitch, and then seeing his father retreat to the basement "for a bit of peace and quiet." Most of the fights simply ended in a stalemate. Gary remembers the frustration and anger he felt, watching his parents hurt and ignore each other. Based on research cited in the text, Gary is most likely to

    a. follow the same pattern—even though he doesn't admire it—modeling his own fighting behavior after that of his father.

b. resort to violence as a result of the frustration he felt as a child listening to his parents quarrel.

c. avoid fighting altogether, having seen how useless it really is.

d. obtain training and counseling designed to help him learn more effective, constructive ways of fighting.

9. Most social scientists would probably agree that the notion of conflict-free love is

a. desirable and ought to be encouraged.

b. a myth—it simply doesn't exist.

c. an ideal worth striving for, though realistically, it's probably not achievable for most people.

d. actually contrary to our cultural ideals, though it's the norm in many parts of the world.

10. Kate and Roger have been attending counseling sessions for about six months now, and feel that they are much more sensitive to each other's feelings, much more capable of fighting in a healthy, productive way. "We've come to realize," Kate tells a friend, "that when you know how to fight the correct way, there's no reason for anyone ever to be hurt. Everyone can come out a winner." The views that Kate expresses in this scenario are

a. an accurate reflection of what happens when people learn to deal with emotions in a constructive, logical manner.

b. fairly egotistical, since her reference to winners suggests that she doesn't understand fair fighting as well as she is trying to imply.

c. ridiculous; conflict is conflict and any time people fight, someone wins and someone loses.

d. a little unrealistic; in real life people do get hurt, even in the most constructive, healthy fighting situations.

## What's Your Decision?

Rudy and Elaine have been married for seven years and are fond of each other, though there's certainly some tension in the air lately. They do not have fights, really. Rudy tries hard to see to that. Though increasingly, it seems, Elaine is finding ways to get on his nerves. He is certain she is doing it purposely, though of course she denies that. When she asks him what she's done to offend him, he usually does not reply at all, though if he's annoyed enough he'll say, "You really don't know, Elaine? That's pretty convincing." There are times when Rudy feels he'll literally explode with anger, but he believes that any physical display of anger is morally wrong, so he finds a way to hold it in, or he tries to work it out jogging or just being alone tinkering with his car. During these times, he does not allow Elaine to intrude on his privacy.

A few years ago, Rudy usually found he could forget most of Elaine's faults. Now, however, things seem to be building up. Even when he's jogging, trying to relax, he finds himself going over and over a list of grievances in his mind. He'd like to forget them, but how can he? She is always there, adding to the list. She's gotten careless with money, he feels, and she's temperamental whenever he tries to discuss it. Where once she was warm and affectionate, she now seems as cold and distant as the rest of her family. Sometimes he feels she cares more about that dog of hers than she does about him. He feels like giving the dog away. Maybe that would get her attention. Other than that, what is there to do but keep quiet and go on with life?

Rudy thinks of his father, Roy. Whenever Roy felt really angry, he just retreated to the basement and worked on model ships until the anger went away. That's the best way to deal with it, Rudy feels. Keep it under control—otherwise, somebody just winds up getting hurt.

Based on what you know of Rudy and Elaine's relationship, do you think Rudy should keep quiet and suppress his anger? What are some of the most important factors for him to consider in making this decision? If he does hold his anger inside, what are some of the most significant ramifications of that decision?

❑ Should Rudy continue to suppress the anger he feels?

❑ What factors support that view?

❑ What factors support the opposite view?

❑ What will happen immediately if he acts as you suggest?

❑ What will Rudy and Elaine's situation probably be five years from now if Rudy acts as you suggest?

❑ Are there research studies cited in the text that offer support for your position?

❑ If you needed additional research-based information to support your position, how or where would you go about getting it?

# Lesson 14

# Power Plays

## Love, Need, and Power

Power. What, you might wonder, does power have to do with interpersonal relationships? Sometimes quite a lot. Ours is a competitive society, and for many people, power is a way of life.

In many ways, we're conditioned to compete from a very early age. Our games and sports are competitive. Most have winners. Those who win a lot are termed champions. Has a nice ring—champion. A word associated with victory, glory, attention, adoration. Love, perhaps. And who couldn't use a little more of all those good things?

Schools are competitive, too. Students are forever striving for the best grades, the highest recognition. We're continually testing students to see who has mastered the necessary skills, who can solve the problems, who knows the right answers, who can demonstrate the best performance. Throughout school, we nurture a competitive spirit that carries right over into the marketplace, where the rewards of grades are replaced by other symbols of achievement: titles, prestige, high pay, pleasant office with a view, and so forth. So, you see, it wouldn't be so very surprising if some of that will-to-win were to carry over into other phases of life, such as courtship and marriage. And in fact, that is precisely what happens.

Before going further, we ought to define what we mean by power. Power, as discussed in this lesson, is the ability to exercise one's will. Notice that this definition is a rather neutral one. It doesn't suggest that power is either good or bad—be-

**Personal, Social, and Conjugal Power**

cause inherently, power is neither. It's how power is used that determines its effects.

Power exists in various forms, depending on context. *Autonomy*, or *personal power*, gives a person a sense of independence. Some autonomy is essential to individual growth and development, to a strong self-concept. In many ways, growing up is a process of acquiring (and learning to use judiciously) personal power.

*Social power* is the ability to exercise one's will over others. Dozens of examples of this exist all around us. Parents have social power over children. So do teachers. Law enforcement officers and others in positions of authority have social power as well, as do politicians, religious leaders, business leaders, and others who have influence over large groups of people. Obviously, one can have a great deal of autonomy, or personal power, without having very much social power at all. And many of us might classify ourselves that way.

Within a marriage, individuals have *conjugal power*—to varying degrees. If the married partners are competitive, there may be a real struggle to see which of them will attain the greatest amount of power within the relationship. How is such power determined? Money? Social status? Age? Responsibility? Physical strength? All these factors, and others, can play a part in determining marital power. Some factors, however, seem slightly more important than others. (Perhaps you already have some guesses about which those might be.) Let's take a closer look at the sources of conjugal power.

## Sources of Power

According to tradition, the man has most of the power in a marriage. He is the unquestioned head of the household. In many societies throughout the world, this situation continues to be the norm. And in our society, despite the influence of the women's movement, some vestiges of that male-centered norm remain.

Most people—men and women alike—do not openly profess this value system, and some may not even be aware of its influence. Yet in many families, there continues to be a certain deference accorded the husband simply by virtue of the fact that he is male. And there are some subcultures—certain religious groups, particularly—which continue to encourage this tradition. Male dominance is by no means universal, however, and many other factors influence power within marriages.

One theory, the *resource hypothesis*, suggests that power comes from the resources that one brings to a marriage. Usually, this means money (or its equivalent—say, land) or the ability to earn money. It might also come from such things as good judgment or education—which again, relate to the acquisition of money or the ability to manage money and investments wisely.

Research conducted by Blood and Wolfe tended to bear out this hypothesis, but their findings were widely criticized. It was suggested, among other things, that Blood and Wolfe's definition of power, which tended to center on which partner made decisions, was simply too narrow.

Power, some sociologists argued, also relates to such issues as relative autonomy and division of labor. Further, critics charged, Blood and Wolfe's research failed to focus on such important marital decisions as when to have sex, how many children to have, how often and when to see relatives, and so on.

Some critics also felt that Blood and Wolfe were operating on the assumption that the patriarchal norm had been generally supplanted in our society by a more egalitarian model of marriage. Not so, most argued. On the surface it might look that way, but in reality, the patriarchal norm had not lost its grip. Not yet. On the positive side, though, even critics admitted that this research did encourage people to see that conjugal power is shared. In other words, it was recognized and accepted that women had power in marriage, too. But how much? How did they get it? These questions were still to be answered.

Later research confirmed Blood and Wolfe's original hypothesis that resources make some difference in marital power. A woman with great wealth probably has more power in a marriage than one who depends solely on her husband for a source of income. Similarly, a well-educated woman probably has more power than one who hasn't finished high school. But of course, we're dealing here with extremes. And other factors, such as self-concept and assertiveness, may be intertwined with factors like education.

While resources tend to make a difference, it's usually the man who has the greater resources. Men tend to be older and physically stronger. Often they're better educated, and even when they're not, their earning power may be far greater than that of a woman. Factors relating to education and earning power are changing; for example, more women are working at higher paying jobs. But we're still far short of achieving true equality in terms of the financial resources with which men and women typically enter marriage.

Women may also lose a certain economic edge through their roles as mothers. Of course, to some extent, parenting affects both partners. But face it: it's the woman who carries the child, bears the child, and often takes primary responsibility in caring for the child—at least during the early months of the child's life.

A woman who bears several children (especially if they come close together) may have a relatively long period during which she cannot attain the economic autonomy she otherwise might. Depending on the kind of work she does, her earning capacity is likely to be either mildly or severely restricted during at least part of her pregnancy. Obviously, the impact is greater for a woman who breaks horses than for one who writes computer programs. But realistically, most women find that pregnancy is a deterrent to their ability to compete in the workplace. For this reason, a woman may also find herself more financially dependent during pregnancy and for sometime thereafter, unless she has access to other childcare.

Further, she's likely to be physically tired during this period. Pregnancy, childbirth, and especially the care of small children are all physically and emotionally draining experiences that can leave a woman feeling exhausted. The last thing she may feel like doing is fighting for greater power within her marriage, even if she feels shortchanged.

Research indicates, as we might expect, that mothers who have small children and who do not work outside the home have considerably less power than women earning income. They lose both economic and sexual attractiveness power to some degree—at the very time when their physical and emotional needs may be greatest. Further, many have the added burden of housework. A woman who does work outside the home, and who has small children besides, is likely to feel—at least much of the time—that she is doing three jobs: working at her career, caring for children, and maintaining the household. The considerable skill and energy required to perform this balancing act is not, however, likely to accord her greater privilege within her marriage. Whether that might be different some time in the future will depend on evolving cultural values.

## Power and Need

Thus far, we've considered the influence of tradition and the influence of resources. What other factors contribute to power within marriage? Social scientist Willard Waller has proposed a theory based on the *principle of least interest*. According to this theory, the partner who feels he or she has the least to lose by dissolving the relationship will be the one with the greater power. Obviously, a high level of self-esteem would be helpful here. If you feel that you have a lot to offer within a marriage, that your partner would be lost and desolate without you (whereas you might trundle on through life relatively unscathed by the breakup), then that very attitude—according to Waller's theory—is likely to give you a real edge.

Of course, practical considerations come into play here as well. If you're a woman with small children, it may occur to you that even if you're not emotionally dependent on your husband, or even fond of him for that matter, that you're better off to remain with him at least until you can figure out some other means of support for you and your family. Similarly, aging partners may feel that their prospects of remarriage, or of just finding a satisfactory relationship outside marriage, are not as great as they once were, and thus even a blissless marriage may provide an element of security.

How needy are you when it comes to love? Well, according to the *relative love and need theory*, that very need for love might be, in part, a measure of your vulnerability. Theoretically, it would seem that according to this hypothesis, women would be as likely to have power within a marriage as men. After all, men are emotionally needy, too. Many may feel very reluctant to give up the love they receive from their wives and families. Still, in reality, it seems that men have greater power. Why? Some sociologists suggest this is because women are more conditioned to love and need husbands than men are conditioned to love and need wives. In short, women are perhaps more in tune with the needs they feel and thus more ready to admit to them.

Further, some sociologists suggest, Americans tend to believe women are more dependent on marriage for happiness and satisfac- tion—regardless of whether this is actually true. Think about a family with five small, dependent children. Which would you find more surprising? To learn that the husband had left his wife and children behind? Or, that the wife had left her husband and children? Most of us have at least some expectation that the wife will do her best to hold the family together, regardless of how cooperative the husband is in that effort. Of course, our expectations may not reflect people's real-life needs and desires. In the real world, women *do* leave marriages to begin new lives—even when it means leaving five small children behind.

**The Exercise of Power**

Power is a funny thing. It exists on many levels, and affects not only the way decisions are made, but also the way in which people interact. It's accurate to say that, to a degree, power takes its definition from the dynamics of the individual family. In other words, what would be a real display of power in one family—a decision to move to another house, for example—might be less meaningful in another family, where value systems are different.

How do you define power within your marriage or family? Is it the big things that matter? Where you'll live? What car you'll buy? Where or how you'll spend your vacation? Who'll take care of the house or pay the bills? Or is it smaller, more subtle things—such as who'll begin talking first following an argument?

There's some evidence to suggest that while men may have dominance in the outside world—deciding such things as whether the family will move to Baltimore—within the home, a woman may have greater power. It may well be the woman who directs the course of the relationship itself. Or, to put it another way, the nature of the intimate relationship between husband and wife is the woman's "turf," and she will make the rules and play this game on her own terms. Social scientists refer to the power struggle within a relationship as *micropolitics*. Some feel that a woman's generally subordinate role in most contexts has given her a certain manipulative advantage in up-close, personal relationships. She may seem to yield to the male's power in some situations when, in fact, she is using that power for her own purposes.

Is the balance of power in marriage changing? Is it likely to become more equal? While this is hardly a simple question to answer, social scientists suggest that equality could come about in several different ways. First, women could attain equal status within the public world. To some extent this seems to be occurring, but as we indicated earlier, progress is not the same thing as equality. A long home stretch remains. Second, society might come to place greater value on the resources generally associated with a woman—nurturing, caring, emotional rewards within marriage. Or, third, the norms of equality might become so strong that men and women would be accorded equal power within a marriage regardless of what resources either might bring to the relationship. In other words, it would no longer matter who had more money, who was better educated, or who made better decisions. The man and wife would simply agree implicitly to view and treat each other as equals, and society in general would accept and support this view. Which of these will happen? We can't say. But studies of current dynamics among married couples may shed some light.

In a recent study by Blumstein and Schwartz, gender still seemed to be the major determinant of power in American couples. Resources, however, were also very significant. The spouse with higher earning power, for example, often seemed to be excused from household chores. Do you agree with this position? If you were the sole breadwinner, would you feel you ought to help with dishes and laundry? Or should that be the spouse's job? Would you get up at night half the time with the baby if your spouse stayed home all day? If you answer no to these questions, then your attitude supports the status quo.

Among those couples Blumstein and Schwartz studied, the lesbian couples seemed most capable of maintaining a sense of equality totally divorced from income. In other words, they did not allow earning power to determine dominance within a relationship. They shared chores and decision-making power equally, regardless of whether one or both worked, or whether their incomes were relatively equivalent or highly disparate. This was not nearly so true among heterosexual couples or among male homosexual couples who tended to be highly competitive about work and income-related matters.

## Power and Happiness Within Marriage

You may be wondering about the relationship between power and happiness within marriage. Is the winner of the power struggle likely to be the happier mate? Even those who've studied power within marriage do not agree on what sort of situation produces most happiness. Some studies indicate that marriages in which the male dominates ultimately produce greater satisfaction for both spouses. Other studies support the theory that *egalitarian* marriages, in which power is shared, lead to greater satisfaction.

It may be that in comparing male-dominated to egalitarian marriages, we need to pay more attention to the influence of society. To the extent that equality is still not universally accepted, and that the patriarchal norm still prevails, couples with egalitarian marriages may feel some discomfort, even rejection. And this, rather than the relationship per se, may be the cause of their lesser satisfaction. Similarly, couples in which the man dominates may experience a degree of social sanction that makes their lifestyle more rewarding than it otherwise might be.

With all this talk of dominance and power politics, you may get the idea that marriage is one big power struggle. Sometimes that's so. It doesn't have to be like that, however. Psychologists tell us that we can, with effort, achieve a *no-power relationship*. This is not, as its name might suggest, one in which neither partner has power; rather, it's a relationship in which partners have equal power, and in which the whole concept of playing power politics is generally rejected. If you wanted to establish such a relationship, how would you go about it?

Well, first, you would need to avoid power games. For example, if you want the right to play golf on Saturdays, or more say in how family income is spent, you would use communication and negotiation to establish your viewpoint. You would not, however, engage in veiled threats (e.g., "If I were single, I could do what I wanted on Saturdays"), sulk, refuse to speak, or withhold sex and affection until your recalcitrant spouse comes around. Such tactics have no place in a no-power relationship. Here are some things you might do, however.

Let's suppose that you're the spouse without as much power. There are effective ways you can go about neutralizing your spouse's power without playing games or becoming overtly aggressive. For example, if the spouse's power comes, in part, from greater income, you might get a full or part-time job in order to have some money to spend that's just yours, or you might simply decide to cut back spending in certain areas. If your spouse gains a measure of power from always being the one to make the social arrangements, you can decide you'll do it or find your own social outlets from now on.

You can also decide that you'll no longer feel obligated for every favor the spouse provides. Say that your spouse cleans the house; do you owe him or her something for this? If you feel you do, you weaken your power position. If your answer is no—since this is a shared responsibility, and your turn is next—then you're on your way to having a no-power relationship.

Now let's suppose that you're the spouse with power. Why would you want to abdicate it? Well, power—as enticing as we think it is—gets in the way of intimacy. You're likely to find your relationship more satisfying in the long run if you learn to share the power.

You can do some neutralizing from your side too. For example, you can give the spouse responsibility for his or her own life. Let's say it's the spouse's responsibility to balance the checkbook, but it doesn't seem to get done, so you take over. Quit taking over the responsibility. Let what happens happen. (Notice that this alternative demands strong nerves and a willingness to live with the consequences if the spouse doesn't see the light and checks begin to bounce.)

Which brings us to alternative two: Do it yourself. If your spouse is unwilling to help take care of the baby, stop using this as a power issue. Simply decide that the child will be your responsibility, and your spouse will do something else. In the most egalitarian marriages, roles are assigned according to ability and interest, not according to tradition or expectations. Also, provide rewards to get your spouse to do what you want. For example, you might agree that if you get to choose the new car, your spouse can make most of the vacation plans. Or, if your spouse will spend Thanksgiving with your family, you'll spend Memorial Day weekend with your in-laws. And finally, here's what some sociologists would say is the most effective neutralizing strategy of all: "Join with joy." In other words, find a way to work together, and try to make it an enjoyable time. The strategy is to take advantage of opportunities to share equally in completing tasks. It may not make doing the dishes fun, but it does increase equality while making the job less distasteful.

## Communication and Honesty

While all these strategies for neutralizing power have great potential, it's vital to communicate with your spouse about what you're doing while you're doing it. Otherwise, your behavior is likely to be misinterpreted. For example, if you suddenly refuse to handle the banking when you've done it for ten years, your spouse is not likely to immediately conclude that you're neutralizing power within the relationship. She's more likely to assume you're inconsiderate and impulsive. If you go out and get a part-time job so that you can buy new golf clubs without feeling guilty, is your spouse likely to see this as an effort to improve the relationship? Probably not—unless you make your motives clear.

Further, let's be honest. Changing patterns that have been set up over many years is likely to prove difficult. Even for partners who talk it all through; even for partners who believe strongly in equality and sincerely want to achieve it. Our society does not support equality in marriage—not strongly, at least. And few of us had good role models to emulate. If your parents (or other influential adults in your life) had what you would regard as a truly egalitarian marriage, consider your experience highly unusual.

In order to get through what is probably going to be a turbulent period while you work toward equality, you may find it useful to employ the services of a good marriage counselor. You need a person you can trust. For some couples, this means—among other things—getting a couple to work with them, a man and a woman, so that both male and female perspectives are represented. And while trust is vital, you've also got to be realistic. Counselors are human, too. They have biases. Some believe strongly in divorce, for example, if a relationship is not going smoothly or if one spouse's autonomy seems seriously threatened. So unless you take an assertive position in controlling your own life, you may find yourself in the very uncomfortable position of feeling you must apply someone else's solution to your problem. Would you consider divorcing your mate to make a marriage counselor happy? Don't laugh—it isn't so preposterous as it sounds. We tend to give great weight to the opinion of a recognized authority.

Can you have a marriage that's totally free of power politics? Probably not. Not even if you're a flag-waving advocate of marital equality with love in your heart and the gift of communication on your tongue. You can, however, choose to emphasize no-power politics. In other words, you can strive for a balance of power, rather than an imbalance. You use your energies and resources to ensure that you and your partner are equals, rather than using them to win the game of marriage.

By committing yourselves to self-disclosure, fair fighting, and open communications, you and your spouse can achieve a no-power marriage. Nobody says it will be simple. And, you might have to give up some degree of personal power to reach that goal. But, as we've said all along, life is a series of choices.

## Learning Objectives

On completing your study of this lesson, you should be able to

❑ Define power and describe several different forms of power.

❑ Explain the resource hypothesis and its relationship to conjugal power.

❑ Discuss the relationship of gender to conjugal power, both traditionally and as it exists now.

❑ Name several factors that affect power in white-collar and blue-collar families.

❑ Define the principle of least interest theory and discuss its relationship to conjugal power.

❑ Discuss the implications of the love and need theory of conjugal power, and explain how this theory relates to the least interest theory mentioned in the previous objective.

❑ Explain how relative conjugal power may vary between the public and private spheres.

❑ Name and discuss three factors that could bring about greater equality between spouses in the future.

❑ Describe the characteristics of a no-power relationship, and identify several strategies by which higher-power and lower-power spouses can bring about such a relationship.

❑ Name and discuss several alternatives to power politics in marriage.

## Key Terms

Conjugal power
Love
Micropolitics
Neutralization of power
No-power relationship
Personal power
Power
Power politics
Principle of least interest
Relative love and need theory
Resource hypothesis
Social power

## Assignments

❑ Before viewing the program, be sure you've read through the preceding overview and familiarized yourself with the learning objectives and key terms for this lesson. Then read Chapter 10, "Power and Violence in Marriages and Families," pages 286–303, of *Marriages and Families* by Lamanna and Riedmann.

❑ After completing these tasks, read the video viewing questions and watch the video program for Lesson 14, "Power Plays."

❑ After viewing the program, take time to answer the video viewing questions and evaluate your learning with the self-test. You'll find the correct answers, along with text page references, at the back of this telecourse guide.

❑ Read the "What's Your Decision?" scenario at the end of this lesson and answer the questions about the decision you would make based on what you've learned from this lesson. Give these questions some serious thought; they may be used as the basis for class discussion or the development of a more complex essay.

## Video Viewing Questions

1. According to Gail Pinkus, Marsha Lasswell, and Joshua, in what ways does power manifest itself in relationships? How do men and women use power differently? What is/were the dynamics of power in the "traditional" family? Refer to the comments of Michelle Harway and Alice Laviolette in your response.

2. Discuss what Carlfred Broderick, Glenn, and Donna mean by "equal access" or "pooling" of resources. Relate your analysis to Bob and Carol's "totally equal" situation and why Margo Kaufman abandoned it.

3. Can true equality exist only in a dual income relationship? Consider the realities of women not being paid equal wages for equal work and the need to take time off for pregnancy and children. Note the comments of Irene Cruz and Carrie.

4. Discuss Gail's comments on the use of power. Does dependency on another person open the door to exploitation? How can this be resolved with the need for trust in a relationship?

5. Why do you think gay couples have been found to be more egalitarian overall than heterosexual couples? In considering this question, note the comments of Jake and Bill, Barbara and Linda, regarding the traditional roles of the sexes in modern society.

6. How is power an obstacle and how can therapy help couples to overcome the problems power causes in relationships? Note the comments of Michelle Harway, John and Muriel Olguin, Margo Kaufman, and David Viscott. Discuss Alice Laviolette's statement on "the roles" and what they mean in friendships and relationships. What do you think the bottom line is in terms of power?

1. _____ power is based on the more dominant individual's ability to claim authority or the right to request compliance.

   a. Legitimate
   b. Referent
   c. Expert
   d. Coercive

2. The ability of one person to exercise his or her will over the wills of other people is *best* defined as

   a. autonomy.
   b. conjugal power.
   c. parental power.
   d. social power.

3. According to the *resource hypothesis*, which of the following would likely have the greatest conjugal power?

   a. *All* of the following would be about equal in conjugal power.
   b. A male blue-collar worker with a high school diploma.
   c. A female surgeon with two small children who has just finished her residency.
   d. A female secretary with one year of business school.

4. In the study by Blood and Wolfe, which of the following groups seemed to have a relatively greater share of decision making power?

   a. Women with small children.
   b. Blue-collar workers.
   c. Persons who did not work outside the home.
   d. Older spouses with more education.

5. According to studies cited in the text, which of the following best sums up the relationship between conjugal power and gender?

   a. Ultimately, gender is probably the sole determining factor of conjugal power.
   b. Gender is perhaps the most significant factor in determining conjugal power—though other factors, such as resources, are highly significant too.
   c. Though gender was once highly significant, it now plays a relatively minor role in determining conjugal power.
   d. There is no relationship whatever between gender and conjugal power.

6. In Blumstein and Schwartz's study of married heterosexuals, cohabiting heterosexuals, gay male couples, and lesbian couples, which of the four types of couples stressed cooperating, worked very hard at their relationship, and often deferred to each other?

   a. married heterosexuals
   b. cohabiting heterosexuals
   c. gay male couples
   d. lesbian couples

7. The equalization of power between spouses in the future could be aided by

   a. the endorcement of matriarchal authority by society.
   b. the political importance of "family values."
   c. the attainment by women of social status and resources that are similar to men's.
   d. men encouraging women to be more assertive.

8. According to the relative love and need theory, a wife is likely to hold less power than a husband within a marriage because

   a. her need for love is inherently greater than a man's.
   b. she is not capable of expressing love as honestly and openly as a man, and therefore has trouble establishing an intimate relationship.
   c. she is likely to be more socialized to loving and needing her husband than he is to loving and needing her.
   d. though capable of expressing love if she wants to, she's likely to withhold love as a manipulation—thus destroying trust.

9. In a no-power relationship, which of the following tends to be true?

   a. Neither spouse has very much personal or social power.
   b. Spouses have equal conjugal power, and work hard at maintaining the balance of power.
   c. Both spouses work at gaining dominance within the relationship, but each uses neutralizing tactics to undermine the power of the other.
   d. Both spouses have extensive social power (outside the marriage), but neither wields much personal power within the marriage.

10. The best way to work through power changes is
    a. to follow the advice of a good therapist and allow the husband to be dominant.
    b. for each spouse to follow her or his inclination, and if this doesn't work out, to either divorce or accept the inevitable.
    c. to discuss power openly and fight about it fairly.
    d. to keep silent about the differences while one works quietly to change the sources of those differences.

## What's Your Decision?

Ned and Becky have had what their friends see as an ideal marriage. They're happy. They have beautiful, bright children. A nice home in the suburbs with a sunroom and a hot tub.

Becky, however, is discontent. She feels restless. She tries not to let it show, and often her feelings give her a strong sense of guilt, but still, she wants something more out of life. In subtle ways, she feels Ned dominates her. He doesn't yell or carry on or order her around, yet she feels that it's Ned who makes most of the decisions, controls most of the money, and generally directs their life. A good life, to be sure—but one in which she seems to have no real say. She tries expressing these feelings to her parents, but they are not especially supportive. "Most wives would give anything for your situation," her mother tells her. "What are you complaining about? Are you just looking for problems? You have everything. Why don't you just enjoy it?" Friends aren't especially helpful either. They think Becky is lucky not to have to work to pay bills. They're generally nonsupportive, if not downright envious. They tell her she's crazy to feel discontent. "You're just spoiled," Myrna tells her over lunch. "I work 50 hours a week—on the average. Try it before you complain about your life in the hot tub."

Still, Becky resolves to make her own decisions. She takes a part-time job, and it feels good to have income she doesn't get from someone else. When Ned lets her decide where to vacation, she no longer feels she owes him something in return. She's less solicitous about watching the television shows Ned likes; she makes some choices now, even when he doesn't agree. She doesn't always cook his favorite dinners, either. "I eat here, too," she reasons to herself. "Why shouldn't we eat what I like for a change?" Ned asks her what is going on, if something is different, if he's done something to offend her. She shrugs off his inquiries. Perhaps she should tell him how she feels... or should she? After the responses she's gotten from family and friends, she's afraid Ned will think she's spoiled and crazy, too. She's afraid he'll come on so strong she'll never be assertive enough to stand up to it. "I'll just cave in," she thinks to herself, "and then the little bit of freedom I've gained will be over. Better to just keep my ideas to myself."

Based on what you know of the situation, do you think Becky should be open with Ned about her feelings, or should she continue seeking personal autonomy without letting Ned know her motives? What are some of the most important factors for her to consider in making this decision? If Becky does confide in Ned, what are some of the most significant ramifications of that decision?

❑ Should Becky be open with Ned about her desire for more autonomy?

❑ What factors support that view?

❑ What factors support the opposite view?

❑ What will happen immediately if Becky acts as you suggest?

❑ What will their situation probably be five years from now if she acts as you suggest?

❑ Are there research studies cited in the text that offer support for your position?

❑ If you needed additional research-based support for your position, how or where would you go about getting it?

## Lesson 15

# Behind Closed Doors

## Violence in the Home

---

Each year, in one out of every six couples, one partner or the other commits an act of violence toward their spouse. And that rate of violence increases sharply if it's based on the entire length of the marriage. In fact, if you are married now, the odds are about one in three that at some time during your marriage, your husband or wife will hit you.

Unfortunately, marital violence is nothing new. It's as old as recorded history. But it's just recently that spouse abuse has been clearly labeled a serious social problem.

**Overview**

The Justice Department estimates that approximately 623,000 cases of family abuse occur each year, about 50 percent of which involve spouses or ex-spouses. And even this high figure, experts suggest, is not likely to be accurate. Many persons are reluctant to report incidents of family abuse for any of several reasons. They may not know the correct procedures for reporting abuse—particularly if the victims are children. They may feel embarrassed. Or they may be afraid of retaliation from the family member who committed the acts of violence in the first place. Many acts of husband abuse may go unreported because the husband would rather suffer the abuse than the humiliation of admitting the incident.

Some people tend to think of marital abuse as a typically blue-collar phenomenon, and there is some statistical evidence to support this impression. It may be that middle class families have greater access to counselors, psychologists, and others who can intervene and help resolve marital problems

**The Scope of the Problem**

before they precipitate violence—or at least before they're brought to the attention of the police. Or it may simply be that middle class families have greater privacy, and thus are more able to conceal problems that do exist.

Regardless of small statistical differences, marital violence is common to all social classes and economic groups. No one is exempt. Further, despite what we might expect, violence is common to both men and women. That is, wives are just as likely to be violent as husbands—though the results of that violence may be quite different.

Just what is *wife abuse*? In many respects, how one defines the term is a rather personal thing, and it's probably fair to say that a wife who *feels* abused *is* abused in a very real sense. But for legal purposes, wife abuse consists of wife beating and some other forms of violence such as kicking, pushing the spouse down stairs, hitting her with an object, attacking her with a weapon, sexually abusing and raping. Verbal abuse is not generally regarded as true wife abuse, but needless to say, it can be very psychologically damaging and can certainly threaten a relationship.

## The Cycle of Violence

If you've ever been involved in a violent personal relationship, or spoken with someone who has, then you may already know that the first act of serious violence generally comes as a shock to the wife—and often to the husband, as well. Both may tend to view it as an isolated incident, one that will never be repeated. The husband may seem very contrite, and may even be genuinely horrified by his own behavior. He may promise that it will never recur, and the wife will tend to believe this promise—not only because she wants to believe it, but also because the violent behavior may seem so utterly shocking, so out of character with the person she has known.

In fact, however, such incidents are rarely isolated when the victim is the woman and the perpetrator the man. (Wives are somewhat more likely to commit isolated acts of violence.) The first act of violence is far more likely to be part of a cycle which repeats itself, building in intensity—and danger—with each recurrence. This cycle, psychologists tell us, consists of three phases.

The first phase involves a building of tension over time. Any number of factors may contribute to this: difficulties on the job or at home, lack of money, health problems, poor self-concept, personality conflicts—and any other of a dozen tension-producing factors you might think of. Of course, all of us seek ways to relieve tension—recreation, time off, exercise. And when these methods work, the cycle may never go beyond this first phase. But if the tension builds to an unbearable point, the cycle enters phase two.

In this second phase, the tension escalates beyond an individual's power to contain it, and explodes in sudden violence. And in the third phase, the husband recognizes what he has done and vows to reform. But then the cycle repeats itself. Why? What are some of the reasons behind this violence? And, if husbands are truly repentant, and truly realize the potentially devastating consequences of their behavior, why can't they stop?

Psychologists suggest that husbands who beat their wives generally do so to compensate for feelings of inadequacy, either on the job or within the relationship itself. A husband who is unable to feel superior to his wife or to demonstrate his superiority in any other way can at least establish his male supremacy in the physical realm. Husbands who beat their wives are more likely than other husbands to have serious dissatisfaction with their jobs, to be high school or college dropouts, or to have an income that doesn't contribute significantly enough to pay the bills, or keep pace with their wife's growing income. Such husbands are often married to women who are more articulate than they. Even a husband who contributes his share of income may feel outdistanced by a wife who is clearly intellectually superior—particularly if she doesn't mind showing it.

It is not so very difficult, even for those of us who are not trained psychologists, to construct some of the reasons that marital violence might occur. The question that's sometimes more difficult to answer is, "Why would a wife put up with it?"

**Why Women Stay in Abusive Marriages**

If you've ever known a woman who was abused by her husband, you may have asked yourself (or her) why she didn't simply leave—get out—get away. That would seem to be the logical solution. But, as we shall see in this lesson, it isn't quite that simple. They *do* want to escape, and many seek various alternatives. However, most do remain married. Why?

The most common reason is probably fear. Husbands who abuse their wives do not, after all, wish to be found out. There can be serious legal, social, and psychological ramifications to such a disclosure. Thus, a husband who beats his wife may threaten her with more serious abuse—even with death—if she betrays him. The wife, therefore, may be afraid of leaving or of telling the police. If she has children, she may fear for their safety. Statistically, she has reason to be afraid. Data indicate that in 1992, 70 percent of victims killed by intimates were women.

Further, cultural traditions encourage wives to put up with a lot, even abuse. Under English common law, what today we define as abuse might have been considered chastisement for misbehavior in earlier periods. While wife beating is no longer legal, the social influence of the older tradition remains.

Fear of retaliation and fear of social disapproval or downright rejection keep some women unhappily married. But there's another important consideration, too. If a woman does decide to leave her husband, where will she go? A fortunate woman might have friends or family to take her in. But barring that alternative, there were not many places of refuge—until recently. In fact, there was little legal protection for battered wives.

The police might be called, but in order to make an arrest, they were required to witness the violence directly. Obviously, not many husbands were likely to be accommodating enough to time their violent acts accordingly. Further, severe injury was required to ensure prosecution. How severe? Well, that was open to interpretation. But suffice it to say, a woman could suffer a great deal of physical and mental anguish without any real legal recourse.

Other factors play a role as well. Often, wives truly love their husbands, and hope they will reform. Some—especially those without sufficient levels of education or a satisfying career—may lack self-esteem. They may feel that without their husbands, they are nothing. A life of abuse, terrible as it is, may seem preferable to being alone.

Some abused wives come from a history of abuse. If they were also abused by fathers or other family members, they may see abuse—at least anything short of extreme violence—as fairly normal, a natural part of family life.

And for some women, practical considerations enter the picture. A woman may be reluctant to break up the family if she has children, for example. She may feel it's better to keep the family together if at all possible, especially if she feels she might not be able to provide for those children. A wife may also fear loss of income or social prestige if her husband is found out. Suppose he should lose his job? And then the house? Who wants to be the cause of all that? It's a weighty responsibility.

She may even see the loss of social prestige as reflecting on her; in some strange way, friends and neighbors may feel she is to blame for the situation, even though she is in reality the victim. Is there a way out of this dismal picture? For most women, we can answer with a qualified yes.

In many parts of the country, shelters for battered wives are becoming more common. Such shelters offer a number of services, designed to meet a range of needs. First, they offer housing, food, and clothing to battered wives and their children. They also offer security, safety from the battering husband who will be refused access to his wife, and may not even know of her whereabouts. (The address of such shelters is often kept secret, and a number of security measures are used to limit access.)

In addition, such centers offer counseling to wives who want it. They may also offer legal assistance as needed, or help in obtaining employment. In short, the goal is to provide the battered wife with the means to achieve increased independence. And not just economic independence, but social and psychological independence as well. That means helping her create a stronger self-image, as well as providing practical skills that will be useful in establishing her identity in the workplace.

Psychologists agree that shelters can only be successful if they focus on long-range goals. If a man is threatening his wife with a shotgun, then getting her off the premises to a place of safety may seem paramount. But in reality, short-term solutions are only temporary fixes. Often, husbands whose wives leave may seek retaliation. Thus, a woman who seeks help from a shelter may be taking a step she can never retrace. It is a big step for her, a decision to begin a new life altogether—usually, one apart from the husband. Therefore, simply providing her with a place to sleep for a few nights and some hot meals will not suffice. She needs the direction, the skills, and the courage required to start over. And such assistance is not easily provided. But shelters are growing in number, and gaining community support and respect.

One might logically suppose that the women's movement would have some positive impact in decreasing the incidence of wife abuse. In fact, however, the movement seems to have mixed effects. On the one hand, it is true that dependent

**Escaping the Cycle of Violence**

wives seem to tolerate more abuse than those who consider themselves independent. On the other hand, independent wives may precipitate more violent feelings in husbands, and thus tend to incur greater abuse. Ultimately, though, financial dependency is likely to go hand in hand with more abuse. The better jobs, higher wages, and available childcare that proponents of the women's movement seek all help women gain the independence they require to free themselves from an abusive relationship. The goal of such independence is not to eliminate marriage as a desirable goal, but to offer alternatives, to ensure women that they need not remain within a bad marriage. This simple freedom, so elusive to many women, is taken for granted by most men.

**Husband Abuse**

Earlier, we mentioned the fact that husband abuse does exist, and for the husbands involved, it poses a real and serious problem. The problem is aggravated by the fact that an abused husband may feel extremely embarrassed and humiliated about admitting to the situation. For this and other reasons, husband abuse has not received widespread recognition, and there has been relatively little support for abused husbands. That situation is not likely to change in the near future, for several reasons.

First, even a cursory analysis of the situation reveals that the most severe violence is perpetrated by men—as a rule. True, some husbands are seriously injured, even killed, by wives. But the reverse situation is far more common. Further, women are more likely to be seriously injured by men than the reverse simply because men tend to be bigger and stronger than women. In addition, while studies show that women are somewhat more likely to threaten a spouse with a gun or knife, men are more likely than women to actually use such a weapon. In addition, as we've noted already, violence initiated by a man tends to be part of a recurring pattern. That is not true of violence initiated by women, however, which is often isolated and situation-specific. In many cases—though by no means all—wives become violent only in self-defense. Overall, wives are less likely than husbands to initiate violence.

Finally, as many social scientists and other observers point out, it is generally easier for a man to walk away from domestic violence. He may feel less commitment to maintaining the family or ensuring care for the children. He is also less likely to be financially dependent on his spouse, so leaving may not seem as difficult—nor as serious a step.

Is spousal abuse likely to become less a problem in the future? There are some hopeful signs. Society is becoming more sympathetic to the plight of battered women. Social support is stronger, and so is legal support. Police protection is getting better, and research indicates that arresting the abusing spouse does help. Whereas once an abused wife might have been scorned for even daring to suppose that she might have a legal leg to stand on, she might now expect to make a very arguable case for herself even if she goes so far as to kill her husband in self-defense.

One of the most promising factors in limiting spousal abuse is the increased direct assistance to abusers. Psychologists believe that many abusing husbands do, in fact, love their wives. They want to stop, want to control their behavior, and are receptive to receiving help. Men who abuse their wives, like the abused wives themselves, may feel that they have no choice, that they lack control over their own lives. Counseling assistance may help them regain that control.

Ultimately, spousal abuse is related to the issue of power. And where there is a struggle for dominant power in a relationship, spousal abuse is likely to increase. Where power is divided equally between spouses, or used to control one's own life and destiny, abuse is much less likely to occur.

## What Does the Future Hold?

Upon completing your study of this lesson, you should be able to

## Learning Objectives

❑ Explain how and why spousal abuse has only recently become a social issue, even though it has existed throughout history.

❑ Discuss the prevalence of spousal abuse in modern society.

❑ Describe the three-phase cycle of male-initiated domestic violence.

❑ Identify and discuss the reasons men commit domestic violence.

❑ Identify and discuss the reasons women may put up with domestic violence.

❑ Describe the advantages and potential disadvantages of shelters in providing protection for battered wives.

❑ Discuss the influence of the women's movement on spousal abuse.

❑ Explain why the abuse of wives is generally considered a more significant problem than abuse of husbands.

❑ Name several factors that could help lessen the incidence of domestic violence in our society in the future.

❑ List several reasons for the large incidence of family violence within American homes.

**Key Terms**

Battered woman syndrome
Husband abuse
Marital rape
Patriarchal terrorism

Three-phase cycle of
   domestic violence
Wife abuse

**Assignments**

❑ Before viewing the program, be sure you've read through the preceding overview and familiarized yourself with the learning objectives and key terms for this lesson. Then read Chapter 10, "Power and Violence in Marriages and Families," pages 303–319, of *Marriages and Families* by Lamanna and Riedmann.

❑ After completing these tasks, read the video viewing questions and watch the video program for Lesson 15, "Behind Closed Doors."

❑ After viewing the program, take time to answer the video viewing questions and evaluate your learning with the self-test. You'll find the correct answers, along with text page references, at the back of this telecourse guide.

❑ Read the "What's Your Decision?" scenario at the end of this lesson and answer the questions about the decision you would make based on what you've learned from this lesson. Give these questions some serious thought; they may be used as the basis for class discussion or the development of a more complex essay.

**Video Viewing Questions**

1. Joshua says that domestic violence is a male problem. Discuss the implications of this statement in terms of the "pattern" of escalating violence and refer to the comments of Sandra Carr regarding her first experience with domestic abuse.

2. Donna discussed the gradual change in her children's attitude toward her husband's abuse. Can children eventually become immune to domestic violence? What can be the long- and short-term effects of such a reaction? Discuss this question based on the assumption that children of batterers become batterers/battered themselves.

3. Describe some of the forms domestic abuse can take. Why is it often difficult for a woman to identify what is happening and what it will likely lead to? What is the honeymoon state; how does it often add to the confusion and perpetuation of abuse?

4. Why is it difficult for many women to leave such terrible circumstances? Avoiding the stereotypical rationales of the battered woman's love and psychological dependence on her batterer, describe the reasons (including genuine fear, financial, and logistical) a woman could become trapped in this type of situation.

5. Victims of domestic abuse usually do not receive support from family and friends when they decide to leave. Why is this? Why is this type of abuse often seen as a woman's problem?

6. Many women who do gather the courage to leave, go to temporary shelters to get back on their feet. What did Sandra Carr have to say about the shelter she went to? Why are the group discussion sessions at many shelters important and effective?

7. Based on the comments of Janet, Tim, and Mary, how is low self-image a factor, both in the men who abuse and the women who are abused? Explain in detail the role low self-image plays in each case.

8. What do Gail Pincus, Tim, Lynne Azpeitia, Joshua, and Janet say about the need for control and the way boys and girls are taught and socialized to think about aggression? Why is this often a generational cycle within families? How can the cycle be broken?

9. Outline the way the legal system deals with domestic violence. Discuss in detail the limitations of this system.

10. Based on the testimony of Joshua, Gail Pincus, Mary Leaming, Tim and Janet Hann, is it possible for a batterer to change?

## Self-Test

1. It is only recently that spousal abuse has been identified as a serious social problem. Of the choices below, the best explanation for this is that

    a. until the 1970s or so, spousal abuse was not a serious problem in our society.
    b. better statistics have given the problem widespread attention for the first time.
    c. though the problem was always recognized as serious, most people have not wanted to talk about it openly.
    d. in our rather violent society, most people tend to condone domestic violence, even now.

2. Statistics on domestic violence are sometimes thought to understate the extent of the problem *primarily* because

    a. many persons are probably reluctant, for one reason or another, to report incidents of domestic violence.
    b. those gathering the data are not as thorough in their procedures as they ought to be.
    c. no one has a clearcut definition of what violence really is.
    d. our definition of wife abuse has narrowed considerably in recent years.

3. Lou and Barney were talking over a beer one day when Lou made this comment: "All this talk about wife abuse is misleading. If the truth were known, women are just as capable of violence as men." Lou's comment in this scenario is

    a. ridiculous. Women simply are not involved in domestic violence—except as victims.
    b. justified in some respects, although women, while just as capable of violence, inflict fewer injuries than men.
    c. highly justified, since men are injured just about as often as women in domestic quarrels.
    d. understated if anything. In fact, women are more likely than men to commit serious acts of violence, including murder.

4. If you are married, what are the odds that at some time during your marriage your husband or wife will strike you?

    a. About one in fifty.
    b. About one in ten.
    c. About one in three.
    d. Almost zero, according to the most recent data.

5. Under traditional law, marital rape was not considered rape at all because
    a. violence is seldom associated with marital rape.
    b. prior to the women's movement, the laws were written and interpreted exclusively by men.
    c. the wife was considered her husband's property and he was entitled to unlimited sexual access.
    d. All of the above.

6. According to what psychologists have observed about the three-phase cycle of domestic violence, the first time a husband beats or strikes his wife, her *most likely* response is
    a. acceptance.
    b. indifference.
    c. understanding, despite her pain.
    d. shock.

7. Studies indicate that husbands who beat their wives are *usually*
    a. honestly trying to improve their wives' behavior—even though their methods look extreme to most rational people.
    b. legally insane, and incapable of knowing right from wrong.
    c. under the influence of alcohol or drugs, and thus acting in ways that they normally would not.
    d. attempting to compensate for deep-seated feelings of powerlessness or inadequacy on the job, within the relationship, or both.

8. Which of the following is *not* likely to be a reason that a wife would remain in a marriage where she is abused?
    a. She truly loves her husband, and despite their difficulties, believes he'll change.
    b. She comes, after a time, to accept and even enjoy abuse, and encourages it.
    c. She fears that if she tries to escape, he'll retaliate with further abuse—and possibly even kill her.
    d. She feels simply helpless, and sees no other alternatives.

9. According to studies, mandatory arrest of domestic violence offenders
    a. deters new assaults.

b. is less effective than simply removing the husband from the premises.

c. can often backfire, angering the husband and triggering further violence.

d. is ineffective in detering new assaults.

10. When low self-esteem interacts with fear, depression, confusion, anxiety, feelings of self-blame, and general helplessness to make a wife feel incapable of making any changes, it is called

a. marital rape.

b. the three-phase cycle of violence.

c. wife abuse.

d. the battered woman syndrome.

## What's Your Decision?

For Ruth and Jethro, domestic violence is a way of life. It began during courtship, but it's worse now. Ruth has never really questioned Jethro's absolute authority over her, or his right to take out his aggressions on her either verbally or physically. That's the way it was in her own family growing up, and she doesn't view it as unusual or abnormal in any way. She knows, furthermore, that she isn't the perfect wife, and supposes that she does plenty of things to annoy Jethro, who is only trying to make a decent living and provide for his family. Still, the thought of putting up with more abuse frightens her and makes her sick to her stomach. She is losing her self-respect and fears she'll lose the respect of her children, too.

Ruth has never had a job and doesn't even have a high school education, so the chances of getting a good job are slim. She thinks of leaving sometimes, but where would she go? She has two small children to think of, and with no job, well, it just isn't very realistic. She has no family to turn to. Their sympathies are with Jethro. Ruth isn't the best housekeeper in the world, and as her mother has said, "No wonder he gets fed up."

Recently, however, a friend told her about a women's shelter where she and the kids could go "if things ever get to where you just can't stand it." Well, that might be a last resort, but it sure seems like a big step. Besides, what if Jethro found out? She remembers his last words after their most recent fight—one in which she suffered two broken ribs: "If you ever try to leave me, if you ever tell anyone about this, you'll be sorry." She knows he means it. Maybe he's capable of killing her. She isn't sure. He keeps a loaded gun in the house—somewhere. If she could find out where, maybe she could use it herself. The thought has crossed her mind more than once, but it scares her to realize she'd even contemplate such a thing. She must be losing her grasp of reality. The shelter seems like a better solution—more peaceful, more sane. Only, what will become of her and the kids next week? Next month? They can't keep her there forever. Is it worth the risk?

Based on what you know of their situation, do you think Ruth should go to the shelter? What are some of the most important factors for her to consider in making this decision? If she does go to the shelter, what are some of the most significant ramifications of that decision?

❏ Should Ruth go to the shelter?

❏ What factors support that view?

❏ What factors support the opposite view?

❏ What will happen immediately if Ruth acts as you suggest?

❏ What will her situation probably be five years from now if she acts as you suggest?

❏ Are there research studies cited in the text that offer support for your position?

❏ If you needed additional research-based information to support your position, how or where would you go about getting it?

# Lesson 16

# Working Husbands/Working Wives

## Rewards and Costs

Very few people make it through their adult lives without work playing a central role in their existence. How often are you asked—sometimes before someone inquires about your name—"What do you do?"

Our jobs define not only how we spend our working hours but also how we spend much of our leisure time: thinking over problems and imagining ways to improve things. We establish many of our friendships through work. For most people, work provides the ultimate identity. Thus, finding or creating meaningful work is a challenge that continues for most of our lives.

Jobs provide one measure of self-worth. A truly happy person usually has satisfying employment that complements other aspects of personal life. Traditionally, the world of work has been male oriented and controlled, with a limited range of job opportunities open to women. One of the most exciting aspects of the women's movement has been the expanding range of career possibilities for women. In fact, probably no job is impossible for women, though attitudes still lag behind what women are actually doing.

Many women, of course, choose not to work outside the home and prefer the role of homemaker. This unpaid job has strongly defined women's roles for generations.

What has your personal experience been? Did either or both of your parents engage in meaningful work? Did their jobs fall into traditional stereotypes? Or did they do work that helped provide a different sense of possibilities for you?

**Overview**

What about you? Has your work experience been largely designed to provide you with an income, or have you been fortunate enough to learn from and grow in the jobs you've held? As you go through this lesson, keep your own attitudes about work and its role in marriage in mind. Perhaps they'll change as you consider the issues presented.

## The Evolving Labor Force

Prior to the industrial revolution, the vast majority of people worked, but not for wages. The whole notion of a labor force and the expectation that the workplace should have a claim on an individual's time is very recent historically. Today, we live in a society where good jobs are not available to everyone, and where many of those that are available require substantial, specialized skills. Many people do find meaningful work, but a growing proportion of the workforce finds neither security nor personal satisfaction in the workplace.

Once upon a time, or so the legend goes, businesses were responsible for paying good steady workers an adequate income. Most men earned enough to support single-handedly an entire family. The man was expected to be a good provider or breadwinner for his family. Women were expected to stay at home to raise the family and maintain the household. Of course, this is still the way of life for some families, but mostly it serves as a model of socially accepted behavior during a period that no longer exists.

Today it is difficult for a man—or a woman—to provide sole support for a family. One of the reasons women have increasingly entered the workforce is the need to increase family income. In doing so, they inevitably become more independent, and less deferential, and this often leads to tension within marriage. For many men, their sense of inadequacy as breadwinners, coupled with the awareness that their wives are gaining a newfound sense of freedom and occupational success in their own right, makes the traditional marriage bargain less satisfying.

The expectation that a man will be provider for his family appears to be present in all social classes, but it is most firmly entrenched in lower- and working-class families. Despite the fact that many blue-collar workers earn high hourly wages, their jobs often don't provide incomes consistent or high enough to allow accumulation of savings. And with plant closures, shortened hours, and eroded fringe benefits, economic difficulties are common.

Preparing for a stable career with an adequate income often helps circumvent such problems. But it's no guarantee.

Even the most stable trade or business is subject to unexpected fluctuations. As a result, most people today can expect to change jobs or even careers several times.

Parents find themselves at a competitive disadvantage in the workplace. Singles and childless couples have no day care to arrange, no sick children to stay home with, and fewer special scheduling problems with which to trouble employers. Although some corporations are providing child care facilities, the great majority do not. And in the absence of greater public commitment, both men and women will continue to pay a stiff price for what has become the privilege of parenthood.

**Shifting Roles in the Family**

A few men are relinquishing the breadwinner role completely, devoting the majority of their time to caring for home and family. The number is still limited, however, if for no other reason than that few women make incomes adequate to support a family. In assessing the experience, househusbands cite closeness to their children as an advantage, and disruption to their careers, financial dependency, and the tedium of housework as negatives. (If you know couples who have reversed traditional roles—and if they're willing—you might ask what advantages or disadvantages they are discovering.)

In fact, the role of homemaker is itself a recent phenomenon. Prior to the industrial revolution most women combined income-producing work on the farm or in a cottage industry with their fa- milial role. But as the economy shifted from agriculture to industry and then to services, most women found themselves devoting increasing amounts of time and energy to the care of home and family.

Because housewives are not *direct producers*, and are thus dependent on their husbands for both income and status, the job of homemaker has few social or economic rewards. This can be stressful in a society where individual achievement is so highly prized. In more traditional familistic societies, the homemaker role is much more valued. Even there, however, studies have found that employed women are generally less stressed than their homebound counterparts.

Of course, some women derive great satisfaction from their husbands' accomplishments, and actively invest time and energy into helping their husbands professionally. Such work is neither highly visible nor openly rewarded; few employers give more than nodding recognition to a spouse's support. As a result, this kind of personal sacrifice has lost much of the appeal it once had. Today's woman is more likely to seek the fulfillment and financial reward of having her own career, and increasing opportunities make her goal more realistic than it was even a few years ago.

A *New York Times* poll found, as one might expect, that women who are not employed generally tend to prefer staying at home, while those in the workforce generally prefer working to home responsibilities. Among employed women, however, fully a third thought home life preferable, if it were financially feasible. The poll also found younger women much less inclined to prefer the homemaker role than women of an older generation. In short, a significant proportion of homemakers find the work satisfying; yet as the number of women in the workforce continues to grow, the homemaker role is increasingly defined as unimportant.

Whether your mother worked or combined work with homemaking depends a great deal on your age. Working mothers were not at all common earlier in the century. Prior to World War II, less than 15 percent of married women worked outside the home. Now 60 percent work outside of the home. The greatest increase in employment levels in recent years has been among Caucasian women. Black women have traditionally had a much higher rate of employment. Two groups with rapidly increasing employment rates are wives of higher income husbands, who've had the option of staying at home if they chose, and mothers with very small children.

This surge in employment, however, has not meant widely expanding opportunities for women to enter various fields. On the contrary, most women's work is still related to the roles women play in the home: health, teaching, assisting someone else. Such relegation to supportive roles has left women earning far lower pay—only about 77 cents for every dollar earned by men.

Some of the discrepancy is due to discrimination, as many women who've tried to break out of stereotypic female low-level jobs can testify. Some women, however, want jobs that will allow them the freedom to return home during the period when their children are very young—and this requirement may place some restrictions on potential income. But even those women who work throughout their lifetimes do not earn substantially higher wages than those who work intermittently. As a result, women are usually able to contribute only 30 to 40 percent of their family's income. This leaves them at a comparative disadvantage in terms of power and decision making within the family unit.

Not all women work out of choice. It is increasingly difficult to maintain a family on one income. Yet for many women the income is secondary. They choose to work primarily because their work provides a sense of identity and an outlet for their talents. Almost 60 percent of college-educated women choose to work for reasons other than money. With family size shrinking and people living longer, more active lives, an increasing number of women are choosing to work rather than stay at home.

Job satisfaction does not, of course, guarantee marital satisfaction. Employed women are more likely to feel inadequate in their parenting, to experience lower levels of interaction with their husbands, and be more upset when marital conflict occurs. In addition, the very fact they are less dependent and have a greater sense of self-worth makes them more likely to feel irritated by their spouse's behavior.

**Two-Paycheck Marriages**

At the same time, working wives are still perceived by many men as threatening. Working class husbands may be somewhat more likely to express their fears and resentments overtly, but many middle class and professional husbands share the same sense of inadequacy. However, once they've grown used to what the additional income provides, few families feel they can afford to live without two incomes for long.

While two-paycheck families are more likely to be egalitarian than those where one partner is the provider, this partnership rarely extends to equivalent efforts on the domestic front. Studies have shown that employed women still spend a great deal more time on "second shift" activities—family work—than do their husbands. Because many men (like many women) consider housework tedious and unfulfilling, they may set low standards which their wives can't accept, or pick specific tasks to perform that represent far less than their fair share of what needs to be done.

One solution, employed by higher income, dual-earner couples, is to spend a portion of their combined income on goods and services that reduce the work load: eating out, childcare, housekeeping help, and so forth. The growth of the low-wage service industry reflects the growing tendency to buy it or hire it done (whenever we can afford to do so). It is also giving us a more class-defined society than we had earlier this century.

There are advantages—people doing interesting work often make stimulating marriage partners—but there are also unexpected costs. Many professional careers implicitly assume the presence of an unpaid, supportive partner. When two employed spouses try to play careers without the wifely support of an unencumbered party, both may find career advancement a real strain. Although husbands feel the effects of the inevitable overload, it's generally the wife who succumbs to demands for familial attention—meal preparation, caring for the sick child, and so on—giving employers yet another justification for keeping a woman's wages lower, and treating her career with less professional respect.

Research shows that women tend to downplay their accomplishments and overestimate the minimal support they actually receive from their husbands—both on the job and at home. And even in cases where the wife holds a prestigious job, her opportunities for advancement and higher wages are seldom decisive in determining whether a family will move.

In this mobile society, careers in business, education, government service, and many other fields require geographic mobility. Wives tend to follow their husbands, and then resume their careers—which sometimes means starting over. This pattern is changing somewhat, however, as women continue rising professionally and men become increasingly accepting of nontraditional family roles.

One alternative that's gaining some popularity is the "commuter marriage," in which husband and wife live and work at separate locations. Such an arrangement poses obvious strains on a marriage, and works best for established couples without dependent children. Since research on commuter marriages began in the early 1970s, scientists have drawn different conclusions. Some studies suggest that the benefits of such marriages—greater economic and emotional equality, and the potential for better communication—counter its drawbacks. Subsequent research, however, reveals the difficulties couples experience in managing the lifestyle.

## Making a Dual-Career Relationship Work

To be successful, two-paycheck marriages will require social-policy support and workplace flexibility. To date, the actions of policymakers have done little to support families with children. Work leave for new parents, for example, is far from becoming a national reality. And the lack of tax-supported day care undoubtedly places a particular hardship on working couples and their children. But there are some things the couple themselves can do to facilitate their management of a working-couple family.

A working-couple relationship requires thoughtful planning and commitment—as well as increased sensitivity on the part of both spouses. It's important for husbands and wives to recognize that both will have positive and negative feelings, especially since few of us were raised in egalitarian two-career families. For the relationship to succeed, conflicts and misunderstandings must be discussed, even if not resolved. And in some way, both partners must be given the opportunity to win. Changing roles take adjustment and compromise. Yet these same changes offer new potential for shared power, and greater intimacy within marriage.

## Learning Objectives

On completing your study of this lesson, you should be able to

❑ Describe, in general terms, the evolution of the concept of the labor force, from before the industrial revolution to today's post-industrial society.

❑ Explain how the role of good provider developed and what new forces make it a difficult role to sustain.

❑ Discuss the traditional roles women have played in marriage, and how the homemaker's role is evolving in response to women's increasing labor participation.

❑ Suggest several reasons women choose to work, and outline differences between social classes on this issue.

❑ Describe the reasons why women still do a disproportionate share of housework and why that can become a serious issue in a working-couple families.

❑ Explain ways in which many couples are struggling to establish more democratic and egalitarian relationships.

❑ Summarize the principal advantages and disadvantages of a two-career family.

❑ Discuss the elements of the balancing act a two-career couple must play.

## Key Terms

Commuter marriages
Good-provider role
Househusbands
Occupational segregation
Pink-collar jobs

Second shift
Two-career marriages
Two-earner marriages
Two-location families

## Assignments

❑  Before viewing the program, be sure you've read through the preceding overview and familiarized yourself with the learning objectives and key terms for this lesson. Then read Chapter 13, "Work and Family," of *Marriages and Families* by Lamanna and Riedmann.

❑  After completing these tasks, read the video viewing questions and watch the video program for Lesson 16, "Working Husbands/Working Wives."

❑  After viewing the program, take time to answer the video viewing questions and evaluate your learning with the self-test. You'll find the correct answers, along with text page references, at the back of this telecourse guide.

❑  Read the "What's Your Decision?" scenario at the end of this lesson and answer the questions about the decision you would make based on what you've learned from this lesson. Give these questions some serious thought; they may be used as the basis for class discussion or the development of a more complex essay.

## Video Viewing Questions

1.  In deciding whether to work or not to work, Warren Farrell says women have three options, whereas men have none. Why? Do you see this changing? According to Margo Kaufman, what pressures does this put on men?

2.  Why do Robin and Chris think "American family values" do not value the family at all?

3.  Why does Arlee Hochschild believe redesigning work to allow parents more time with children is better for both society and business? Discuss this notion in detail.

4.  In Question 1, you discussed how men have no options and women have several. Based on the testimony of Anita Allen and Irene Cruz, is this true? Are these options real or just hypothetical?

5.  When looking at American history, it is typically thought that women did not work in significant numbers, excluding wartime, until after the feminist movement began. However, this is not the experience of the African-American woman. Why is this true? How might this relate to culture? Discuss why, for a great many people, history simply ignores the facts and generalizes. What does this suggest?

6. What does Carrie think about leaving her baby to return to work?

7. What does Arlee say about women in the labor force and the difference between male and female jobs? What does Carlfred Broderick have to say on the subject?

8. Carlfred Broderick says you can't be giving baths while giving 200 billable hours. Discuss the complexity of juggling a career and a family. Will both inevitably suffer? Is society set up to handle the pressures? If so, what needs to change to make it all come out in the wash?

## Self-Test

1. The concept of a labor force
   a. can be traced back to the earliest evidence of man.
   b. is a social invention.
   c. began in the nineteenth century.
   d. both b and c.

2. Job security has increasingly become an issue as employers adjust to new market forces. Which of the following *best* describes the current situation in the U.S. labor market?
   a. Increased employment prospects for any citizen, as long as they know English and are willing to work odd hours.
   b. Meaningful work for a significant part of the labor force, especially in jobs that are directly created by government.
   c. Relatively fewer full-time positions, but far more part-time positions that offer few, if any, benefits.
   d. Decreasing job opportunities for all but the best-educated managerial employees.

3. Men traditionally have been led to believe they should be the principal providers for their families. When this is no longer possible, the *best* solution (according to the lesson) is usually
   a. divorce—it is best for each partner to begin fresh in a new relationship where the husband can assume his proper traditional role.
   b. just to make the best of things; many families these days live on the borderline of poverty, and doing without is no disgrace in tough economic times.

c. for the husband to face the fact that he has failed in his role, assume the household duties without complaint, and give his wife a chance to succeed in the workplace.

d. to alter the process of exchange, with both partners negotiating what portions of the other's traditional role each can comfortably accept.

4. A serious "cost" of the good-provider role is that

a. it assumed there would always be some who needed to be provided for.

b. many males—perhaps as many as 45 percent—never fully accepted the role.

c. the economic system sometimes did not lend itself to the definition of this role.

d. too much of a man's self-esteem was wrapped up in this one role.

5. Which of these is a good example of the "second shift"?

a. Paul works from 9:00 a.m. until 5:00 p.m., and then moonlights for more income.

b. Felicity works from 9 a.m. until 6 p.m., and then comes home to work for several more hours around the house.

c. Shelly Lynn has a full-time job during the day, but she has a mail-order business that she runs from her apartment during the evening hours.

d. Around the age of 40, Robert quits his job as a meatcutter and enrolls in a college program leading to a B.A. degree in psychology.

6. Women's wages have not grown as fast as has their participation in the labor force. On the average, employed wives contribute only 40 percent of family income, a figure unchanged since 1970. Which of the following is most likely the *key* underlying reason for this difference in earning power?

a. Women generally choose jobs with limited responsibility or irregular, part-time hours—and in such jobs they cannot expect equivalent wages or opportunity for advancement.

b. Most women—by choice, lack of experience and opportunity, or discrimination—work in jobs that are not held in very high esteem, leading to segregation and inferior wages.

c. With few exceptions, women lack both the aggressiveness and the serious, long-term commitment to be serious contenders with men in the marketplace.

d. Minority women's stagnant average incomes make the overall picture look worse than it really is; nonminority women are actually making great advances.

7. When their second child begins school, Fred finally agrees to let his wife Myrtle go back to work. Within a year her income equals his. She seems to be happier with life but her work has become a common subject of mutual discussion. He's happy to have the additional income but wishes she would pay more attention to his needs and what he thinks. Based on information from the text, is this marriage likely headed for a breakup?

a. Yes, definitely. Fred clearly lacks the self-confidence necessary to adjust to an egalitarian relationship, and it's doubtful Myrtle will want to return to the old way of doing things.

b. No, definitely not. Myrtle will most likely give up her job once she realizes that the relationship—which is, after all, more important than a job—is threatened.

c. A breakup is possible, but unlikely; most couples in their position manage to work out their problems with negotiation and compromise—though it's never a simple process.

d. In all likelihood they'll remain together only so long as their children are small; then the desire for independence that Myrtle has now experienced will become stronger than her desire to hold the family together.

8. Studies show which of the following to be true of the amount of time spent on housework in two-earner housholds?

a. *All* of the following are true.

b. Employed wives do nearly twice as much housework as employed husbands.

c. Despite the assumption of an earning role by a majority of women, there has been little change in responsibility for household work.

d. In a comparison of black, Hispanic, and non-Hispanic white men's household labor time, the men in all three categories had a similar pattern of spending considerably less time than the women.

9. Attempts at solving work/family issues include
   a. Family leave and flexible scheduling of jobs
   b. "Family-friendly" workplace policies
   c. The "mommy track"
   d. All of the above

10. Couples who have been married for shorter periods of time seem to have more difficulties with
    a. two-person single careers.
    b. two-location family life.
    c. the wife having a pink-collar job.
    d. the wife having a career equal in prestige to that of the husband's career.

## What's Your Decision?

Harry and Kim, a third-generation Chinese couple, both have advanced professional degrees. Kim worked hard as wife, hostess, and housekeeper for the first years after they completed their graduate studies. Now, with their kids in their teens, she has taken a junior engineer position with a large chemical company. Her income is only one-third of Harry's and he is complaining that her decision to re-enter the working world is costing them more money for a housekeeper and increased transportation costs than it brings in. Kim feels that she is entitled to resume her career and that Harry shouldn't expect her to earn what he does right away. She also resents his insinuation that his work is more important than hers.

Their parents still play significant roles in their lives—with only Harry's widowed mother encouraging Kim to continue what she is doing: "I sacrificed everything for his dad and look what it got me!" Kim doesn't want her relationship with Harry to become petty and cynical—yet she doesn't want to give up her work, either. Harry claims his being passed over for a recent promotion was all Kim's fault: "If you weren't so bound up in your own work, so I could still talk to you like in the old days, it would be a whole lot less stressful for me. I need you right now, and you're turning your back on me just at the most important time in my career. You're making it hard on both of us." He asks her to quit the chemical company so she can give her full attention to supporting him in his career "for just five more years"—after which he will support her decision to pursue any activity she chooses.

Based on this scenario, how would you rate the pros and cons of Kim and Harry's disagreement over her employment? Should she keep her job? What positive outcomes might result? What negative outcomes? What factors should they consider especially carefully in making their decision?

❑ Should Kim continue her work, despite Harry's objections?

❑ What factors support that view?

❑ What factors support the opposite view?

❑ What will happen immediately if she acts as you suggest?

❑ What will their situation probably be five years from now if she acts as you suggest?

❑ Are there research studies cited in the text that offer support for your position?

❑ If you needed additional research-based information to support your position, how or where would you go about getting it?

# Lesson 17

# To Parent or Not to Parent

## Children by Choice

Having a child can be an act of love and sharing, the ultimate statement two people can make as a couple. Before they have children, many couples imagine that parenting will be among life's most rewarding and fulfilling experiences. And often, that proves to be true.

That's not the whole truth about parenting, however. It's also a stressful, high-risk experience fraught with sleepless nights, unfulfilled expectations, and considerable financial expense. Which is not to say that people should avoid parenthood. After all, life itself is risky. The point is, parenthood changes one's life in major and irreversible ways, and is therefore not a decision to be undertaken lightly. Of course, many children are brought into the world with little or no planning; but laying some groundwork can make the experience more fulfilling and less stressful—for everyone. As in any context, good decision making requires a thorough understanding of the potential consequences—both positive and negative.

**Fertility**

The circumstances facing a young family today are considerably different than they were even 30 or 40 years ago. In fact, family patterns in the United States have been changing for the past 200 years. This once largely rural nation has become urban-suburban. The national fertility ratio has dropped considerably since the 1800s, except during the post-World War II baby boom period. Even that anomaly didn't last for long. The U.S. birth rate has remained below actual replacement levels since the mid-1970s.

225

Many people in this country today are deciding not to have children. Others are consciously limiting family size to what has become the new American standard, the two-child family. And many couples are waiting longer—into their early thirties and beyond—before having a first child, and then allowing more time between births. This downward trend in the birth rate corresponds directly with the dramatic rise in employment for women.

Today, having children is rarely seen as an economic advantage. Normally, children do not do any significant amount of work to sustain the family (as they often did in the past). Then, too, there was a time when parents felt the need to produce many children in order to ensure the survival of a few. With the present low rates of infant mortality, that need has disappeared. Most children born today survive and grow—and consume their share of family resources.

Caring for and educating a child, as most parents will verify, is extremely expensive. In addition, of course, the presence of children often makes it more difficult for parents to work. All things considered, couples with children are at an economic disadvantage in comparison to singles and non-parenting couples.

Research indicates significant differences in fertility rates among ethnic groups. True, religion has been a key determinant; but many families today, regardless of religion or other cultural factors, regulate the number of children they choose to have. So whereas once the idea of a large family—many children to help with the family business or assist with the family's agricultural activities—was almost an imperative, today's more active lifestyles place different demands on couples. These days, couples are concluding that limiting childbearing makes good sense.

## The Views of Society on Parenthood

The decisions about parenthood we tend to take for granted today were not always so objective. Earlier generations simply had children, and then coped with the mouths eagerly expecting to be fed. We tend to believe that deciding whether to have children, how many to have, and when to have them is up to us—not to fate, chance, or the dictates of various political or religious groups.

When parenthood was considered the only natural order of things, society was termed *pronatalist*. Now that the tide is shifting, society is becoming increasingly *antinatalist*.

Still, traditions die hard. Those who are currently deciding whether or not to have children are likely to feel pressures from both sides. On the one hand, there's the promise of a wonderful and unique experience: the promise of children whom we can love and from whom we hope to get love in return. Our parents may be vocal in expressing their desire to become grandparents, and have the family name and traditions carried on.

If you live in a neighborhood where having children is the norm, you may feel very left out if yours is the only yard not overflowing with toys, or you're not involved in local school functions, or you're excluded from conversations that center around the needs and experiences of children. Having children not only seems desirable; sometimes it seems to be the passport to a full life.

On the other hand, pressures from the other side can be equally strong. Single and nonparenting friends may discourage a couple from having children. Employers may openly oppose a couple's decision to have children, fearing that it will hinder their professional productivity. Couples themselves may feel ambivalent about giving up the freedoms they've become accustomed to. What will it mean to share space, income, time, and emotional energy with a child on a daily basis, *with no opportunity to turn back*? Increasingly, couples are giving more thought to what is now considered an opportunity rather than an obligation.

## A Practical Look at Parenting

For many people, children provide the single greatest satisfaction and justification for being. A child provides continuity, the promise that the family line will survive into future generations. Especially in their early years, children are full of fresh insights into the world. They offer pure, unquestioning love, and provide an outlet for their parents' love.

A first child is tangible proof that a couple's love "amounts to something." It's evidence, even for couples in their thirties, that adulthood has finally been reached. And for those who are largely powerless in our society, children offer a chance to exercise the authority missing in other aspects of their lives.

Such pleasures, however, carry a price. In addition to the direct costs of food, clothing, and sundries, there can be a hefty *opportunity cost*—the estimated unrealized income for a primary caretaker who might have worked outside the home had children not been present. To these monetary costs can be added the emotional costs: lost free time, the end of sexual spontaneity, worries about a child's safety, and the finality of it all—once a parent, always a parent.

For many, childbirth signifies the end of the honeymoon. Even the most loving parents find children disruptive. And many parents find themselves doing something they never imagined doing—playing the traditional mother and father roles they learned from their own parents. It's a rare parent indeed who has not inadvertently replayed some parent-child confrontation from an earlier time—this time around in the parent's role—and later regretted it. "Why did I do that? I swore I'd be different with my kids!"

So you might wonder, given the many inherent pitfalls, why so many people decide to have children. It would be easy to give the traditional answer—that life without children isn't as happy. For many people, however, that simply isn't true.

While four-fifths of those who have children express satisfaction in their decision, not having children doesn't doom one to a life of misery. Leaving aside those who never mate, many couples decide to remain child-free for an extended period, if not their entire lives. What's more, mutual happiness seems to be highest between couples with few or no children.

It's important to realize, however, that what seems a good solution at one point may be less satisfying later on. In fact, ambivalent feelings on the subject of having children are common. A once satisfying career can turn sour, or the desire to have a child can surface. And it's indeed a serious matter when a husband and wife who agreed to remain childless suddenly find themselves divided on the issue. If you are married, and if you've discussed the possibilities of having children with your partner, then you already know how important it is that the two of you agree on the decision. Yet if one partner merely acquiesces to the other's wishes, later conflicts and regrets are all but inevitable.

Even when it's clear that children are desired, it's common these days to defer childbearing until a time when the partners agree they are ready. The trick is determining the point of readiness. When is there enough money, enough room, enough freedom from other responsibilities, a sufficiently well established career? Sometimes it's hard to know. Many parents would probably tell you that the perfect moment never arrives, that it's a mirage. Couples who postpone childbearing too long, waiting for some biological instinct to whisper "Now," often feel resentful when they see their contemporaries who had early families moving on to increasing freedom. Combining career and family, at any age, is a major challenge.

Limiting family size is one way of coping. The fewer the children, the less disruption to the normal routine. A growing number of couples have only one child. And they're unlikely to feel any social stigma attached to this decision since many of the earlier negative stereotypes of the only child have been found to be untrue. Plus, there are definite advantages. A smaller family is generally more democratic and can afford to do more things together. The choice to limit family size became considerably simpler in the early 1960s, when the Pill appeared on the scene.

Birth control has long been a controversial subject, in part because the brunt of responsibility has usually fallen on women. Though the use of condoms is strongly advocated today as a barrier to AIDS, most forms of contraception are designed with women in mind. Women run the health risks associated with the Pill and other forms of contraception, undergo abortions, bear the children, and are most likely to take major responsibility for them after birth. Most men continue to assume the woman will protect herself, reinforcing the time-honored double standard.

**Regulating Conception**

With the sexual revolution which began in the 1960s, attitudes toward sex and childbirth outside of marriage changed considerably. It's ironic that during this period, when contraception and information about birth control became more available, the rate of illegitimate births also rose. In fact, the children of the baby boom generation are much more likely to have an illegitimate child than those of any previous generation. A significant percentage of young unmarried mothers are keeping their children, which has a generally negative effect on their educational and occupational well-being.

Even though the free sex mentality of the 1960s doesn't seem to be carrying over from one generation to the next, public resistance to sex education and open provision of contraceptives to teenagers has helped create an epidemic of premarital pregnancy. Nearly one-third of sexually active teenage women use no contraception and even those who claim to be practicing birth control often use inadequate techniques.

In addition, many young women fail to use contraception because of the guilt they associate with the sexual act. The term *paradoxical pregnancy* is used to describe the common outcome of such neglect. Many women fear they will be thought of as "too active" if they prepare for sex beforehand. And some, who do not have ready access to good information through family or school may be reluctant or unable to secure the information they need about contraception. Sex and birth control are uncomfortable subjects for many people. The very parents who oppose sex education in the schools may find it difficult to discuss the subject themselves.

Unwanted pregnancies are not the sole province of teenagers; they occur to women of all ages. Increasingly older, professional women are choosing to bear and raise children on their own. But, whether a woman is 13 or 33, if she is not prepared to bring a baby to life, she may find herself choosing one of several legal forms of abortion to terminate the pregnancy. In 1973, the U.S. Supreme Court's decision in *Roe versus Wade* made abortion legal nationwide. Though certain recent decisions have abridged women's access to abortion somewhat; safe, legal abortions have by and large replaced the self-induced and illegal abortions which had caused high rates of death and serious injury. Obviously, a decision to have an abortion is never easy, and most women and their partners find the experience emotionally difficult.

## Additional Options for Parenting

Many couples who want to have a child have trouble getting pregnant at all. *Involuntary infertility* affects one in five couples, due to a wide range of factors. Such a discovery is often emotionally painful, but a number of medical solutions exist to remedy the problem. Options include *in vitro fertilization*, *artificial insemination*, *embryo transfers*, and *surrogate* motherhood. But while each offers hope for people with impediments to pregnancy, all carry legal and ethical complications. Even adoption, by far the most traditional option for the involuntarily infertile, carries its own risks and difficulties.

With parenthood, as with any major decision, broadening the range of options makes the decision-making process much more difficult. In many respects, it was simpler when people simply took whatever fate sent—ten children, two children, no children. Now, it isn't simple at all. We're all expected to decide whether to have children, how many to have, and when to have each one, in a socially responsible manner—all the while taking into account the needs and wants of spouses, parents, friends, employers, and others.

Knowing something of the advantages and disadvantages of parenting may make the decisions somewhat easier. But the fact remains that each person's life situation is different.

No one else can say what is right for you. You must make the decisions that govern your future. And, for the first time in history we have both the knowledge and the supporting technology we need to control some of that future in a way never dreamed of previously. Small wonder that we sometimes find the responsibility just a little intimidating.

On completing your study of this lesson, you should be able to

❑ Discuss the variations in the total fertility rate in the United States, including some of the principal reasons for the changes that have occurred.

❑ Describe the impact of education and economic factors on family size.

❑ Explain the social pressures that have moved today's society toward structural antinatalism.

❑ Enumerate several positive reasons for having children, both today and historically.

❑ Summarize the principal costs of having children, both economic and emotional.

❑ Discuss the three "emerging options" facing couples today.

❑ Describe the shift in family patterns brought about by the Pill and other birth control options.

❑ Compare the incidence of teen pregnancy and child bearing by older single women, and the consequences of each for mother and child.

❑ List the principal forms of abortion, including the term in which each is appropriate; discuss the personal and medical factors one should consider in deciding whether to have an abortion.

❑ Summarize the primary reasons for infertility and the current medical and legal alternatives available to infertile couples.

**Learning Objectives**

Antinatalist
Embryo transfer
Fertility
*In vitro* fertilization

Involuntary infertility
Opportunity costs
Paradoxical pregancy
Pronatalist bias

**Key Terms**

## Assignments

❑ Before viewing the program, be sure you've read through the preceding overview and familiarized yourself with the learning objectives and key terms for this lesson. Then read Chapter 11, "To Parent or Not to Parent;" Appendix C, pages 563–569; Appendix D, pages 570–580; and Appendix E, pages 581–582 of *Marriages and Families* by Lamanna and Riedmann.

❑ After completing these tasks, read the video viewing questions and watch the video for Lesson 17, "To Parent or Not to Parent."

❑ After viewing the program, take time to answer the video viewing questions and evaluate your learning with the self-test. You'll find the correct answers, along with text page references, at the back of this telecourse guide.

❑ Read the "What's Your Decision?" scenario at the end of this lesson and answer the questions about the decision you would make based on what you've learned from this lesson. Give these questions some serious thought; they may be used as the basis for class discussion or the development of a more complex essay.

## Video Viewing Questions

1. Discuss how American attitudes toward children have changed since the 1950s. What effect do the ideas of "choice" and "priorities" have on these attitudes? Include the testimony of Carol, Glenn, and Kathy Wexler in your analysis.

2. What does Dr. Anwyl say about the need to be "ready" for children? Do you agree?

3. There have always been pressures and anxieties about having children. Now, with so many dual income households, things are more complicated than ever. What additional pressures are felt by both men and women in these households?

4. Discuss the role of the "biological clock" in relation to the desire to have children. Is it better to wait to have children? List the pros and cons.

5. Many people believe it is "irresponsible" to have a large family given the problems of overpopulation and shortages in a variety of natural resources. Why do Chris, Anita,

and Julie believe it is important to have more than one child? Do you agree? Justify your answer.

6. Deciding not to have children has become an acceptable alternative for couples, although some people still believe this desire is rooted in selfishness. Contrast the testimony of Bob versus Barbara and Dick. Do you think Barbara and Dick are imposing by sharing their love of parenting in that way? Does democracy and modernization allow for selfishness?

7. Thanks to medical technology, infertile couples have enormous conception options. What does Dr. Marrs say about American society and the importance of the family? What does Kathy Wexler think about laying blame? What do you think about a single woman having a child through artificial insemination?

## Self-Test

1. Declining American birth rates is a long-term pattern dating back to about 1800. Which of the following has been a *primary* factor in perpetuating this pattern?

   a. Despite medical advances, we've never succeeded in bringing the infant mortality rate under control in this country.

   b. Women could combine productive work and motherhood in a preindustrial economy, but when work moved from home to factory, the roles of worker and mother were not so compatible. As women's employment increased, fertility declined.

   c. Though fertility increased in direct relationship with women's newfound income, birth control became widespread at the end of the seventeenth century.

   d. As more and more women have entered the workplace, there has simply been less opportunity for partners to have a sexual relationship.

2. Our society may have a pronatalist bias, despite multiple forces working against it. Which one of the following has been the strongest influence maintaining this bias?

   a. grandparents
   b. organized religion
   c. the military
   d. media, especially television

3. It is sometimes suggested that children can provide a sense of continuity of self, "the advantage of seeing something of yourself passed on." Which of the following is a related reason often cited as an important reason for parenthood?

   a. Raising children provides an opportunity to watch one's personal characteristics develop in another generation and to see which negative ones should be consciously eliminated in one's own being.

   b. Having children provides a logical reason for acquisitive behavior, which otherwise is too often perceived to be greed.

   c. Parenthood goes hand in hand with behavior often labeled childlike, a chance to live out the fantasy of eternal youth.

   d. It offers the chance to develop a close-knit family unit, one in which sharing and nurturing become primary links and challenges.

4. According to the text, opportunity costs of parenting are best defined as

   a. the loss of free time.

   b. the loss of economic opportunities for wage earning and investment

   c. the loss of spontaneity.

   d. loss of the personal resources required for personal growth and development.

5. Studies comparing marriages with and marriages without children indicate

   a. All of the following are true.

   b. children stabilize marriages.

   c. children cause marital strain.

   d. marital happiness is higher in child-free unions.

6. When Edward Foote advocated use of the cervical diaphragm in 1864, it was a rare example of a male supporting a woman's right to make reproductive choices. Which of the following *best* describes our current state of contraceptive responsibility?

   a. The traditional double standard is still in place, leaving women responsible for being prepared for sex and birth control.

   b. New scientific discoveries have made men and women equally responsible for birth control.

    c. Given the problems associated with the Pill and AIDS, sexual relations are so problematic that no one really has much sense of who is responsible for what anymore.

    d. Increasingly, innovative birth control methods place the responsibility for contraception on the male.

7. Studies show that use of birth control is *most likely* among teenagers who

    a. have frequent sex with a number of different sexual partners.

    b. are aware their parents disapprove strongly of their sexual behavior.

    c. being in school or employed.

    d. have taken a sex education course together.

8. Sally is 21 years old and has just had an abortion. Her partner Felipe, who opposed her decision, was out of town when it happened. Her parents were supportive, but live across the country. There were no complications. Still, she feels empty and remorseful afterward. A social psychologist would *probably* characterize Sally's feelings in this scenario as

    a. a sign that Sally is a relatively immature person and that her relationship with Felipe is likely to be severely damaged.

    b. perfectly normal since abortion is emotionally upsetting—at least temporarily—for most women, and often for their male partners as well.

    c. an indication that Sally may have made a mistake. She should not have had the abortion, and she is likely to suffer some severe psychological ramifications.

    d. really unrelated to the abortion. She is simply lonely without Felipe or her parents and is transferring those feelings onto the current situation.

9. Which of the following is one of the *primary* reasons genetic counseling has become such a controversial field of medicine?

    a. Science is now capable of determining the genetic structure of a fetus, leading to fear of potential cloning and possible development of a "super race."

    b. Because couples can now be advised of a potentially abnormal fetus and elect to have an abortion rather than give birth to the child.

c. In order to protect themselves from potential lawsuits, genetic counselors are forcing parents to undergo unnecessary and sometimes risky tests with few, if any, benefits.

d. As with all new, experimental medical fields, costs have risen so high that only the very privileged can afford genetic counseling services.

10. Surrogacy, *in vitro* fertilization, artificial insemination, and embryo transplants are relatively new ways otherwise involuntarily infertile couples can become parents. These techniques raise legal and ethical questions, as well as previously unimagined emotional ones. Of these methods, which one has, for most couples, the greatest potential for emotional problems?

a. surrogacy
b. *in vitro* fertilization
c. artificial insemination
d. embryo transplants

## What's Your Decision?

Rick and Barbara have been planning to raise a family together ever since they met and married in their mid-twenties. They purposely chose to get their careers off the ground before having children. Rick is now a medical technician and has just been promoted to a position of much greater responsibility in a large city hospital. Barbara teaches the deaf and hard of hearing and recently decided, at 38, that she did not want to wait any longer for an opportunity to love and nurture a child of her own. She had planned to continue working part-time even after their first child was born. Now they find, however, after years of careful contraception, that Rick's sperm count is low and thus it's unlikely they can conceive.

After sharing an acute sense of failure, Rick brings a book home from the hospital with a list of options they could try to bring their child into being. Barbara has always wanted to experience childbirth, so they reject adoption and surrogacy. Rick says he will support any decision she makes, but is quietly encouraging the use of in vitro fertilization, one of his hospital's specialties. Barbara thinks the technology is too expensive and is leaning toward artificial insemination. Rick grows further reluctant when he learns his sperm might have to be mixed with those of an anonymous donor. "I'd rather not have a child than wonder if I'm the father," he tells her.

"If you raise and love the child, it is your child," Barbara counters. "The important thing is that we'll be parents, we'll be using the safest technology available, and we'll be having a child as 'naturally' as possible. Since it can't be totally natural, this is the next best option."

Based on this scenario, how would you rate the pros and cons of Barbara's and Rick's arguments over their reproductive choices? Should they still try to have a child together, in your opinion? What positive outcomes might result? What negative outcomes? How are the positive and negative factors affected by their choice of method? What factors should they consider especially carefully in making their decision?

❑  Should they have a child together?

❑  What factors support that view?

❑  What factors support the opposite view?

❑  What will happen immediately if they act as you suggest?

❑  What will their situation probably be five years from now if they act as you suggest?

❑  Are there research studies cited in the text that offer support for your position?

❑  If you needed additional research-based information to support your position, how or where would you go about getting it?

# Lesson 18

# One Plus One Equals Three

## Parents and Children

Most of us can probably remember at least one incident in which our parents seemed extremely unfair, closed-minded, unreachable, unrealistically demanding, or just plain insensitive. Whatever the conflict—over dress or hair, friends or homework—it likely happened when our need for independence clashed with our parents' need to maintain control. Remember wondering how it was that the same old mom and dad who occasionally appeared to be such wise authorities could turn into such ignorant tyrants on such short notice? They, in turn, were probably busy wondering what had transformed their sweet, lovable child into a snarling stranger.

It's disturbing to be angry with and frustrated by the children you love, especially when nothing that society told you about being a parent prepared you for those emotions. But virtually all parents feel these emotions. A mother who is home all day with young children may resent the limited opportunities to pursue her own interests. Or a father may become angry when his young child fails to perform up to his expectations. Worse yet, sometimes these perfectly normal feelings get out of control and lead to physical abuse—a problem that appears to be increasing in a rapidly changing society that puts stress on both parents and children. In short, we've been led to expect the rewards but not the frustrations of parenthood . . . and not even the experts seem to agree on the right way to handle them.

If you grew up assuming you'd be a parent yourself someday, you probably looked forward to the joys of loving and caring for a child. As you imagined life as a parent, you may not have anticipated just what it would be like to have continuous responsibility for a fragile and mysterious infant. You may not have been prepared for the emotional and financial strain that a child places on a marriage. Above all, you probably weren't counting on the feelings of guilt, doubt, and confusion that accompany parenthood today.

What is your image of the ideal parent? A pal to the children? Their policeman? A teacher-counselor? An athletic coach? Do you think that taking care of an infant is primarily the mother's responsibility? Are fathers cut out for child care at all? Would you ever strike your child? How can you best protect your child from danger; his or her own mistakes? With so little training for parenthood, there's never a shortage of questions.

We assume, sensibly enough, that children should be treated differently from adults, that they need special care to ensure their safety and healthy development. But who is the best person to provide that care?

Remember the Cleavers and the television sitcom "Leave it to Beaver"? In the idyllic television world of the 1950s, the mother, June, calmly waited with her apron on to greet the boys with a snack each day after school; while their dad, Ward, put in a brief and sometimes perfunctory appearance after a hard day at the office. The two children inhabited a carefree world, under the protection of a tolerant and financially secure mom and dad—a world in which the roles and responsibilities of parents and children were clearly defined.

Those romanticized images don't match the realities of today, or for that matter, the realities most of us grew up with. For example, although Ward and June Cleaver may have been irritated occasionally by the Beaver's antics, they were never really angry. Unfortunately, they were never very real, either. And as a result, Ward and June had little to offer as role models for those of us whose kids—unlike the Beaver—aren't always so easy to manage.

Mothers sometimes find parenting particularly stressful. Do the roles of full-time mother and full-time homemaker that June Cleaver filled so effortlessly really go together? Not necessarily. When the burden of full-time child care is added to full-time care of the home, mothers often find themselves isolated in a world of diaper pails, television cartoons, and vacuum cleaners. Not surprisingly, many don't like it there, and women who have arranged for time away from their children tend to be happier with their role.

But things get even tougher when they take a job outside the home. Can they still meet their children's physical and emotional needs? Will their children suffer "maternal deprivation"? That depends. Getting the kids up, dressed, fed, and ready for school or day care; dressing and feeding oneself; then working a full day and returning home to prepare dinner, do a little housecleaning, review the notes for that morning meeting, and get the kids ready for bed is quite a load. And women who attempt it may have little time or energy for their children and feel guilty as a result. On the other hand, quitting the job and simply being at home doesn't guarantee that a mother is spending quality time with her kids. And if a working mother likes her job and has a supportive husband to help, employment outside the home can have a positive effect on the children. Still, the attitude persists that children will miss a working mother more than they do the usually absent father.

What should a father's role be? Should he share child care duties equally? Most fathers feel that they should, though in practice they participate less than mothers. But beyond simply sharing the load with the mother, do fathers have something unique to offer that mothers can't provide?

Infants seem to attach equally to both parents, but fathers give their children different experiences, including more physically stimulating play and unpredictable games. They also play a significant role in influencing the gender role identification and cultural values of both their daughters and sons.

But despite the fact that today's fathers are more motivated than previous generations to meet the emotional needs of their children—a role formerly assigned almost exclusively to mothers—the absent, silent father is still with us. Just when he's needed most by his children—during their early years—the economic demands of parenthood take him away from the home. Many would contend it's as hard to be a full-time working father as it is to be a full-time working mother.

Parents today—exposed as they are to psychologists telling them how much parents can influence their child's IQ or self-esteem—worry more than parents ever did before. How can they give their kids the time they need? What's the right way to discipline them? Should a parent be a friend or an authority figure?

If your parents picked up after you, bought anything you asked for, and planned family vacations around your wishes,

**Styles of Parenting**

they fit what social scientists call the *martyr* style of parenting. Now that may sound all right from a kid's point of view, but parents who consistently deny their own needs to please their children cannot really enjoy the parenting role.

Would it be better to be a *pal* to your children instead? Would it be better to let them set their own goals, rules, and limits? That way, you may avoid the conflicts that inevitably result from the generation gap, but that style is probably unrealistic in a society in which parents *are* held responsible for their children. Besides, this *laissez faire* discipline policy sometimes results in juvenile delinquency, drug use, or running away from home. But the answer doesn't appear to lie on the other extreme either, where parents assume the role of *police officers* who apply *autocratic discipline*. These parents make sure that their children obey the rules at all times and punish even the smallest infraction. But they risk alienating the children with such a heavy hand. So what style of parenting does work best?

At first glance, acting as a *teacher-counselor* appears to be a better approach than trying to be a policeman or a pal. Such parents believe that, if they do the right things at the right times, their children will turn out happy, intelligent, and successful. The problem with this style of parenting is that very few parents are experts in child rearing—a fact that makes them anxious and fearful of doing the wrong thing. Further, most of us realize from experience that parents don't really have unlimited power over their child's development. Children have inherited abilities and needs, and they're born with a mind of their own.

The approach that recognizes the needs of both parents and children is called the *athletic coach* style. Coaches understand that, in many sports, once the event has begun it is up to the players to win or lose. Some parents emulate this approach. They set up house rules—sometimes democratically—and then enforce appropriate penalties when the rules are broken. The goal is to teach the children that it's necessary to accept discipline and subordinate their needs to the interests of the "team." But in the end, these parents have to trust the child to apply what's been learned on his or her own.

You may be wondering where your experiences fit within these categories. You may find yourself saying, "Yes—that sounds something like us—but no, that part doesn't sound like the way we do things at all." That's normal. Most families reflect some mix of these various parenting styles. And just as children go through a number of distinct stages in their lives—walking, talking, then thinking abstractly, for instance—so do parents perform different tasks and have different needs as they and their children change. From the time couples become parents for the first time, to the time they become grandparents, they must respond to a changing array of problems and needs—both their own and their children's.

For most parents, the most challenging transition comes with having the first baby. As an example, let's look at a young couple—call them Hal and Kate—who didn't think about having a child until several years after they were married. They then read books about pregnancy and infants and attended a birthing class together, but nothing—not even the experiences of friends and relatives—prepared them for the distress Kate feels at the weight she'd gained during pregnancy or the trauma of having their sleep interrupted three or four times each night by a screaming child.

Hal often wonders if it had been the expectations of his family that pushed them into having a child. It was great fun thinking of names and remodeling the spare bedroom, but Kate's personality change is something he hadn't bargained for, nor had he expected her lack of interest in the problems he is having at the office.

And Kate, who has been working for five years, finds that since she is home all day now, Hal expects her to take care of housework he used to share. Their son, Jon, seems to cry a lot for no apparent reason, too; Kate's mother always told her what an easy baby she'd been, and she wonders what she is doing wrong.

While her friend's child walks by the time she is a year old, Jon doesn't master it until he was almost 18 months. Is that normal? Once on his feet, however, he seems to find a way to get into everything, and by the time he reaches three, broken household items scattered across the floor are a daily occurrence. Is she being too lenient? It's all very confusing.

Social scientists distinguish between permissiveness and overpermissiveness as a way to guide parents like Hal and Kate. Permissiveness means accepting the childishness of childhood and not restricting a child's wishes or feelings. But overpermissiveness allows children to express those feelings in undesirable acts. Hal and Kate soon learn that it is acceptable for their son to be angry, but also they decide that he should never be allowed to express anger by hitting his parents or damaging things. But their lives change again when their son enters school and they have their second child.

Hal and Kate are more confident with their new daughter, Erika, but unexpected demands soon pile up. Different tasks and different problems—juggling Jon's afternoon soccer matches with work and taking the new baby to a sitter, helping with Jon's homework when they are both tired and the baby needs attention; and, as the years pass, the constant fighting between son and daughter. When Jon gets a present, should they give one to Erika, too? Must they intervene in the kids' every little squabble? Other questions puzzle them, too: What household chores should their son be required to do? Does he really need a room of his own?

By the time both children reach their teens, Hal and Kate turn 40, and both they and their children are undergoing major biological and psychological changes. Just when they need the satisfaction of guiding their kids the most, both son and daughter seem determined to avoid their care and control. Hal and Kate feel a vital stake in how their kids perform in school; they don't want them to get into trouble, they want to be proud of them. But the children seem bent on rejecting their values—experimenting with alcohol, staying out late, dressing as they please. Would their kids fall apart and turn bad in their late adolescence? Studies suggest that Hal and Kate are worrying too late. Patterns are established in childhood, with few drastic changes occurring after age 15.

Fortunately, instead of engaging in power struggles which they could not hope to win, Hal and Kate realize that they could continue to *influence* their children by being models and consultants for them. We learn values from those around us whom we admire, and parents can continue to model important values for their older children, too.

Should they pretend to be paragons of virtue with no problems of their own? If they adopt this approach, it's probable that they'll appear to be phonies, and will offer their children no model for solving their own problems. A more effective way to continue to influence teenage children is to act as a "consultant" who can offer information about alternatives a child may be considering. Again, think of the parent as an athletic coach who must allow the players to make their own choices once on the field.

Above all, researchers have found that the parent-child bond is most likely to continue when parents set limits through *democratic discipline* in which all family members have some say and compromise is sought whenever possible. Even when adult children return home to live, parents must renegotiate their earlier "contracts," relinquishing control while requiring greater contributions to the household from those grown children.

Parent-child relationships need not be inflexible. In fact, it is often vital to redefine roles as responsibilities shift and children prepare for their own independence. Yet clear role definitions are important; without such definition, power struggles can ensue. Even when children are completely independent with children of their own, the stress and conflict inherent in the parent-child relationship may continue.

Family relationships are extremely intense. That's good, in that the relationships forge bonds that become a vital form of support during times of stress. Unfortunately, that intensity also creates stress that can culminate in physical or mental abuse.

**Child Abuse**

What causes parents to mistreat their children? Studies have shown that abusive parents were usually abused as children themselves. As a result, they come to believe that children are innately "bad," and require physical punishment. Child abusers often have unrealistic expectations about their childrens' capabilities, and since physical punishment is legally and culturally approved in the U.S. today, it is easy for parents who are under stress to go beyond reasonable limits in disciplining their children. The definition of "reasonable limits" may vary with the culture and social class of the family.

It's difficult for those outside the family to know what may be going on behind the closed doors. Many of us feel uncomfortable—sometimes horrified—when we hear stories of child abuse. Yet, because children are relatively helpless individuals, it's often difficult to protect them without invading a family's right to privacy. Would you want state agents to have the right to enter your home at any time to find out if you were abusing your children? Most of us would probably object to that kind of intrusion. So, in the absence of watchful neighbors, friends, and relations, the stage is set for physical or psychological abuse that may go undetected for years.

It's easy to tell that a child has been abused when he or she has severe burns, or is malnourished, or near death from a beating, but most maltreatment of children never requires hospitalization. In fact, often the only scars the abuse leaves are psychological. And since hostile feelings towards one's children are as normal as occasional feelings of hate between lovers, psychologists have come to believe that the potential for child abuse exists even in families we consider normal.

The maltreatment of children can take many forms, from the overt acts of physical or sexual aggression that we always call abuse, through the overly harsh emotional demands that constitute *emotional maltreatment*, to the acts of omission (failing to provide food, clothing, protection, or other care) that are called *child neglect*.

Should abusive parents be punished like criminals? Or should the problem be viewed as a family problem that requires psychological treatment? The first response mentioned is called the *punitive approach*, while the latter—which has become the favored strategy among those who work with abused children—is called the *therapeutic approach*. The therapeutic approach is designed to help parents increase their self-esteem and knowledge about children through meetings, classes, and hotlines. At the same time, special programs give parents some desperately needed "time out." For example, "crisis nurseries" offer a place where parents can take their children when they need to get away for a few hours.

Unfortunately, it's become increasingly difficult to involve members of the community in helping abusive parents. Recent media attention to child molestation, combined with the fear of kidnapping and murder by strangers, has created an attitude of mistrust in this country. Even teachers, day-care workers, and others who deal with children every day are reluctant to hug or touch them for fear of false accusations of molestation.

Should we teach our children to fear and mistrust strangers as a way of protecting them? Before forming an opinion, keep in mind that a child's chances of being kidnapped or molested by a stranger are extremely small when compared to the likelihood of that same child's being physically or sexually abused by a member or friend of the family.

## Building Successful Parent-Child Relationships

Perhaps you've concluded that being a parent sounds like a mysterious and difficult endeavor. Professionals suggest, however, that building a successful parent-child relationship is no more difficult than establishing an intimate relationship with anyone else. In any relationship, we need to accept our own limitations and mistakes, as well as those of the other person. Such acceptance will contribute to a better parent-child relationship—just as it does in marriage or friendship.

What makes this acceptance so difficult for parents today is the fact that we rarely have a network of relatives or close neighbors to help meet our children's needs. While some families can count on grandmothers, uncles, or other members of an extended family to help out, many urban dwellers can rely only on cooperation among a dwindling number of neighborhood families with children of the same ages, or upon the institutions set up specifically to help them, such as schools and day care centers.

If you've ever dropped your child at the local day care center, then driven away watching a small, teary face in the rear-view mirror, then you have probably asked yourself a question that plagues millions of parents: "Is day care good or bad for children?" Formal day care—in which parents hire one or more persons to take care of children in their own home or pay a nursery school for the same service—can provide an environment just as healthy and stimulating as the child's own home. Does it harm a child to spend long hours away from home and family every day? Provided the day care is of good quality, the answer is no. Nevertheless, every child needs to spend time each day with someone who loves him and whom he loves in return.

For working parents, there simply are no easy answers. It is often difficult for parents to maintain their basic "contract" with their children—support and commitment in return for loyalty and commitment—at a time when they have to work to maintain the household. Meanwhile, the emotional and financial costs of caring for their children are continuing to rise.

Social scientists suggest that one of the most constructive things parents and children can do is to accept their anger when it occurs, and recognize that fair fights can bond as well as separate participants—when those struggles end in negotiation and compromise, that is. In fact, the same guidelines that govern positive fighting between married partners—using "I statements" and presenting specific grievances along with concrete suggestions for resolving them, for instance—are just as valuable between parents and children. Supportive communication with children is the best way to help them become adults who relate well to other people.

To build better relationships with their children, parents need to recognize their own needs as well as their child's and avoid feeling unnecessary guilt. They need to learn to accept help from friends and the community at large as well as professional caregivers. And finally, they need to try to build and maintain flexible, intimate relationships that will enhance the quality of interaction between parent and child through all the growing years.

## Learning Objectives

On completing your study of this lesson, you should be able to

❑ List the reasons why parenting and stepparenting is often characterized by increased frustration.

❑ Explain how the myth of motherhood leads us to overlook the stressful realities of the mother-child relationship.

❑ Discuss the positive and negative effects a mother's employment has on her children.

❑ Explain how the myth of fatherhood leads us to overlook the importance of the father's role in raising children.

❑ Discuss the advantages and disadvantages of each of the five parenting styles described in this lesson.

❑ Describe the different tasks and needs that characterize each stage of the parenting role.

❑ Define child maltreatment and differentiate it from child abuse.

❑ List the society-wide conditions and beliefs that can lead well-intentioned parents to mistreat their children.

❑ Explain the difference between the punitive and therapeutic approaches to combating child abuse.

❑ Describe the ways in which parents can improve their relationship with their children.

## Key Terms

Autocratic discipline
Child abuse
Child care
Child neglect
Democratic discipline
Developmental model of child rearing
Emotional maltreatment

*Laissez-faire* discipline
Parenting styles
Permissiveness
Punitive approach to child abuse
Supportive communication
Therapeutic approach to child abuse

## Assignments

❑ Before viewing the program, be sure you've read through the preceding overview and familiarized yourself with the learning objectives and key terms for this lesson. Then read Chapter 12, "Parents and Children Over the Life Course," and review "Child Abuse and Neglect,"

248

pages 313–318, in Chapter 10 of *Marriages and Families* by Lamanna and Riedmann.

❏ After completing these tasks, read the video viewing questions and watch the video program for Lesson 18, "One Plus One Equals Three."

❏ After viewing the program, take time to answer the video viewing questions and evaluate your learning with the self-test. You'll find the correct answers, along with text page references, at the back of this telecourse guide.

❏ Read the "What's Your Decision?" scenario at the end of this lesson and answer the questions about the decision you would make based on what you've learned from this lesson. Give these questions some serious thought; they may be used as the basis for class discussion or the development of a more complex essay.

**Video Viewing Questions**

1. According to Kathy Wexler, new parents are often told "You don't have to be a good parent, just good enough." Relate this advice to the comments of Don and Martha, Rob and Carrie, and Doug and Julie. Based on their comments, what is "good enough"?

2. New challenges and problems arise with each developmental stage of a child's growth. Note Kirby Alvy's statements regarding parental development and compare them to those of the teenage mothers interviewed. How can the developmental stage of a parent come into serious conflict with that of a child, and what can result from the mismatch?

3. Even mature parents find raising children to be stressful. Compare and contrast Dr. Alvy's statements to the 10-year-olds interviewed on this subject. What role does communication play at this stage of the game? How do Jess and Irene's comments fit into the picture?

4. Communication between parents and children becomes all the more important during the teen years. How do the comments of Luke, Jennifer, and Irene address this subject? What does Dr. Alvy say about the relationship be-

tween communication and acceptance of children? Explain Anna's comments in these terms.

5. Most experts agree that parents need to form consistent boundaries and expectations with their children in order to enforce discipline and teach their children guidelines. With this in mind, compare the comments of Irene, Andrea, Chris, and Robin to those of Jennifer and Luke. What effect can different disciplinary styles between parents have on the persuasiveness of the discipline?

6. Note the statements of the teenagers: Johnny, Luke, Jennifer, Rosario, and James. What do each of them find frustrating about being a teenager? Discuss the comments of Nancy Weber, Dr. Nobles, and Linda Poverny. How might a parent prevent a child from "cutting off his nose in spite of his face"?

7. When all is said and done, Barbara believes all we can give our children are roots and wings. Discuss the complexity of this simple statement.

## Self-Test

1. Which of the following is *not* a legitimate difference between the parenting styles of mothers and fathers?

   a. Men lack confidence in their own competence as fathers; women tend to be both supportive and fully confident of their husbands' competence as parents.

   b. Mothers tend to "worry" (anticipate and cope with problems) more than fathers.

   c. Fathers tend to seek emotional closeness with children, while mothers tend to be concerned with attending to their childrens' needs.

   d. Mothers tend to a sense of shared identity with children, while fathers tend to maintain a separateness in identities.

2. One social scientist has concluded that "Despite the highly publicized rhetoric of the 'new' fatherhood, the tradition of the absent, distant, silent father is still with us." What factor *best* accounts for this?

   a. Fathers aren't really cut out for parenting.

   b. Infants attach more strongly to their mothers than to their fathers.

c. Fathers can best affect their children indirectly, through their relationship with the mother.

d. The heavy economic demands of supporting children tend to keep the father more focused on work than his children.

3. Which of the following statements *best* accounts for the frustration that parents feel today in trying to raise their children?

a. There are more working mothers today, and the demands of parenthood are, by their very nature, incompatible with holding a full-time job.

b. In a society that doesn't offer them much support to begin with, parents are asked to learn attitudes about child rearing that often differ from their parents' attitudes.

c. Children are growing up faster than ever today, and their desire for independence at an ever-earlier age conflicts with their parents' need to maintain control.

d. Most parents follow the developmental model of child-rearing today, which leaves them feeling constantly frustrated from placing the needs of the child ahead of their own.

4. In analyzing the advantages and disadvantages of the "pal" style of parenting, most psychologists would probably say that

a. while children may not always make the right choices, this style works well because it eliminates conflicts caused by the generation gap.

b. this style is a big improvement on the "police officer" style since it virtually eliminates inevitable value clashes between generations, and puts responsibility for action where it belongs—with the children.

c. while it may eliminate conflicts caused by the generation gap, this style is unrealistic because it attempts to absolve parents from responsibilities they should rightfully assume.

d. while there are risks in this approach, parents do not have great power to influence their children's development, anyway; for this reason, it is best to build a mutual relationship early in order to maintain intimacy.

5. The transition to parenthood is the most difficult stage of the parenting process, *mainly* because

   a. new parents are usually under great financial strain, and this causes stress that a baby only aggravates.

   b. society encourages people to become parents with little or no preparation, with the result that many new parents are unprepared—especially for the negative aspects of parenting.

   c. fathers aren't affected in the same way that mothers are by the birth of the first baby, and this creates stress in their relationship.

   d. the demands of meeting an infant's needs are much greater than the demands placed on parents by older children.

6. Jason, Maria's new baby, is difficult—he sleeps and eats irregularly and cries endlessly for no apparent reason, even though Maria spends all of her time trying to make the child happy. This has upset Maria a great deal because she feels it means she is probably a bad parent. What advice would child-care experts be most likely to give Maria?

   a. She shouldn't make any changes in her life; over time, Jason will mature and will no longer cause problems.

   b. She should see a child development specialist; this abnormal behavior may be due to a physical condition of which she is not aware.

   c. She is probably not meeting Jason's needs in some way and should learn to "read" his messages better so that she can give him what he needs.

   d. She should not treat the baby as a problem, but should try to strike a balance between his needs and hers; she may need to spend more time away from the baby.

7. Adolescence tends to bring with it increased parent-child conflict. Which of the following would social scientists recommend as the best way to dealing with this conflict?

   a. Parents should try to influence their children by modeling desirable behavior and discussing the potential consequences of their children's choices.

   b. Parents should negotiate their control, offering continued economic support in exchange for control over their children's choices (and, thus, as children become financially independent, parents should relinquish control).

c. Parents should realize that both they and their children are going through biological changes that will be over in a few years. Both parents and children should try not to engage in much serious discussion until these changes are over.

d. Parents should realize that by adolescence, most habits are formed anyway, and should generally allow children whatever freedom and independence they desire.

8. Which of the following is most likely to be a significant factor in contributing to the incidence of child abuse, even among well-intentioned parents?

a. Unemployment among male heads of household.

b. A culturally supported belief in the appropriateness of corporal punishment as discipline for children.

c. Hostile feelings that parents sometimes experience toward their children.

d. Our society's emphasis on family privacy, which means that parents usually have little support and little guidance in dealing with parenting problems.

9. Which of the following best describes the therapeutic approach to combating child abuse?

a. The court places the abusive parent in jail.

b. The police and court system become involved, removing the abusive parent from the home or placing the abused child in foster care.

c. Social workers help abusive parents to build their self-confidence and self-esteem through group counseling programs.

d. Abusive parents are referred to "crisis nurseries" where they can take their children at any time of the day or night when they feel the need to get away for a few hours.

10. Which of the following parenting styles do social scientists and counselors hold to be the most effective with adolescents?

a. Autocratic discipline

b. *Laissez-faire* discipline

c. Authoritative discipline

d. Neither of these parenting styles has been associated with behavior problems or juvenile delinquency.

## What's Your Decision?

George and Marie are in their mid-forties and both work, Marie only part time. They have two children—Lisa, 18, who lives at home, works part time, and attends a nearby community college; and Michael, 16. Lisa is only an average student at best, and lately her grades have been getting worse. She has a boyfriend of whom George and Marie do not approve, and—as they've recently learned—she has been spending several nights a week at his apartment. Last night, they got a call from the police station: Lisa's boyfriend had been arrested for possession of a controlled substance and Lisa was with him.

Michael has also begun to cause them problems. Marie has to nag him about everything—he won't even brush his teeth unless she gets after him, and although he's always been a good student, he doesn't seem to try. Marie finds mercenary soldier magazines and empty beer cans when she cleans up his room. They've always let the kids pretty much set their own rules, but now they wonder whether being more restrictive would direct their children toward more positive choices and productive values.

Based on what you know about this family, how should George and Marie deal with Lisa and Michael? Should they be more restrictive—set down more rules—in an attempt to gain Lisa's and Michael's attention? What are some of the factors they should consider in making this decision? If they do "crack down" on their kids, what are some of the most significant ramifications of that decision?

❑ Should George and Marie attempt a more authoritarian approach with their children?

❑ What factors support that view?

❑ What factors support the opposite view?

❑ What will happen immediately if they act as you suggest?

❑ What will the situation probably be five years from now if they act as you suggest?

❑ Are there research studies cited in the text that offer support for your position?

❑ If you needed additional research-based information to support your position, how or where would you go about getting it?

# Lesson 19

# For Richer or Poorer

## Family Economics

---

"American Express—Don't leave home without it," the ads used to say. And for years we took that message (and others like it) to heart, using dozens of credit cards to finance purchases that were beyond the dreams and incomes of families before World War II. Vacation homes, recreational vehicles, travel, and electronic gadgets no longer looked to us like luxuries; these were everyday necessities that middle-class families came to take for granted.

Then, in the mid-1970s, the economy finally stopped growing, and the standard of living for many Americans started a downward spiral that continues, even today. This decline has severely diminished spending power for many families. As a result, more women are working outside the home, families are cramped in apartments or rented living quarters instead of their own homes, grown children are returning to live with their parents, and the strains placed on marriages have contributed to a rising divorce rate.

Perhaps you and your family have developed ways of coping with the economic crunch, such as preparing a monthly budget, shopping more carefully, restricting credit purchases, or "doing it yourself" whenever possible. You may also have found yourself depending more on relatives than on banks or other institutions for school or home loans, or sharing living space with others in order to keep expenses down. The rising costs of health care may have put a comprehensive health insurance policy out of your reach, and you may depend more than ever on the help of family rather than doctors during an illness. Most families have had to adapt in

## Overview

some ways to new economic realities, even if it means simply learning to live with less.

## Economic Pressures on the Family

But families and individuals can only do so much on their own to solve the problems caused by a changing economy; governments must also adapt to deal with the new conditions. In the past, government policy in America has not been supportive of families, in part because the diversity of family styles in this country has made it difficult to develop programs that will satisfy everyone. But the problems that families face in America today raise a number of difficult questions. As you go through this lesson, try to answer these questions for yourself. You may discover problems you weren't aware of, or find ways of dealing with financial hardship that you hadn't considered. At the end, ask yourself whether your ideas about coping with the financial challenges facing families have changed.

What effect has the end of America's post-World War II economic boom had on family relationships? The combination of double-digit inflation, recession, and record unemployment in recent decades has hurt minority families, women, the disabled and the retired even more than it has the white majority. Even so, many white, middle-class women have been forced to work to supplement family income. In a number of families, the wife's return to work has changed the balance of power between husband and wife—sometimes for the better, as husbands, through necessity, have assumed more housework and child-care responsibilities; and sometimes for the worse, when already overloaded wives have had to maintain their usual household responsibilities while working.

Economic pressures on a family vary over the course of its life, as its members' earning power and needs change. A two-paycheck couple without children tends to be financially comfortable, whereas a couple with children approaching school age finds that demands often exceed income. A middle-income family's standard of living tends to decline until the oldest child reaches 18—unless that child goes on to college, that is.

Until recently, most middle-class parents could look forward to a better standard of living once their children reached 18. But that has changed somewhat now with college costs soaring. In addition, many young adults without work continue living at home, and middle-aged couples increasingly are called on to help their own aging parents financially. Even after retirement, when couples used to be able to look forward to some security, our contracting economy has caused new problems—health insurance costs are on the rise, serious illness or nursing home care can wipe out a life's savings, and federal programs such as Medicaid and Social Security face cutbacks.

Of course, this is a highly simplified scenario. People have many choices to make at each of those stages, and their decisions will have an impact on their finances. Some couples, realizing the financial consequences, may choose not to have children. Some parents may choose to give their children more advantages while they are young rather than saving for a college education.

The financial pinches that families suffer in these various stages affect the way they live and the way members feel about themselves. Is there a way to deal with these problems that will minimize the strain and turmoil? The best advice seems to be to plan ahead by creating a family budget—a spending plan for a definite time period.

**Effective Budgeting and Credit Use**

Although the idea of creating a budget may sound restrictive, this kind of planning can increase the amount of goods and services your money will buy by as much as 10 percent. How? Well, have you ever found yourself wondering what happened to all your money just a few days after cashing your paycheck? Budgeting forces people to stop and consider whether they really need an item before they buy, and it helps them plug leaks from expenses they may not have been aware of—since records will show exactly where the money went. In addition, a budget helps determine just how much money can truly be considered *discretionary income*—uncommitted funds that can be spent as the family pleases.

Budgeting also makes it easier to adjust an irregular income to regular expenses; and in an economy with unpredictable layoffs, keeping some money in reserve is a strategy not to be overlooked. Planning ahead is a necessity when the amount that families need and spend varies over the years.

But the best reason to budget is that it encourages families to examine goals and values: Just how much do we need a bigger color television? Would we be just as happy vacationing nearby as we would going to Hawaii? And the planning process itself, in which all family members are involved, leads to negotiation and cooperation that promotes intimacy.

Planning a budget may also be a way to avoid the disappointment and shattered illusions that many couples experience when they move from the romance of courtship to the realities of marriage. Are you assuming that one or both partners will bring a car into the marriage? That both partners will work? What if the woman gets pregnant and you lose her income? Would you be willing to give up eating out, new furniture, a second car? How important is your membership in an athletic club? Would you give it up in order to support a child?

One study reports that only about one-third of American households have significant amounts of money left over after paying for what they perceive as a comfortable standard of living. Whether you are looking forward to your first year of marriage or your fifteenth, you may want to sit down with your partner and plan a budget. Here are some general types of planning a budget that can be adapted to your own interests and needs. First, assess your situation; prepare a balance sheet that lists your financial assets and liabilities so you know where you stand. Next, decide on your priorities and goals and realistically estimate your income for the next year.

Before creating your budget, try to get an accurate picture of current expenses. Keep track of everything you spend for at least a week, and then prepare a budget for the year, listing anticipated expenses for each category that will require an expenditure of funds.

Planning a budget is not all that's needed, though; daily and monthly records should be kept as well. If excessive expenditures occur in successive months, you may have to eliminate some purchases you intended to make, or find ways to earn additional income.

Saving regularly is highly improbable, if not impossible, for low-income families. But financial advisors recommend that middle-income couples regularly save 10 percent of their gross income. If that seems too difficult, start with less and work up, taking advantage of payroll deductions and other savings plans that many employers offer.

What about purchases on credit? Should you use credit to buy a car? A swimming pool? To finance a college education? Financial writer Sylvia Porter counsels people not to use credit for purchases intended to boost their morale or social status, nor to finance purchases on the strength of a hoped-for raise or windfall. There are other ways to borrow money besides using high-interest credit cards.

Many people use installment buying—contracting with a dealer to pay for an appliance or other major item in a series of monthly payments—as a way to get the car or washing machine they can't pay for in a lump sum. This approach can be deceptive, however. You should consider the *real* cost of an item purchased on an installment plan—not just the purchase price but also the cost of financing the purchase, which will greatly increase the cost.

If there is simply not enough money to pay the bills—if a family finds itself overextended—the first step in solving the problem is to make a conscious choice to change things. This may mean changing spending habits, giving up credit cards for a time, and consulting with a credit counselor. Some families attempt to solve their credit problems by taking out a *consolidation loan*, a single loan large enough to cover all outstanding debts that can be repaid over an extended length of time through relatively smaller monthly payments. The total interest that must be paid, however, is much greater. Such an approach can't replace the simpler tactic of using credit wisely in the first place so that the family income is not overcommitted.

In the decade of the 1990s, it has become increasingly difficult for families to secure adequate housing and health care. Even in relatively stable economic times, many families find that being careful consumers isn't enough.

**Paying for Housing and Health Costs**

The drive to secure a home is, for most families, very strong. After all, a home represents more than physical shelter—it is psychologically and symbolically important to binding a family together and providing a feeling of safety and security. While some experts say that a family should not pay more than one-quarter of its monthly income for housing, many low-income families have no choice but to pay close to 50 percent of their income to house their family.

Housing needs for most families change over the years. Newlyweds may live with parents or rent a small apartment, but they're likely to feel cramped once children are on the way. Later, when children begin to leave home, living quarters may seem too large—a smaller home is needed. Of course, these various needs aren't always met. The high cost of housing has kept the American ideal of home ownership out of reach of many younger families, and has even made renting a financial strain.

For some segments of the population, choices are particularly limited. Home prices have increased much faster than income in recent years, and unless families are willing to consider a smaller home, duplex, or townhouse, home ownership will remain beyond their reach. If a large down payment is the only stumbling block, gifts from relatives may provide the necessary assistance. If the payments are the bigger problem, sharing a house with others can be a creative solution.

Will current trends in housing will affect family relationships? For example, will tension between parents and adult children increase if parents finance their children's purchase of a home? Will families feel more or less secure if they share a home with another family? Perhaps. But some social scientists point to potentially positive benefits, too. Economic hard times and the tight housing market may be encouraging more extended family cooperation.

Let's return to your budget for a moment. Have you considered the rising cost of health care? We often tend to think there isn't much we can do about these rising costs, nor about improving the quality of services we get for our money. But that may not be true.

Do you have a family doctor? Does he or she always explain your illness or treatment to your satisfaction? Have you ever questioned your doctor's fee? One social scientist suggests that families can receive better health care when they demand information and become actively involved in their care rather than passively submitting to it. If you are called upon to make life and death choices for parents, children, or spouse, will you leave the decision of whether to use life-support systems up to doctors and technicians? Or will you insist upon having the information you need to decide for yourself?

Becoming involved in your own health care is one way to adapt to a changing economy, to get the most for your diminished purchasing power. Still, as we noted earlier, there's a limit to what individuals can do alone. Many of the troubles that families are having with health care and housing are also public issues.

## Social Policy Toward Families

Family policy addresses the problems families face within the context of the larger society. It includes the effects that other social institutions—such as churches and corporations—have on families. In a narrower sense, family policy is all the procedures, regulations, and attitudes of government that affect families. With our individualistic values and ethic of self-reliance, Americans have so far been unwilling to support costly family programs. Increasingly, however, we are beginning to see that the results of this neglect may be costing our society even more in unemployment compensation, welfare benefits, and the expense of more prisons and mental hospitals.

Of course, fixing these problems takes more than money alone. We must also question whether our state, federal, and local bureaucracies are equipped to deal with family needs effectively. And whether or not we really want government playing an even bigger role in family life. The experience of European countries suggests that more government intervention could be beneficial, but on this, like every other family policy issue, opinion remains divided. We like the freedom and the opportunity to make our own decisions, particularly where issues are close to home and hearth. The problem is, with our economy in its current fragile stage, many of us are finding our options eroding along with our paychecks. Expanded leave policies . . . national health insurance . . . are these good ideas, or just more examples of government interference? While we struggle to answer these questions, families all about us struggle to keep financially alive.

## Learning Objectives

On completing your study of this lesson, you should be able to

❑ Describe how the end of the post-war economic boom affected American families.

❑ Explain the changes in spending patterns that occur over the course of family life.

❑ List the reasons for planning a family budget.

❑ List the steps in planning a family budget.

❑ Discuss the advantages and disadvantages of buying on credit and borrowing money for major purchases.

❑ Describe current trends in the housing market that affect the ability of families to meet their changing housing needs.

❑ Discuss the ways in which cooperation among an extended family can help to lower housing and health care costs.

❑ List some ways in which families can meet the challenges of finding affordable, accessible health care.

❑ Compare the advantages and disadvantages of a government sponsored and supported family policy program, and speculate on its overall impact on the economy.

**Key Terms**

Budgeting  
Consolidation loan  
Discretionary income  
Extended family living  
Family physician  

Family policy  
Financial overextension  
Inflation  
Installment financing  
Post-war economy  

**Assignments**

❑ Before viewing the program, be sure you've read through the preceding overview and familiarized yourself with the learning objectives and key terms for this lesson. Then read Appendix I, "Managing a Family Budget," pages 593–595, of *Marriages and Families* by Lamanna and Riedmann.

❑ After completing these tasks, read the video viewing questions and watch the video program for Lesson 19, "For Richer or Poorer."

❑ After viewing the program, take time to answer the video viewing questions and evaluate your learning with the self-test. You'll find the correct answers, along with text page references, at the back of this telecourse guide.

❑ Read the "What's Your Decision?" scenario at the end of this lesson and answer the questions about the decision you would make based on what you've learned from this lesson. Give these questions some serious thought; they may be used as the basis for class discussion or the development of a more complex essay.

**Video Viewing Questions**

1. A growing number of people are finding it extremely difficult to provide basic needs to their families. How might a change in circumstance for one member of a family spell poverty for the rest of the group? Explain your answer using the information Dr. Sneiderman supplied on "income sharing."

2. Dr. Sneiderman states the stress of poverty brings a sense of depravation, alienation, and non-participation in soci-

ety. Based on the comments of Josh, Kathy Icenhower, Dr. Alvy, and Dr. Zimmerman, describe how the stress of poverty manifests itself in other ways. Differentiate between the experiences of children and adults.

3. Is the traditional family a ridiculous notion? Discuss the challenges double-income families face in the caretaking of dependents. Refer to the comments of Drs. Zimmerman, Sneiderman, and Broderick in your response. Do the observations of Anita Allen and Marsha Lasswell fit into your analysis?

4. Financial concerns are the source of continuing stress for the majority of middle class families as well as the truly impoverished. What creative means did Rob and Carrie, Jess and Irene, and Marsha and Don come up with to handle money problems? Describe how buying on credit can lead to serious financial problems down the road.

5. Julia Hare and Dr. Wade Nobles contend that the media gives false images and expectations to children regarding what they can expect to have. How do Jess, Peter, Robin, and Chris address their children's "wanting it all"? How do they try to bring the expectations back to a realistic level? What else might the children learn in the process?

6. Explain why the elderly often face financial difficulties despite the fact that they worked hard all of their lives.

7. Both Dr. Zimmerman and Dr. Sneiderman contend that multiple financial pressures not only take an inevitable toll on families, but also on society as a whole. In what way is society affected by this seemingly individual problem?

8. Many countries offer a variety of services and support networks to help alleviate additional stresses on families. What steps might the United States take to assist families in maintaining their general financial stability and thus lowering the stress level and improving the quality of life? Research your answer and fully explain what you think should be done, why steps have or have not been taken in the past, and possible road blocks to implementation of your suggestions.

## Self-Test

1. When the post-World War II economic boom ended, which of the following resulted?

   a. The oil shortage of 1973–74.

   b. A drop in workers' real purchasing power due to inflation, recession, and unemployment.

   c. A more equal distribution of income among different working classes.

   d. A shift in conjugal balance of power favoring women.

2. Which of the following best defines discretionary income?

   a. Income that does not come from sources that might be questioned by the Internal Revenue Service (IRS).

   b. Money or other assets that have been earned for use at a later date.

   c. Income that is either earned or not earned, according to the desire of the wage-earner.

   d. Uncommitted money that can be spent as the family pleases.

3. Families go through different stages and experience different financial situations during each. Based on the economy over the last ten years, during which of the following stages is a family *most likely* to suffer financial hardship?

   a. Before they have children.

   b. When they have young children living at home.

   c. When they have older children living at home.

   d. After they retire.

4. The Smiths both worked for years before they had a child and had grown accustomed to the discretionary income that resulted from two paychecks. They didn't save money; in fact, they ran up a large credit card balance after the baby was born in addition to existing accumulated debts. Now they can't seem to make their monthly debt payments and still take care of necessities. They've cut back their spending and don't use their credit cards, but they still don't have enough to pay the bills and have fallen behind. What should they do?

   a. Grit their teeth, cut back more by getting rid of health insurance and whatever else they can, sell their house—in general, do whatever necessary to make those monthly payments.

   b. Declare bankruptcy so they can start fresh.

c. Take out a consolidation loan that will enable them to get over this rough period.

d. Plan a budget, consult a credit counselor, and ask creditors to spread payments over a longer period.

5. Some good reasons for budgeting include *all but one* of the following.

a. Budgeting makes each adult member of the family accountable for their own expenditures.

b. Budgeting encourages two-paycheck families to decide whether the second salary is to be considered temporary or permanent.

c. Budgeting helps in adjusting irregular income to regular expenses.

d. Budgeting encourages family members to examine personal and family goals and values.

6. A danger of installment financing is

a. not being able to take advantage of real bargains when you don't have cash available.

b. that the interval between purchase and receipt of goods is too long.

c. instant gratification becomes a habit.

d. that the real cost of the item purchased—including the cost of financing—is often overlooked.

7. Financial advisors recommend saving _____ percent of your gross income.

a. 1

b. 5

c. 10

d. between 15 and 20

8. In the context of marriage, money issues are

a. a frequent cause of disagreements between couples.

b. often a source of power and control struggles.

c. both a and b

d. seldom reported to be a source of friction between partners.

9. In a sense, _____ is all the procedures, regulations, attitudes, and goals of government that affect families.

a. the political state

b. Family Organization Compendium

c. family policy

d. conjugal law

10. Of the options given, the rationale *most* proponents would cite as the reason we need a comprehensive family program is

    a. to bring support for families more in line with support provided by other industrialized countries, consequently strengthening our political ties with them.

    b. to free middle-aged Americans from worry about how they will meet the medical, housing, and social needs of their elderly relatives and of themselves as they become older.

    c. to bring about a single definition and structure of the American family, eliminating current problems caused by trying to plan for the multitude of family structures that now exist.

    d. because the costs of comprehensive services to families would likely be less than the long-term social and financial costs of the approach now in existence.

## What's Your Decision?

Mike and Pete have been friends since high school and are now in their late twenties. Both are college graduates with roughly equal incomes. Both are single, but Pete has a steady girlfriend, while Mike appears to be a confirmed bachelor. They are tired of renting, and they would each receive substantial tax breaks for the interest payments on a home, but houses and even condos are so expensive in their area that neither can afford to buy a place alone. Together, however, they could afford to buy a new two-bedroom condominium unit in a development with tennis courts and a pool where other people their age are living.

They could qualify for the loan on the basis of their combined incomes, although Mike is a free spender who likes expensive gadgets and has seriously over-extended his credit card balance a number of times. They can see the advantages of going in to buy the unit together, but they can also see some disadvantages—what if Pete and his girlfriend decide to marry? What if Mike gets over-extended again and can't keep up his half of the payments? They can't decide what to do.

Based on what you know about them, do you think they should buy the condo unit together? What factors should they consider in making the decision? If they do buy it together, what are some of the problems they may face as a result of that decision?

❑ Should they buy the unit together?

❑ What factors support that view?

❑ What factors support the opposite view?

❑ What will happen immediately if they act as you suggest?

❑ What will their situation probably be five years from now if they act as you suggest?

❑ Are there research studies cited in the text that offer support for your position?

❑ If you needed additional research-based information to support your position, how or where would you go about getting it?

# Lesson 20

# Turning Points

## Crossroads in Family Living

In fairy tales, marriage is the beginning of bliss. The hero and heroine, who have resolved all problems and overcome all obstacles, ride off together into eternal happiness. Do you believe it? No, of course not . . . well, maybe a little. Ridiculous as the fairy tale sounds when we take it apart and analyze it, many of us accept it to some extent. There is a tendency to believe that the secret to happiness lies in avoiding problems and keeping life on an even keel.

Psychologists tell us, however, that true happiness comes from a realistic attitude, not a belief in romantic myths. The happiest families are not necessarily those with the easiest, most trouble-free lives, but those with the capacity to weather stress and cope with crisis. This lesson looks at the course of crisis as it affects a family, and some ways in which families handle various kinds of crises.

**Overview**

Let's begin with a definition. When you hear the word crisis you may tend to associate it with major disasters: floods, earthquakes, towering infernos, and so forth. But the term has much broader application as a social psychologist would use it. It refers to a turn- ing point in the life of a family, a period of crucial change, or of unstable conditions and upheavals in relationships. Often, crisis signifies a time for decision making, for altering one's behaviors, attitudes, or roles.

A crisis may be precipitated by something as significant and emotionally jarring as a death in the family, or by something as relatively routine as moving to a new neighborhood.

**Definition of a Crisis**

As we shall see, it isn't just the event that defines the crisis, but the way in which each individual family defines its situation, and the resources they can bring to bear in dealing with that situation. What one family views as stormy weather, another may see as a veritable hurricane.

People within a family develop particular ways of relating to one another. When a crisis hits, all that may change. Suddenly, new routines, new relationships are required. And establishing those may take time, not to mention patience and understanding.

For example, let's say that in one family, the father is laid off for a time. He isn't sure how long he'll be out of work. To make ends meet, the mother decides to take a job. But now, since she's out of the house all day, most of the child-care responsibilities fall either to the father (who may resent this new role) or to the oldest child (who may also feel resentful or fearful of not coping adequately).

Notice that in this situation, everyone's role is shifting in some way. The father, who was once the breadwinner, now relinquishes that position to the mother—who in turn relinquishes her homemaker position to either the father or the oldest child (whose role is still unclear for the moment). Younger children, in turn, may no longer know who has primary authority in controlling their behavior or primary responsibility for their welfare. And this confusion adds to what is already a stressful situation.

## The Realities of Family Life

Most families have difficulty coping with crisis situations. There are pressures from many directions. Most of us are struggling to juggle a career with some sort of home and family life, and never seem to find quite enough time for either. At the same time, we have obligations to the community. And of course, we're supposed to stay young and healthy through all this. Exercise. Eat right. And while you're at it, don't let yourself get too dull or stuffy. Be adventurous. Find yourself. Fulfill yourself. Be thinner. . . richer. . . happier. . .

Few families consist solely of self-fulfilled, capable, independent adults with strong self-concepts and impressive money-earning capabilities. Families generally are a mix of people—some adults, some children. Some independent, some dependent. Some stronger, some weaker. The family is generally the place you can find unconditional acceptance. Even if you're somewhat incompetent, somewhat helpless, and more than a little obnoxious, you probably won't get "fired" from your position within the family.

Of course, this kind of acceptance places something of a burden on the stronger members of the family. Sometimes it is a burden they accept willingly. Parents, for example, generally expect to support their children for a number of years. Children do not always, however, expect to support their parents—though they may eventually wind up doing so because of economic hardship or illness. Sometimes, conversely, parents who feel their child rearing days are over are surprised to find their fledglings returning to the nest—divorced, or out of work. Sometimes one spouse or the other becomes unable to work. And if this situation creates economic hardship, it's likely to produce tension and resentment.

**Stressors**

What triggers a crisis? Something called a stressor. This stressor might be the loss or addition of a family member. It could be a sudden change such as a move, loss of a job, or unexpected promotion. Or a demoralizing event such as loss of health or mobility, alcoholism or drug problems, an illegitimate pregnancy, abortion, imprisonment of a family member, or attempted suicide. Notice that stressors are not always negative. While many of our examples have negative overtones, such things as marriage, promotion at work, birth of a child, vacations—even holidays—can be stressors because they cause real change in the way people go about their daily lives and relate to one another.

Some families, for example, might view the Christmas holiday season as a time of joy and happiness. Yet it can be a highly stressful period because it disrupts daily routines, requires extra energy (mailing cards, wrapping gifts, shopping, etc.), sometimes strains family budgets, reinforces feelings of loneliness among persons who are separated from loved ones, and may even require some reevaluation of interpersonal relationships. ("Should we invite Uncle Bill to Christmas dinner even though we haven't spoken in ten months?") Similarly, a promotion at work or the birth of a child, while welcomed on the one hand, still bring new and unfamiliar responsibilities that not only disrupt accustomed routines, but may cause people to question their own capabilities or to feel anxiety about the future.

Further, crisis isn't always triggered by one big event—such as a flood. Sometimes, as they say, it's the little things that get you. And they get you when they come in succession, not allowing you time to recover from any one before the next mini-catastrophe strikes. For example, let's say a family moves to a new house. It may be a happy event for the most part. Still, the family has to reorient itself, make new friends, develop new patterns for shopping or obtaining medical services, and so forth. All mildly stressful. However, if other events in the family's life remain relatively calm for a time, chances are they will adjust well enough, so the stressor—moving to a new house—is not likely to cause a full-blown crisis.

But let's make the life of our hypothetical family a little more interesting (some would say realistic). Let's say that they discover the plumbing isn't working in their new house, and won't be working for another week. Shortly after they move in, Dad is involved in a minor car accident. He isn't injured, but the car needs extensive repair, and meanwhile Dad needs Mom's car to get to work; she is less than pleased. While they're in the midst of making other arrangements, their dog kills the neighbor's kitten. And so it goes...

As you can see, none of these events might seem disastrous in itself. But coming together, one right on top of the last, the total effect can be overwhelming. Sometimes, undercurrents of ongoing stress add to the situation. Let's say the economy isn't doing well right now; Dad isn't entirely sure his new job is secure. Maybe they shouldn't have made the move. Inflation seems to be growing worse; the cost of living is rising. While none of these problems might have kept Mom and Dad awake at night prior to the move, they may now cast a very large shadow over what started out to be a happy event.

## Factors Affecting the Impact of Stress

About 30 years ago, sociologist Reuben Hill constructed an ABC-X model for explaining how a crisis affects family life. In Hill's model, A is the stressor event, B is the family's ability to cope with crisis, and C is the way in which the family defines the event (internal versus external). These three elements all interact to determine X—the crisis itself.

The point of the model is that the dynamics influencing the birth of a crisis differ from family to family. In the preceding example, one family tended to see the mother's losing her job as the result of external influences. And that way of defining the crisis affected their way of dealing with it. The second family blamed the mother for the situation, and again, their way of defining the crisis determined their method of dealing with it.

Hill also notes that crises are influenced by family hardships and prior strains. Hardships are additional sources of stress brought about by the original stressor. The breadwinner loses his job and suddenly there is no money for a vacation or other luxuries. Other family members may need to work outside the home; the house may even have to be sold. Prior strains are unresolved stressors or ongoing tensions. For example, the everyday stress and strain of being a new parent may be intensified when other problems exist. If both parents are working outside the home to make ends meet, and getting up at 6:00 each morning, the 2:00 a.m. feeding for the new baby may seem more stressful than it would otherwise.

Other factors affect the degree of stress families experience as well. One is the extent to which they feel a situation is beyond their control—either temporarily or permanently. A person who is laid off from work, for example, not only faces unemployment, but the daily stress of not knowing when he or she will be reemployed—or how. A family whose child has run away lives with the agony of not knowing that child's fate. Is she all right? Still alive? In the same city or state? Will she ever return?

In addition, it's important to realize that the way we define various crises as a society tends to change over time. Two hundred years ago, such a grievous event as the death of a child might have been handled in a way that today might seem rather matter-of-fact. Because childhood mortality was common in the 1700s, most families expected to experience it, and tended to see it as more "natural" than we do today. In our society, we expect children to outlive their parents, and find it distressing when the reverse occurs.

On the other hand, the loss of a child through miscarriage or death during the birth process may be seen, by our society today, as more of a medical problem than a family tragedy. There may be no religious or other ritual signifying the death; it is as if society does not recognize the fetus or newborn as a human being or family member. A mother grieving over the loss of a baby through miscarriage may find little sympathy or support within her family or in the larger society. Left alone with her grief, she may even feel a little guilty in the absence of any strong empathy for her feelings, and she is likely to find the situation difficult. Regardless of the stressor, most psychologists agree that crises are harder to deal with alone.

## Family Transitions as Stressors

As we mentioned earlier, family transitions can serve as stressors. They call for dramatic changes in behavior, attitudes, or beliefs, but they're predictable in the sense that most families experience them, and there are established ways of coping with these events.

Take parenthood, for example. The birth of a baby can be a kind of stressor, especially for parents who have not been around children or infants much, and know little of what to expect. Suddenly, their lives are disrupted to an unbelievable extent. They no longer eat, sleep, work, or relax in any sort of orderly, routine way. They must take responsibility for the health, welfare, and very life of a person who cannot communicate his or her needs in intelligible language. And the result can be fatiguing, bewildering, and at times even frightening. Gradually, parents do adjust, particularly if they're able to view the situation as a challenge—one that will strengthen their coping skills.

Midlife transition can be another stressor. At some point during midlife (however you define that term) partners begin to experience the first physical effects of aging, and with those effects may come a somewhat diminished self-concept. Maybe the image in the mirror doesn't look quite as it once did. Maybe it isn't so simple to sink a jump shot. At the same time, careers may peak—or bottom out. One or both spouses may feel that there are no interesting goals on the horizon, or perhaps, that the best is over. Neither is going to win a Nobel Prize or even get to be a particularly important part of the company. Questions may arise. Did we raise our children as well as we might have? Were we good parents? Did we make the most of our careers? Jealousy can be a problem, too, if grown children just entering the world seem to face new opportunities that are now behind Mom and Dad forever.

The "empty nest" syndrome can be a stressor—at least according to some psychologists. In her studies, Pauline Bart discovered that women who had devoted their lives to the care and nurturing of children experienced a personal sense of loss and emptiness when the last child left home. More recent studies, however (Borland and Rubin), tend to dispute those findings somewhat. True, many mothers do experience some temporary sadness when the last child leaves. Some question the future, wonder what life will bring. But many—despite some doubts or melancholy—seem on the whole to look forward to that time as a period of opportunity. It's a chance to get that part-time job that sounded so interesting, or to return to school for a degree, or just to pursue a hobby that's been neglected. In short, the stress may be rather short-lived.

Further, some studies show that what may be more stressful to parents than having children leave home is having them leave sooner than expected (because of an early marriage or deciding to work rather than finish school), or having them return home (because of divorce or financial problems). And some studies show that having children leave home isn't stressful just for mothers; it's often stressful for fathers, too. But it tends to affect either parent less if he or she has other activities and interests to fill the time—in other words, has some role other than that of mother or father to fill.

## The Course of a Family Crisis

The first response to crisis is frequently denial. While denial may seem irrational, it is simply a human way of gearing one's personal resources up for the job of coping. The death of a family member or loss of one's home may seem too terrible to face at the moment.

Within a short time, however, reality sets in, and with it, disintegration. Routines are disrupted. Roles and relationships seem uncertain and confused. Family members may experience anger, fear, resentment. They may feel their situation is unfair; that others have it easier.

Families who receive the support of friends and extended family during this period seem to fare better. And of course, the support that immediate family members extend to one another is invaluable. But it may not be easy to achieve. Remember, tension is affecting everyone. And if there is conflict, an atmosphere of blame, or ambiguity over roles, then family members may have a difficult time finding ways to express their support.

For example, suppose a member of the family suffers from a terminal illness that is physically debilitating. How do other members of the family respond to this condition? Do they overtly express sympathy, provide assistance whenever possible? Or do they insist the person to be self-sufficient, in the interest of dignity, even when self-sufficiency is physically difficult? These are not simple questions to answer, and finding a way of relating that's comfortable for everyone takes considerable patience and sensitivity. Suppose you're trying to assist a handicapped family member and told that you're only interfering; that you don't understand how it feels to experience a debilitating illness. How will you respond?

The complexities inherent in sorting out relationships bring us to another issue: anger. Tempers tend to run short during periods of great stress. Is it all right to express anger, to let such feelings out? Psychologists tend to say yes. In fact, they encourage the open expression of feelings—*if* it does not involve blaming of other family members. That can be a difficult balance to achieve.

Sooner or later, the period of disorganization or disintegration comes to a close, and the family enters the recovery phase. At some point, the worst seems to be over, and things begin to improve. Rarely, though, does the family emerge from the crisis looking quite the same.

For some families, the crisis proves too much—as our high divorce rate indicates. Others may remain together, but may be so shaken by the experience that their relationship never regains its former closeness. A destructive cycle may be set into motion if the family member viewed as perpetuating the crisis continues to receive blame for future problems. This is often the case with a family member who is an alcoholic, or an inveterate gambler.

But some families emerge from a crisis with renewed strength and commitment. They may see the crisis as an opportunity to create ways of building their personal resources. For instance, if one family member takes drugs, the whole family may seek counseling. It is as if the problem serves as a signal that overall, things could get better. This sort of approach tends to boost everyone's self-concept.

## Death and Dying

Of all the potential sources of stress, the death of a loved one is perhaps the most profound in its personal and familial impact. A sudden, unexpected death can rock a family to its very foundations. The personal impact on each family member, and the effect on the family unit can be devastating.

Coping with a terminal illness involves the additional stress of watching helplessly as a loved one's condition deteriorates, being unable to offer anything more than comfort and emotional support while trying to handle the personal implications of the situation. Each day we wonder what we could have done better—how we can improve the dying person's quality of life in the days that remain.

Impending death isn't something we feel very comfortable talking about, especially with someone who is dying. Yet research indicates that a dying individual may become very depressed if people around them talk around the situation or in optimistic terms all the time. This attitude—while perhaps meant to be helpful—may seem to deny the person's fears, problems, and reality.

No one can promise you a life free of stress. Nor can anyone predict what all the stressors in your life will be—though as we've seen, you can anticipate and plan for some of them. What we do know, however, is that it's possible to find peace of mind despite stress, given a supportive environment, free of blame, in which family members work together to meet the crises that inevitably affect them all.

On completing your study of this lesson, you should be able to

❑ Define the term crisis.

❑ Explain the role of a stressor in precipitating a crisis, and give several examples of common stressors.

❑ Describe the ways in which family transitions can act as stressors.

❑ Describe the interrelationships inherent the ABC-X model of family stressors and strains proposed by Reuben C. Hill.

❑ Discuss some of the ways in which social attitudes, evolving over time, affect the ways we personally define crisis.

❑ Explain some of the reasons why recovery from crisis is different for different families.

❑ Summarize the course of a family crisis.

**Learning Objectives**

ABC-X model     Predictable crises
Crisis     Recovery
Empty nest     Transitions
Period of disorganization

**Key Terms**

❑ Before viewing the program, be sure you've read through the preceding overview and familiarized yourself with the learning objectives and key terms for this lesson.

**Assignments**

Then read Chapter 16, "Managing Family Stress and Crises," of *Marriages and Families* by Lamanna and Riedmann, with particular emphasis on pages 526–543.

❑ After completing these tasks, read the video viewing questions and watch the video program for Lesson 20, "Turning Points."

❑ After viewing the program, take time to answer the video viewing questions and evaluate your learning with the self-test. You'll find the correct answers, along with text page references, at the back of this telecourse guide.

❑ Read the "What's Your Decision?" scenario at the end of this lesson and answer the questions about the decision you would make based on what you've learned from this lesson. Give these questions some serious thought; they may be used as the basis for class discussion or the development of a more complex essay.

## Video Viewing Questions

1. Stress is a part of everyday living. It can be caused by single or cumulative events, adding excitement and tension to one's daily activities and responsibilities. What do Anita, Michelle, Linda, and Robin find to be consistent sources of stress in their lives? How do each of them cope with this stress?

2. In addition to everyday pressures, most individuals and families have to face a crisis situation at some point. How can ordinary events trigger a crisis? Describe through examples what Marsha Lasswell means by "second order change." Why is this kind of pressure harder to deal with than everyday stress?

3. Carlfred Broderick contends that the way a family interprets and defines a crisis can often predict how the family will function during and after the crisis. How does this relate to the commentary of Julia and Nathan Hare? Be specific in your analysis.

4. Perhaps the most devastating crisis a family can face is the impending death of a loved one. But even in the face of tragedy, basic daily needs and obligations continue. How did Margaret, Charlie, and Deborah each meet their regular responsibilities in spite of what loomed in the future? In what way did their approaches differ? How did

their personal priorities change during the progression of the illness?

5. Based on the testimony of Charlie, Deborah, Margaret, and her son, describe why communication between family members is so important in this type of crisis, especially in the later stages. Is there a link between stress and communication? In what ways did Charlie and Deborah differ in terms of the stress they experienced and how it was or was not communicated?

6. Explore comments by Margaret and her sons regarding Carlin's eventual death. Could their perspective be a result of their initial interpretation of the crisis? Considering all that Margaret said, can the way in which she will emerge from this crisis be predicted? Fully explain your response including what factors help to determine how one emerges from a serious crisis.

## Self-Test

1. Some psychologists would argue that an event such as the birth of a baby is better termed a "transition" than a "crisis." The *main* reason for this is that

   a. it's obviously a happy, welcome event.
   b. it tends to be predictable.
   c. unlike a true crisis, it involves no real changes in beliefs, attitudes, or behaviors.
   d. unlike a true crisis, it has no serious debilitating effects on the family.

2. An event which precipitates a crisis is *best* termed

   a. a stressor.
   b. a predictable transition.
   c. a tragedy.
   d. a strain.

3. Which of the following is the *best* example of a boundary change?

   a. Al and Rita move to Chicago when Rita gets a better job offer.
   b. Bob and Sally adopt a Korean orphan child.
   c. David is expelled from school for rowdy behavior.
   d. When Ruth gets promoted to vice-president, Ed agrees to take on more homemaking responsibilities.

4. The concept of "stressor overload" applies in which of these instances?

   a. Family resources enable family members to overcome the stressors with their problem-solving abilities.

   b. A stressor finds too much family resilience and vanishes as a problem for the family.

   c. Stressors may accumulate without family members knowing it until a crisis is precipitated.

   d. One family takes on another family's excess stressors.

5. Which of the following would *not* be categorized as a stressor?

   a. loss of a family member

   b. winning the lottery

   c. a demoralizing event

   d. all of the above are stressors

6. Husbands' retirement often precipitate far-reaching adjustments;

   a. the consequences are often more negative than positive for most men.

   b. adjustments are also expected to occur for their homemaker wives.

   c. most companies and/or corporations now have effective retirement training programs to facilitate adjustment.

   d. most educated husbands discover retirement to be relatively uneventful.

7. According to the ABC-X model presented in the text, the nature of a crisis is affected by

   a. All of the following—b, c, and d.

   b. the nature of the stressful event that triggers it.

   c. the inherent ability of the family to cope.

   d. the way in which the family defines the crisis.

8. A family has just learned that their child is physically disabled. Probably the *most constructive* attitude or behavior that they could adopt at this point would be to

   a. believing that the crisis is surmountable.

   b. refusing to accept the diagnosis.

   c. accepting the fact that they are responsible, as a family, for this situation.

   d. trying to figure out which family member has primary responsibility for bringing on this tragedy.

9. In the 1800s, a family whose young child died suddenly of disease would probably be *most likely* to see that loss as

   a. retribution for sin—a judgment of God.
   b. unnatural and untimely, though not a real cause for grief.
   c. the most grievous loss any family could suffer.
   d. fairly natural and expected, though unfortunate.

10. Which of the following is probably the *most important* factor in prompting a family's recovery from crisis?

    a. Recognizing that what was perceived as a crisis wasn't really so very serious after all.
    b. Having strong support from the immediate family as well as friends and kin.
    c. Finding who was to blame for the crisis in the first place so that person's behavior can be modified.
    d. Ensuring that roles and attitudes weather the crisis relatively unscathed or unchanged.

## What's Your Decision?

In Jack's family, things seem to have gone from bad to worse. What started out to be a three-month layoff for Jack has now turned into a nightmare of endless unemployment, and there seems to be no way out. Jack has tried desperately for several months to get a job, but to no avail. "They just don't seem to be hiring anybody like me," he tells his wife Lucy. "Or if they are, there are eighty other guys like me waiting in line, gripping souped up resumes in their hot little fists—man, it's hopeless."

Depressed and dejected, Jack begins to drink. Not too much at first—just a beer or two at the end of the day. Soon, however, he is drinking heavily, on a daily basis. And some days, he doesn't feel well enough to get out of bed and look for work. Lucy feels frustrated, resentful, and very angry. "If you would get yourself together," she tells Jack, "if you would try—really try—you'd find a job, and we wouldn't be in this mess."

Jack feels too that he is primarily to blame for the family's hard times, but it is too much responsibility for one person to bear. "You try it," he tells Lucy in self-defense. "See what kind of a job you can come up with—see how easy you think it is out there." She retorts, "What a grand idea. And who do you propose will take care of the baby? The baby-sitter we cannot afford to hire since we have no money?"

A friend who's acquainted with their situation suggests that they go together with their two older children to get some family counseling. Jack is for the idea. He is willing to try almost anything at this point. Lucy opposes it. "Our problem is not poor communication," she tells her friend. "And we don't need fancy psychoanalysis to solve it. Jack knows what the problem is. I know. Everyone knows. He's too lazy and too incompetent to get work. And now with the drinking thing—I don't know. It's not a family problem. There's nothing the kids can do or I can do. It's Jack's problem. If he were willing and able to make a decent living, everything would be great."

Based on what you know of their situation, do you think Jack and Lucy should seek family counseling? What are some of the most important factors for them to consider in making this decision? If they do seek counseling, what are some of the most significant ramifications of that decision?

❏ Should they seek counseling?

❏ What factors support that view?

❏ What factors support the opposite view?

❏ What will happen immediately if they act as you suggest?

❏ What will their situation probably be five years from now if they act as you suggest?

❏ Are there research studies cited in the text that offer support for your position?

❏ If you needed additional research-based information to support your position, how or where would you go about getting it?

# Lesson 21

# The Strained Knot

## Families in Crisis

Are you the sort of person who comes unglued under stress? Or do you thrive on a challenge—are you at your best when pressured to marshal resources hidden deep inside yourself? In this lesson, we hope to help you define the term crisis realistically, and to learn some creative ways of coping with the various crises all of us face within our lives. And if you relate the lesson to your own attitudes and behaviors as we go, you may also learn a great deal about your personal crisis management style.

Crises tend to follow predictable patterns. Some event— or stressor—sets off the crisis. It might be a significant or catastrophic event, such as a hurricane or a death in the family. Or it might be something that would seem more routine— graduation from college, moving to another state.

How do families tend to react to a crisis? First there is a period of disorganization, during which personal and family routines are disrupted, roles shift a bit, and things seem generally out of focus. Sometime during this period, the crisis hits what social scientists term its *nadir*—the lowest point. Things can only improve from here. But the extent to which they do so depends on whether the people involved allow the crisis to overwhelm and control their lives, or take control and find creative ways of managing the crisis.

In the recovery phase, the family that deals creatively with the crisis may emerge with an organizational structure that is equal to, if not stronger than, that which it had prior to the crisis. In real-life terms, this means that family members generally have a stronger self-concept, communication lines

## Overview

are more open, roles and relationships are more flexible, and the family has a strong sense of itself as a community capable of coping.

## Resources for Coping with Crisis

As we have discussed, stress in some form is common to virtually all modern families. What makes families different is their capacity to cope with stress, and the resources they bring to bear.

What is meant by "creative" coping, anyway? Well, if you think about it, creating is making something new. Creative stress management often means the design of a new family structure—new roles, new patterns of relating, new ways of living life.

For some people, creative crisis management might mean divorce. It's extreme in one sense, but in another sense it's simply the creation of new roles for those involved outside the family structure. Generally, though, families attempt to find ways of realigning roles and responsibilities and relationships within the family unit.

A family's power of creativity, as it were, depends on two primary factors: how they define the crisis confronting them, and what resources they're able to bring to bear in handling the crisis. Let's talk about each.

First, two families faced with the same problem may define that problem very differently. Let's say that a 42-year-old woman, herself a grandmother, unexpectedly becomes pregnant. One family may view this event as disastrous—particularly if it means disruption to a blossoming career, a decline in financial resources (just when they're needed to send other children through college), and a return to a way of life that is no longer appealing. In another family, however, the same circumstances might be received with great joy. Perhaps the woman will see the impending birth of a child as precisely what's needed to give her life new meaning, a chance to escape a job she wasn't particularly enjoying anyway, an opportunity to return to a period of self-fulfillment she remembers with warmth and satisfaction. Just by virtue of her attitude, the woman in the second scenario is already better equipped to deal with this "crisis" than the woman in the first scenario. But attitude isn't all that's important.

Resources count, too. When we mention resources, most of us think of money. And economics are an important part of family resources, of course. Having sufficient income to support and educate a child, for example, is an important consideration. But the resources required to cope with crisis extend beyond material wealth. Resources also include such things as the sense of harmony and well-being within the family, personal health, communication among family members, a satisfactory sex life for both spouses, creative and fulfilling use of leisure time, a supportive network of family and friends, and overall satisfaction with one's family and lifestyle. Think about your own family situation for a moment. If you would rate your family life a strong plus in many of these categories, then you can feel confident that your family is probably well equipped to deal effectively with crisis—especially in comparison to a family that lacks many of these resources.

Other factors are important in dealing with crisis as well. One relates back to attitude. An ability to focus on the positive can strengthen your crisis combatting forces. If, on the other hand, you have a tendency to think you've been singled out by fate for especially hard knocks, your combat reserves are likely to be depleted.

Religious faith can be important, too. Research seems to point to a strong correlation between religious faith and family cohesiveness in the face of crisis. In addition, high self-esteem is important. For one thing, people with a strong sense of self may believe they're somewhat more invincible, that they'll weather whatever comes along. They're more likely to view hardship as a challenge.

But self-esteem is important for another reason, too. During periods of crisis, everyone expends a great deal of energy just dealing with the problems at hand. There may not be a whole lot left over for expressing affection, showing special consideration, being warm and sensitive. Tempers may grow short. People may become snappish—or just quiet. A strong self-concept can help a person weather this period without feeling picked on or rejected.

## Maintaining Flexibility Through a Crisis

If there's one consistent theme that runs through all experiences of marriage and family life, it's change. No matter what individual experiences each of us has, all of us experience change in many forms. And success in marriage, or in family life, means—among other things—learning to adapt. A kind of flexibility seems to give a family some resiliency in meeting crises.

Further, families in which the atmosphere is more democratic, relationships more egalitarian, appear to be stronger as well. Think for a moment about your own experience growing up. Was your father the primary decision maker in the household? Your mother? Someone else? How would that person have responded to having his or her authority and position as decision maker challenged?

In the traditional family, one person (usually the father) was responsible for all or most decisions. Realistically, however, there may be instances when someone else is better qualified. This could come about either because the circumstance is special, or because the decision maker is temporarily or permanently incapacitated—through illness, for instance, or an alcohol problem.

Let's consider an example. Suppose that an unmarried teenage girl becomes pregnant and must decide whether to continue the pregnancy and keep her baby. In a traditional household, the father may have wielded a great deal of decision-making power in this instance. In a flexible household, however, the decision might fall primarily to the teenager herself, with support from other household members.

Decision making is certainly facilitated when the person most affected by the decision has something to say about outcomes. On the other hand, if the person normally responsible for the decision in a traditional family is asked to abdicate that power—even temporarily—he may feel that his authority or ability is being questioned. The resentment that results can persist even after the crisis itself passes.

Adaptable families adjust to crisis in other ways, too. For example, they're open to new schedules, new use of space, trying new activities, following new rituals. In short, they do what has to be done to cope with the problem at hand, without agonizing over the loss of old, treasured routines.

A flexible family will also be open to external help in coping with a crisis. There are two external resources that are particularly important. One is the availability of counseling or support groups within the community. Increasingly, we're recognizing that counseling is not just for people in trouble. It's a useful resource for anyone facing a major decision: whether to get married, to have children, to retire or accept a new job, or move. Counselors and support groups cannot relieve us of decision-making responsibilities. But they can be helpful in sorting through the complex factors, including our own submerged feelings, that make decisions difficult sometimes.

The second resource is support from an extended family. Traditionally, kin networks have been stronger among black and blue-collar families. But that picture is changing a bit, and throughout society we're witnessing some reaffirmation of kin networks. Why? Well, for one thing, the need seems greater now than it has been in the past. More wives are working, the need for reliable childcare is at an all-time peak, and economic expectations often mean that two persons within a household must work to meet all expenses. Further, kinship groups provide a source of help that many of us feel we can turn to with less embarrassment in times of need. A family requiring childcare but lacking resources to pay for it may feel far more comfortable asking Grandma Jones or Aunt Alice to help out than going to friends or neighbors for support.

There are potential problems, however. The first, obviously, is that the family has to be open enough to ask for help in the first place. But even if they do, the amount of help kinship networks can provide in the future is still questionable. For some of us at least, family patterns are changing in ways that mean, not much of a network is likely to exist as we enter old age. Families are having fewer children these days; many have just one or two, and increasing numbers of couples have no children at all. Even when there are one or two children, increasing divorce rates and the high mobility of our society decrease the chances that a grown child will be there to provide support as we age. And, obviously, fewer numbers of children also mean that many of us are now growing up either not having or not knowing aunts, uncles, or cousins. For some of us, the immediate family may be all the network there ever is.

Open communication during a crisis situation is critical. Even relatively small problems can seem ominous if people cannot talk about them freely. But there are some subjects that leave most of us tongue-tied.

**Communication During a Crisis**

Consider a family with a disabled child. If one or both parents feel some embarrassment or discomfort about their situation, and do not discuss this openly—at least with each other—repressed anger, frustration, despair, or humiliation may seek another, more destructive, outlet. Further, lack of discussion may make a problem seem insurmountable. It may encourage a "well, what's the use?" sort of attitude that can be unhealthy and unproductive for everyone involved. The disabled child may experience a deep sense of rejection and frustration from having no one with whom to discuss personal fears—or hopes.

A communication model commonly adopted in talking with dying persons is significant because it has application for the way in which we discuss other sensitive issues related to crisis. Psychologists suggest that there are three patterns of such communication: avoidance, confrontation, and reaction. The avoidance approach, as its name suggests, consists of talking about everything and anything except the impending death or other crisis issue at hand. Confrontation is quite the opposite; it consists of taking the initiative in raising the subject in order to give the person a chance to express any fears, worries, or wishes. And reaction consists of simply being a good listener—allowing the person to talk about whatever he wants, and just being there to listen.

Which approach is best? Psychologists agree that no one approach works in all situations, with all persons; probably some combination of the three is best, though this implies that we will have the sensitivity to use the right approach at the right time. No one likes to dwell on the down side of life all the time. But on the other hand, ignoring problems may seem to deny the very real fears that live within all of us—and that is, in a sense, to deny ourselves.

## Disaster versus Opportunity

How do you think of a crisis? As a misfortune? A disaster? Or an opportunity for growth? This is not the sort of question that one answers for all time and then forgets about. It is the sort of question that recurs with each new crisis.

Inherent in any crisis is the chance for creative decision making. But taking that chance requires changes—sometimes major changes—in the way people think and act. To the extent you resist change, you're likely to find crises somewhat harder to deal with.

One thing is certain: no one escapes. Crises in some form come to us all. Not everyone will have the house carried off in a flood, not everyone will be struck by lightning. But all of us will face major transitions in our lives. Most of us will marry, and at some point, we may lose our spouses—through divorce or death. Many of us will have children. Most of us will work—and will change the nature of our careers one or more times. All of us will face the death of our family members, friends, and ourselves. Some situations may push even the most resilient of us to our creative limits. Still, psychologists contend, even the grimmest of these circumstances contains within it the potential for some positive effects—if we manage the crisis well.

What are the chances that your family will have the capabilities it needs to meet crisis effectively? Or emerge from a crisis with an even stronger capacity for supportive interaction among its members? You may already have a good sense of that based on your reading so far. As a final sort of checklist, though, we can suggest that the most successful families seem to be those which:

❑ Have a positive outlook—even in the face of what would appear to be the most devastating circumstances, such as terminal illness.

❑ Avoid blaming any one family member for the problem— even if blame seems to be deserved. Successful families look for ways to creatively solve problems together.

❑ Work on deliberately strengthening communications, even about topics that make people uncomfortable.

❑ Keep leadership flexible, so that everyone has a voice in making decisions that influence his or her own life, as well as the future of the family.

Opportunity may seem an odd word to associate with crisis. But remember, we're not talking about the opportunity to lead a carefree existence. We're talking about the opportunity to become more capable in making the sorts of decisions that make the inevitable crises manageable.

On completing your study of this lesson, you should be able to

❑ Identify and describe at least four factors that help families deal with crisis creatively.

❑ Discuss the importance of counseling and informal social support in helping families cope with various types of crisis.

❑ Define the concept of adaptability as it relates to crisis management, and provide specific examples of adaptability and lack of adaptability in dealing with crises.

❑ Describe three different styles of communicating with a dying person, and explain how these styles relate to communication in other crisis situations.

## Learning Objectives

❑ Discuss, in general terms, the philosophical connection between crisis and disaster; crisis and opportunity.

❑ Name and discuss several factors that help determine whether a family will view a particular crisis as a disaster or an opportunity.

## Key Terms

Crisis                                   Stress
Extended family                   Support group
Self-esteem

## Assignments

❑ Before viewing the program, be sure you've read through the preceding overview and familiarized yourself with the learning objectives and key terms for this lesson. Then re-read Chapter 16, "Managing Family Stress and Crises," with particular emphasis on pages 541–550, and Appendix H, pages 591–592, of *Marriages and Families* by Lamanna and Riedmann.

❑ After completing these tasks, read the video viewing questions and watch the video program for Lesson 21, "The Strained Knot."

❑ After viewing the program, take time to answer the video viewing questions and evaluate your learning with the self-test. You'll find the correct answers, along with text page references, at the back of this telecourse guide.

❑ Read the "What's Your Decision?" scenario at the end of this lesson and answer the questions about the decision you would make based on what you've learned from this lesson. Give these questions some serious thought; they may be used as the basis for class discussion or the development of a more complex essay.

## Video Viewing Questions

1. Bob, Debbie, and Mary each recall never knowing what to expect at home and the uncertainty this caused in their childhoods. What effect can this instability have on children? How does the issue of communication between family members influence the function of the family unit? How does Debbie's recollection of her feelings as a child fit into your analysis?

2. Both Debbie and Bob vowed never to make some of the mistakes their parents made, and yet the cycle of abuse continued. Based on the narrated information regarding problems adult children of alcoholics often face, why do you think the cycle of abuse perpetuates? Discuss emotional and behavioral factors including the common problems with self-perception and personal relationships.

3. The difficulty associated with the teenage years is legendary, even if the family environment is caring and supportive. What reasons do Paul, Angie, Debbie, and David give for using drugs? Why did they choose this avenue of escape when each had witnessed first hand the problems and pain substance abuse brings to a family? What role do the pressures of adolescence assume?

4. How do the relationships between family members change when drug abuse becomes the center of the family's interaction? (Note the comments of Mary, Paul, and the Scruggs family.) Did Mary's or Melody's actions help perpetuate role distortions within the family? What were the consequences for each of them individually?

5. Why may the family unit collapse after a drug user cleans up? Use both narrated information and the testimony of Mary, Angie, Bob, Debbie, and Melody in your response.

6. Explain why many treatment facilities for alcohol and drug dependencies insist that the entire family participate. Refer to both the Scruggs and Krause families in your explanation.

## Self-Test

1. Meeting crises creatively usually implies that following the crisis, a family emerges

   a. just as prepared or even more prepared to support one another emotionally.

   b. intact, though not necessarily prepared to offer one another emotional support.

   c. with greater knowledge of problem solving strategies, but no real differences in emotional support patterns.

   d. with each of its members having a newfound independence and freedom from old emotional ties.

2. Which one of the following factors makes it difficult for many American families to meet crises creatively?

   a. Simple lack of imagination.
   b. Too much influence from kinship networks.
   c. Ongoing levels of high stress.
   d. Unwillingness to assign blame for the crisis.

3. One day Elmer and his friend Clyde were talking about how families handle problems. "It was simple for Doris and me," Elmer remarked. "The best way we knew how to handle our problems was divorce. That seemed to solve everything!" *Most* social psychologists would probably say that Elmer's comment in this scenario is

   a. ridiculous, since divorce isn't a solution to anything.
   b. truthful and accurate for his situation, since divorce is one way of creatively reorganizing—though it's obviously not the answer for everyone.
   c. remarkably insightful, since divorce is probably the best solution to 90 percent of the crises Americans face.
   d. honest but unrealistic, since the stigma associated with divorce keeps many people from pursuing this creative approach to crisis management.

4. How important are personal resources in helping families cope creatively with crisis?

   a. Not at all important; while personal resources afford some comfort, in the final analysis it's the nature of the crisis itself that counts.
   b. Slightly important in the sense that families without a strong kinship network seldom manage crisis well.
   c. Quite important, though no more important than attitude or the nature of the crisis itself.
   d. Critical; in fact, resources are the determining factor in predicting whether a family will cope well with crisis.

5. When Arnie learned that his wife Hilda was terminally ill, this was his immediate response: "Well, what else would you expect with my luck? Fate has been against me from the beginning—and now this. There must be some reason I deserve this." What influence is this attitude likely to have on Arnie's crisis management capabilities?

   a. Little or no influence.

b. It could have a negative influence unless he's successful in hiding these feelings in communicating with his wife.

c. It will probably have a positive influence; realistic assessment of one's responsibility for misfortune is generally helpful.

d. It will likely have a negative influence; what Arnie needs is a more positive attitude, even in the face of his severe misfortune.

6. According to research, seriously ill or terminally ill patients may feel better adjusted within their families *if*

a. communication is totally open and honest, even though some topics may cause discomfort.

b. communication is mostly open, but doesn't touch on the subject of death.

c. all communication is positive, and death is associated with passage to a better life.

d. the family worries first about dealing with the practical side of problem solving—and second about establishing good communication.

7. Which of the following does *not* help to foster a positive attitude in times of crisis?

a. Establishing blame when it is deserved

b. Accepting the negative feelings of family members

c. Developing more open communication

d. Neither a nor b help to foster a positive attitude

8. Holly is a 13-year-old girl with a drug problem. She has not taken drugs herself, but several of her friends are doing so, and they're urging her to do it, too. Holly isn't sure herself how serious her problem is; she just knows she feels a need for help. She would prefer to get this help from a counselor. Probably the most creative and effective approach her family could take at this point would be to

a. allow Holly to make her own decision about seeing the counselor, even if they do not feel totally comfortable with it.

b. insist that Holly try to work out the problem with her family first, then rely on outside resources only as a last resort.

c. leave the decision up to her father or mother; she is too young and inexperienced for such responsibility.

d. ignore the problem entirely for now; taking Holly to a counselor or making too much of it will just escalate the whole situation.

9. Most social psychologists would probably agree that the importance of kinship networks in helping families cope with crisis is likely to

a. increase among blacks and blue collar families, but diminish among the white middle class.

b. increase somewhat throughout society, though the increase will likely be held in check by declining birth rates.

c. diminish throughout society as people come to rely more on the government to provide social services.

d. escalate markedly so that by the year 2000, few families will look outside the kinship network for emotional or social support.

10. It is probably *most realistic* to say that crisis

a. affects many unfortunate families, but is something most of us will never experience firsthand.

b. affects most families sooner or later—though by no means all.

c. touches everyone's life in some form, though the degree and frequency are highly variable.

d. is pretty much a way of life in modern American society; we are all in the midst of some crisis virtually all the time—though we may be unaware of it.

## What's Your Decision?

Joe is 12. He lives with his parents and two sisters, both older. Joe and his sisters are all honor students. His is a middle class family, with a moderately high income. They live in a house in the suburbs, where Joe has many friends and is widely involved in sports activities. Recently, Joe has begun drinking. It was kind of a joke at first, something to do after school with friends. He would have a beer, tell some jokes, play some basketball. Lately, he and a group of friends have started going to one friend's house or another's—wherever no adults are present—so that they can drink more freely. Sometimes getting the money for the liquor—or getting the liquor when no one has the money—can be a problem. But they manage. It's rare now for Joe to go past the lunch hour without sneaking at least one drink. It's dangerous keeping liquor in his locker at school, but it's worth the risk—most of the time, anyhow.

Lately, he's been getting a little worried, though. His grades are falling—not that much, but enough so that someone is likely to ask questions. He has headaches a lot, and it's hard to concentrate. Sometimes he feels guilty—though why should he? His parents both drink. It isn't such a big deal, is it? Then one day, the bottom falls out of everything. Joe's father finds a whiskey flask in Joe's backpack—and the whole story comes out. Most of it, anyway.

Amidst the shouting and general clamor, Joe makes it known that yes, he is willing to work on solving the problem, but he wants to do it his way. He wants to join a support group for alcoholic teenagers. His parents are appalled. "It's like you don't trust me," his father declares. "I think you ought to give your family a chance to work with you on this first. If we can't solve it together, fine. Then give your group a try. But let's not involve the whole world right off the bat if we don't need to. You should consider yourself lucky that I'm the one who found out about this and not some school official. This is not the sort of thing you need on your record. You ought to think about the advantages of keeping this private, keeping it right in the family. We care about you and we can work this out together."

Based on what you know of the situation, do you think Joe's father should encourage Joe to attend the support group, or insist on letting the family try to work with Joe in solving the problem? What are some of the most important factors for them to consider in making this decision? If Joe does attend the support group, what are some of the most significant ramifications of that decision?

❏ Should Joe be encouraged to attend the support group?

❏ What factors support that view?

❏ What factors support the opposite view?

❏ What will happen immediately if Joe and his family act as you suggest?

❏ What will their situation probably be five years from now if they act as you suggest?

❏ Are there research studies cited in the text that offer support for your position?

❑ If you needed additional research-based information to support your position, how or where would you go about getting it?

# Lesson 22

# Irreconcilable Differences

## Separation and Divorce

Divorce is a devastating experience, both for the couple whose marriage is failing and for their family. Divorce undermines self-esteem, provokes endless betrayals, and creates feelings of rejection and despair for almost everyone it touches. Yet in the last 25 years the divorce rate for Americans has nearly doubled; and though the increase has recently begun to level off, our divorce rate is still the highest in the world. Why are so many of us choosing divorce when it causes such pain for ourselves and those we care about?

Most Americans who divorce do so hoping to escape an unhappy marriage and replace it with a better one. They see divorce not as a permanent way of life but as an important step on the way to another, happier relationship. Fifty years ago, many people expected marriage to provide practical economic benefits and a stable environment for raising children. Today, however, many of us expect our marriages to be more personally fulfilling, to provide a relationship based on love and shared intimacy. When a relationship fails to meet our expectations, we're likely to consider divorce as a way to free ourselves to seek a new and more satisfying union.

## Who Gets Divorced and Why?

Although social changes—more women working outside the home, less emphasis on the family as a unit of economic survival—have altered the nature of marriage over the past few generations, it is our shifting attitudes that have contributed most to the rising divorce rate. Before the 1930s (and even for some time thereafter), being a divorcee carried a social and moral stigma. But today, even mainstream advice columnists like Ann Landers counsel us to leave a loveless marriage, and religions are less critical of divorce than they were in the past. In short, our society is coming to value the happiness of the individual over commitment to the family. Personal happiness is the highest goal in our marriages, and we appear determined to pursue that goal even if it means stumbling through a divorce to do it.

Chances are, your life or the lives of those close to you have been touched by divorce, and you have probably developed some ideas of your own about it. Does it appear to you that people are divorcing too quickly, that they are "taking the easy way out," that their expectations about marriage are too high? Is it realistic to view contemporary matrimony as only semi-permanent? Perhaps you have had to decide for yourself whether you would be happier after ending your marriage. You may have experienced firsthand the stress and expense that a divorce is likely to bring. Or you may have had to suffer through your parents' divorce, with the attendant feelings of fear, guilt, and betrayal.

As you go through this lesson, you might ask yourself under what circumstances you feel divorce offers an appropriate resolution to marital problems, and whether our changing social attitudes toward divorce are—from your own perspective—healthy or socially damaging. You might also ask whether any of your attitudes toward divorce have changed.

Some demographers predict that in the near future two-thirds of first marriages will end in divorce. But is it possible to predict, statistically, your own chances? Not with much accuracy, according to social scientists. They use several methods—from counting the number of divorces in a given year to comparing the number of divorces with the total number of women eligible for divorce—none of which provides an ideal measure. And the divorce rate, while higher than ever for all social groups, still varies among economic and racial groups, although differences among groups have narrowed in recent years.

Teenagers of all groups, however, have the highest divorce rate, undoubtedly because they tend to have lower earning power, less education, higher incidence of premarital pregnancy, and less emotional maturity. All these factors work to create stress within teenage marriages. In fact, the recent stabilization in overall divorce rates may be due in part to the fact that fewer people are marrying at a younger age today than a few years ago.

Waiting to marry, however, is no guarantee of marital stability. Indeed, there are no guarantees at all. Regardless of the economic or racial group to which we belong, changes in American culture have weakened the bonds that used to bind families together, making divorce far more likely for us than it ever was for our grandparents.

**Income, Employment, and Divorce**

Are the practical, economic benefits of marriage enough to keep couples from divorcing anymore? Not necessarily. Today, more women are working outside the home than in the past, and divorce rates have increased along with women's employment opportunities. Employed women do have higher divorce rates than nonemployed women. But research indicates that wives' employment makes no difference in marital quality. It may, however, give *unhappily* married women the economic independence and self-confidence to view divorce as a realistic out. And they're even more likely to take that course of action if their total family income is low. Up to a certain point, in fact, the *higher* a couple's income, the less likely they are to divorce.

At the same time, a very high income creates a certain sense of freedom for married partners. The fact that there will be enough money for both partners' needs after the divorce leaves partners free to focus on whether the marriage is worth saving for its own sake, without worrying over the economic benefits.

It is often the middle-income couple that is most affected by economic concerns. Few persons at this economic level can expect to live as comfortably after divorce as before. And today, with *no-fault divorce* laws—in which settlement awards are no longer tied to fault (or guilt)—divorced women often receive less income through property settlements and alimony awards than before. Nevertheless, in general, the economic benefits of marriage do not seem to prevent unhappy couples from divorcing.

**Marriage— A Practical or Emotional Convention?**

Today, there are also fewer social, legal, or moral reasons not to divorce. Divorce is not an issue in most political campaigns—nor are most of us likely to be aware of which candidates are divorced and which are not. Corporations are more willing to hire divorced executives than before; religious leaders rarely criticize parishioners for divorce; and many of us accept the belief that a marriage ought to be happy if it is to continue. In the past 50 years, we have shifted the emphasis in marriage from the practical to the emotional.

Consider a 30-year-old woman with two children—we'll call her Gina—who has elected to divorce her husband (Rob) after 10 years. A middle-income couple, Rob and Gina had an idyllic marriage for the first five years and were very compatible, but as Gina explains it, they just grew apart. She still loved her husband, but not in a romantic way anymore, and she felt unhappy. Unfortunately, her husband still loved her and didn't want a divorce. Gina decided, however, that life was too short to remain in an unhappy marriage where she had to hide her true feelings in order to avoid hurting her husband. It was the right decision for her, she feels, but it has caused a great deal of pain for others—including her husband, parents, and children. Some years ago, very few people would likely have seen much cause for Gina to divorce her husband. And some of us may still feel that way. Others of us, though, are likely to agree that her unhappiness within the marriage was cause enough. But what went wrong, really?

For one thing, Gina expected a happy, emotionally supportive relationship with her husband, one in which the romantic love that first brought them together would remain strong. But romance is difficult to maintain, partly because the rules that used to govern the roles of husbands and wives are not as clear as they once were. The result is often an endless round of negotiation over who is to do what, especially with more wives working outside the home. Perhaps the single life began to look restful by comparison to Gina. So when she realized that her feelings had changed, she was ready to consider divorce as an alternative—despite the guilt and pain that divorce was to cause for herself and others.

## Attitudes About the Permanence of Marriage

Like Gina, many of us consider marriage a permanent relationship only so long as intimate, romantic love remains alive and well. Some couples even strike the phrase "until death do us part" from their wedding ceremonies. This mutation of the concept of permanence may become a self-fulfilling prophecy. When couples behave as if their marriage is likely to end, chances are that it will.

Let's return to our hypothetical couple (Rob and Gina) for a moment. Before she told her husband of her desire to separate, Gina had to weigh the attractions of divorce against the practical and emotional benefits of remaining in her marriage. Most unhappily married couples who eventually divorce express the same sort of dissatisfaction with the emotional quality of their relationships that Gina felt. In choosing divorce, Gina decided that she would be happier if she were no longer married to Rob.

But that doesn't necessarily mean that she will choose to remain single after her divorce. Most people considering divorce, in fact, weigh their chances of future happiness in another marriage against the benefits of staying in their current relationship. Compared to unhappily married people, divorced individuals have better physical and emotional health and higher morale. Yet when compared to all married people in general, divorced individuals have poorer health, are more often depressed, and are more inclined to suicide.

The big question facing anyone contemplating divorce is this: Will I be happier if I divorce? It's not a simple question to answer. First, an individual must decide whether her current unhappiness is really the result of the marriage or the product of an individual problem. Counselors often advise couples to try improving their relationship or to work out their individual problems before resorting to divorce. They point out that marriages which end in divorce do not actually differ very much from other marriages. In other words, the real difference between good and bad marriages often lies in the attitudes of the persons within those marriages. How committed are they to staying together? Do they look upon adversity as a curse? Or as a problem to be mutually resolved?

Often the answers to such questions are not clear, and in attempting to weigh their alternatives, couples often go through an agonizing process of indecision. They still feel an attachment to their partners, and yet a sense of urgency compels them to "do it now." Counselors often suggest, therefore, a period of "structured separation," during which a couple lives apart, continues counseling, and avoids forming new attachments. After such a trial separation, couples may be better able to determine whether they can feel comfortable over an extended period of time with the decision to divorce. Nevertheless, some—like Gina's husband Rob—may never feel comfortable with the decision, particularly when, as in Rob's case, the decision seems to have been made by someone else.

## Getting Divorced

When they consider divorcing, few partners recognize the difference between *emotional divorce* and *legal divorce*. In emotional divorce, one or both partners withhold their love and affection from the relationship, and behave in ways that undermine the spouse's self-esteem and cause alienation. When a husband wants comfort after a disappointing letdown at work, for example, the wife may respond by blaming him for his own problems: "If you were more committed to the job, you'd probably have gotten the promotion." As a result, he's likely to feel misunderstood and rejected. To minimize the emotional destructiveness that often accompanies emotional divorce, counselors have begun to offer "divorce counseling," in which partners try to negotiate their conflicts and grievances so that the feelings of hostility and lack of cooperation that are usually produced by the legal divorce are less painful.

Legal divorce, which dissolves the marriage by court order, compounds the pain of a marriage breakup. Divorce is an emotional experience, and like a death in the family. It creates the need to grieve for what has been lost. But our rational, unceremonious system of divorce seldom provides an orderly or socially-approved mechanism for discharging the emotional aspects of divorce.

The attorneys who represent us in these proceedings have been trained to deal with divorce in a detached, businesslike manner. They do not usually have the time or inclination (or training, for that matter) to listen to our anger, anxiety, and self-doubts. Trained in the adversary system, their goal is to get the most for their clients, not to balance the interests of both parties and strive for an outcome that promises *mutual* benefit. In divorce court, attorneys suddenly become the principal actors in what had been our very personal drama. We are left on the outside, spectators at the dissolution of our own life as we knew it.

Doesn't seem like much of an alternative, does it? Yet, other than a permanent separation, in which couples live apart while still legally married, divorcing couples used to have little choice. Since the 1970s, however, the legal divorce process has been undergoing some changes. As a means of allowing couples to work out a settlement best suited to their mutual needs, lawyers and therapists now offer "divorce mediation" services as an alternative to the adversary system.

## The No-Fault Divorce

Perhaps the most significant change in the process of legal divorce, though, has been the advent of "no-fault divorce." Under this system, the partner seeking divorce no longer has to prove that grounds for divorce exist, that one partner is guilty and the other innocent. Their union is legally dissolved because the relationship is "irretrievably broken." In theory, this no-win/no-lose settlement offers real advantages. Couples are no longer required to destroy each other in order to regain their freedom. But in practice, some partners still feel a need to vindicate themselves while publicly denouncing the other. Given no other battlefield, they may challenge the partner in a child custody suit. Just because society is willing to forego fault finding is no sign that divorcing partners will share this attitude.

Another result of the no-fault system—which demonstrates how it sometimes works better in theory than in practice—is its impact on the *economic divorce.* What happens to the house, cars, savings accounts, debts, and other shared obligations of a husband and wife after their divorce? If a husband has been the primary breadwinner throughout most of the marriage, should he receive the bulk of their assets in a divorce settlement? Or, if the wife gains custody of the children, should the bulk of the assets go to her because her need is greater?

To determine how to break up a couple into distinct economic units, two contradictory legal assumptions come into play. First, there's the assumption that a family is an interdependent economic unit. Gina's husband, for instance, could not have made the money he earned without the moral support and domestic assistance of his wife. Second, there's the assumption that a wife's work in the home is "nonproductive" (which is to say, non-income-producing), and hence she does not contribute to their acquisition of property.

In the few states that have "community property laws," the first assumption prevails, and all property is considered jointly owned by husband and wife. In all other states, however, the wife gets *some,* but not always an equal share, of the family property.

Should a wife receive one-half of the couple's property and assets? Would this be fair even if her future earning power is considerably less than her husband's? How should child support payments be figured into the settlement? In the case of Rob and Gina, should the fact that she (not her husband) wanted the divorce carry any weight?

One of the consequences of no-fault divorce is that the economic status of divorced husbands often improves—one report puts the increase at 42 percent—while the standard of living for ex-wives with minor children declines by 73 percent. While other studies dispute the precision of these figures, they agree that children in single-parent families suffer an economic disadvantage in comparison to children in two-parent families. This can be partly explained by the fact that divorced women with children are often forced into the job market without the training or skills to succeed. But our changing attitudes about alimony—now generally called "maintenance" or "spousal support"—especially under the no-fault law, also contribute to this startling difference.

People used to believe that ex-wives lived comfortably on large alimony awards, but the truth is that courts only awarded alimony in about 15 percent of all cases. And with no-fault divorce, alimony in marriages lasting less than five years has been virtually eliminated. Further, like child support payments—in which the average award is less than half of what it costs to maintain a child at poverty level—less than half of alimony awards are paid regularly. Responding to this problem, state and federal governments have passed legislation to facilitate collection of child support payments.

Despite the fact that their children are probably grown, economic divorce is particularly difficult for older divorced women who were full-time homemakers and who now have few marketable skills. Despite *rehabilitative alimony* awards, which specify payment from the ex-husband while a wife goes to school or receives training, divorced women are unlikely to ever support themselves in a lifestyle comparable to what they knew in marriage, nor are many of them likely to remarry. For these and other reasons, some persons believe that these displaced homemakers should receive "entitlement" awards which compensate them for their contribution to a husband's career—a contribution some wives make in lieu of developing personal skills that would make them employable.

The experience of divorce is almost always more painful than people expect. Ironically, they often choose to undergo this process because they are unhappy in their present relationship and hope to find fulfillment in a subsequent marriage. Sometimes, anything looks better than the reality with which we're currently coping day to day.

Yet the consequences of divorce, for women especially, are financially as well as emotionally devastating. True, society has changed, freeing more people to divorce than in the past. Most of the social stigma has been erased, and with it, much of the personal guilt that once accompanied divorce. The no-fault divorce also acknowledges that even when no one is to blame, some marriages simply do not work out. And our society is willing to say that's reason enough to end a marriage. We don't necessarily have to think of family first, last, and always. We're allowed to pursue personal happiness—but at what price? Often, ironically, we find ourselves seeking personal happiness at the cost of short-term emotional turmoil and long-term economic deprivation.

Legal reforms are making divorce a more fair proposition—though many would argue that much remains to be done. Yet, nothing seems capable of repairing the emotional damage that divorce creates. Like marriage itself, divorce often seems to promise more happiness than it actually delivers.

## Learning Objectives

On completing your study of this lesson, you should be able to

❑ Describe trends in the divorce rates in the United States.

❑ Explain the reasons for the high divorce rate among teenagers.

❑ List the social changes that have contributed to the rising divorce rate.

❑ Discuss the relationship between divorce and income.

❑ Explain why marriage is often viewed as not necessarily permanent, and explain why that has sometimes become a self-fulfilling prophecy.

❑ Describe some of the advantages and disadvantages of divorce that unhappily married couples usually consider.

❑ Explain what happens to a couple during the emotional divorce.

❑ Define no-fault divorce.

❑ Discuss the two contradictory legal assumptions behind the idea of fair divorce property settlements and their effect on ex-wives.

❑ List some unanticipated consequences of no-fault divorce.

## Key Terms

Adversary system
Alimony
Child support
Community property laws
Displaced homemaker
Divorce counseling
Divorce mediation
Economic divorce

Economic interdependence
Emotional divorce
Entitlement
Legal divorce
No-fault divorce
Refined divorce rate
Rehabilitative alimony
Separation

305

## Assignments

❑ Before viewing the program, be sure you've read through the preceding overview and familiarized yourself with the learning objectives and key terms for this lesson. Then read Chapter 14, "Divorce," of *Marriages and Families* by Lamanna and Riedmann, with particular emphasis on pages 450–468.

❑ After completing these tasks, read the video viewing questions and watch the video for Lesson 22, "Irreconcilable Differences."

❑ After viewing the program, take time to answer the video viewing questions and evaluate your learning with the self-test. You'll find the correct answers, along with text page references, at the back of this telecourse guide.

❑ Read the "What's Your Decision?" scenario at the end of this lesson and answer the questions about the decision you would make based on what you've learned from this lesson. Give these questions some serious thought; they may be used as the basis for class discussion or the development of a more complex essay.

## Video Viewing Questions

1. The divorce rate has skyrocketed in recent years, and now only one out of two marriages will last. Explain some of the reasons for this increase in the divorce rate, including socioeconomic and attitudinal factors. Refer to the comments of Daphne Rose Kingma, Constance Ahrons, and Richard Varnes.

2. The breakdown in communication between couples represents a significant problem in the vast majority of failed marriages. What begins to occur when a couple fails to communicate? What does Paul Bohannan say about communication, conflict, and divorce? What suggestions do Daphne Rose Kingma and David Viscott have for keeping the lines of communication open and resolving conflicts?

3. Divorce is emotionally traumatic for everyone involved. Do you agree with Carlfred Broderick's assertion that men and women are affected differently by divorce, but with equal severity? If so, how do the sexes differ? Draw your conclusions from the statements of Lily, Sam, Alma, Alan, Renee, Jackie, and Tom.

4. Why is it important not to view divorce as a single incident, but as a slowly evolving process, as described by Richard Varnes?

5. Children are often upset and alienated by divorce. How do custody battles further alienate children from parents? What does the trend toward joint custody suggest about changing attitudes in both custody proceedings and parenting? What is it hoped joint custody will change or do about the treatment of children within the judicial system and between estranged parents? What problems can arise from joint custody? Consider the lengthy testimony of parents, experts, and members of the judicial system in your response.

6. What purpose does mediation serve? Is it a feasible alternative to the judicial system? Does it seem to be a sound plan to refocus the attention to the interests of the children? What other alternatives exist? Justify your answer.

## Self-Test

1. The current divorce rate in the United States is

   a. among the highest in the world.
   b. less than in many developed nations, but certainly not the lowest.
   c. about comparable to that of most other countries.
   d. lower than that of most other countries—for the first time in several decades.

2. Which of the following *best* expresses the relationship between the divorce rate and the increase in the number of single-parent families?

   a. Contrary to what one might logically expect, these two factors are really unrelated.
   b. Divorce is partially responsible for the increase in singleparent families, but lags far behind such factors as death of a spouse or illegitimate birth.
   c. Divorce is a major contributing factor to the existence of single-parent households in upper socioeconomic groups, but is a minor factor in lower socioeconomic groups.
   d. Overall, divorce is the major contributing factor to the growth in single-parent families among all socio-economic groups.

3. The text predicts that in the future, _____ of all marriages will end in divorce.

   a. less than one in ten
   b. about half
   c. two-thirds
   d. 75 percent

4. Eleanor married her high school sweetheart, Joe. After about seven years of marriage, they divorced. Two years later, Eleanor married her boss, Jim. Jim had been married to his first wife, Val, for about ten years prior to their divorce. Statistically, based on what we know of their situation, which of the following future scenarios is probably *most likely*?

   a. If they divorce, they will do so within three years, and both will go on to marry a third time.
   b. They will be divorced within a few months.
   c. They will remain married for a period of seven to ten years, but will eventually divorce.
   d. If they divorce, it will be within five years.

5. According to research studies, which of the following couples would probably be *least likely* to wind up divorced?

   a. An extremely wealthy couple—both partners have independent sources of income and neither has to work.
   b. A moderately well-off couple—both are professionals and work, but they could live on one income if they had to.
   c. A low-income couple—neither is a college graduate, and money is a problem.
   d. These couples are equally likely to divorce eventually; there is little relationship between income and divorce rates.

6. According to statistics, divorce rates have risen somewhat as a result of growing employment opportunities for women. Probably the *most likely* explanation for this is that

   a. many women lack the energy to deal with a marriage and a career at the same time—ultimately, they're forced to make a choice.

b. educated women tend to prefer a life of independence to the relatively more demanding role of homemaker, wife, and mother.

c. employment opportunities provide women who are in an unhappy marriage to begin with some means of escape.

d. many men dislike the idea of having their wives work, and the resulting stress within the marriage leads to divorce.

7. Which of the following *best* characterizes the current prevailing attitude toward divorce in our society?

a. Surprisingly, it's still generally considered immoral.

b. Though not necessarily viewed as downright immoral, it's definitely frowned upon, and still carries a certain social stigma.

c. Thanks to the influence of no-fault divorce laws, divorce is now viewed in a very positive light, as an important stage in personal growth.

d. While still widely viewed as unfortunate, divorce is generally accepted and no longer carries any social stigma.

8. Which of the following *best* explains how marriages that end in divorce tend to differ from other marriages? Marriages that end in divorce

a. tend to be inherently more violent.

b. almost always involve partners that are ill-matched in terms of age, race, religion, or other important factors.

c. usually reveal a history of economic hardship or quarrels over financial matters.

d. none of the above; surprisingly, marriages that end in divorce aren't very different from other marriages.

9. Fay and Elroy have been married for 15 years. Fay can't quite put her finger on the problem; she just feels she'd be better off outside the relationship. "Elroy isn't a bad husband," she confesses. "He's thoughtful, makes a good living, and he's good company—a good father, too. I'm just bored, smothered. I want to explore my own talents a little, and right now an independent life with my own

place doesn't sound all that bad." According to research, if Fay divorces Elroy, she is *likely* to feel

  a. some real stress and depression—even if she continues to feel it was the right decision.

  b. a general sense of relief, but no real emotional highs or lows.

  c. a continued sense of restlessness and boredom, not very different from what she feels now.

  d. real joy and happiness—perhaps for the first time in her life.

10. Ben and Morris are talking over lunch one day about their friends who have gone through divorce. "You know how it is," Ben remarks. "These guys support a wife for years—kids, too—and then they go to court and get wiped out financially with alimony payments. The wife ends up living in luxury, while some poor guy kills himself to support her." Ben's comments in this scenario are

  a. slightly biased in tone, but statistically quite accurate since most divorced wives receive a generous alimony.

  b. quite true for wives in upper socioeconomic brackets, but much less true for those in other income groups.

  c. often accurate since the no-fault divorce laws came into existence, though prior to the 1980s they would have been a gross exaggeration.

  d. a real exaggeration even now since alimony payments tend to be very small and are actually awarded in fewer than one out of five divorce cases.

## What's Your Decision?

Art and Sylvia are in their early forties, have three adolescent children, have been married for 20 years, and recently separated. Art is an accountant with a private practice and makes over $80,000 a year, while Sylvia has never worked outside the home. Her primary responsibility has been for caring for the children and Art, and entertaining Art's business associates and clients at home at least once a week. Sylvia began taking classes in photography when her youngest child started junior high school, and her instructors told her that she has a lot of talent. She began meeting many people through her classes and at the art gallery where she volunteered her time twice a week. She is trying to make a career as a freelance photographer.

Art was not supportive, however, and wanted her to continue to be available to entertain his guests, keep house, spend time with the kids, and devote herself to him. He didn't take Sylvia's photography seriously, and he felt jealous of and threatened by her new friends. After fighting about her new direction for over a year, they decided to separate.

Art moved out of the house leaving Sylvia with the children. Despite the fact that her new career shows great promise, and even though Art spent little time at home before they separated, Sylvia is devastated. She feels abandoned, and overwhelmed by the prospect of facing the financial and emotional burden of being alone with three children. She is surprised by how much she misses Art and is hurt by the hostility that has developed between them. She had envisioned a "civilized" separation—a real opportunity to come to grips with the situation and evaluate their feelings toward each other and the marriage without the constant arguing. But their mutual anger is making it impossible to be civil to each other and seems to be pushing them into a divorce that Sylvia is beginning to think may be a mistake. If she really doesn't love Art any more, why does she feel so lost without him? The situation seems to have taken on a life of its own, propelling them ever closer to a conclusion she is not at all sure is the right one for her, for Art, or for the children. All she really wanted was the opportunity to pursue her own interests.

Based on what you know of their relationship, do you think Art and Sylvia should proceed on to divorce? Whether or not they divorce, how will they cope with their anger toward each other and the effect it is having on the children? What are some of the important factors they should consider in making this decision? If they do choose to divorce, what are some of the important ramifications of that decision?

❏ How should Art and Sylvia proceed, given Sylvia's ambivalence about divorce and the anger that is interfering with making an objective decision?

❏ What factors support that view?

❏ What factors support the opposite view?

❏ What will happen immediately if they act as you suggest?

❏ What will their situation probably be in five years if they act as you suggest?

❑ Are there research studies cited in the text that offer support for your position?

❑ If you needed additional research-based information to support your position, how or where would you go about getting it?

# Lesson 23

# Single, Head of Household

## The Single-Parent Family

What's your image of the typical American family? Mom, Dad, Buddy, and Sis together in the family car on a summer vacation? Twenty-five years ago, before the divorce rate for Americans nearly doubled, that picture might have been accurate. Today, however, over one-quarter of all family groups in this country are headed by one parent, and over one-half of those are women. Today, Mom and Sis may be spending the summer at home while Buddy visits Dad in another city. This change in the American family has happened rapidly; between 1970 and 1987, the number of children living with one parent more than doubled. This increase in single-parent families is in part a result of rising unwed birth rates, but the major cause is divorce.

**Family Consequences of Divorce**

What are the consequences of divorce for the family? While children of two unhappily married parents are likely to suffer stress and lower self-esteem, they will suffer both financially and emotionally if their parents break up. Single-parent families that result from divorce may offer some advantages to children—the chance for real responsibility and increased closeness to the parent they live with. But it also creates distance between children and the absent parent, and makes it difficult for the single parent to form new romantic attachments or remarry.

Divorcing parents face a host of difficult personal problems, ranging from the stress of custody disputes to the psychological healing they must achieve before they are ready for

313

remarriage. Although both spouses suffer from divorce—and can be considered equal victims of the experience—divorce affects men and women differently, particularly given that women usually retain custody of the children. While the courts and some psychologists favor sole custody—and in the majority of cases custody still goes to the mother—joint custody may offer more advantages to both parents and children. Whatever the arrangement, however, a high divorce rate and single-parent families result in a host of problems.

If you grew up in the last 20 years, chances are good that you or your friends were part of a single-parent family. If you were in that category, you may have felt depressed, confused, or even guilty about your parents' divorce. You may have suffered a lower standard of living because of it, or you may worry that you won't be able to achieve a stable marriage yourself.

If you're presently divorced and heading a family alone, you may find yourself resenting your ex's social and financial freedom and wondering how your desire to date again might affect your children. If you're a divorced woman, you may be having a hard time making ends meet. If you're a divorced man whose ex-wife has custody of your children, you may feel lonely and fearful—fearful that your children are slipping away or that your ex-wife is turning them against you.

All of us have either observed or directly experienced the effects of divorce and the single-parent families that resulted from the dissolution. As you go through this lesson, you might ask yourself, "What are the most important disadvantages to single-parent families? What advantages, if any, are there? How should custody be decided? Why does divorce affect husbands and wives so differently, both economically and emotionally? Can anything be done to help people adapt to these painful changes in family structure?"

## The Effects of Divorce on Children

What do we know about the effects of divorce on children? If your parents divorced, you may remember it as a devastating process that still affects your ability to make romantic commitments. On the other hand, you may have had few problems.

Most social scientists now agree that living in an intact family where there is unresolved tension and conflict between parents causes greater emotional stress on children than living in a supportive single-parent family. And there is no evidence that divorce *necessarily* makes children unhappy.

But there's no denying that divorce is psychologically stressful for children, who often feel depressed, guilty, and scared.

Living in single-parent families, most researchers contend, has its disadvantages. For example, studies have shown that girls raised without a father present may begin premarital sex earlier and have difficulty relating to men. Another study revealed that 37 percent of the children of divorced parents were moderately or severely depressed even five years after the divorce. Many fantasize about their parents reuniting—and some even take steps (including undermining new relationships) to bring it about.

Children of divorced parents suffer a certain loss of identity as members of an intact family, as well as losing daily contact with one parent. Depending on the community, they may also suffer the social stigma of being from a broken home, although as divorce becomes more common that stigma is eroding rapidly. Further, watching one or both parents simply walk away from a relationship—perhaps for the second time in a child's life—may leave children with the fear that nobody can be trusted or that they weren't worth their parents' love. This may make them hesitant to marry or fearful they will be rejected by the opposite sex. "How can you expect commitment," asks one young woman whose parents divorced, "when anyone can change his mind?" All the evidence, however, makes one conclusion clear: children are *most* likely to adjust positively when their parents cooperate during and after divorce and the children maintain ties with the noncustodial parent.

Are there any advantages for children in single-parent families? For adolescents, it may be an opportunity to share real decision-making power—not just what to have for dinner but where to live and how to allocate resources in the family budget. A single parent is more likely to discuss a wide range of issues with children. On the other hand, the closeness in a single-parent family can also have its painful side, especially when children leave home or the parent decides to remarry. Following the emotional trauma of divorce, letting go becomes just that much more difficult, for both sides.

But the primary disadvantage to children in many single-parent families is financial. Divorce is an expensive process, and the cost of maintaining two households often creates a lower standard of living for everyone. Divorced women with sole custody often find it difficult to provide their children with the clothes, toys, or outings they were accustomed to while their parents were married. And since divorce settlements usually include no provision for paying for college, children from single-parent families may find that they cannot afford the kind of higher education they had hoped for.

One of the major consequences of our high divorce rate has been increasing attention to the question of *custody*—which parent will assume the primary responsibility for the children's upbringing? For most divorcing couples with children, custody is worked out as an extension of the basic exchange that existed during the marriage: divorced fathers take legal responsibility for financial support while divorced mothers continue the physical, day-to-day care of the children. Social scientists call this a "coparental divorce".

For many parents, determining custody is a complicated and emotional issue. Some mothers voluntarily give up custody for financial reasons; some fathers are fighting to retain custody. According to one study, two-thirds of fathers who request sole custody receive it. Even in cases where mothers fight the request, fathers are awarded custody about one-third of the time.

## A Divorce Scenario

Let's consider the case of a recently divorced couple—Marsha, a 36-year-old mother of two children, ages 11 and 8, who hasn't worked since her marriage; and her husband, Ed, a 39-year-old office manager making $42,000 a year. Like 90 percent of divorcing couples, they have agreed that Marsha will have sole custody of the children. Ed is paying $600 a month in child support, which only covers Marsha's house payment. Marsha earns about $16,500 a year working five days a week in a clerical position and two or three nights a week as well as weekends at a shopping center drugstore. Marsha is having a hard time making ends meet on her limited income, especially since she must spend so much on baby sitters.

At first, Ed takes the kids every weekend, spending more time with them than he spent when the family was together. In the hours they are together, Ed tends to indulge their every whim in order to make the visits as happy as possible—a propensity known as the *Disneyland Dad* syndrome. This situation creates enormous stress because it allows Ed to be a pal, someone who sees the kids only during the good times, and who rarely has to say no. Meanwhile, the overworked, cash-short mother becomes a sort of combination martyr and killjoy, left out, unable (and perhaps unwilling) to indulge the children with gifts and permissiveness.

It is understandable when Marsha, who truly doesn't have much time to spend with her kids, begins to resent Ed's higher income, free time, and lack of responsibility. She begins to make negative remarks about the children's "playboy father" when they return on Sunday afternoons. Some weekends she goes so far as to cancel trips that Ed has planned with the kids, and as the months pass, he takes them less and less often.

Ed feels that he is losing influence over his son, and in addition to the loneliness he suffers all week, he is depressed and angry about his ex-wife's interference with his plans for the weekends. As a result, his visits begin to taper off. It was Ed who wanted the divorce, and therefore, Marsha believes, he deserves to suffer a little, too. It's certainly not much, she reasons, compared to what she has to handle every day.

Notice that it isn't only Marsha and Ed who endure the brunt of their mutual ill will. Fighting through their children is likely to have negative consequences on the children's adjustment to the divorce, just as the lack of a continuing close relationship with the absent father will take its toll. The lack of cooperation between Marsha and Ed makes the whole situation more painful for everyone.

Ed's way of coping is to ease himself out of the picture. But not all fathers in Ed's position would respond so passively. In more extreme cases, lack of cooperation and understanding can lead to *child snatching*—kidnapping one's children from the other parent. Child snatching is not legally considered kidnapping, however, but a misdemeanor called *custodial interference,* although the recently passed federal *uniform child custody acts* has caused states to do more to extradite offenders.

Is there any antidote to the destructive feelings that eat away at divorcing couples? Well, counseling often provides some answers. It won't necessarily eliminate the reason for divorce, nor will it do away with the pain of divorce, but regular counseling can help married couples work through the conflicts they still have after divorce, rather than fighting those battles through their children.

In addition to their interpersonal difficulties, divorcing couples go through something called the *community divorce*. It's the sudden realization that one is now out of place among former friends and colleagues—many of whom are likely to be married. Being the only divorced person at the party is a

**Consequences of Divorce**

notoriously uncomfortable feeling. Friends do not know how to act (sympathy? good humor? direct confrontation?), and the divorced person isn't quite sure what role to play either.

This separation from one's former social circle—which may comprise people one has known for years—can be almost as painful as separation from one's spouse. The old familiar landmarks are gone, the familiar ways of relating to others are gone. And one is left feeling adrift, in limbo.

Remember Marsha? Perhaps she finds the community divorce not so very difficult at first. She may be too busy with her two jobs, or rather disinterested in continuing relationships with friends whom she views as "mostly Ed's anyway." She may prefer to seek the company of new single friends, women who have also been divorced and who share her feelings. But after a while, she is also likely to become interested in meeting available men. For most divorced persons, building a new community involves dating and the possibility of a new romantic attachment. It sounds exciting, perhaps, but it isn't always easy—especially for a person who is dating again for the first time in years.

One study shows that separated persons who date have fewer adjustment problems with their new status than those who do not. But inevitably, there are some hurdles to overcome. Children may resent a dating partner, and their resentment can make both the parent and the date very uncomfortable. Then too, a person fresh from the pain of divorce may be wary of another commitment. Lack of confidence can make a relationship difficult to establish as well. The majority of divorced individuals, however, do seek a postmarital sexual relationship—often within a year. Yet, they're not likely to feel ready for anything more permanent until they have passed through the stage social psychologists term the *psychic divorce*.

Immediately following a divorce, an ex-spouse (especially if he or she did not initiate the divorce) may feel shock and an inability to accept the situation. Some people become extremely depressed, more prone to accidents, even physically ill. Some attempt suicide. Psychologists call this experience the *mourning process* stage of the psychic divorce. During this process, divorced persons gradually regain their freedom through emotional separation from the personality and influence of the former spouse. It isn't a freedom easily won, and not all divorced persons successfully complete the process.

In the final stage of the psychic divorce, both ex-mates take responsibility for their part in the demise of the relationship, forgive themselves and the partner, and proceed with their lives. This stage is easier if one isn't burdened with too many outside pressures—e.g., a new job, too little income, having to relocate, insufficient time for oneself. But the biggest obstacle of all is often the nagging feeling that one is the victim in a divorce.

Who really *is* the victim? The partner who didn't want the divorce in the first place? The non-custodial parent who feels he or she is losing touch with the children? Or the children themselves? Psychologists argue that *both* husband and wife are victims—both suffer loss of self-esteem, feel they have failed as spouses and parents, and worry that they won't be able to make a successful remarriage. Yet husbands and wives suffer the consequences of divorce very differently.

Divorced mothers with sole custody of their children often undergo severe overload as they try to provide for their own financial support as well as daily care of their children. Child care is expensive, and it can take an intolerable bite out of a paycheck. In addition, it may be difficult for a woman to secure the kind of employment that makes child care affordable. A woman who hasn't worked or who hasn't worked for a long while may have relatively few saleable skills.

Further, women often face discrimination in hiring and promoting practices. These problems are compounded when the everyday problems of raising children require energy that a woman would like to devote to herself or to meeting new people. It may well appear to her that the man has the best of the situation—more money, fewer responsibilities, fewer heartaches, and greater opportunities on the horizon.

From the man's perspective, however, things are not likely to look so rosy. More opportunities? Fewer heartaches and responsibilities? Get serious. Family counselors point out that in reality, men take divorce much harder than ex-wives usually think. Even when a man initiates the divorce, he may realize later just how much his wife and family meant to him. And at that point—ironically, some would say—his loneliness is aggravated by having no one with whom to share his pain. The carefree single life may turn into a monotonous routine of evenings in the same old restaurants and theaters or nights plunked in front of a monotonous television that drones on in an empty house or apartment.

The divorced father may find himself with many of the financial obligations of fatherhood, and few of its joys. Shut off from his children and the family closeness of the past, recreational opportunities inhibited by financial obligations, he may feel he has limited control over his life and that divorce has brought little real benefit save to escape the immediate stress of a difficult relationship.

**Custody Arrangements**

Sometimes, the problems of divorced parents and their children can be ameliorated by a *joint custody* arrangement, in which both parents continue to take equal responsibility for important decisions affecting their children's upbringing. This is most likely to work in cases where there are only one or two children, the parents live near each other, and they are committed to working out the details of child rearing together. Ideally, both parents should be equally employable as well, since most joint custody arrangements involve a fairly equal sharing of financial responsibility for the children, and assume that both spouses will support themselves. Remember Ed and Marsha from our earlier scenario? They would have found such an arrangement difficult at best because Marsha's limited earning power would make it impossible for her to maintain a home without Ed's child support payments—which are often not awarded when custody is shared.

Another reason that sole custody tends to be favored over joint custody is that ex-spouses who had trouble making joint decisions while they were married are not likely to become skilled joint decision makers after divorce. In our highly mobile society, moreover, joint custody might well require children to split their lives between distant schools and communities. Often, children have enough difficulty adjusting to divorce without having to cope with new surroundings, friends, and teachers every few months. A workable alternative for many couples is shared *legal custody* (giving both the right to participate in important decisions and a symbolically important authority), while one parent has *physical custody* (primary residential care of the children).

Clearly, joint custody has some drawbacks. But when conditions are right, it offers several advantages. It gives children the chance for a more normal relationship with each parent, who can then feel that he or she can have some hand in shaping the children's values and goals. Neither feels as overloaded with responsibility or loses the freedom to form new relationships. Fathers especially seem more comfortable with joint custody arrangements because their involvement is increased. Even without official joint custody, though, ex-spouses can improve their relationships with their children by arranging visits from the noncustodial parent and otherwise taking steps to ensure that the noncustodial parent and the children do not drift physically or emotionally apart.

Joint custody . . . physical custody . . . just two attempts to restructure relationships that no longer seem capable of functioning within the context of family and marriage. There have been few studies of the long-term effects of such arrangements, so we can only speculate. But it is clear that the single-parent families that have resulted from our high rate of divorce present serious problems for parents and children. Anything that can make the consequences of these changes in our social structure less painful should be welcomed. The trick is to find solutions that everyone can agree are fair to all concerned—ex-spouses *and* their children. Perhaps one day we'll have what social scientists can refer to as "victim-free" divorce.

On completing your study of this lesson, you should be able to

❑ Describe the consequences of divorce for children.

❑ Discuss the advantages and disadvantages of living in a single-parent family for children.

❑ Explain why mothers are more often awarded sole custody of their children than fathers.

❑ Describe ways ex-spouses fight through their children.

❑ Describe the three stages in the mourning process necessary for the psychic divorce to be complete.

❑ Discuss the major differences between the effects of a typical divorce for the husband and for the wife.

❑ Discuss the advantages and disadvantages of joint custody for both parents and children.

**Learning Objectives**

Child snatching
Community divorce
Coparental divorce
Custody
Disneyland Dad syndrome
Father absence
Joint custody
Legal custody
Martyred Mom

Maternal custody
Noncustodial parent
Physical custody
Postmarital sex
Psychic divorce
Sole custody
Uniform child custody acts
Visitation

**Key Terms**

## Assignments

❏ Before viewing the program, be sure you've read through the preceding overview and familiarized yourself with the learning objectives and key terms for this lesson. Then re-read pages 468–488 from Chapter 14, "Divorce," of *Marriages and Families* by Lamanna and Riedmann.

❏ After completing these tasks, read the video viewing questions and watch the video for Lesson 23, "Single, Head of Household."

❏ After viewing the program, take time to answer the video viewing questions and evaluate your learning with the self-test. You'll find the correct answers, along with text page references, at the back of this telecourse guide.

❏ Read the "What's Your Decision?" scenario at the end of this lesson and answer the questions about the decision you would make based on what you've learned from this lesson. Give these questions some serious thought; they may be used as the basis for class discussion or the development of a more complex essay.

## Video Viewing Questions

1. Single-parent households have increased dramatically in the last 20 years. One in every four households is now headed by a single parent; 90 percent of them women. Discuss the difficulties all single parents experience, and those faced primarily by women in this area. Refer to the remarks of Richard Varnes, Leonard Sneiderman, and Elaine Zimmerman in your response.

2. For single parents, building a career and raising children can become a huge burden. Discuss Elaine Zimmerman's comments regarding the lack of parental leave provided by employers and problems that occur when children are sick. What alternatives or governmental action would you recommend to help alleviate some of these pressures?

3. Describe the "lack of balance" single parents often experience, as depicted by the single parents who were interviewed. How do they try to regain some balance? Why is it so important?

4. It has been shown that two-thirds of all children of divorced families adjust in a positive way to their new fam-

ily environment. However, the initial adjustment is certainly a tough one. Consider the comments of Troy, Krysta, Bill, and Susan. How does their testimony relate to the statement above?

5. Do mothers necessarily make better parents than fathers? Note the comments of Lamont, Walter, Bill, and Ray. What has helped to change the view of parenting responsibilities and gender? Do you consider the change positive?

6. What do Susan, Bill, Judy, and Aaron think about single parents and dating? Why can even the idea of dating be frightening for a single parent? How does Ray maintain a social life without excluding Aaron? Do you think this is an appropriate approach? What negative consequences might it have?

7. Sixty percent of all children in this country will spend at least some time in a single-parent household. How do Kirby Alvy, Jackie, Ray, Nancy, and Bill make the best of this complicated situation? In what ways do they each utilize quality time?

## Self-Test

1. As a result of the divorce rate, a certain percentage of children now under 16 can expect to spend some portion of their childhood in a single-parent family. About what percentage of children are affected?
   a. Well over 90 percent.
   b. About 60 percent.
   c. Perhaps 25 percent—though the figures are slightly higher for black children.
   d. Fewer than 5 percent.

2. How is divorce *most likely* to affect children economically?
   a. It has little, if any, measurable effect on their economic status one way or the other.
   b. Most children find themselves slightly better off following divorce, thanks to alimony and child support.
   c. Most children are much better off economically following divorce—perhaps because both parents usually work following a divorce.
   d. The truth is, most children suffer some degree of economic deprivation as a direct result of divorce.

3. Which of the following is probably the most accurate generalization we might make about the emotional health of children affected by divorce?

   a. Emotional adjustment is never easy, but most children can adjust well if both parents are cooperative and supportive.
   b. Despite the best efforts of parents, divorce invariably has a negative influence on children's self-esteem and confidence.
   c. Most children of divorced parents carry a burden of suppressed anger that may eventually erupt in violence.
   d. Surprisingly, most children of divorced parents are better adjusted and happier following the divorce.

4. According to the text, how do separation and divorce affect children?

   a. The divorce experience is psychologically stressful for children
   b. Divorce is usually financially disadvantageous for children
   c. While many children adapt to their parents' divorce, they often express a great sense of loss
   d. All of the above are true concerning the affect of divorce on children

5. Rene and Mario have been married for about 10 years and have no serious problems, but both are currently having affairs with other persons, and both would like to dissolve the marriage. They feel bored, restless, ready to move on. "The only thing that keeps us together," Mario explains, "is the high cost of divorce. We just can't afford not to stay married—crazy, isn't it?" Mario's comment in this scenario is

   a. crazy indeed; it's marriage that's expensive, not divorce.
   b. understandable. Divorce has traditionally been expensive—but cost is no longer an issue, thanks to no-fault divorce.
   c. simply reflective of his personal economic level; most people in even the lower ranges of middle income brackets take the cost of divorce in stride.
   d. quite accurate; legal fees are high and so are the expenses incurred in the division of assets.

6. Dudley and Sara, now married four years, are both from broken homes. Both sets of parents have long since remarried. What impact, if any, is this situation likely to have on the probability that Dudley and Sara will also divorce?

   a. It will increase the odds that they'll divorce—particularly if the parents themselves approve of the divorce.

   b. It will make divorce for Sara and Dudley almost a certainty, regardless of how the parents now view divorce.

   c. Actually, it will decrease the probability that Sara and Dudley will divorce; they have witnessed the difficulties inherent in divorce firsthand.

   d. It will have little effect one way or the other.

7. For some time, our society has held the belief that a mother should almost always be awarded custody of the children from a marriage. To what extent is this belief borne out statistically?

   a. It is virtually always true; fathers almost never receive custody unless the mother is physically or psychologically incapable of caring for her children.

   b. It is generally true, but not always; in fact, growing numbers of fathers are being awarded custody—with or without the mother's consent.

   c. Role reversal has become so prominent in our society that about half of all divorcing fathers now receive custody.

8. While it was once a given that the mother would receive custody, that trend is now reversing itself, and custody is more likely to go to the fathDuane's parents have been divorced for about a year. Duane lives with his mother, who received custody largely because his father was not employed at the time of the divorce. Duane's father has weekly visitation rights, but rarely comes around more than once a month, and monthly visits seem to be growing farther apart all the time. It's as if they hardly know each other anymore. What effect, if any, is this likely to have on Duane?

   a. No measurable long-term effects; eventually, he will adjust to his new life, and will forget about the monthly visits.

b. It's likely to increase Duane's sense of loneliness and depression, but will not have any negative effect on his own emotional growth or adjustment.

c. Research suggests that Duane's dissolving closeness with his father could have some serious, long-term negative effects on Duane's self-esteem.

d. In fact, it's likely to have a positive effect in the long run, especially given that Duane's unemployed father may be a bad influence on a young child.

9. Darlene has been divorced for almost three years. For a long time following the divorce, she never left the house except to go to church or work. Now she socializes regularly, belongs to a yacht club, and takes a class in oil painting. "I hardly think of Dick," she tells a friend. "And when I do, I just try to wish him well, think about the good times we had and forget the rest. I guess I finally got all the meanness, depression, grief, and resentment out of my system." The feelings that Darlene describes in this scenario would best be labeled

a. community divorce.
b. coparental divorce.
c. autonomy.
d. psychic divorce.

10. During the period when a person is recovering from the emotional trauma of divorce, which of the following would a social psychologist be most likely to advise?

a. Be completely open about experiencing the pain and grief you feel; don't pretend you aren't hurt or angry.

b. If possible, bury yourself in work or hobbies that will take your mind off your miserable feelings and yourself.

c. Think about the possibility of rekindling the old relationship—maybe it isn't too late, after all.

d. Review the relationship prior to the divorce; try to determine who was responsible so you won't find yourself in a similar situation again.

## What's Your Decision?

Donna is an art director at an ad agency and her husband, Joel, is a reporter for a daily newspaper. They have been married six years and have two children under the age of five. They have never communicated very well, and they have grown apart because of their different jobs and lack of time together. While neither blames the other for the situation, they have come to realize that they would be happier apart and have decided to get a divorce.

Either one of them could support the children on a single paycheck, but Joel has never been happy with Donna's decision to continue working and place the kids in day-care five days a week. With the impending divorce, he fears that he will lose touch with them and have no control over their upbringing. Even though Joel has offered to assume custody of the children himself, Donna doesn't want to give them up. But she does worry about having enough time for the kids as well as her job if she has them alone. They have been discussing the option of joint custody, but Donna's friends have counseled her against it.

Based on what you know about Donna and Joel, do you think they should seek a joint custody arrangement? What are some of the most important factors for them to consider in making this decision? If they do arrange joint custody, what are some of the important ramifications of that decision?

❑ Should they arrange joint custody?

❑ What factors support that view?

❑ What factors support a sole custody arrangement with Donna taking the children?

❑ What will happen immediately if they act as you suggest?

❑ What will their situation probably be in five years if they act as you suggest?

❑ Are there research studies cited in the text that offer support for your position?

❑ If you needed additional research-based information to support your position, how or where would you go about getting it?

## Lesson 24

# The Second Time Around

## New Families; New Lives

Suppose your own marriage ended in divorce. And suppose further that the divorce involved considerable recrimination, legal squabbling, and expensive property and custody battles. Do you think you'd be inclined to give love a second try? Would you still believe in the existence of love at all?

On the surface, you might say no. But given time, even the traumas of separation generally fade, and most people—however cautiously at first—begin to consider new relationships. In retrospect, a former domestic life can look happier than it felt while we were living it. Many of us tend to tire of our own cooking or our own company after a time. Or we may simply want the emotional or financial security of having a partner.

**Divorce and Remarriage**

Whatever the reasons, statistics show that the overwhelming majority of divorced persons ultimately marry again, most within less than three years of the first union's breakup. Will they be happy? That, as you might guess, depends on a number of things. Those who are able to change pain into wisdom and proceed cautiously with their subsequent relationships naturally have a much greater chance of success than those who are unable to learn from—or even acknowledge—their mistakes. Past experience can be an advantage—or an obstacle—in building a successful remarriage. Attitude toward divorce itself makes some difference, too.

Think back to your own childhood. Chances are, someone in your family—perhaps even your parents—were divorced at some point. Maybe you felt let down, disappointed, even angry at one or both partners in the marriage. Almost certainly, your impressions about the persons involved changed in some way. Given the identical circumstances today, you might feel quite differently.

Let's suppose that you know a young couple, Stuart and Susan. Susan is a friend you've known since middle school—an attractive, successful woman with a gentle sense of humor and a quiet intelligence. Her husband, a graphic artist, can be the most charming and gregarious man you know. But he is given to profound mood swings, and during his down cycles—which are frequent—he is appallingly abusive, especially to Susan. Susan has tried on many occasions to get him to see a doctor or counselor, but Stuart adamantly refuses.

One day Susan comes to work with a cut lip and bruises. If, a few days later, she told you that she and Stuart were breaking up, how do you think you would feel? Would you be disappointed in Susan's lack of commitment? Not likely. You'd probably applaud her decision as eminently sensible—though not so many years ago, such a response would have been fairly rare.

Naturally, most divorces turn on subtler issues of incompatibility and dissatisfaction, and questions of right or wrong are seldom this cut-and-dried. What really matters is their effect on the persons involved. While it may be true that divorce no longer carries the social stigma it did only a few years ago, few divorcees escape the process without a significant alteration in their attitudes toward love and marriage. How do these shifting attitudes affect their future courtships, and what are some of the unique complications that arise during courtship for remarriage?

Whether they're hurt, angry, desperate, or relieved, it's fair to say that few divorced men and women totally write off marriage as an institution. They tend to blame their partners or themselves rather than marriage itself for the marital failure. In fact, paralleling the increase in the number of divorces in the last 30 years is a corresponding rise in the incidence of remarriage. Nearly half the marriages performed today are remarriages, a sign that the thirst for love and companionship remains.

Remarriage has always been fairly common in the United States. Until fairly recently, however, most remarriages came about as the result of widowhood. Immediately after World War II, the incidence of remarriage rose to an all-time peak as thousands of servicemen either returned home to find that they and their wives had become strangers, or failed to return home at all.

Both remarriage and divorce rates fell sharply during the 1950s, a decade of prosperity and stability unmatched in American history. Then, during the social upheaval of the 1960s—with its emphasis on personal freedom and self-awareness, the divorce and remarriage rates rose again. Have those effects faded with time, or are they more powerful than ever today?

It's probably safe to say that as part of the 1960s legacy, Americans as a group are less likely to remain in an uncomfortable marriage—a little more willing to view divorce as preferable to a lifetime of unhappiness. But that hardly means people have given up on marriage. Today, more people than ever before are in the market for new partners. Are they choosing more wisely the second time around? Or do other factors—such as the pressure to find a new mate while one is still young and attractive—impair judgment and spur impulsiveness?

## The Second Courtship

One thing is clear: we make our decisions a little differently the second time around. The final goal—lasting happiness—is the same. But the courtship process in which we weigh the pluses and minuses of a potential partner is filtered through experience and shaped by altered expectations.

Even the questions are different. Instead of "Do you want children?" we might to ask, "Do you have children who would resent me, but whom I would have to support?" Instead of "What do you like to do in your spare time?" we might wonder "Will your love for tennis drive me crazy?"

In courtship for remarriage, this assessment process might proceed at a slow, cautious pace, or it might move right along because two experienced adults, who've been through the motions before, know just what they want this time around. Either way, the relationship is likely to involve sexual intimacy a little sooner than in a first courtship. But both sexual activity and the basic process of assessment are complicated by the presence of children—whom one or both partners are likely to have.

Think back to your first serious relationship, the first time you dated someone and you began, however faintly, to consider the possibility of marriage. Perhaps you went to dinner, or a movie, or sat and talked uninterrupted for hours at a time. You went for long walks, to concerts, met for a weekend rendezvous. You got to know one another at your own pace, when you wanted, where you wanted. In courtship for remarriage, partners seldom enjoy the luxury of this leisurely, reflective pace.

If children from the first marriage are present, establishing intimacy—especially sexual intimacy—becomes a delicate and difficult matter. Awkward morning-after confrontations in the kitchen or accidental late-night interruptions can be embarrassing or even painful for everyone involved. If a custody battle is still in progress, the relationship can be further complicated by the need for discretion. Additionally, most children, especially those bruised by the traumas of divorce, resent anyone who intrudes on the already-strained family unit. Ex-spouses, especially those who have not yet begun dating themselves, may feel resentful if not downright hostile toward a dating partner.

With such complications, you might wonder how it is that so many of us survive a second courtship and make it all the way to remarriage. With financial and emotional security at stake, to say nothing of domestic harmony, companionship, the chance for real family life, and all the other things that make marriage so desirable, small wonder that most people risk some difficult moments to achieve future happiness. What's more, most are confident that—given their increased maturity, more realistic expectations, and a wiser choice of mates—their second marriage will be more successful than their first.

And that's the key question. Is it really possible to find happiness and fulfillment in a second marriage? The answer is yes. Many couples are able to find the companionship, love, and security they crave the second time around. In fact, 95 percent of the divorced and remarried men and women in one study said their second marriage was better than their first. Why do you think this might be? Well, divorced men and women tend to have more reasonable expectations about marriage the second time around. They have the advantage of maturity, and often, some increased insight regarding their own needs. And don't forget—they're comparing that second marriage to one that ended in pain and discord.

Still, the comparative happiness of remarriages is more than a little amazing given the array of factors working against it, such as complications involving children and former spouses. As a result, while statistically remarriages are as happy as first marriages, they tend to be less stable. While happiness in marriage may contribute somewhat to stability, it is no guarantee.

Part of the problem, experts say, is our unrealistic expectations about how happy we'll be once we find that special person. This kind of thinking can be a problem even for those who have had earlier illusions dispelled by on-the-job experience. Sometimes one dose of reality just isn't enough. We tend to feel that if we can just find someone sensitive, thoughtful, bright and caring, all the old problems will melt into the mist. Of course, it doesn't work out like that. Day-to-day problems follow us from the gloom of one marriage into the fog of the next.

Part of the trouble with remarriage is the fact that society has yet to develop any norms or models of what is expected from re-wedded spouses. We're essentially on our own, breaking new marital ground. One solution might be the negotiation of a remarriage contract that spells out precisely what each partner expects from the other.

What kinds of factors might be covered in a personal remarriage contract? Things like inheritance. Adoption. Housework. Financial and emotional support. In short, anything we might assume the other person would intuitively know about our own needs and desires—but often doesn't.

Some couples may be reluctant to construct a remarriage contract. If the pain of divorce is still fresh, the last thing new partners may want to do is reopen old wounds by raising potentially controversial issues. But ignoring potential problems is unwise at best. In fact, a personal remarriage contract makes good practical sense, from several perspectives. It allows a couple to discuss major issues *before* their emotional involvement becomes too deep, at a time when partners are more likely to be capable of rational negotiation. It encourages both partners to take a realistic view about marital expectations. And it provides some assurance of commitment on both sides.

## Staying Single

Remarriage may be more popular than ever, but sheer numerical reality says that not everyone is going to find a partner the second time around. Is this a tragedy? Probably not. Many people find happiness even though they're single all their lives. And we're learning that many are probably far happier than they would be if they were married.

Although the American dream may still consist of a good job, a comfortable home, a loving spouse and dutiful children, we all know that reality wears more than one face. Jobs are sources of stress, houses need repair, mates and children are seldom perfect. Marriage can be fulfilling, but it's certainly not an indispensable component of a happy, healthy life

Single parenthood, as difficult as it is, may be a better option for some people than combining families or complicating matters with stepparents. And if no children are present, it is quite common for both single men and women to prefer a single lifestyle. There is, after all, much to recommend the freedom, financial independence, and self-reliance that single status commands. Many who are divorced enjoy the feeling of self-confidence that comes from being responsible for their own happiness.

In some ways, our society isn't quite ready to deal with someone who is content to be single. Men and women who remain unmarried past their thirties are likely to be viewed—at least by some—as undesirable partners or persons too set in their ways to make anyone good spouses. Parents, siblings, relatives, friends—even the media, to some extent—are all likely to promote marriage as normal, healthy, desirable. As a result, most of us feel considerable social pressure to find a mate at all costs, before it's too late. Combating this pressure isn't easy, but if we've learned anything it's that marriage isn't an inevitable road to happiness. The relationship has to be right, the value systems of the two partners must be compatible—whether it's a first marriage or second.

For better or for worse, most divorcees do choose to remarry, and soon find themselves facing the challenges, joys, frustrations, and compromises that are a part of any vital union. It's not so surprising, really, that even those who have been through the worst a relationship has to offer are generally willing to have another go at romance, once the scars have healed. And the intent of this lesson is not to discourage anyone from doing just that, but simply to say that it's best to enter marriage number 2 (or 3, or 4) with eyes open (and hopes high, of course). After all, love is what we're all taught to pursue and to expect from life. Marriage the second time around can be just as fulfilling as it is for the most star-struck newlyweds. With maturity, hard work, and a grain of realism, even the most hard-bitten divorcees have been known to find connubial bliss. And after all, isn't that what the American Dream is all about?

## Learning Objectives

On completing your study of this lesson, you should be able to

❑ Describe the changes that have occurred in our modern attitude toward divorce.

❑ List a few of the reasons why remarriage is still an attractive option, even for men and women who have experienced traumatic divorces.

❑ Explain some of the ways courtship for remarriage differs from courtship the first time around.

❑ Discuss the reasons why the basic exchange favors men over women in remarriage.

❑ Discuss the concept of heterogamy as it applies to remarriage.

❑ List some of the reasons why remarried couples tend to evaluate their second marriages more positively than their first.

❑ Discuss the relative stability of first marriages and second marriages.

❑ Explain why the presence of children tends to be a complicating factor in remarriage.

❑ List some of the reasons for negotiating a personal remarriage contract.

## Key Terms

Basic exchange
Cultural script
Custodial parent
Heterogamy
Marital happiness
Postmarital happiness

Redivorce
Remarriage
Remarriage market
Remarried families
Stability

## Assignments

❑ Before viewing the program, be sure you've read through the preceding overview and familiarized yourself with the learning objectives and key terms for this lesson. Then read Chapter 15, "Remarriages," with particular emphasis on pages 494–511 and 518–520 of *Marriages and Families* by Lamanna and Riedmann.

❑ After completing these tasks, read the video viewing questions and watch the video program for Lesson 24, "The Second Time Around."

❑ After viewing the program, take time to answer the video viewing questions and evaluate your learning with the self-test. You'll find the correct answers, along with text page references, at the back of this telecourse guide.

❏ Read the "What's Your Decision?" scenario at the end of this lesson and answer the questions about the decision you would make based on what you've learned from this lesson. Give these questions some serious thought; they may be used as the basis for class discussion or the development of a more complex essay.

## Video Viewing Questions

1. How did Tom, Margo, Ray, Glenn, and Donna each view singlehood following a divorce? How did their relationships differ the second time around? Is it valuable to spend some time alone between long-term relationships? Explain your answer.

2. What are monkey bar relationships? Why do Kathy Wexler and Constance Ahrons believe these relationships are often doomed to fail? Do you agree?

3. The courtship process differs greatly between those who have married before and those who have not. Describe courtship after divorce as seen through the comments of Judy and Ray. How has their view toward romance changed?

4. According to experts, most people who have divorced generally view what went wrong in the marriage in terms of their former spouse's faults, not their own. Why does this occur and what are the ramifications? Base your response on the testimony of Alan, Constance Ahrons, and Tom Seibt.

5. When people who have been widowed remarry, what are some of the qualities they tend to look for? Is this list influenced by the fact that widowed persons are typically older? How might a widow(er)'s perspective be quite different from a divorcee regarding the selection of a mate and remarriage?

6. Discuss the problems and pressures that can arise when children are part of a remarriage.

7. How do the financial realities for remarried men frequently contrast with the image the media portray? How can finances tie former spouses together and create problems in a second marriage?

8. What lessons, learned through divorce, can bring greater happiness to a second marriage?

1. Which of the following *best* describes the general trend toward remarriage over the past few decades?
   a. Remarriages have increased significantly in number, and the trend continues upward.
   b. Rates of remarriage have dropped steadily since 1966.
   c. The remarriage rate has pretty much held steady since shortly after the turn of the century.
   d. Because of some social disapproval, the remarriage rate has declined pretty steadily since the 1950s.

2. Research indicates that for the most part, remarried persons tend to consider themselves
   a. quite happy—though not necessarily more so than never-divorced persons.
   b. extremely happy—in fact, much happier on the whole than their never-divorced counterparts.
   c. only moderately happy, and generally not as happy as in their first marriages.
   d. rather unhappy—far less happy, in fact, than they would have predicted prior to remarriage.

3. In our society today, remarriage tends to be viewed as
   a. immoral—even though few of us come right out and admit to this attitude.
   b. not necessarily immoral, but unnatural and undesirable in almost all cases.
   c. somewhat aberrant, though overall, tolerance is increasing markedly.
   d. no different from first marriage.

4. Statistically, which of the following is *most likely* to remarry?
   a. A widowed black woman
   b. A divorced black woman
   c. A widowed white woman
   d. A divorced white woman

5. Betty is a well-educated, professional woman in her fifties with three children, ages 12 to 17, still living at home. She has been divorced for several years. Betty has dated three men during that time, and has been serious

about two of them; she would like to remarry. Based on what you know of her situation, how would you rate her chances of remarriage?

a. Fairly low—given her age and the fact that she has children still living at home.

b. Moderately low, mostly because of her age; some men would see the children as a plus.

c. Quite good because of her education and status; contrary to popular belief, her age will work in her favor.

d. Extremely good; virtually all the factors noted in the scenario are likely to work in her favor.

6. Which of the following *best* describes the tendencies of divorced persons in selecting a remarriage partner?

a. Most persons tend to select someone as much like the first partner as possible.

b. Selected partners may or may not resemble the first partner, but most persons remarry homogamously (i.e., to choose someone like themselves).

c. Younger persons tend to remarry homogamously, but older persons are likely to marry heterogamously (i.e., to choose someone unlike themselves).

d. While older persons often tend to marry homogamously, young and middle-aged divorced persons are more likely to marry heterogamously.

7. Greg has just married for the second time, three years following his divorce. This time, he's sure, things will work out differently. "Everything's different this time around," Greg declares happily. "My second wife is nothing like the first—she's a better housekeeper, more understanding of me and my needs—not to mention better looking. Besides, we have more in common. We're both outdoor people, both like sports—we even both like cats. There's just no way this marriage can fail." Based on this scenario, how would you evaluate the *likelihood* that Greg's second marriage will be more stable than his first?

a. It will definitely be more stable. He and his second wife have more in common, and he has a positive attitude, which is vital.

b. Greg's positive attitude is a very important factor, but he may be a little unrealistic in his expectations, thereby decreasing the chances for stability slightly.

    c. Chances for a stable marriage are probably no more than fair; his expectations tend to be unrealistic, he focuses too much on his own needs, and he bases their compatibility on very superficial concerns.

    d. There is simply no way to answer this question without knowing more about Greg's first marriage and the reasons for his divorce.

8. Which of the following typically gain most financial from remarriage?

    a. Women in general
    b. White women
    c. African-American women
    d. Hispanic women

9. Anthropologist Paul Bohannan has coined the term quasi-kin. To which of the following relationships would he suggest that this term be applied?

    a. Alan, Janet's current husband, and George, Janet's former husband.
    b. Cindy, Robert's child by his first marriage, and Emily, Robert's child by his third marriage.
    c. Rita, the sister of Leslee's first husband, and LeeAnn, Leslee's child by her second marriage.
    d. Nolan, Ed's cousin, and Tracy, Ed's third wife.

10. Many social psychologists believe that constructing a remarriage contract can be just as important as constructing a marriage contract in ensuring the long-term stability of a relationship. Reasons for this include

    a. Most people emerge from divorce unwilling to trust another partner. A contract is nearly essential to reassure them their personal interests are protected.
    b. Society has not yet evolved an effective cultural model for these complex relationships.
    c. It gives couples a way to apply all they learned from their previous marriages.
    d. Both a and c above.

## What's Your Decision?

Lars and Karla have been married for less than a year. Lars' son from his first marriage, Jerry, is turning five next week. Both Jerry and Lars' ex-wife, Barbara, have had a difficult time accepting Karla, and seem to feel that Lars should have waited longer before he remarried. Lars can sense Jerry's resentment when they're together, and suspects that Barbara has gone to no great lengths to soothe Jerry's hurt feelings or explain why his father might remarry. Still, Jerry is excited about seeing his father at his birthday party. And Lars is looking forward to the party, and perhaps an opportunity to talk things over with Jerry. Lars is a little surprised and resentful, then, when Karla tells him she wants to go to the party as well. "You can come if you like," he says after a moment, "but frankly, I'm not sure it would be such a good idea."

Karla, who is trying to make a positive gesture and demonstrate a willingness to get to know both Jerry and Barbara better, is puzzled and angry. "How are things ever going to get better if I'm always excluded?" she demands. But Lars knows his son, and he feels that Karla's presence will spoil what would otherwise be an opportunity to spend some special time with Jerry. More than that, Barbara has pointedly neglected to invite Karla. "This is a special occasion," Lars says defensively. "We'll get together another time. If you love me, you'll just have to accept that for now."

Based on what you know about the situation, do you think Lars should give in and let Karla come? What are some of the most important factors for him to consider in making this decision? If he goes alone, what are some of the most significant ramifications of that decision?

❑ Should Lars take Karla to the party?

❑ What factors support that view?

❑ What factors support the opposite view?

❑ What will happen immediately if he acts as you suggest?

❑ What will his situation probably be five years from now if he acts as you suggest?

❑ Are there research studies cited in the text that offer support for your position?

❑ If you needed additional research-based information to support your position, how or where would you go about getting it?

# Lesson 25

# Yours, Mine, and Ours

## The Challenges of Stepparenting

The ideal American family, as presented by countless television sitcoms over the years, consists of two parents—loving, successful, and judicious—two or three well-adjusted children, and a quirky relative or two thrown in for good measure. Sitcom families have relatively minor problems (they have to be solvable in 30 minutes), and are rarely beset with true emotional trauma. The worst thing that ever happens to anybody is when the jokes fail.

Of course, people are generally sophisticated enough to know that television doesn't depict life as it really is. The trouble is, we don't have many other models—aside from those few families we know well. As a result, many of us are inclined to believe that, real or not, the sitcom world is closer to how things *ought* to be than anything we've observed firsthand. And, unfortunately, even when we learn not to take them too seriously, idealized models can make reality harder to swallow.

In real families parents fight, face insurmountable differences, divorce. Children can be selfish and difficult as often as they are joyful and affectionate. Quirky relatives are more likely to be avoided than chuckled over. In short, the structure of many families has evolved, through divorce and remarriage, into forms they never told you about on "Ozzie and Harriet" or "Leave it to Beaver."

Today, single-parent families, and families where one or both divorced parents have children from a previous marriage, are becoming increasingly common. But until very recently, such families were rarely portrayed on television or in films. And few of us have built-in expectations regarding how the members of such families ought to interact.

Think for a moment about some of the questions created by these new combination family structures: Where do stepparents stand legally? What's the acceptable way to show affection for or discipline a child who is not your own? Is it alright for stepchildren to date each other? And . . . where do they teach you these things?

Being a stepparent is one of the most difficult and demanding roles any of us will ever be asked to play. And when we don't know the answers (which is a good deal of the time), there are no sources to which we can automatically turn for guidance. We're building new traditions as we go.

## The Complications of Stepparenting

In the bargaining process that occurs during courtship for remarriage, children from a previous union tend to weigh against the match for most people. Just what is it about the idea of living with someone else's children that's so frightening or unappealing? Part of it may have to do with responsibility. Not everyone is ready to have children of his or her own, let alone assume emotional and financial responsibility for someone else's. Not only do children from a previous marriage complicate the key financial aspects of the relationship, they may actively attempt to undermine their parents' romantic relationships. Courtship between two people who have never been married is complicated enough. For divorced parents, it means that in addition to building a relationship with each other, they must court one or more potentially hostile children. All things considered, stepparenthood doesn't fit in with the average person's romantic ideal.

All this is not to imply that stepchildren doom a relationship to failure. Many stepparents and stepchildren manage to establish a strong bond that provides mutual emotional support and satisfaction. But there's little question that children complicate the remarriage picture. There are more feelings to consider, more needs to satisfy, more relationships to sort out.

Studies show that child rearing is the single most serious problem facing many remarried couples. Even financial difficulties pale by comparison. Further, studies tell us that the presence of stepchildren makes marital unhappiness and divorce more likely. This is in no way an indictment of children—who are often only acting out of the deep need for the very love and security they feel is threatened. Rather, it's an acknowledgement of the fact that marriage, and especially remarriage, often affects more than just the two central people.

## Negative Feelings of Stepchildren

Let's look at the situation from the child's point of view for a moment. When a child rejects a stepparent—as some do—is it right to label this behavior sabotage? From the adult's perspective, a child may seem irrational, temperamental, stubborn, or even explosive. But, from the perspective of a 5- or 6-year-old whose secure emotional footing has been removed, behavior that looks irrational to us may be the most natural sort of self-defense.

Circumstances vary, of course, but children may disapprove of their parents' divorce for several years afterward. They may even harbor fantasies about their parents' eventual reconciliation and the reunion of their family as it used to be. As an intruder on those fantasies, the stepparent must be prepared for "war."

Stepchildrens' negative feelings may be particularly strong with respect to the issue of their parents' sexuality. It's hard enough for many children to accept their parents as sexual beings, let alone to imagine one of them having sex with a perfect stranger. The child may experience anger, resentment, and confusion—feelings that clash head on with the emotional and sexual needs of the parent.

If half of the horror stories we hear are true, it's easy to see why the very idea of being a stepparent is sufficient to make some people think twice about continuing the relationship. The truth is, children in stepfamilies can be as happy and well-adjusted as kids who live with both biological parents. In fact, a healthy percentage of children ultimately regard their stepparents with affection. But affection doesn't come automatically or easily, and the process of working toward it generally proves to be as hard on the adults involved as on the children.

## Working Toward Affection

It's human nature to want to be liked. Nobody openly invites rejection. But sometimes it's hard to overcome. If you are a man who's fallen in love with a beautiful divorcee, but her kids throw rocks at your car, pour milk in your beer when you aren't looking, and seem to regard you only with contempt no matter how you have tried to win them over, you may soon find the attraction waning. By the same token, if you are the mother involved, the conflict between your need for love and adult companionship and your loyalty to your children may put the damper on romance.

But suppose the courtship persists against these odds, and this hypothetical couple—call them Bob and Molly—

marry. How do you think their relationships with each other and the children might change? Much, naturally, depends on the people involved, particularly Bob, the stepfather-to-be. As the catalyst of change, the approach he decides to take will go a long way toward determining thesuccess or failure of the new family.

Chances are that Molly and her children will have certain expectations about Bob's role within the family—which Bob may or may not be able to live up to. Many divorced mothers and their children form a tightly-bound unit, drawn closer together by the need for self-reliance and responsibility. Tasks are divided; routines are established. The longer the woman has been divorced, the harder it will be for an outsider to break into this closed group. If, as is often the case, Molly and her children fail to tell Bob what they expect from him if he wants to be accepted, chances are he will have trouble fitting in. Psychologists call these undisclosed expectations the *hidden agenda*.

If Bob has lived on his own for a while, he may have trouble adjusting to the pressures of living with others—in other words, he may have a hidden agenda of his own. If Bob decides that the best way to handle the situation is to assume the traditional male role of authoritarian father, how do you think Molly and her kids will react?

You can picture the situation. Bob comes home from work, gives Molly a perfunctory hello without any inquiries about her day, chides his stepchildren about their schoolwork or the mess their toys have made of the living room, retreats to his den demanding silence while he reviews the notes for the board presentation he is making in the morning, and waits impatiently for someone else to prepare and serve dinner. In a formerly egalitarian household, this sort of behavior won't make Bob very popular.

If, on the other hand, Bob makes it a point to get to know the household routine before the wedding, assumes a portion of the duties himself, and trades in that dictatorial demeanor for something a little more accessible and empathetic, chances are the transition will be a lot easier for everyone involved. Of course, there will probably still be some confusion and hostility. But communication and flexibility, so important to any good relationship, are absolutely vital in stepparenting. After all, remarriage with children is the most difficult form of marriage. Its very life depends on compromise.

Many men fantasize about fatherhood. They think about taking their children to ball games or symphonies, and picture themselves passing along generous doses of accumulated wisdom that will help these children avoid their mistakes. Probably very few, however, fantasize about having stepchildren. And in some ways, that's probably too bad. If you don't role-play a little beforehand, it's a little hard to know how to act.

Sometimes children, especially young ones, are willing to accept a stepfather as a new daddy; more often, they're angry, mistrustful, and determined not to like him. When these negative feelings arise, it can help if the stepfather has at least given some thought to how he'll cope. But chances are, he hasn't. And it's hard to feel fatherly and loving when someone is resenting you, shrieking at you, or wishing you weren't part of the family. Further, in the back of our minds somewhere lives a nagging suspicion that society expects remarried families to be as happy as natural ones.

## How to Succeed as a Stepparent

So, what's the answer? Is a good stepparent an authority figure? A friend? A buddy? An impartial bystander? At times, it may seem like an impossible task to sort it all out. Family counselors do have a few suggestions, however. First of all, it's important to know that as a stepparent you're not alone. Many other couples have struggled with the same dilemmas. It is possible to resolve them successfully.

Professional counseling is often available, and can provide help with both the emotional and pragmatic issues that are involved. Groups like Parents Without Partners offer workshops on both remarriage and stepparenting. But while outside help can be invaluable, it's not an option that automatically occurs to most people.

Psychologists also stress how important it is that everyone involved in the remarriage get to know everyone else. Both adults and children need to develop a rapport, and an understanding of the changes remarriage will bring. This means talking together, spending time together, observing each other's lifestyles and behaviors, sharing one another's needs, fears, hopes, frustrations, and expectations for the future. Such openness isn't readily achieved. It takes time, and the opportunity for people to be together in a wide variety of circumstances and situations.

Living together is never simple, even under the best circumstances. Dishes get left in the sink, the stereo is played too loud, curfews and promises are broken, conflicting schedules breed disappointments, misunderstandings simmer and sometimes boil over. But things tend to go more smoothly when there are common understandings and guidelines.

It would be unreasonable for a new stepparent like Bob to expect instant and enthusiastic acceptance into the family unit, no matter how willing he was to establish communication in advance. Molly's son probably won't ask him to coach the Little League team; that's a job for his natural father. His stepdaughter probably would prefer to see her real father at her gymnastics competition. And there are bound to be periods of anger and resentment as the adjustment process continues. But it helps for participants to know that a slow adjustment is natural—that it doesn't mean anyone is doing something wrong, or that the relationship won't work out eventually. Realistic expectations, combined with patience, are critical.

As a remarried family, Bob and Molly are operating at something of an advantage. Theirs is one of the least complicated family structures among the range of possible combinations. Imagine for a moment how the situation might be different if Bob were also a custodial father, and his children, in addition to Molly's, were living with them. Or suppose Bob's children came to live with the family on weekends or in the summer. Or suppose that Molly had three children—two of her own, plus one stepchild from a second previous marriage.

It isn't so much the complexity of the situation that determines whether a stepparenting relationship will succeed. Virtually all situations have built-in complexities of one sort or another. The real keys to success are communication, compromise, and above all—patience.

Establishing a stepparent relationship is, in many ways, like establishing any intimate relationship. It requires sensitivity, give and take, self-confidence, and a capacity for love. It's different in one big respect, though: often the relationship isn't what the child wants at all. Those negative feelings can change over time, given enough love and enough commitment to the family relationship as a whole. But turning them around takes more emotional stamina than some of us may have—or think we have. Is it worth the effort? You have to decide. For some people, it's probably too much challenge for too little reward. But then, who's to say? Perhaps those people are missing something.

## Learning Objectives

On completing your study of this lesson, you should be able to

❑ Discuss some of the factors that make remarriage with stepchildren the most difficult form of marriage.

❏ Explain some of the ways role ambiguity makes stepparenting so difficult.

❏ List a few of the reasons why children may object to a new stepparent.

❏ Compare the relative difficulties facing stepfathers and stepmothers.

❏ Describe the potentially damaging effects of the hidden agenda.

❏ List a few of the ways remarried families can ease the transition involved in learning to live with one another.

❏ Explain why discipline is a special problem for many stepparents.

| | | |
|---|---|---|
| Absent partner | Remarried family | **Key Terms** |
| Additional parent | Role ambiguity | |
| Assimilation | Stepmother trap | |
| Hidden agenda | Weekend stepparent | |

**Assignments**

❏ Before viewing the program, be sure you've read through the preceding overview and familiarized yourself with the learning objectives and key terms for this lesson. Then review Chapter 15, "Remarriages," of *Marriages and Families* by Lamanna and Riedmann, with particular emphasis on pages 511–522.

❏ After completing these tasks, read the video viewing questions and watch the video program for Lesson 25, "Yours, Mine, and Ours."

❏ After viewing the program, take time to answer the video viewing questions and evaluate your learning with the self-test. You'll find the correct answers, along with text page references, at the back of this telecourse guide.

❏ Read the "What's Your Decision?" scenario at the end of this lesson and answer the questions about the decision you would make based on what you've learned from this lesson. Give these questions some serious thought; they may be used as the basis for class discussion or the development of a more complex essay.

## Video Viewing Questions

1. Due to the high rates of divorce and remarriage, blended families are becoming more and more the norm. However, the initial transition is rarely an easy one for any member of the new family unit. Describe the difficulties stepparents, children, and natural parents each face in a combined family situation. Consider the comments of Mary, David, Paul and Angela, and Bill, Peter, Kathy, Pam, and Cassandra.

2. Tom Seibt, Linda, and Tom discuss disciplining each other's children. What do their comments reveal about the difficulty stepparents and children generally experience with regard to discipline? How do the additional comments of Peter and Bill fit into the picture?

3. In what way do the expectations of stepmothers vary from those of stepfathers? Is this discrepancy self-imposed, or is it caused by some other factor? Relate the comments of Constance Ahrons to the commentary of the stepparents and children.

4. How do children manipulate both natural parents and stepparents? To what end? How did Suzanne's response to manipulation efforts differ from the reactions of Pam, Mark, and Kathy? Which of the methods combats the problem most effectively? Why?

5. No rules exist to define or govern the potpourri of relationships blended families create. What kind of relationship frequently develops between an ex-spouse and a current spouse? How do the children generally respond to this situation? Do the children of different marriages living under the same roof get along? In what way can grandparents and in-laws become sources of stress and discord? Utilize at least two of the multiple testimonial examples supplied.

## Self-Test

1. According to research, the greatest problems for *most* remarried couples tend to center around

   a. emotional immaturity.
   b. stepchildren.
   c. sexual incompatibility.
   d. religious differences.

2. Which of the following generalizations tends to be *most* accurate?

   a. There are an array of challenges specific to stepfamilies—both parents and children.

   b. Both stepchildren and stepparents tend to be better adjusted emotionally than children and parents in intact families.

   c. Though stepparents are generally very well adjusted and happy, stepchildren often suffer severe emotional adjustment problems.

   d. Neither stepparents nor stepchildren are usually very well adjusted or happy.

3. Phyllis and Hans have been married for two years. It is the second marriage for both, and both have children from their first marriage. Phyllis is now expecting her first child from her marriage to Hans. What impact, if any, is the birth of this child likely to have on the marriage?

   a. It will have an extremely negative impact on the stability of the marriage.

   b. It will have a temporary positive effect on their overall marital happiness, but in the long run will pose a threat to the stability of the marriage.

   c. Overall, it will have a positive effect on the happiness and stability of their marriage.

   d. The birth of a child is likely to have little influence one way or the other.

4. According to the text, there are three major problem areas that affect emotional adjustment for remarried families. *All but one* of the following are cited as potentially significant problem areas. Which of the following is *least likely* to be a problem area for remarried families?

   a. Role ambiguity

   b. Birth of new children

   c. Financial burdens

   d. Negative feelings of children from first marriages

5. From a legal perspective, a stepparent tends to be looked on as

   a. the equal of a biological parent.

   b. a replacement for the biological parent.

   c. a nonparent with the legal authority of a biological parent.

   d. a nonparent with no prescribed rights or duties.

6. Ed recently married a woman with three children from her first marriage. Though he expected the adjustment to be fairly smooth since they'd dated for well over a year, he's finding it difficult at best. "The kids don't accept me the way I thought they would," he tells his friend Chuck. "What's worse, though, is that I don't feel quite the way I thought I would. I thought I'd feel a lot of affection and the truth is I don't. You know, you're expected to be the loving father right off the bat. Most of the time I find myself wishing the kids were with her ex-husband. Sounds terrible, doesn't it?" The feelings that Ed expresses in this scenario are

   a. quite typical of stepfathers who feel social pressure to love their stepchildren in the same way they might love their biological children.
   b. typical early in a relationship when emotional adjustment is most difficult, but fortunately, only temporary.
   c. rather unusual in the sense that most people do not feel such strong social pressure to love stepchildren—few people regard that as expected.
   d. rather unusual in the sense that most stepparents find they love stepchildren as much as their own biological children—if not more.

7. Studies indicate that by the time parents have been divorced for about five years, *most* children

   a. strongly disapprove of the divorce or at least question its appropriateness.
   b. accept that the divorce was the best solution under the circumstances, though they continue to feel regretful.
   c. not only accept their parents' divorce, but even approve the decision.
   d. no longer think about the rights or wrongs of the divorce at all.

8. The phenomenon known as the "stepmother trap" refers to the fact that

   a. children in a second marriage often pretend to accept a stepmother openly until after the marriage—when their negative feelings emerge.
   b. stepmothers often pretend to be loving and caring, while in reality they tend to be cruel, vain, selfish, and competitive with their stepchildren.

   c. men who remarry often do so simply to find a new mother for their children, with little real affection for the women they choose.

   d. prevalent myths about stepmothers often require a stepmother to be exceptionally loving and giving just to be regarded as acceptable.

9. Rich has been a stepfather for about three months now, and despite the fact that his wife is very happy and his stepchildren seem well adjusted, he doesn't give himself very high marks: "I'd give myself a C+, tops," he jokes with his brother Rod. "I'm just not doing as well as I'd hoped. This fathering business is a lot tougher than it looks." Probably the *main* reason that Rich gives himself such low marks in this scenario is that

   a. he just isn't a very confident person by nature.

   b. the stress of his new role is depleting his self-confidence somewhat—at least for now.

   c. he really isn't doing a good job, and he knows it.

   d. he's just using reverse psychology to elicit some attention and approval; in truth, he probably knows what a good job he's doing.

10. Raymond and Felicia are considering marriage. Felicia has custody of one child from her first marriage. Raymond's wife Bonnie has custody of their two children, whom Raymond sees on weekends. As they're making a final decision about whether to marry, which of the following recommendations would a social psychologist be *likely* to support most strongly?

   a. Don't include children from either marriage on dates or outings; allow the spousal relationship to develop first.

   b. Avoid prying too deeply into the partner's potential motives for marriage; this is likely to generate an air of mistrust.

   c. Don't delay discussing philosophies about child rearing, including potentially touchy subjects like discipline or education.

   d. Maintain a very positive attitude; don't allow doubts, frustrations, or worries to taint your relationship.

## What's Your Decision?

No matter how hard he tries, Carl just can't seem to avoid conflict with his stepdaughter, Jennifer. Jennifer is the 14-year-old daughter of his wife, Ann's, previous marriage. When Carl and Ann were married, they moved into Carl's house. Ever since, Carl's relationship with Jennifer has been a series of running battles. "I try to be patient, and I try to be fair," Carl tells Ann. "But at the same time, we have to have rules." Ann looks harried and a little confused. She tends to think that some of Carl's rules are a little arbitrary, laid down merely to show Jennifer who's boss.

"She's just going through a stage," Ann tells Carl. "She'll grow out of it. You just have to be patient. When I was her age I was the same way. Let's just give her a little time." This is an attitude that infuriates Carl—he thinks Ann is shirking her responsibilities and putting pressure on him to discipline her daughter. One night Carl and Ann walk to a local movie theater. When they return home, they find their car sitting in the driveway with a dented fender. When they confront Jennifer, she shrugs and tells them that she was bored and decided to go for a drive. "That's it," Carl tells Ann. "She's going to live with her father."

Based on what you know of the situation, do you think Carl and Ann should give up on Jennifer, break up the family unit and send her away in order to preserve their own marriage? Or should they try a little more patience, and perhaps seek counseling to help resolve their differences?

- ❏ Should Jennifer be sent to live with her father?

- ❏ What factors support that view?

- ❏ What factors support the opposite view?

- ❏ What will happen immediately if they act as you suggest?

- ❏ What will their situation probably be five years from now if they act as you suggest?

- ❏ Are there research studies cited in the text that offer support for your position?

- ❏ If you needed additional research-based information to support your position, how or where would you go about getting it?

# Lesson 26

# The Later Years

## Aging and Relationships

Remember those old inevitabilities—death and taxes? Some of us might consider old age a close contender for this exclusive group. Not inevitable, exactly (since there is an unattractive alternative), but a growing possibility as longevity expands far beyond what our grandparents and great grandparents would have dreamed of.

Picture yourself as an old person. What do you see? Someone frail, perhaps, or physically slow and awkward? Are you leading a quiet, solitary sort of life, spending long hours gazing out the window, hoping for the phone or doorbell to ring, wistfully dreaming of days gone by? If your picture is anything like this, you may be a victim of stereotyping, which has taught us to see the old as infirm, alone, often lonely and despairing, often sick, and quite frequently leading unfulfilling lives.

This scenario applies to some older people, it's true—as most of us with families can testify. But it's by no means true of all, or even of a majority, as we shall see in this lesson. And it's becoming less typical all the time. Research conducted within the past few years is opening our eyes to the lifestyles of our older citizens. It's a topic we should explore . . . after all, it's where most of us are headed.

One thing research has shown us is that the old are getting younger. How do you define old in years? 65? 75? 90? According to recent definitions, old persons now fall into three definitive categories: the young old, or persons 65 to 74, the moderately old, or persons 75 to 84; and the elderly old, or persons 85 and over. But don't take these figures too liter-

## Overview

ally. Thanks to a phenomenon called *youth creep*, the old are getting younger all the time, both in terms of physical health and in terms of the activities in which they're engaged. All things considered, old age just ain't what it used to be.

**The Changing Elderly**

First, research indicates that older citizens have better mental and physical health and are better off financially than their counterparts of even a generation ago. True, some are living in poverty, particularly members of minority groups. But the majority have incomes that allow them to live productive and comfortable, if not luxurious, lives.

Further, increasing numbers of people are reaching 65, 75, and even older in remarkably good health, with few if any serious problems. They may not be doing gymnastics or running races, but they are golfing, jogging, playing tennis, hiking, biking, and otherwise staying active. Many work, either at regular full- or part-time jobs or in volunteer positions within the community.

Social scientists agree that many older people have a functional age that is far younger than their chronological age. Many men and women in their seventies lead lives comparable to what would have been expected of 50-year-olds a generation or so ago.

If you're an organized, logical sort of person and you like lots of structure in your life, then you may feel that there are "right" ages to do certain things: go to school, get married, have children, start a new business. Now, many people consider this sort of structure old-fashioned, not to mention impractical and, well, boring. Not too many older people are starting families (though some are reliving their parenting days as grandparents), but increasing numbers are remarrying, or just enjoying a courtship, returning to school, even changing careers or beginning new businesses. Don't get the idea that these activities are just whimsical indulgences. These people mean business. And they have an excellent track record, thanks to a combination of experience and dedicated commitment. For example, research shows that older people make outstanding students. They take the work seriously, and often have fewer social and personal distractions to break their concentration. So, if you're feeling slightly sorry for that gray-haired lady across the aisle in Freshman English, watch out. She's the one *most likely* to raise the grading curve!

Once upon a time, old age was considered a rather lonely place to be. People in their eighties or nineties stood out in the community as landmarks of a sort. Today the elderly population is growing rapidly. There are almost 30 million people in this country who are over 65, and it's estimated that by the year 2000, nearly 10 percent of the population in *all* nations around the world will be 80 or older. By 2030, the *biggest* population group in our society will be those 75 and over.

This general shift in the population is a phenomenon social scientists refer to as *squaring the pyramid*, meaning that within the next few years, the numbers of persons in various age groups will come close to being equal. The days when the young outnumbered the very old are past—if anything, the situation may be reversing itself.

For one thing, the baby boom generation is growing older, and in 20 years or so, the first baby boomers will enter the young old phase of old age. At the same time, today's young parents are tending to have fewer children, so that even now fewer than one person in four is under the age of 20.

The growing size of the older population has significant social implications. Perhaps for the first time in the United States, this population is gaining real power. They have more money than previous older generations, and their buying power is increasing, giving them a voice as consumers in the marketplace. They have political power, too. Voting records are better for persons over 60 than for any other age group, and given that the size of this group continues to grow, the political implications are obvious.

As research on older persons continues, we're beginning to dispel a lot of myths about old age. But just exactly where does myth end and reality begin? Let's start by looking at the physical aspects of aging. It's true, doctors tell us, that some dysfunctions are inevitable with age. For instance, eyesight dims eventually—sooner for some than for others—and hearing becomes less acute. The lungs lose some elasticity, and muscles are likely to be less strong or flexible. Such changes are considered the *primary* effects of aging—meaning that there isn't much one can do about them.

The heart, however, can actually grow stronger with age if it's properly cared for through diet and exercise. Many of the physical signs that we assume are inevitable consequences of old age—hardening arteries, for instance—are what medical researchers term the *secondary* effects of aging. That is, they're largely preventable. What we see as a consequence

**Old Age—Myths and Reality**

355

of aging may often be simply the result of abuse. We can live longer and healthier . . . if we want to.

Older people often lead very active social lives, too. Many are dating—an issue we'll return to in a moment. Even the oldest old—those over 85—find ways to socialize. Many belong to church or community groups, or regularly visit with children and other family members.

What about mental health? Many of us tend to associate forgetfulness with old age. We joke about it, remarking that it's old age setting in, when we become absent-minded ourselves. And that might be true. Medical research indicates that as we get older, we do tend to grow forgetful about specific dates, numbers, names, and other facts. However, there are also indications that our capacity to reason, to solve problems, and to conceptualize may actually grow more acute with time. Traditional IQ tests have not reflected this ability because they tend not to draw heavily on personal experience—the older person's built-in repertoire. Newer tests are measuring the ability to use experience in handling problems posed by daily life, and on such tests age provides a clear edge.

There is one facet of older life which has not seemed to keep pace with the general trend toward modernism. That is housing for the elderly. There are a variety of alternatives, most traditional, but a few more innovative. The majority of older people do not reside in nursing homes or similar facilities. Most live in their own homes or apartments; a few live with children (although many would prefer not to). Perhaps 5 percent do live in nursing homes. These are often older people who do not have family or friends to provide care, or who require extensive attention because of physical ailments or medical problems.

We often tend to think of the elderly as abandoned souls, but research indicates that this view is part of the mythology about growing old. In fact, kinship networks—in which support is provided by family and friends—are remarkably strong, particularly for older individuals who still live in their own homes. While it's somewhat rare for an extended family to live together under one roof, the feelings of closeness prevail. Most families find a way of keeping the network strong, even if it means crossing miles to do it. In other words, the family as a social institution that provides loving care has not been supplanted by formal institutions like nursing homes or hospitals. For most older citizens, that's a good thing. Most would prefer to receive care from an informal network, and to turn to formal institutions only when other alternatives are not available or when severe crises limit the family's power to provide effective help.

The dynamics of kinship networks differ a little among various socioeconomic classes. Working- and middle-class families are likely to provide direct assistance; upper-class families are more likely to purchase specialized services from other caregivers. Further, kinship networks tend to be strongest among Hispanic families, but are also strong within the black and white communities.

## The Elderly and the Family

Despite the strength of these networks, formal institutions still serve a purpose, particularly in providing care for the very old or the ill. Such care usually involves everyday, intensive assistance with a wide range of tasks, such as personal care with bathing, cleaning, medication, household chores, and managing finances. In the absence of formal institutional help, such responsibilities often fall to a married daughter, who may have children of her own, a household to manage, and sometimes a career to maintain. The strain of fulfilling these simultaneous roles can be overwhelming. Social scientists say that for *women in the middle*, who are unable to abandon one set of responsibilities before assuming another, the stress can be all but unmanageable. There simply is not time or energy to deal with everything. And until now, our society has been less than creative in coming up with alternatives. But as we've indicated, the older population is growing—and attention to such problems is growing with it, as people in their forties, fifties, and sixties become more concerned about how they will manage.

Adult Family Care, a pilot project which has operated in Massachusetts since 1979, is one example of an alternate care system that is gaining notice and approval. The project works something like a computerized dating system. Elder citizens who are candidates for alternative care submit biographical data detailing their needs and preferences for daily living. They include information relating to mobility and medical care, together with such preferences as whether they like pets, being around small children, and so forth. Families, in turn, provide information about their lifestyle. The system works to provide a good match.

Benefits go both ways. For the elderly person, it means a real family, a feeling of belonging, a chance to be in control of one's own life. For the family, there's the chance to benefit from the wisdom of an older person—a mentor, confidant, and storyteller, who can enrich the lives of everyone, and particularly children who might not otherwise have contact with someone who can recall how life was several generations past.

Other societies have recognized the important role of the elderly, and have given them positions of respect. Unfortunately, our society's emphasis on youth has put real distance between generations, often stripping elders of the respect and dignity they might have had in other times and places. As a result, we have what psychiatrist Arthur Kornhaber calls a nation of *grandorphans*—young children physically and emotionally abandoned by grandparents, neither generation knowing much of the other.

Grandparenting, according to Kornhaber, is a biological instinct—and one he encourages us to nurture since it offers a special bonding afforded through no other relationship. A child with two working parents may grow up knowing only hired caregivers. This child may fail to recognize the value of strong family ties and may raise his or her children the same way—ultimately weakening the total kinship structure. To test your family's attitudes, Kornhaber suggests asking yourself how the birth of a new grandchild might be received. Would it be an occasion for joyous celebration? Or would it be looked on in a ho-hum way: Uh-oh, here's another burden added to our growing list of responsibilities... quick, which way to the golf course?

Make no mistake: Kornhaber puts just as much blame on grandparents as on children and grandchildren for allowing the separation to happen. We must not be so eager to get to the bridge club or retire in the sunshine that we forget the importance of keeping those kinship networks alive and well. Grandparental love may consist of a lot more than warm hugs and cookies; some psychologists feel it is essential to a child's adjustment. Unlike parental love, grandparental love comes with no behavioral strings. In the grandparents' hearts and minds, you can be accepted and loved for just being you—an essential ingredient in strong self-concept.

## Aging and Intimacy

But, you may ask, is it realistic to suggest that Grandma is shirking her grandmotherly duties because she's out on the eighteenth hole, chipping her way out of the rough? You might find her there, or she could be out on the town with her latest flame. For a long time, we've had a tendency to think that interest in the opposite sex for people over 60 meant something like a wholesome game of pinochle or a chat about the old days out on the front porch swing. Well, elders are swinging, all right, but not always on the front porch. Most admit openly to a strong need for intimacy, closeness, and physical contact. Many desire a sexual relationship with a dating partner, and while their intimacy may not always involve intercourse, it involves a great deal of hand-holding, cuddling, and other forms of touching.

Further, the over-60 crowd experiences the same romantic feelings that most of us recall from our teenage days: the so-called "sweaty palm syndrome" that consists of damp hands, dry mouth, fluttering heartbeat, and the rest. Is romance important to the older set? You bet. They still like candlelight and wine, walks in the moonlight, music and dancing, flowers—and sitting on the old porch swing.

There are some differences, though, in dating patterns of the very young and the very old. Older people tend to have monogamous relationships, even during dating. They're loyal. They don't wait too long before moving into a sexual relationship, perhaps because they feel the pressure of the time crunch. On the other hand, they're more reflective about some things. They tend to know the value of companionate love, and to recognize this as a part of being in love. They don't discount passion, but unlike their teenage counterparts, they know it won't last, and they view it as less important than finding a partner with the right personality and character.

Admittedly, the road to true love can be a little bumpy for older people. For one thing, having sex outside marriage may go against religious or personal values that have governed their lifestyles for many years. They may feel guilty about having sex, and may fear social disapproval, or the disapproval of their children or other family members. A perplexing role reversal indeed.

Some begin a relationship fully intending to marry, but when the critical moment approaches, they find they're more reluctant to relinquish their freedom than they might have thought. The usual motives aren't there. They aren't beginning a whole new life with someone, looking to establish a family, raise children; those things are in the past. Marriage may even seem to threaten the stability of existing relationships.

Friends aren't always supportive, either. Most of the very old are women, and they're competing for a relatively small number of eligible older bachelors. A woman with a steady dating companion can expect some jealousy from friends for this reason. And the support she gets from family members may be given with the understanding that she will, sooner or later, marry. Peer pressure, it seems, lives on and on.

**The Logistics of Growing Old**

Old age is a different experience for men and women. By today's projections, women can expect, on average, to outlive men by seven or eight years. This means that a woman is more likely than a man to spend a fair portion of time living alone, widowed. And as we've seen already, she is not likely to be living with her grown children, though she may see them frequently.

Remarriage—because of the disproportionate ratio of women to men—is very much a man's prerogative. An elderly widowed man who wishes to remarry is likely to have a number of willing women from whom to choose. A woman is less likely to have many chances; she may very well have none whatever. Resources do make a difference here, though. A widowed woman who has money or a good education stands a far better chance of remarrying. Ironically, just the reverse is true for men. The greater the resources, the lower the chances of remarriage for a man, perhaps because he has difficulty deciding with whom to share the wealth. Also, men who remarry tend to opt for younger women, reducing the older woman's chances of remarriage even further.

Old age is different for men and women economically, too. Women who are currently in their sixties or older are likely to have spent large portions of their lives as homemakers who worked outside the home sporadically, if at all. This means that in later years they're likely to have less social security, a small pension, and little in the way of personal savings. In other words, a woman in this age bracket is likely to be highly dependent on a husband to provide for her through pension, savings, or insurance. And if he did not, she may need the support of children or social services to keep her life intact.

**A Need for Time and Attention, Not Financial Help**

Despite this very real possibility of financial problems, however, few older people are a true financial drain on their families. In fact, even those at the borderline poverty level are more likely to provide financial help to their grown children than to receive help. Their needs are more likely to focus on personal care and social contact than on bill paying per se.

Some married children spend up to 35 hours a week or more running errands, taking parents to the doctor, cleaning, preparing meals, tending to the home and yard, and just providing company or personal attention. Until recently, there were few alternatives to this personalized care, though some social help groups—such as Care for Caregivers in Maryland—provide supplementary support through trained professionals. More hospitals and clinics have initiated at-home medical care. And nursing homes are sponsoring special programs that provide opportunities for socialization. Laura Huxley's Project Caress, for example, brings visiting children and their parents once a week into nursing homes where the old and the young can exchange ideas and hugs, and where the needs of each group make the other feel important and wanted.

Undoubtedly, projects like Adult Family Care, Care for Caregivers, and Project Caress will increase in number and impact. And as this happens, our awareness of older people's needs, desires, feelings, and capabilities may expand. For now, we're still in the throes of *ageism*—which is to say, myths persist and prejudice still shuts older people out of certain activities or benefits. While many would argue that our society fails to accord older people the respect that is their due, it is probably fair to say that most ageism is the result of misguided compassion, rather than genuine ill will. It's demoralizing just the same. Many older people do not wish to be forced into early retirement, for example. And while some may long for the peace and sunshine of a Southwest retirement community, others find such a prospect dull indeed, preferring an active life surrounded by grandchildren, friends, and general hubbub. If research on the aging has taught us anything, it is that elderly citizens are not all alike. In meeting their needs, we need to be flexible and creative. Having said that, we can point to two specific challenges that lie ahead.

One challenge is to continue searching for more innovative lifestyle alternatives for elderly persons who want to retain independence and control. Basics like food, shelter, and medical attention are important, but they're not enough. That much we know. Research shows that when individuals lose control of their lives, the results can be devastating, even fatal. Even in a nursing home, inhabitants are happier when they can choose their own furniture, decide when to attend a

**The Challenges of an Elderly Population**

movie, care for a pet, and invite visitors on their own schedules. Effective care enables people to create lifestyles that suit their needs and abilities, which we've often underestimated.

The second challenge is to find more ways to take advantage of older citizens' skills and wisdom. It may seem ironic that while some families are allowing generations to drift apart, others are seeking ways to bring older citizens into situations where their stories can be heard by those whose lives are just beginning. The value of this sharing is just starting to make itself known to us.

As our research on old age continues and improves, we're likely to become a good deal more adept at meeting these related challenges. That's good news for most of us, as we enter old age ourselves, and discover it's something quite different from what we expected. Not so quiet and peaceful, perhaps. Less frightening. A lot more demanding. When we used to say that life begins at 40, or 50, or 60, we were joking—mostly. But, surprisingly, we may have been right.

## Learning Objectives

Upon completing your study of this lesson, you should be able to

❏ Explore several myths related to old age and discuss their relative truth.

❏ Summarize trends relating to the population of persons over 65; over 80.

❏ Explain the implications of research in shifting attitudes toward the elderly.

❏ Distinguish between primary aging and secondary aging factors, and relate each to attitudes, behaviors, and lifestyles.

❏ Describe several ways in which the experience of growing old is likely to differ for men and women.

❏ Explain why some social scientists feel the old are actually getting younger all the time (i.e., the phenomenon of *youth creep*).

❏ Discuss the myths and realities related to dating and sexual activity for persons over 65.

❏ Compare the relative advantages and potential disadvantages of various lifestyles for the elderly (e.g., living alone, living with children, living in a nursing home or other formal care facility, living with a family as part of an informal care program).

❏ Define the concept of ageism and give at least one example prevalent in society today.

❏ Explain several ways in which attitudes toward aging and retirement have influenced the role of grandparents, and describe how social scientists see this role evolving in the future.

## Key Terms

Ageism
Alzheimer's disease
Formal (vs. informal) caregiver
Grandorphans
Heirarchical-compensatory care

Kinship networks
Primary aging
Secondary aging
Squaring the pyramid
Women in the middle
Young old (vs. the moderately old, elderly old)

## Assignments

❏ Before viewing the program, be sure you've read through the preceding overview and familiarized yourself with the learning objectives and key terms for this lesson. Then read the articles that follow in Appendix A of this telecourse guide.

— "Families" by Cantor from *Aging*.
— "Never Too Late" by Bulcroft and O'Conner-Roden from *Psychology Today*.
— "Let's Put the PARENT Back in Grandparent" by Rice from *Plus*.
— "The Vintage Years" by Horn and Meer from *Psychology Today*.

❏ Also read the following sections from *Marriages and Families* by Lamanna and Riedmann:

— Chapter 5: "Older Partners" and "Sex and Older Single Adults: The Double Standard of Aging," page 123.
— Chapter 10: "Elder Abuse and Neglect," page 299.
— Chapter 14: "Retirement" and "Widowhood and Widowerhood," pages 445–447.

❑ After completing these tasks, read the video viewing questions and watch the video program for Lesson 26, "The Later Years."

❑ After viewing the program, take time to answer the video viewing questions and evaluate your learning with the self-test. You'll find the correct answers, along with text and readings references, at the back of this telecourse guide.

❑ Read the "What's Your Decision?" scenario at the end of this lesson and answer the questions about the decision you would make based on what you've learned from this lesson. Give these questions some serious thought; they may be used as the basis for class discussion or the development of a more complex essay.

## Video Viewing Questions

1. Dr. Somerville believes that up to a certain point, the common perception of "old age" is 10 to 20 years beyond one's present age. Do you agree? What does Dr. Somerville's observation say about the way American society views old age and the elderly?

2. What do Glenn and Anita fear about aging? Give two examples of the ways in which the media depicts older people. Do these examples help to explain or justify the fears Anita and Glenn expressed? Does the testimony of Joe, Muriel, and Ann strengthen or negate the stereotypes of aging? Explain your answer.

3. How can the physical and emotional aspects of declining health and the loss of loved ones affect the quality of life for seniors? Consider the statements of Marlin, Dr. Somerville, Eugenia, Lou, Herbert, and Mary in your response.

4. For many seniors, the "golden years" can become a demeaning experience because of financial concerns, neglect by loved ones, or a debilitating illness. Consider the remarks of Mary and Dr. Viscott's guest. Why does this type of neglect occur? Why is living with a child not a feasible solution? Do you agree with the contention that nationalized health care would relieve financial burden and return respect for the elderly to society. Support your position with facts.

5. Elaine Zimmerman and Dr. Sneiderman believe the elderly are not being utilized in our society. Explain what they mean by this and how the elderly might be utilized. How will the gradual aging of the baby boom generation affect the attitudes of society?

6. Describe why retirement is often seen as a second beginning.

**Self-Test**

1. *Most* social psychologists would probably agree with which of the following? The activities and attitudes of a typical 70-year-old today are roughly equivalent to those of a

   a. 60-year-old a generation or two ago.
   b. 50-year-old a generation or two ago.
   c. 90-year-old a generation or two ago.
   d. *none* of the above; research reveals no general trends in the attitudes and behaviors of the aging.

2. Which of the following best summarizes population trends among persons over 65?

   a. This population is growing dramatically; faster than ever before in recorded history.
   b. There is a slight increase, though younger groups are still growing at a faster rate.
   c. This population is actually stabilizing, and is expected to remain at about the same level till the year 2000 or so.
   d. A gradual decline in the older population has been noted in recent years; a trend which may reverse itself soon.

3. Which one of the following generalities about older men and women seems best borne out by research?

   a. For most senior citizens, old age is a lonely and sad time.
   b. With few exceptions, most older people experience poverty at some time in their lives after age 65.
   c. While most persons over 65 desire an active life, few have the health to pursue it.
   d. For a variety of social and financial reasons, old age is a very different experience for men and women.

4. Warren is 80 and lives alone, as he has for the past 20 years. His only regular companion is his dog, Fred. Which of the following is most likely to be true of Warren's functional capabilities and limitations, according to research?

   a. He's likely to be mentally alert, but to be physically unable to care for himself without extensive assistance.
   b. He's unlikely to be either physically or mentally capable—unless he's the rare exception to the rule.
   c. Most likely, Warren lives with some illness or disability, but it's unlikely to seriously affect his ability to carry out everyday activities.
   d. If he's like most persons his age, Warren has no illness or disability, and is probably as fit as many 30-year-olds.

5. Sally and her friend Madge are talking one day, thinking about the prospect of growing older. Sally makes this remark: "I for one dread it. You know how it is for old people. You're alone—totally. Your family deserts you. You're nothing but a burden and you know it. There's nothing to do but sit by a phone that never rings and wait for the end to come." According to research summarized in the text, Sally's remarks are

   a. very accurate—unfortunately.
   b. accurate for about half the elderly but no longer typically true.
   c. fairly inaccurate, but only because formal support networks have taken the place of the family in providing the care and attention older citizens need.
   d. typical of a prevalent myth about old age—but in reality, inaccurate since kinship networks provide extensive, continuing support to most older people.

6. According to research, which of the following is most likely to be a prominent source of stress to families that provide care to aging parents and other older persons?

   a. The overwhelming financial drain on the family.
   b. The sheer time and energy involved.
   c. The stress of pretending to care for someone who is no longer very important in one's life.
   d. Feelings of inadequacy that stem from general inability to meet an older person's needs as well as a qualified social agency might.

7. About how important is the sexual aspect of a relationship likely to be for older people who date?

  a. There is no way to answer this question satisfactorily since research indicates that very few older persons date as we think of it.

  b. Very important; research shows that older persons value intimacy and physical contact.

  c. Modestly important, though really secondary to the partner's income level and other concerns.

  d. Of no consequence whatever; older persons have learned the value of companionship, and most prefer not to have any sexual involvement.

8. According to studies cited in the text, which of the following is probably the main thing that older couples look for in an out- of-marriage relationship?

  a. They hope eventually to be married.

  b. Most want financial security, whether or not this involves marriage or some other contractual arrangement.

  c. Sadly, many are simply escaping the misery of their current lives, and may prefer living with a friend to living with their own families.

  d. Most want companionship first and foremost; few want marriage, however.

9. Psychiatrist Arthur Kornhaber coined the term "grandophans" to describe persons who

  a. are totally out of touch socially with their grandparents.

  b. have lost one or both parents through death or divorce.

  c. have little respect for the role of grandparents as keepers of wisdom and history.

  d. spend some portion of their childhood under the supervision of hired caregivers.

10. According to psychiatrist Kornhaber (Question 9), which of the following best characterizes the primary difference between the love provided by parents and that provided by grandparents?

  a. The love provided by parents is stronger and more lasting.

  b. Grandparents' love, unlike parents' love, tends to be sporadic and unstable.

c. Unlike parents' love, grandparents' love is wholly unconditional, thereby creating a special emotional bond.

d. Grandparents' love tends to grow stronger over time, while that of parents starts out strong but gradually fades.

## What's Your Decision?

Alice is 78. She has been a widow for two years, since her husband of 51 years died of a heart attack. She lives alone with her pets, whom she treasures—two dogs, a cat, and several birds. Though Alice is capable of seeing to most of her daily needs, and her house is small and modest and on one floor, she needs increasing amounts of attention to keep everything functioning. While she doesn't need to visit the doctor daily, she is diabetic, and must perform blood and urine analyses and give herself daily injections. All of this seemed simple and routine while her husband Arnold was alive, but now it's difficult having no help or even moral support. Further, Alice has become frightened to drive. She's had several close calls; her eyesight and hearing are poor, and she admits her reflexes aren't what they were. Thus, she needs someone to run errands—buy her medication and groceries, get pet supplies, and so forth. It's nice to have someone help feed the animals, too. Alice feels guilty asking for all this assistance, but feels she'd be unbearably lonely without her pets. She knows it isn't easy for her family to provide the care she increasingly requires.

Her daughter-in-law Maureen is employed as a teacher and has three children of her own, the youngest of whom is only three. Maureen has asked Alice to live with them, but realistically there isn't space. The children already share bedrooms. And Alice has repeatedly said no. There is one other possibility—a family down the road from Alice has offered to provide ongoing care for Alice and her animals. They have small children, too, but have lots of space, and the woman—Nora—is home all day and welcomes the additional responsibility. "I'd like to do it—really," she tells Maureen and her husband Dave. "Caring for others is what I like. Besides, our kids have never known their own grandmother—this would be a real opportunity for them. She can keep the animals—everybody will be happy." Dave isn't sure about the idea, though. "It just doesn't seem right to send Mom off to live with strangers," he tells her. "What will people think? It would seem more natural, more justifiable, if we put her in a good nursing home. Besides, there she'd get the medical care she really needs. Nora means well, but she's no nurse. Is she going to give shots, test blood? This is serious stuff. You can't just dump your own mother at the neighbors."

Based on what you know of the situation, do you think Maureen and Dave should let their mother live with the neighbor, Nora? Or, would it be better to put her in a qualified nursing home with professional care? What are some of the most important factors for them to consider in making this decision? If Alice does go to live with Nora, what are some of the most significant ramifications of that decision?

❏  Should Alice live with Nora?

❏  What factors support that view?

❏  What factors support the opposite view?

❏  What will happen immediately if Alice and her family act as you suggest?

❏  What will their situation probably be five years from now if they act as you suggest?

❏  Are there research studies cited in the readings that offer support for your position?

❏  If you needed additional research-based information to support your position, how or where would you go about getting it?

# Appendix A

# Families: A Basic Source of Long-Term Care for the Elderly

by Marjorie H. Cantor, Ph.D.

The growing need for services for the aging, whether formal or informal, is directly related to changes occurring in the world's population. Demographic projections indicate that the fastest-growing population group in the world continues to be the elderly. In 1980, there were an estimated 258 million persons aged 65 and over, with the number expected to rise to 396 million by the year 2000.

Since women tend to outlive men, the majority of older people are women, who also make up an increasingly large proportion of the extremely old—those 80 and older. In the United States, for example, women comprise 57 percent of persons 65 to 74, 63 percent of those 75 to 84, and 70 percent of those 85 and over. This sex imbalance has serious implications for the provision of care, since women are more likely to be widowed and living on limited incomes.

Equally significant, in terms of the need for social supports, is the rapid increase in the population of elderly aged 80 and over. It is estimated that by the year 2000 more than 10 percent of the aged populations of nearly all nations will be 80 and older. In the United States as in other developed countries, the proportion of these "old old" persons will be even higher, and is expected to double from the current 9 percent to approximately 18 percent of the elderly population by the year 2000. This continued increase in the number of old old coincides with the expanded involvement of women in the labor force and the resultant reduction in the pool of persons potentially able to provide family care.

**The Growth in the Aged Population**

371

**Disability and
Chronic Illness**

Older people differ in their need for assistance. Although most older people suffer from one or more chronic illnesses, the majority are not disabled or dependent. Brody notes that "most older people do not need any more help than the normal garden variety of reciprocal services that family members of all ages need and give each other on a day to day basis and at times of emergency or temporary illness" (Brody and Brody, 1981).

Data on disability and the need for services in the United States support this view and suggest that there are roughly three distinct age groups of elderly with differing degrees of support needs. The largest group, about 60 percent of the aged population, are the young old, aged 65 to 74. The majority of the young old are relatively fit and active. Sixty-one percent have no major functional limitation, and their need for family supports are minimal, except in times of crisis. The next largest group consists of the moderately old, aged 75 to 84. Persons in this group, comprising 30 percent of the elderly, have increasing rates of illness and disability, and yet half of them have no limitations in their ability to carry out the activities of daily living. Thus, most are still independent, although they may increasingly need some assistance with more arduous tasks such as carrying heavy shopping bundles or heavy cleaning.

The oldest elderly, those aged 85 and over, are the most vulnerable and in need of assistance. Although they comprise only 9 percent of the elderly, the majority in this group either are limited in the kind or amount of major activity they can undertake, or are totally unable to carry out the major activities of daily living. This group requires the most extensive support, which often includes personal care such as washing, bathing, and supervision of medical regimes.

There are also sex and socioeconomic differences among the elderly. Women have a higher rate of illness, both acute and chronic, and are more likely to suffer limitations in their ability to perform normal routines. But, the diseases associated with women tend to be less life-threatening than those prevalent among men, suggesting one reason why women tend to outlive men. Furthermore, the burden of illness and chronic disability falls most heavily on those in the lowest socioeconomic position and members of minority groups.

Most older people who need care live in the community, not in institutions. A national health survey by Shanas found that among community-based elderly about 8 percent to 10 percent were bedfast or homebound and as functionally impaired as those in institutions (Shanas, 1979a and 1979b). Thus, there were twice as many bedfast or homebound elderly at home as in institutions. (Elderly persons in institutions are estimated to constitute 4 percent to 5 percent of the elderly population at any given time.) In addition, another 7 percent of the community residents surveyed were able to go outside, but only with difficulty.

While the amount of help needed by the elderly living in the community varies greatly, estimates of the overall proportion requiring some kind of supportive services range from 12 percent to 40 percent (depending on the services included). The majority of experts suggest that one-third of the elderly, or about eight million people, need some help.

Given the growing number of older people and particularly the rapid expansion in the number and proportion of the old old (who need the greatest amount of care), we can see that the role of the family is indeed crucial, from both the individual and societal points of view.

## The Role of the Family

Is the family really involved in assisting older people? To what extent are family members responsible for the long-term care of the elderly? And what of the future of family care?

The long-standing pervasive myth of the elderly as isolated and abandoned without meaningful kin relationships has been destroyed by study after study. What has emerged instead is a picture of urban industrial society in which the social support system of the elderly increasingly involves an amalgam of informal assistance provided by family and significant others (such as friends and neighbors) and formal services offered by large-scale organizations, both governmental and voluntary, usually supported by public funds. We have seen an evolution of the traditional extended family to a modified extended family characterized by a coalition of separately housed, semiautonomous, semidependent families. Often possessing a quality called intimacy at a distance, these family units—some nuclear, some female-headed single-parent, others composed of nonrelated adults—share with formal organizations the functions of family. As a result, there has been a shift in the importance of familial and societal roles, with regard to the elderly in such areas as income maintenance, health, and housing, but the family has by no means been supplanted by formal organizations. And nowhere has the family been more crucial than in the provision of social supports, particularly in the case of the long term care needs of the frail elderly.

What are the social supports needed by the elderly and how are they provided? Three decades of gerontological research and practice have shown that the conditions of the elderly that require supports are usually chronic, calling for sustained assistance. And, although purely medical or medically related services are sometimes involved, in general the supports are social and health related in nature and are needed to help an older person maintain physical, psychological, and social integrity over time. Thus, a social support system provides assistance to older people fulfilling three major needs:

❏ Socialization and personal development,

❏ The carrying out of daily living tasks such as shopping, cleaning, and laundry, and

❏ Personal assistance during times of crisis or illness.

Research has also shown that older Americans perceive the informal network of kin (particularly spouse and children), friends, and neighbors as the most appropriate source of social supports in most situations, and they turn to this network first and most frequently. Only when assistance from the informal system is unavailable or no longer able to absorb the burden of such care is help sought from formal organizations. The social support system in the United States can therefore be categorized as hierarchical-compensatory, with kin as the first and preferred avenue of assistance, followed next by friends and neighbors and lastly by government and other formal organizations.

Research in New York City and elsewhere discloses a pattern of reciprocal aid between generations, including emotional support, economic aid, child care, household management, and health care. The amount of help that parents receive from their children is related to the level of the parent's frailty and the paucity of his or her income, suggesting that as older people become more vulnerable, children respond with more assistance. Although research in New York and Los Angeles shows that the role of family as a support giver is strongest among the Hispanic population, where the traditional extended family is more in evidence, white and black elderly also have substantial informal support networks, involving one or more children usually living close by.

Interestingly enough, the extent of informal supports does not vary much by social class, although the form of interaction may differ. Working- and lower-middle-class families interact with direct assistance. Upper-income families rely more heavily on gifts of money or the purchase of outside services. But no matter the form, the family remains the prime caretaker of its older members in the United States today.

However, focus on the family should not obscure the fact that there are a significant number of elderly, probably at least one-third, without children or with no children nearby. For such older people, other relatives, friends, and particularly neighbors can and indeed often do compensate as primary social supports. Even though most elderly live in age-integrated neighborhoods and the majority of neighbors may be younger, this does not preclude the development of mutual systems of assistance between the elderly and their younger neighbors. Thus neighbors and the elderly socialize, shop for each other, and help in emergencies; and neighbors, like family members, accompany older people to the doctor or clinic. However, the most frequent form of assistance is help during illness or emergencies.

In most cases, assistance from neighbors during illness is either short-term or sporadic, with the longer-range care of the more seriously or chronically ill generally assumed by kin. However, because neighbor-friends often play an important surrogate family role with respect to those elderly who have no kin, it is not uncommon in such cases for a neighbor to be involved in more long-range responsibilities, or those involving crucial decision making, such as hospitalization. The degree of involvement of a neighbor or friend at times of illness or in assisting with the chores of daily living is therefore not only a function of the intimacy of the relationship and the nature of the task, but is heavily influenced by the presence or absence of kin.

Perhaps most striking is the role of family and significant others in providing services in the home when older people are sick or grow frail with increased age. An analysis of two studies that sought to estimate the extent of current family responsibility to the functionally disabled suggests that between 60 percent and 85 percent of all impaired elderly are helped by the family in a significant way. Further, family members, not professionals, give the bulk of the care to the impaired elderly. Eighty percent of medically related care and personal care, and 90 percent of home help services, to say nothing of extensive emotional support and response in crisis are provided by family members.

**Assistance to the Moderately and Severely Impaired Elderly**

As older people become more frail and dependent, a shift occurs in the kinds of social supports they need and the patterns of assistance. Families respond with more help. Studies involving the impaired elderly (ranging from persons with moderate functional limitations to the homebound and bedfast) indicate that the helping patterns are different from those involving the well elderly in the following ways:

❏ The time frame of assistance changes from intermittent and crisis-oriented to continual and long term.

❏ The degree of family involvement in the day-to-day lives of the elderly increases from relatively minimal to considerable.

❏ Assistance patterns between generations are no longer reciprocal, and assistance flows more clearly from children to parents.

❏ The nature of the tasks changes from peripheral to more central, including direct intervention in housekeeping, personal care and total management.

Perhaps most important is the fact that family members often continue to care for the frail elderly even at great personal sacrifice. In a recently completed study, what emerged as the overriding problem for all types of caregivers—spouse, children, and friends—was not the physical or financial strain, but the emotional impact of dealing with increased frailty in a person with whom one is close. We find caregivers, mainly women, often working outside the home and already committed to a variety of roles, extending themselves even further to encompass the additional regular tasks involved in the care of a frail parent or relative. Even when a homemaker service provided some relief, the families continued to remain in the picture, merely shifting the focus of their caregiving from cleaning and personal care to emotional support, socialization, and overall care management tasks.

But what of the future of the family as a provider of social care? In any consideration of an appropriate balance between informal and formal long-term care for the elderly, there are some important trends and issues that require research and policy attention in the period ahead.

The number of older people in the population relative to younger adults is expected to increase worldwide, and the fastest-growing segment of the elderly, particularly in developed countries, are the older elderly. These are the very people who will need the greatest amount of assistance. Thus the need for long-term care will be greater, not less, in the coming decades.

And yet women, the very group now involved in providing most of the informal social care, are increasingly entering the labor market and remaining in it, even during the years of child rearing. The trend toward more working women is certainly influenced by the increase in divorce and single-parent households. But working women are found as well in the traditional nuclear husband-wife household, where two-wage-earner families are one answer to inflation and unemployment. Particularly significant is the continued rise in working among women aged 45 to 54, the very women who have traditionally contributed many hours to volunteer service and the informal support of elderly parents.

However, there is no indication that today's women, including those who work outside the home are abandoning their filial responsibilities. Work as such does not seem to be a reason for relinquishing responsibilities to the old. Rather, research suggests that these "women in the middle" appear to be extending themselves further to assume the multiple roles of caring for their own families and for aged parents, in addition to working at paid jobs. Furthermore, in interviews with children who care for frail parents, there emerges a deep sense of moral obligation on the children's part to both their own families and their older relatives. The dilemma of conflicting demands, in most cases, is handled not by denial of responsibility but through considerable personal sacrifice.

Coping mainly involves restricting life to the minimum essentials of family, work, and care for dependent elderly. Thus free time, relaxation, socializing with peers, and the pursuit of personal interests are sacrificed under the relentless time and energy constraints of caregiving. How long this pattern will continue we do not know. However, the strain involved is considerable, and some way must be found to lessen the burden in order to prevent both younger and older families from suffering.

Furthermore, spouses, friends, and neighbors are also involved as informal caregivers. Much less is known about the difficulties they can reasonably be expected to endure and still continue as viable sources of long-term care. Most important for elderly spouses, who are often in poor health themselves, are in-home and respite services, sponsored by public or voluntary agencies, at a cost that the elderly can afford.

Friends and neighbors, although not usually as centrally involved in the care of the frail homebound elderly, are also a source of help. Their geographic proximity makes them particularly suitable for providing time-limited neighborhood-based assistance, such as shopping, escorting people to medical care, friendly visits, and acting as "spotters" who alert family or community agencies in case of crisis. More attention needs to be directed to such secondary informal support groups, as well as to the appropriate involvement of other neighborhood helpers, such as churches, block associations, and the mail carrier.

If informal supports are to continue to be a principal mode of social care for older people, serious consideration must be given to methods of assisting family, friends, neighbors, and other informal groups in their efforts. Many forms of assistance merit consideration, including home care, respite services and counseling, training, and self-help groups for caregivers. Is support best given in the form of direct services, vouchers for service, cash allowances, or a combination thereof? Throughout the world there is a growing awareness that methods of assisting informal networks are essential, but widespread and comprehensive family-oriented policy in this area has yet to emerge.

Taking care of a frail dependent person often involves considerable emotional strain, particularly for the informal caregiver. Special services geared to caregiver needs should, therefore, be considered. Support groups for caregivers under the auspices of a church or social agency are a growing response. Through the sharing of experiences, information on the aging process, and available community resources, the burden is eased, to the benefit of all concerned.

Such groups, sponsored by unions or employee assistance programs, could function equally well in the workplace and, along with flexible work schedules, could make a difference in the well-being and productivity of caregiving employees.

Of great importance to the informal support system, particularly spouse and children, is gaining access to those community resources that exist. Given the fragmented nature of the social-health-care system in the United States, caregivers need information on resources and the availability of professionally supervised social services, including assessment and some form of care management. We often speak of "one-step entry points" for older people, but too often children and others giving care are enmeshed in time-consuming and bureaucratic duplications of effort.

With informal care playing such a crucial part in the social care system, the question of the proper interaction between informal and formal subsystems becomes critical. To bring about a positive interaction we need to know more about the appropriate balance among individual, familial, and societal responsibilities for the care of dependent elderly.

Furthermore, positive interaction requires training the formal system in the value and importance of the informal. Formal helpers of all disciplines must learn to appreciate the role of family, friends, and neighbors, must take the time to work with them and include them in care planning for older persons. Such an interface probably involves radical reexamination and changes in prevailing attitudes about professionalism, status, and the importance of technical expertise. A shortage of resources may force such a reappraisal, but it is hoped that the new working relationships which must emerge can be built upon a positive appreciation for the respective roles of each sector, formal and informal.

If we accept the premise that both informal and formal social care have unique values and that the welfare of older persons is advanced by cooperative efforts, we must be careful not to upset the delicate balance between the two subsystems. The tendency to formalize the informal system, regulate it, and bureaucratize it, in our desire to enhance and support, poses a real and serious threat. Does filial responsibility under law really promote informal support, or is the widely accepted moral imperative of caring for parents the more important motivating force? How does one help such mediating structures as churches and neighborhood groups to play a role with the elderly, without interfering with those structures? Even the granting of modest sums for development costs involves issues of accountability and regulation.

In a similar vein, although direct or indirect financial incentives may require less regulation, can the frail elderly realistically assume responsibility for obtaining and supervising home services, without the supervisory assistance of a case manager or younger family member? These are complex issues requiring more study. Solutions will differ, depending on the mix of public and private services, and the value systems, in particular countries. However, the basic issue of how to strengthen informal networks without transforming them into formal entities and creatures of government is crucial everywhere.

Finally, in a climate of service retrenchment and economic restraint it is particularly important that the role of community-based, publicly supported social-care services be reaffirmed. It is clear that the family and other informal supports have a unique and valuable role to play in the long-term care of the elderly. It is this informal system to which older people turn naturally, and there is little indication that the moral responsibility to care for the old will be eroded in the coming period.

At least one-third of the elderly, however, are childless and perhaps without other family members to act as substitutes. In other cases, families are not close by, or can no longer carry the burden of in-home care without assistance. Thus, the informal system, in highly industrialized societies, cannot function adequately unless there is a floor of comprehensive social care entitlements and services in place in the community. Only with such a floor of services can we ensure, on the one hand, that older persons without kin are adequately cared for and, on the other hand, that assistance will be readily available when the need for care is beyond the capacity of the informal network.

There is always the danger, in periods of presumed limited resources, that the informal care system, whether it consists of family, friends, or neighbors, will be offered as a viable alternative to community-based services. Such an approach would not only destroy the balance between informal and formal but would result in a serious reduction in care for older people. Only when both systems are in place and functioning at optimum levels will the increasing number of elderly be assured the long-term care they need and desire.

# Never Too Late

by Kris Bulcroft and Margaret O'Conner-Roden

What is the age of love? The star-crossed lovers Romeo and Juliet were teenagers; Anthony and Cleopatra's torrid affair occurred at the prime of their health and beauty; Lady Diana Spencer was barely 20 when she married her Prince Charming. How old is too old for the sparkle in the eye and the blush in the cheek?

The message our culture often gives us is that love is only for the young and the beautiful—people over 65 are no longer interested in or suited for things such as romance and passion. Few of us imagine older couples taking an interest in the opposite sex other than for companionship—maybe a game of bridge or conversation out on the porch. But, in fact, there are quite a few older single people who not only date but are involved sexually with someone.

Statistically there are good reasons for older people to be dating. At the turn of the century only about 4 percent of the total American population was 65 years of age or older. Today that number has soared to approximately 11 percent, with the total expected to increase to about 20 percent by the year 2050. In addition, older people are living longer and staying healthier, and they are less likely than before to have children living at home. And an increasing number of divorces among the elderly is casting many of these older people back into the singles' pool. All of these factors create an expanded life stage, made up of healthy and active people looking for meaningful ways to spend their leisure.

The question of whether older people date, fall in love and behave romantically, just as the young do, occurred to us while we were observing singles' dances for older people at a senior center. We noticed a sense of anticipation, festive dress and flirtatious behavior that were strikingly familiar to us as women recently involved in the dating scene. Although our observations indicated that older people dated, when we looked for empirical research on the subject we found there was none. We concluded this was due partly to the difficulty in finding representative samples of older daters and partly to the underlying stereotype of asexual elders. So we decided to go out and talk to older daters ourselves. Once we began looking, we were surprised at the numbers of dating elders who came forward to talk to us. We compared their responses to those from earlier studies on romance and dating, in which the people were much younger.

Dating, as defined by our sample of older people, meant a committed, long-term, monogamous relationship, similar to going steady at younger ages. The vast majority of elder daters did not approach dating with the casual attitude of many younger single people who were "playing the field." All respondents clearly saw dating as quite distinct from friendship, although companionship was an important characteristic of over-60 dating.

One of our major findings was the similarity between how older and younger daters feel when they fall in love—what we've come to call the "sweaty palm syndrome." This includes all the physiological and psychological somersaults, such as a heightened sense of reality, perspiring hands, a feeling of awkwardness, inability to concentrate, anxiety when away from the loved one and heart palpitations. A 65-year-old man told us, "Love is when you look across the room at someone and your heart goes pitty-pat." A widow, aged 72, said, "You know you're in love when the one you love is away and you feel empty." Or as a 68-year-old divorcee said, "When you fall in love at my age there's initially a kind of `oh, gee!' feeling . . . and it's just a little scary."

We also found a similarity in how older and younger daters defined romance. Older people were just as likely to want to participate in romantic displays such as candlelight dinners, long walks in the park and giving flowers and candy. Older men, just like younger ones, tended to equate romance with sexuality. As a 71-year-old widower told us, "You can talk about candlelight dinners and sitting in front of the fireplace, but I still think the most romantic thing I've ever done is go to bed with her."

A major question for us was "What do older people do on dates?" The popular image may suggest a prim, card-playing couple perhaps holding hands at some senior center. We found that not only do older couples' dates include the same activities as those of younger people, but they are often far more varied and creative. In addition to traditional dates such as going to the movies, out for pizza and to dances, older couples said they went camping, enjoyed the opera and flew to Hawaii for the weekend.

Not only was the dating behavior more varied, but the pace of the relationship was greatly accelerated in later life. People told us that there simply was "not much time for playing the field." They favored the direct, no-game-playing approach in building a relationship with a member of the opposite sex. As one elderly dater commented, "Touching people is important, and I know from watching my father and mother that you might just as well say when lunch is ready . . . and I don't mean that literally."

Sexuality was an important part of the dating relationship for most of those we spoke to, and sexual involvement tended to develop rapidly. While sexuality for these couples included intercourse, the stronger emphasis was on the nuances of sexual behavior such as hugging, kissing and touching. This physical closeness helped fulfill the intimacy needs of older people, needs that were especially important to those living alone whose sole source of human touch was often the dating partner. The intimacy provided through sex also contributed to self-esteem by making people feel desired and needed. As one 77-year-old woman said, "Sex isn't as important when you're older, but in a way you need it more."

A major distinction we found between older and younger daters was in their attitudes toward passionate love, or what the Greeks called "the madness from the gods." Psychologists Elaine Hatfield, of the University of Hawaii in Manoa, and G. William Walster, of Los Gatos, California, have similarly defined passionate love as explosive; filled with fervor and short-lived. According to their theory of love, young people tend to equate passionate love with being in love. Once the first, intense love experience has faded, young lovers often seek a new partner.

For older daters, it is different. They have learned from experience that passionate love cannot be sustained with the same early level of intensity. But since most of them have been in marriages that lasted for decades, they also know the value of companionate love, that "steady burning fire" that not only endures but tends to grow deeper over time. As one older man put it, "Yeah, passion is nice . . . it's the frosting on the cake. But it's her personality that's really important. The first time I was in love it was only the excitement that mattered, but now it's the friendship . . . the ways we spend our time together that count."

Nonetheless, the pursuit of intimacy caused special problems for older people. Unlike younger daters, older people are faced with a lack of social cues indicating whether sexual behavior is appropriate in the dating relationship. Choosing to have a sexual relationship outside of marriage often goes against the system of values that they have followed during their entire lives.

Older couples also felt the need to hide the intimate aspects of their dating relationship because of a fear of social disapproval, creating a variety of covert behaviors. As one 63-year-old retiree said, "Yeah, my girlfriend (age 64) lives just down the hall from me . . . when she spends the night she usually brings her cordless phone . . . just in case her daughter calls." One 61-year-old woman told us that even though her 68-year-old boyfriend has been spending three or four nights a week at her house for the past year, she has not been able to tell her family. "I have a tendency to hide his shoes when my grandchildren are coming over."

Despite the fact that marriage would solve the problem of how to deal with the sexual aspects of the relationship, very few of these couples were interested in marriage. Some had assumed when they began dating that they would eventually marry but discovered as time went on that they weren't willing to give up their independence. For women especially, their divorce or widowhood marked the first time in their lives that they had been on their own. Although it was often difficult in the beginning, many discovered that they enjoyed their independence. Older people also said they didn't have the same reasons for marriage that younger people do: beginning a life together and starting a family. Another reason some elders were reluctant to marry was the possibility of deteriorating health. Many said they would not want to become a caretaker for an ill spouse.

Contrary to the popular belief that family would be protective and jealous of the dating relative, family members tended to be supportive of older copules' dating and often included the dating partner in family gatherings. The attitude that individuals have the right to personal happiness may be partially responsible for families' positive attitudes. But more importantly, many families realize that a significant other for an older person places fewer social demands on family members.

Peers also tended to be supportive, although many women reported sensing jealousy among their female friends, who were possibly unhappy because of their inability to find dating partners themselves and hurt because the dating women didn't have as much time to spend with them.

Our interviews with older daters revealed that the dating relationship is a critical, central part of elders' lives that provides something that cannot be supplied by family or friends. As one 65-year-old man told us, "I'm very happy with life right now. I'd be lost without my dating partner. I really would."

Our initial question, "What is the age of love?" is best answered in the words of one 64-year-old woman: "I suppose that hope does spring eternal in the human breast as far as love is concerned. People are always looking for the ultimate, perfect relationship. No matter how old they are, they are looking for this thing called love."

# Let's Put the PARENT Back in Grandparent

by Berkeley Rice

Arthur Kornhaber thinks millions of American grandparents need a collective kick in the pants. He accuses them of "dropping out" of family life when they retire, and "abandoning" their children and grandchildren.

"A lot of older people are emotionally selfish this way," says Kornhaber. "They look on family attachments as restricting rather than fulfilling, and view emotional bonds as bondage. But their goal as grandparents should be to nurture the younger generations, not to run off and play shuffleboard in the sun."

If this message makes you squirm a bit in self-recognition, you must be wondering just who this Arthur Kornhaber thinks he is, and what gives him the right to talk this way? The answer: *He's a man with a message*, a 53-year-old psychiatrist who has just written a book entitled "Between Parents and Grandparents" (St. Martin's Press). He's also the president of the Foundation for Grandparenting, an organization he's created to educate Americans about what he considers one of the country's most pressing social problems. According to Kornhaber, "powerful social trends and forces have weakened the relations between parents and grandparents, creating a nation of 'grandorphans' who are totally out of touch with their grandparents." These social trends are fairly well known: families move, or are transferred across the country; grandparents retire to Florida or Arizona or another sunbelt area; divorce and remarriage destroy the ties that used to bind the traditional three-generation family together.

While part of "the grandparent problem" can be attributed to increases in the divorce rate and social mobility, much of it is the result of the changing roles and attitudes of the grandparents themselves, Kornhaber contends. "Grandparents should be the emotional leaders and keepers of the extended family," he says. "They should fulfill a variety of vital roles for the younger generations. For openers, consider these five: 1) mentor, 2) wizard, 3) confidante, 4) historian and 5) storyteller. They should serve as negotiators when there are conflicts between generations, and as role models for their children's and grandchildren's old age. They must view themselves in terms of these family roles, and not as isolated individuals.

"Primitive societies knew this, and gave their elders a prominent role in village and family life, as repositories and teachers of tribal experience and wisdom. Our society has changed since then, but our biology hasn't. Grandparenting is a biological instinct that must be encouraged for the preservation of the species. If there are social forces that interfere with that natural urge, we must change our society."

When he gets rolling like this on his favorite topic, Kornhaber combines the rhetorical flourish and compelling enthusiasm of an old-fashioned preacher, a talent that makes him a persuasive lobbyist for his cause. In interviews with reporters or talk-show hosts, Kornhaber makes it clear that grandparenting is more than an academic interest for him—it's a crusade, one he's convinced is needed to preserve the American family.

Fifty years ago, when Kornhaber was growing up in New York's Bronx, life was different. The neighborhood was filled with closely knit multi-generation families. He was the oldest of eight children with dozens of aunts, uncles and cousins living nearby. "My grandparents lived just one block away," he recalls fondly, "and they were terrific. We were always going back and forth between each other's houses. With them, and all our aunts and uncles, there was an abundance of emotional attachments and security."

Kornhaber started out practicing general medicine, but soon shifted to pediatric psychiatry. For about 15 years he had a busy and successful clinical practice in Westchester County, a prosperous suburban area north of New York where he and his wife, Carol, also 53, raised their own four children.

Among the many children he saw in his office, Kornhaber was frequently struck by the importance of—but more often the absence of—a strong relationship between children and their grandparents. He particularly remembers Billy, a nervous eight-year-old, constantly in motion. "Billy believed that life was pretty terrible," says Kornhaber, "except when he was with his grandparents. They made him 'feel good', he used to tell me. What Billy loved most about them was their complete acceptance of him just as he was, in contrast to his parents, who were always critical of his behavior and performance."

For years Kornhaber treated many children like Billy. Becoming increasingly interested in the role of grandparents in family relationships, he searched through the psychological literature but found discouragingly little research devoted to this topic. Faced with this gap, he and wife Carol embarked on a three-year study of the relationship between grandchildren and their grandparents.

Their research showed that we have become a nation of "grandorphans," with the generations separated by cross-country moves, retirement, divorce and indifference. Among the children they interviewed, only 15 percent had close relationships with their grandparents. As Kornhaber had found in his own practice, those who did were "much healthier emotionally" than those who lacked this added dimension.

"When grandparents and their grandchildren are closely bonded," Kornhaber concluded, "they confer on each other a form of emotional immunity that no one else can give—certainly not the parents. The emotional conflicts that commonly occur between children and their parents rarely exist between children and their grandparents. (Grandparental love comes with no behavioral strings attached.) With them, the children do not have to 'perform' as they do for their parents and teachers."

Kornhaber's study resulted in a book entitled, "Grandparents/ Grandchildren: The Vital Connection." Published in 1981, the book led to lectures, TV appearances and radio talk shows, which brought hundreds of letters from people who poured out moving accounts of how they were cut off from their grandchildren.

To Kornhaber, the need for an organization for grandparents was plain. "At the clinic we were treating the daily problems on an individual basis. But once I realized the magnitude of this problem, I knew I had to take my ideas outside my own private practice and put them into action on a broader scale. I wanted to do preventative medicine, to practice social psychiatry."

In a major mid-life career change, Kornhaber has taken an "indefinite sabbatical" from his practice to launch the

Foundation for Grandparenting. It's a non-profit educational organization that serves as a clearinghouse for news, information and "networking," designed to raise public consciousness about the social, psychological and emotional importance of grandparents. The Foundation's newsletter, "Vital Connections," gives advice on such problems as "long-distance grandparenting," and reports on issues involving visiting rights for grandparents when families are separated by divorce.

With their own children grown and gone from home, the Kornhabers have used this career shift as an opportunity to move upstate to Lake Placid, N.Y., to the heart of the Adirondacks. There, in a handsome cedar-beamed lodge, they have created a comfortable new base for their own widely dispersed family. This winter all four of their children returned for Christmas, one bearing what will soon become the Kornhaber's first grandchild.

A husky, gray-haired six-footer, Kornhaber keeps in shape by splitting logs for his massive stone fireplace, and by jogging nearly every morning, even when the temperature hovers near zero. Up here in the mountains, his usual working uniform consists of sweaters, corduroys and boots, instead of the jackets, ties and polished shoes more appropriate to his former suburban medical practice.

I drove up to the Adirondacks to interview Kornhaber at the Foundation's headquarters in the small village of Jay, a 20-minute drive from Lake Placid over the winding Wilmington Notch road. I drove right past the Foundation at first because it's housed in a converted ski lodge at the foot of a small mountain. There, Kornhaber and his wife work out of adjacent pine-panelled offices. The casual atmosphere around these offices is deceptive, however. At work, at home, or at dinner in town, anyone who gets into a discussion with Kornhaber on the topic of grandparents quickly discovers that his interest is far from casual: he's clearly a man with a mission.

Although at this point the Foundation essentially consists of Arthur and Carol Kornhaber, both have abundant energy and a deep commitment to their cause. They already have several projects in the works or on the drawing boards: an "expectant grandparents" program; a summer camp for grandparents and their grandchildren; an "adopt-a-grandparent" program that would bring schoolchildren into nursing homes; and an "adopt-a-grandchild" program that would bring the elderly into daycare centers. These projects are now at various stages of development: the expectant grandparent project has already been tried out at one hospital; the summer camp will have a short trial run this summer at nearby Sagamore Lodge; the others are still in the planning stage, awaiting funding or under discussion with public officials in local communities.

One of the Foundation's most ambitious ideas is the "Centrum Project," which would put volunteer "grandparents" in the schools as teachers' aides. Each one would be assigned to several "grandchildren" in the first grade, and would be "promoted" along with them until they graduated from elementary school. One day a week the grandparents would attend their own training classes.

As Kornhaber sees it, the Centrum Project would "intergenerationalize" the schools, providing emotional support for both the children and the elders. "Our goal for this project," says Kornhaber, "is to produce a generation of children who have received the love and attention of their elders, and who will therefore be more emotionally secure and more socialized in the community."

In addition to running the Foundation, Kornhaber has found time to write his new book on the relationship "Between Parents and Grandparents." In it he deplores the decline of the "natural" or traditional family, and its replacement by what he calls "the contractual family." He describes the latter as a nuclear unit whose members are isolated and emotionally estranged from each other—within the family and between the generations. Since both parents often work, they hire "paid strangers" such as nannies or day-care centers to care for their children. Parents and children are cut off from grandparents, either because the parents or grandparents have moved, or because of divorce. The decline of the family farm and the family business, where the elders could offer valuable experience and assistance, has added to this unfortunate pattern.

In such families, Kornhaber feels, too many children grow up supposedly "independent," but emotionally insecure because they don't have the emotional support system of the extended family. As a result, when they grow up and start their own families, they tend to repeat the same pattern of intergenerational isolation. Like their own parents, they too will turn to friends and neighbors for emotional support, rather than their own family. Parents who raise their children this way are implicitly teaching them that family elders can be forgotten and discarded, a fate that parents will also suffer when they eventually become grandparents themselves.

Kornhaber lays part of the blame for this predicament on the grandparents themselves. "Grandparents in such contractual families tend to greet the birth of each new grandchild with ambivalence," he writes. They spend only token time with their children and grandchildren, preferring to associate with people their own age. Except for brief visits, generally around the holidays, they have essentially abandoned their children.

In his book, Kornhaber describes a couple in their thirties who typify this situation. The wife was raised in a warm and loving family, but her husband came from a family she refers to as "the coldest group of fishes I ever met. They have no closeness, no interest in what Bob and I are doing, and they couldn't care less about our kids. They don't give a hoot about anyone else in the family. If someone is in trouble and asks for help, they say, `Let him stew in his own juices.'"

Kornhaber sees hope even for these troubled, alienated families because the arrival of a grandchild provides an opportunity to rebuild relationships that have lapsed. "Grandparents should seize this chance to offer assistance and non-critical advice," he says. The new parents must also make an effort to include the grandparents in celebrating the newborn child, and to welcome whatever help they provide. Such help must be offered, however, not forced. Grandparents must learn to be "on call," helping to share the burdens of child-rearing.

As grandchildren grow, grandparents can overcome the separation of geographical distance with frequent notes, cards, pictures, videotapes and gifts. Kornhaber tells of one grandmother who records stories on tapes and sends them to her grandchildren to play at bedtime or during long trips. Many grandparents organize family reunions, or invite their grandchildren to spend part of their vacations with them. If the parents or grandparents must move, Kornhaber feels the grandparents must remain flexible enough to make frequent visits possible, and to be involved when family emergencies occur. When retirement comes, he says, it means not moving so far away that contact becomes impractical.

For many modern American families, it will take a concerted effort by both parents and grandparents to retain the bonds that keep traditional families together. But Kornhaber is convinced the effort is necessary and highly worthwhile, for only in this way will grandparents fulfill their natural and instinctive role as useful, respected and beloved family elders.

Inspired by Kornhaber's message, I called my own mother soon after I returned home, and tried for a third time to talk her into joining us for Christmas, using our two children—her grandchildren—as bait. The previous two years she had come up with enough excuses to avoid the visit: the prospect of bad weather; the long bus ride; various minor medical problems. She tried them all again, but this time I insisted, threatening to make the five hour drive myself to pick her up. Persuaded or perhaps overwhelmed by my insistence, she finally gave in and came on her own. She had a great time, and the kids enjoyed having her with us again. Kornhaber is right. It does take an effort, on both sides. But it's worth it.

# The Vintage Years

by Jack C. Horn and Jeff Meer

Our society is getting older, but the old are getting younger. As Sylvia Herz told an American Psychological Association (APA) symposium on aging last year, the activities and attitudes of a 70-year-old today "are equivalent to those of a 50-year-old's a decade or two ago."

Our notions of what it means to be old are beginning to catch up with this reality. During the past several decades, three major changes have altered the way we view the years after 65:

❑   The financial, physical and mental health of older people has improved, making the prospect of a long life something to treasure, not fear.

❑   The population of older people has grown dramatically, rising from 18 million in 1965 to 28 million today. People older than 65 compose 12 percent of the population, a percentage that is expected to rise to more than 20 percent by the year 2030.

❑   Researchers have gained a much better understanding of age and the lives of older people, helping to sort out the inevitable results of biological aging from the effects of illness or social and environmental problems. No one has yet found the fountain of youth, or of immortality. But research has revealed that aging itself is not the thief we once thought it was; healthy older people can maintain and enjoy most of their physical and mental abilities, and even improve in some areas.

Because of better medical care, improved diet and increasing interest in physical fitness, more people are reaching the ages of 65, 75 and older in excellent health. Their functional age—a combination of physical, psychological and social factors that affect their attitudes toward life and the roles they play in the world—is much younger than their chronological age.

Their economic health is better, too, by almost every measure. Over the past three decades, for example, the number of men and women 65 and older who live below the poverty line has dropped steadily from 35 percent in 1959 to 12 percent in 1984, the last year for which figures were available.

On the upper end of the economic scale, many of our biggest companies are headed by what once would have been called senior citizens, and many more of them serve as directors of leading companies. Even on a more modest economic level, a good portion of the United States' retired older people form a new leisure class, one with money to spend and the time to enjoy it. Obviously not all of America's older people share this prosperity. Economic hardship is particularly prevalent among minorities. But as a group, our older people are doing better than ever.

In two other areas of power, politics and the law, people in their 60s and 70s have always played important roles. A higher percentage of people from 65 to 74 register and vote than in any other group. With today's increasing vigor and numbers, their power is likely to increase still further. It is perhaps no coincidence that our current President is the oldest ever.

Changing attitudes, personal and social, are a major reason for the increasing importance of older people in our society. As psychologist Bernice Neugarten points out, there is no longer a particular age at which someone starts to work or attends school, marries and has children, retires or starts a business (see "The Changing Meanings of Age" this issue). Increasing numbers of older men and women are enrolled in colleges, universities and other institutions of learning. According to the Center for Education Statistics, for example, the number of people 65 and older enrolled in adult education of all kinds increased from 765,000 to 866,000 from 1981 to 1984. Gerontologist Barbara Ober says that this growing interest in education is much more than a way to pass the time. "Older people make excellent students, maybe even better students than the majority of 19- and 20-year-olds. One advantage is that they have settled a lot of the social and sexual issues that preoccupy their younger classmates."

Older people today are not only healthier and more active; they are also increasingly more numerous. "Squaring the pyramid" is how some demographers describe this change in our population structure. It has always been thought of as a pyramid, a broad base of newborns supporting successively smaller tiers of older people as they died from disease, accidents, poor nutrition, war and other causes.

Today, the population structure is becoming more rectangular, as fewer people die during the earlier stages of life. The Census Bureau predicts that by 2030 the structure will be an almost perfect rectangle up to the age of 70.

The aging of America has been going on at least since 1800, when half the people in the country were younger than 16 years old, but two factors have accelerated the trend tremendously. First, the number of old people has increased rapidly. Since 1950 the number of Americans 65 and older has more than doubled to some 28 million—more than the entire current population of Canada. Within the same period, the number of individuals older than 85 has quadrupled to about 2.6 million.

Second, the boom in old people has been paired with a burst in the proportion of youngsters due to a declining birth rate. Today, fewer than one American in four is younger than 16. This drop-off has been steady, with the single exception of the post-World War II baby boom, which added 76 million children to the country between 1945 and 1964. As these baby boomers reach the age of 65, starting in 2010, they are expected to increase the proportion of the population 65 and older from its current 12 percent to 21 percent by 2030.

The growing presence of healthy, vigorous older people has helped overcome some of the stereotypes about aging and the elderly. Research has also played a major part by replacing myths with facts. While there were some studies of aging before World War II, scientific interest increased dramatically during the 1950s and kept growing.

Important early studies of aging include three started in the mid or late 1950s: the Human Aging Study, conducted by the National Institute of Mental Health (NIMH); the Duke Longitudinal Studies, done by the Center for the Study of Aging and Human Development at Duke University; and the Baltimore Longitudinal Study of Aging, conducted by the Gerontological Institute in Baltimore, now part of the National Institute on Aging (NIA). All three took a multidisciplinary approach to the study of normal aging: what changes take place, how people adapt to them, how biological, genetic, social, psychological and environmental characteristics relate to longevity and what can be done to promote successful aging.

These pioneering studies and hundreds of later ones have benefited from growing federal support. White House Conferences on Aging in 1961 and 1971 helped focus attention on the subject. By 1965 Congress had enacted Medicare and the Older Americans Act. During the 1970s Congress authorized the establishment of the NIA as part of the National Institutes of Health and NIMH created a special center to support research on the mental health of older people.

All these efforts have produced a tremendous growth in our knowledge of aging. In the first (1971) edition of the *Handbook of the Psychology of Aging*, it was estimated that as much had been published on the subject in the previous 15 years as in all the years before then. In the second edition, published in 1985, psychologists James Birren and Walter Cunningham wrote that the "period for this rate of doubling has now decreased to 10 years . . . the volume of published research has increased to the almost unmanageable total of over a thousand articles a year."

Psychologist Clifford Swenson of Purdue University explained some of the powerful incentives for this tremendous increase: "I study the topic partly to discover more effective ways of helping old people cope with their problems, but also to load my own armamentarium against that inevitable day. For that is one aspect of aging and its problems that makes it different from other problems psychologists study: We may not all be schizophrenic or neurotic or overweight, but there is only one alternative to old age and most of us try to avoid that alternative."

One popular misconception disputed by recent research is the idea that aging means inevitable physical and sexual failure. Some changes occur, of course. Reflexes slow, hearing and eyesight dim, stamina decreases. This *primary aging* is a gradual process that begins early in life and affects all body systems.

But many of the problems we associate with old age are *secondary aging*—the results not of age but of disease, abuse and disuse—factors often under our own control. More and more older people are healthy, vigorous men and women who lead enjoyable, active lives. National surveys by the Institute for Social Research and others show that life generally seems less troublesome and freer to older people than it does to younger adults.

In a review of what researchers have learned about subjective well-being—happiness, life satisfaction, positive emotions—University of Illinois psychologist Ed Diener reported that "Most results show a slow rise in satisfaction with age . . . young persons appear to experience higher levels of joy but older persons tend to judge their lives in more positive ways."

Money is often mentioned as the key to a happy retirement, but psychologist Daniel Ogilvie of Rutgers University has found another, much more important factor. Once we have a certain minimum amount of money, his research shows, life satisfaction depends mainly on how much time we spend doing things we find meaningful. Ogilvie believes retirement-planning workshops and seminars should spend time helping people decide how to use their skills and interests after they retire.

A thought that comes through clearly when researchers talk about physical and mental fitness is "use it or lose it." People rust out faster from disuse than they wear out from overuse. This advice applies equally to sexual activity. While every study from the time of Kinsey to the present shows that sexual interest and activity diminish with age, the drop varies greatly among individuals. Psychologist Marion Perlmutter and writer Elizabeth Hall have reported that one of the best predictors of continued sexual intercourse "is early sexual activity and past sexual enjoyment and frequency. People who have never had much pleasure from sexuality may regard their age as a good excuse for giving up sex."

They also point out that changing times affect sexual activity. As today's younger adults bring their more liberal sexual attitudes with them into old age, the level of sexual activity among older men and women may rise.

The idea that mental abilities decline steadily with age has also been challenged by many recent and not-so-recent findings (see "The Reason of Age," *Psychology Today*, June 1986). In brief, age doesn't damage abilities as much as once believed, and in some areas we actually gain; we learn to compensate through experience for much of what we do lose, and we can restore some losses through training.

For years, older people didn't do as well as younger people on most tests used to measure mental ability. But psychologist Leonard Poon of the University of Georgia believes that researchers are now taking a new, more appropriate approach to measurement. "Instead of looking at older people's ability to do abstract tasks that have little or no relationship to what they do every day, today's researchers are examining real-life issues."

Psychologist Gisela Labouvie-Vief of Wayne State University has been measuring how people approach everyday problems in logic. She notes that older adults have usually done poorly on such tests, mostly because they fail to think logically all the time. But Labouvie-Vief argues that this is not because they have forgotten how to think logically but because they use a more complex approach unknown to younger thinkers. "The [older] thinker operates within a kind of double reality which is both formal and informal, both logical and psychological," she says.

In other studies, Labouvie-Vief has found that when older people are asked to give concise summaries of fables they read, they did so. But when they were simply asked to recall as much of the fable as possible, they concentrated on the metaphorical, moral or social meaning of the text. They didn't try to duplicate the fable's exact words, the way younger people did. As psychologists Nancy Datan, Dean Rodeheaver and Fergus Hughes of the University of Wisconsin have described in their findings, "while [some people assume] that old and young are equally competent, we might better assume that they are differently competent."

John Horn, director of the Adult Development and Aging program at the University of Southern California, suggests that studies of Alzheimer's disease, a devastating progressive mental deterioration experienced by an estimated 5 percent to 15 percent of those older than 65, may eventually help explain some of the differences in thinking abilities of older people. "Alzheimer's, in some ways, may represent the normal process of aging, only speeded up," he says.

Generalities are always suspect, but one generalization about old age seems solid: It is a different experience for men and women. Longevity is one important reason. Women in the United States live seven to eight years longer, on the average, than do men. This simple fact has many ramifications, as sociologist Gunhild Hagestad explained in *Our Aging Society*.

For one thing, since the world of the very old is disproportionately a world of women, men and women spend their later years differently. "Most older women are widows living alone; most older men live with their wives . . . among individuals over the age of 75, two-thirds of the men are living with a spouse, while less than one-fifth of the women are."

The difference in longevity also means that among older people, remarriage is a male prerogative. After 65, for example, men remarry at a rate eight times that of women. This is partly a matter of the scarcity of men and partly a matter of culture—even late in life, men tend to marry younger women. It is also a matter of education and finances, which, Hagestad explains, "operate quite differently in shaping remarriage possibilities among men and women. The more resources a woman has available (measured in education and income), the less likely she is to remarry. For men, the trend is reversed."

The economic situations of elderly men and women also differ considerably. Lou Glasse, president of the Older Women's League in Washington, D.C., points out that most of these women were housewives who worked at paid jobs sporadically, if at all. "That means their Social Security benefits are lower than men's, they are not likely to have pensions and they are less likely to have been able to save the kind of money that would protect them from poverty during their older years."

Although we often think of elderly men and women as living in nursing homes or retirement communities, the facts are quite different. Only about 5 percent are in nursing homes and perhaps an equal number live in some kind of age-segregated housing. Most people older than 65 live in their own houses or apartments.

We also think of older people as living alone. According to the Census Bureau, this is true of 15 percent of the men and 41 percent of the women. Earlier this year, a survey done by Louis Harris & Associates revealed that 28 percent of elderly people living alone have annual incomes below $5,100, the federal poverty line. Despite this, they were four times as likely to give financial help to their children as to receive it from them.

In addition, fewer than 1 percent of the old people said they would prefer living with their children. Psychiatrist Robert N. Butler, chairman of the Commonwealth Fund's Commission on Elderly People Living Alone, which sponsored the report, noted that these findings dispute the "popular portrait of an elderly, dependent parent financially draining their middle-aged children."

There is often another kind of drain, however, one of time and effort. The Travelers Insurance Company recently surveyed more than 700 of its employees on this issue. Of those at least 30 years old, 28 percent said they directly care for an older relative in some way—taking that person to the doctor, making telephone calls, handling finances or running errands—for an average of 10 hours a week. Women, who are more often caregivers, spent an average of 16 hours, and men five hours, per week. One group, 8 percent of the sample, spend a heroic 35 hours per week, the equivalent of a second job, providing such care. "That adds up to an awful lot of time away from other things," psychologist Beal Lowe says, "and the stresses these people face are enormous."

Lowe, working with Sherman-Lank Communications in Kensington, Maryland, has formed "Caring for Caregivers," a group of professionals devoted to providing services, information and support to those who care for older relatives. "It can be a great shock to some people who have planned the perfect retirement," he says, "only to realize that your chronically ill mother suddenly needs daily attention."

Researchers who have studied the housing needs of older people predictably disagree on many things, but most agree on two points: We need a variety of individual and group living arrangements to meet the varying interests, income and abilities of people older than 65; and the arrangements should be flexible enough that the elderly can stay in the same locale as their needs and abilities change. Many studies have documented the fact that moving itself can be stressful and even fatal to old people, particularly if they have little or no influence over when and where they move.

This matter of control is important, but more complicated than it seemed at first. Psychologist Judith Rodin and others have demonstrated that people in nursing homes are happier, more alert and live longer if they are allowed to take responsibility for their lives in some way, even in something as choosing a plant for their room, taking care of a bird feeder, selecting the night to attend a movie.

Rodin warns that while control is generally beneficial, the effect depends on the individuals involved. For some, personal control brings with it demands in the form of time, effort and the risk of failure. They may blame themselves if they get sick or something else goes wrong. The challenge, Rodin wrote, is to "provide but not impose opportunities. . . . The need for self-determination, it must be remembered, also calls for the opportunity to choose not to exercise control. . . ."

An ancient Greek myth tells how the Goddess of Dawn fell in love with a mortal and convinced Jupiter to grant him immortality. Unfortunately, she forgot to have youth included in the deal, so he gradually grew older and older. "At length," the story concludes, "he lost the power of using his limbs, and then she shut him up in his chamber, whence his feeble voice might at times be heard. Finally she turned him into a grasshopper."

The fears and misunderstandings of age expressed in this 3,000-year-old myth persist today, despite all the positive things we have learned in recent years about life after 65. We don't turn older people into grasshoppers or shut them out of sight, but too often we move them firmly out of the mainstream of life.

In a speech at the celebration of Harvard University's 350th anniversary last September, political scientist Robert Binstock decried what he called The Spectre of the Aging Society: "the economic burdens of population aging; moral dilemmas posed by the allocation of health resources on the basis of age; labor market competition between older and younger workers within the contexts of age discrimination laws; seniority practices, rapid technological change; and a politics of conflict between age groups."

Binstock, a professor at Case Western Reserve School of Medicine, pointed out that these inaccurate perceptions express an underlying ageism, "the attribution of these same characteristics and status to an artificially homogenized group labeled 'the aged.'"

Ironically, such ageism is based on compassion rather than ill will. To protect older workers from layoffs, for example, unions fought hard for job security based on seniority. To win it, they accepted mandatory retirement, a limitation that now penalizes older workers and deprives our society of their experience.

A few companies have taken special steps to utilize this valuable pool of older workers. The Travelers companies, for example set up a job bank that is open to its own retired employees as well as those of other companies. According to Howard E. Johnson, a senior vice president, the company employs about 175 formerly retired men and women a week. He estimates that the program is saving Travelers $1 million a year in temporary-hire fees alone.

While mandatory retirement is only one example of ageism, it is particularly important because we usually think of contributions to society in economic terms. Malcolm H. Morrison, an authority on retirement and age discrimination in employment for the Social Security Administration, points out that once the idea of retirement at a certain fixed age was accepted, "the old became defined as a dependent group in society, a group whose members could not and should not work, and who needed economic and social assistance that the younger working population was obligated to provide."

We need to replace this stereotype with the more realistic understanding that older people are and should be productive members of society, capable of assuming greater responsibility for themselves and others. What researchers have learned about the strengths and abilities of older people should help us turn this ideal of an active, useful life after 65 into a working reality.

# Appendix B

# Answer Key

Many of the self-test questions in this telecourse guide can be answered based on information provided in the text, telecourse guide, *and* video. For purposes of this answer key, however, only the text references will be cited.

1. b  (Page 4)
2. c  (Page 24)
3. c  (Page 9)
4. b  (Page 20)
5. d  (Page 37)
6. c  (Page 44)
7. d  (Pages 44–47)
8. a  (Pages 44–49)
9. d  (Page 10)
10. c  (Pages 24–25)

**Lesson 1 – Family Portraits**

1. c  (Page 12)
2. b  (Page 20 and entire lesson)
3. d  (Pages 12–13 and entire lesson)
4. d  (Page 14)
5. c  (Page 17)
6. d  (Pages 17–18)
7. d  (Pages 17–18)
8. d  (Page 30)
9. a  (Page 39)
10. b  (Page 32)

**Lesson 2 – The Seasons of Life**

**Lesson 3 – When I Grow Up...**

1. c (Page 54)
2. b (Page 55) Intelligence and height (Options A and C) would not be considered either instrumental or expressive. Competitiveness (D) would be considered an instrumental character trait.
3. a (Page 54)
4. c (Page 65)
5. d (Page 57 and entire lesson)
6. c (Pages 65–66)
7. a (Pages 57–58)
8. d (Page 66)
9. c (Page 62)
10. d (Page 65)

**Lesson 4 – Adam's Equal or Adam's Rib?**

1. c (Page 67) Notice that in Options A, B, and D, the persons do not seem particularly influenced by social pressure. Only the person in Option C (based on what we know) is allowing outside social pressures to have a strong influence on her decision. She is adopting the attitudes she feels society would wish her to adopt, and that is part of internalization—making society's attitudes our own.
2. a (Page 67)
3. b (Page 68) In fact, it is usually the mother who provides most early care and affection (Option D), but the link with the mother appears very strong even if another caretaker is present.
4. d (Page 68–69)
5. a (Page 69)
6. a (Page 73) Options B, C, and D may all contain elements of truth, but none is accurate as stated. Men do have an expressive side to their nature (Option B), but it is not accurate to say that the expressive side dominates. True enough, men are competing with more women for jobs (Option C), but it is the pressure to succeed per se, not the competition of women versus men, that produces stress. Option D suggests that women are more able to cope with the stress of a constantly competitive environment; it is probably more accurate to say that the pressures of competition take a toll on everyone.
7. c (Pages 75–76)
8. d (Pages 78–80)

9. b (Pages 76–81) Only Option B shows a person torn by an internal struggle that is characteristic of ambivalence—the conflict between opposing attitudes or viewpoints, sometimes between what one feels and what society expects. Joe, Bill, and Larry are pretty clear about their feelings—though they may still have some problems to resolve. George, on the other hand, is reluctant to express what he feels—vulnerability, fear, anxiety –which would conflict with his image as a successful professional person capable of filling the role of sole breadwinner.

10. b (Page 79)

1. b (Page 86)
2. a (Page 86)
3. a (Page 94)
4. d (Page 94) Manipulators tend to feel guilty; martyrs tend to feel angry because—despite the fact they themselves are the givers, and they contribute to their own situation—they realize they're not receiving as much from the relationship as the other person. Sylvia would feel in love if she were romanticizing, which she is not. She would feel content and satisfied only if this were an equitable relationship, which it is not.
5. c (Pages 95–96) Research indicates that in a symbiotic relationship—which this martyr-manipulator relationship is—stability depends on the partners continuing their roles. If either becomes more independent, the relationship tends to lose its stability, and the other partner—no longer sure what role to play or how to play it—may feel lost.
6. b (Pages 92–94)
7. b (Page 93)
8. d (Page 88)
9. c (Pages 96–98) John obviously needs lots of approval from others. He tends to lack conviction, to question the value of his own work and performance, to be easily led by others, and to be surprised (though pleased) when others like him. A person with no more self-esteem than this is likely to have a hard time giving love or receiving it without doubting the other person's motives—e.g., "Do I really deserve it?"

**Lesson 5 – Learning to Love**

10. a  (Page 99) A person with relatively low self-esteem is likely to exhibit highly dependent behavior; thus fitting best into an A-frame relationship, characterized by strong mutual dependence. John lacks the independence and self-esteem to fit into either the H- or M-frame models.

**Lesson 6 – The Pleasure Bond**

1. a  (Page 108)
2. b  (Page 109)
3. c  (Pages 561–562)
4. d  (Telecourse guide)
5. c  (Telecourse guide)
6. d  (Page 110)
7. a  (Pages 109–110) Social scientists tend to believe that sexual preference is the real determining factor in classifying persons as relatively homo- or heterosexual. True, Bill did have one homosexual relationship. But it was short-lived, and he did not enter another similar relationship. This suggests that he was probably exploring his own feelings rather than expressing his true sexual nature.
8. c  (Page 111)
9. b  (Pages 116–117)
10. c  (Page 127)

**Lesson 7 – Epidemic Proportions**

1. d  (Pages 137–139)
2. c  (Page 132)
3. a  (Page 137) While it is likely that the commitment to treating and curing AIDS will outdistance the efforts directed at herpes, the *initial* commitment to AIDS is recognized as having been less than that for herpes. This may be because middle class America saw herpes as more of a threat and problem for itself, while it saw AIDS as a problem restricted to lower socioeconomic and disfavored social groups. Indeed, gay rights activists have often charged that the lack of commitment to research on AIDS is the result of discrimination. Option C is incorrect; AIDS has received significant media attention.
4. b  (Page 135, 139–140, Box 5.3) It seems fair to say that Eunice has a moral obligation to share what information she has with Frank. There is no particular reason to stop dating altogether or to become reclusive (Option D). But at the same time, it might be

wise to cease sexual activity until she can be quite certain that she could not transmit AIDS to another person. This may require that both Eunice and Bob be tested for AIDS. If Eunice simply says nothing (Options A and C), regardless of whether she has sex with Frank, her silence about such an important matter could well threaten their relationship.

5.  c  (Page 130)
6.  b  (Page 131)
7.  c  (Page 132)
8.  b  (Page 131) Even if Burt has no reason to believe his friends are currently carriers of AIDS, the fact that they (both as homosexuals and as drug addicts) are already members of high-risk groups puts Burt at high risk as well. Burt could contract AIDS from such persons either by homosexual contact or the sharing of intravenous needles. Option D addresses a relevant issue; Burt's general state of health might well be a factor, but he is still at high risk regardless of whether his addiction has damaged his overall immunity to disease.
9.  b  (Page 136)
10. a  (Page 132)

1.  b  (Page 146 and entire lesson)
2.  a  (Pages 149–150 and entire lesson)
3.  a  (Pages 146–148 and entire lesson)
4.  b  (Page 149) Having grown up during the Depression, Ed is most likely—according to research—to have a very strong sense of family that will shape his decision-making throughout life. He is less likely, all other things being equal, to divorce or separate from his wife, or to take any steps that threaten the integrity of the family, which he (as a typical child of the 1930s) holds in very high regard.
5.  d  (Pages 157–164)
6.  d  (Pages 150–153 and entire lesson) Emily's attitudes and feelings cannot be characterized as typical, since there is no typical single person. At the same time, it's also accurate to say that many singles do share Emily's perspective, and hope ultimately to marry. It is inaccurate, however, to describe these people as typically depressed or lonely.
7.  a  (Page 175 and entire lesson)

8.  d  (Page 153)

9.  c  (Page 157 and Table 6.2, page 160) Martha fits the pattern of the involuntary temporary single because she plans to marry, despite her earlier commitment to singlehood. Even if she is never successful in her search for a mate, she continues to be classified as an involuntary temporary single as long as she does not give up on the idea of eventually marrying. In other words, Martha has not accepted the state of singlehood as permanent.

10. d  (Page 178 and entire lesson) Singles do not necessarily prefer to live alone (Option C), and while some people may have a need to see singles as lonely (Option B), an equal number of us may tend to view them as happier than they really are. The research—which is not limited (Option A)—tends to suggest that singles are often lonely, and that it can be difficult to establish primary relationships outside of marriage. It can be done, of course. But often, unmarried people tend to have secondary relationships, which are less fulfilling because they are not as intimate and because they may focus on only one part of an individual's personality—the person as worker, for instance. A whole world of only secondary relationships can leave a person feeling fragmented, misunderstood, and lonely.

**Lesson 9 – The Marriage Market**

1.  d  (Page 184–185)

2.  a  (Page 185)

3.  a  (Pages 203–204) Though people are not precisely "buying and selling" in this marital marketplace, it is quite accurate to say that they are engaged in trade. A woman, for example, may exchange her household management and childbearing capabilities for some combination of emotional satisfaction and financial security. The precise nature of the trade varies with virtually every marriage, of course; some people are more interested in love, some in finances, and so on. The array of resources with which people can bargain is as varied as people themselves.

4.  a  (Page 205)

5.  b  (Pages 203–206 and entire lesson) While there is no way to predict for certain what will happen to people like Bob and Rita, the important factor to consider

here is their relative happiness with the relationship. It may be that Rita, herself an ambitious and successful person, is more interested in having a domestically oriented, nurturing mate than another ambitious person like herself. And if Bob is happy in his role, and derives what he needs from the marriage, there is no reason it cannot succeed.

6.  d   (Pages 208–209) Homogamy implies similarity with respect to race, culture, religion, age, educational background, and social class. Each example in the question presents some difference between the two partners which disqualifies it as an example of true homogamy.

7.  d   (Pages 208–209)

8.  c   (Pages 213–218) True, George and Mina have the odds against them. They differ in age, religion, race, and culture. Their occupations suggest, however, that they may share some similarities in educational background, and perhaps in values as well. If that value structure is strong enough, it will tend to be a more powerful bond in the long run than commonalities of religion, race, age, and so on.

9.  a   (Pages 189–190) For better or worse, most of us tend to base at least some of our initial judgment on a person's appearance. Thus, physical attractiveness does play a role in initiating most relationships. As people learn more about one another, though, that role tends to diminish—though obviously, a partner's looks are more important to some people than others. There's no evidence, however, that the relative importance of physical appearance is different for men and women.

10. b   (Page 197)

1.  a   (Pages 32–37)

2.  b   (Pages 4–10) Option D may seem to have some validity, given the increasing diversity in family structure. But note that diversity is not equivalent to lack of structure. Further, families are defined according to interpersonal relationships—not residence; although in fact, families tend to live under the same roof. Options A and C are both false.

3.  d   (Page 33)

4.  b   (Telecourse guide and video)

**Lesson 10 –
Variations on a
Theme**

5.   c   (Page 548) A commune (Option B) would have to include several smaller family units. Both a nuclear
family and a stepfamily include a man and a woman.
The nuclear family consists of two married partners
and their offspring; the stepfamily includes a man
and a woman, at least one of whom has been married
before, and one or more children from previous marriages.

6.   c   (Telecourse guide)

7.   d   (Pages 164–165)

8.   a   (Telecourse guide and video)

9.   b   (Pages 164–165)

10.  c   (Pages 4–10 and entire lesson) Option A is not really
accurate. It isn't so much that we've had difficulty
defining the concept of family; it's more that that
definition is shifting and expanding. Yes, laws (Option B) are having an impact on family structure and
practices, but overall, the trend is toward liberaliza-
tion. Option D is simply inaccurate. If anything, the
sense of family commitment is stronger than ever for
most people; however, the kind of family in which
they choose to express that commitment may be
changing dramatically.

**Lesson 11 – Great
Expectations**

1.   d   (Pages 229–235 and entire lesson)

2.   c   (Pages 235–237)

3.   b   (Page 237) In fact, many Americans do not practice
sexual exclusivity, though most (not all) give lip service to it as part of their wedding vows. For most of
us, such exclusivity is an assumption—whether expressed or not. And our belief in "strict monogamy,"
as the social scientists sometimes call it, is well
founded in Judeo-Christian tradition. Indeed, our
culture tends to emphasize sexual exclusivity more
than most other cultures.

4.   a   (Page 239) Any of the options—B, C, or D—can play
a part, but the truth is that most people seem to have
affairs for a combination of reasons, not just one reason. Further, their motivation may be a little unclear
even to themselves.

5.   d   (Page 241) We usually think of jealousy as centering
around a person, and often involving a threat to a
sexual relationship. However, jealousy may center
around anything which seems to take one spouse's

attention away from the other—in this case, the bowling night is making Marie feel that she is no longer a part of Bernie's life.

6. a (Page 229)
7. d (Page 229)
8. c (Pages 232–233) John and Martha's marriage could probably best be defined as conflict-habituated. In such marriages, psychologists suggest, many couples derive satisfaction despite the constant tension. They may even thrive on it. Such marriages, outward appearances notwithstanding, may be very stable, and do not necessarily end in divorce. Conflicts, however, are rarely resolved—partly because partners seem to have a vested interest in keeping the tension alive, and partly because arguments rarely focus on the real subject of controversy.
9. b (Pages 232–236)
10. d (Pages 252–253)

**Lesson 12 – Intimate Connections**

1. a (Page 258 and entire lesson)
2. c (Pages 258–259) Notice that Rodney's father pretends to be listening, giving Rodney token attention out of a sense of duty, perhaps—but not really caring about Rodney's performance. This message is bound to get through eventually, even if Rodney is a little puzzled (Option D) at first. It is almost certain that Rodney cares very much about his father's opinion and reaction to his performance; for that reason, he'll be very tuned in to all verbal and nonverbal cues—which in this case, unfortunately, do not reflect much concern or interest.
3. b (Pages 258–259) Alice's early experience within her immediate family (as a child) is likely to have a stronger influence over self-concept and self-image than later experiences. If she enters marriage seeing herself as a strong-willed, intelligent, and resourceful person, that image is not likely to be greatly changed.
4. d (Pages 258–260) People tend to become the selves that we create through our descriptions of them.
5. d (Page 259)
6. a (Page 279)
7. b (Pages 279–280) Option C may look right; however, what matters is spending some family time together.

It is certainly not necessary that persons give up their individuality and all take up the same hobby—in fact, that could lead to more frustration than unity. There is no evidence to suggest that Option A is correct either; again, what is important is ensuring that neither work nor other outside activities eliminate all possibility of family time together. Option D is incorrect.Arguing is a natural part of life in any family; what matters here is how the arguments are conducted and whether fight tactics turn out to be damaging to individuals.

8.  a   (Page 259)
9.  b   (Page 259)
10. a   (Pages 258–259) The significant others in Emily's life—in this case, parents and friends—are likely to have a strong impact on the way she perceives herself. If the early messages Emily receives say "talented singer," then Emily is likely to adopt those messages as true, even if objective facts argue otherwise.

**Lesson 13 – For Better or Worse**

1.  b   (Page 270) Option A is partially correct, but it is really a secondary outcome. The real goal of bonding fighting is better communication and improved intimacy between the partners. Options C and D are both false and, in fact, would be counterproductive goals.

2.  a   (Pages 261–263) What Jack needs to do in this instance is level with Jane—be honest about the feelings he has, even if he feels guilty or ridiculous. Until he's honest, nothing can be done about the real problem.

3.  d   (Page 273) Psychologists suggest that "I statements" are generally more productive in fair fighting than those that focus on *you* or on ways of accusing the partner.

4.  d   (Page 272–273) Research indicates that body language and facial expression may speak louder than words.

5.  d   (Page 274)

6.  d   (Page 274) Options A, B, and C are all likely to be counter-productive. Note, however, that it isn't desirable to be overly aggressive or tactless (Option C); yet no matter how hard we try, if we're honest with

another person feelings are likely to be hurt some-times, even when we would wish otherwise.

7. c (Pages 274–275) Crying is a natural response to emotional upset, and *may* signal that a partner has simply had enough for the time being. There is no reason to conclude that Amy is weak or over-emotional because of this response; another person might give the same message by becoming quiet or very angry. The point is, the discussion is not likely to be very productive when one or both partners are under severe emotional stress. Some arguments may need to proceed in stages.

8. a (Pages 275–276) Option D is possible, of course, es-pecially if Gary really wants his own life to be differ-ent. Nevertheless, change does not come easily; the motivation must be very strong. Indications are that most of us repeat the patterns we see modeled by parents.

9. b (Pages 260–261)
10. d (Pages 277–279)

**Lesson 14 – Power Plays**

1. a (Page 287)
2. d (Page 286)
3. c (Pages 287–288) The woman in Option C has the greatest potential earning power by far—even though she is just completing her training and has two children. According to the resource hypothesis, then, she would have the greatest power.
4. d (Page 288)
5. b (Page 290) Gender continues to be the primary fac-tor in determining conjugal power, partly because of the influence of tradition, but also because it is often the man who brings the greater resources (more money and earning power) to the marriage in the first place. Further, because men do not bear chil-dren, they are less vulnerable to having their power reduced during the course of the marriage.
6. d (Page 295)
7. c (Page 294)
8. c (Page 293) Both men and women need love, but the wife may be conditioned to believe that her need is greater—and society often reinforces this condition-ing, suggesting in subtle (and overt) ways that it is

usually the woman who holds the family together, while the man has a lesser emotional investment.

9.   b   (Page 297) Option C is almost correct, but misses the point. In a no-power relationship, spouses are not competing for power or dominance over each other. Both, rather, are working hard to achieve a balance of power, and their neutralizing strategies are directed toward achieving and maintaining this balance, not toward furthering their personal ambitions.

10.   c   (Pages 299–302)

## Lesson 15 – Behind Closed Doors

1.   b   (Pages 303–305)
2.   a   (Page 304) If anything, our definitions of wife abuse have grown broader (Option D). Data-gathering procedures per se are not to blame for the fuzziness; the problem has been the reluctance of victims to report abuse out of fear, ignorance, and a host of other motives.
3.   b   (Pages 310–312)
4.   c   (Page 305)
5.   c   (Page 307)
6.   d   (Page 307)
7.   d   (Page 307) Certainly, some wife abuse is carried out while under the influence of alcohol or drugs (Option C), but the drinking or drug abuse do not *cause* the feelings leading to the beating.
8.   b   (Pages 307–308)
9.   a   (Page 313)
10.   d   (Page 309) Options A, B, and C are all false. And while husband abuse may be more humiliating, most social scientists would argue that it is less a problem than wife abuse, for a wide range of reasons—not the least of which is the fact that wives are more likely than husbands to suffer serious physical injury as a result of domestic violence.

## Lesson 16 – Working Husbands/ Working Wives

1.   d   (Page 405)
2.   c   (Page 405) Though the U.S. has managed to create jobs at a far higher rate than many European nations, they are often low-paying, part-time service jobs that don't contribute as much to per-capita income. Industrial and white-collar employment have both been hard hit as the U.S. has been forced to compete directly in the world market.

3. d (Page 406) This adjustment is central to both partner's sense of worth, whatever their economic or educational status. Because the traditional expectations of both husbands and wives have not caught up
with the emerging service society, considerable negotiation and compromise on both sides are often required for such an adjustment to occur.
4. d (Page 406)
5. b (Pages 419–420)
6. b (Pages 410–411)
7. c (Pages 427–428)
8. a (Pages 417–418)
9. d (Pages 432–438)
10. b (Page 432)

1. b (Page 325)
2. a (Page 329)
3. d (Page 331)
4. b (Page 332)
5. a (Pages 332–333)
6. a (Page 337)
7. c (Page 344)
8. b (Page 347)
9. b (Page 347) Also read pages 566–567, "Monitoring
Fetal Development," in Appendix C.
10. a (Page 351)

**Lesson 17 – To Parent or Not to Parent**

1. a (Page 365)
2. d (Pages 364–368) Options A, B, and C are all false.
3. b (Pages 363–364)
4. c (Pages 386–387) While no single style of parenting is
correct for every situation, the abdication of responsibility inherent in the *Pal* model is thought by most
social scientists to have serious negative effects.
5. b (Pages 380–381)
6. d (Page 381–382) Option B is probably too dramatic;
after all, babies who cry for no apparent reason are
probably more normal than babies who don't.
7. a (Pages 383–384) Option A is a good summary statement of what is considered the most effective way of
modifying adolescent behavior. Options B and (particularly) C would be much less successful. Option D
is partially correct. Many of a child's habits are
formed prior to adolescence, but that shouldn't sug-

**Lesson 18 – One Plus One Equals Three**

gest that the child doesn't need continued guidance in dealing with new situations.

8. d (Page 316) While a belief in corporal punishment (Option B) can contribute to child abuse, it is not sufficient on its own to cause it. Likewise, loss of a job (Option A) may trigger abuse in some situations, but unemployment is not considered a *cause* of abuse. Hostile feelings toward children (Option C)—though they can, of course, get out of hand—are normal and virtually universal. All in all, OptionD is the best explanation.

9. c (Page 317)
10. c (Page 388)

**Lesson 19 – For Richer or Poorer**

1. b (Telecourse guide)
2. d (Telecourse guide)
3. c (Telecourse guide) While most couples experience a decline in income after they retire (Option D), cost-of-living increases built into Social Security payments did a better job of keeping pace with inflation than did earned income over the past ten years. Families with older children, on the other hand, must face soaring college tuition costs, young adults forced to live at home because of a lack of work, and often the added expense of caring for their own aging parents.
4. d (Pages 594–595) The other options *might* be plausible under certain circumstances, but none is anywhere near as likely to help as the steps in Option D.
5. a (Telecourse guide)
6. d (Page 594)
7. c (Page 594)
8. c (Television program)
9. c (Telecourse guide)
10. d (Telecourse guide and Television program) Most other industrialized countries far outstrip the U.S. in the attention they give to the needs of families, but that's not a reason to change by itself, and there's no indication that improving our policies would strengthen political ties (Option A). And while there is a clear need to deal with the elderly's full range of needs, the reason for doing so is not simply to free people from worry (Option B). Option C is incorrect; many people would say that a comprehensive policy

should *not* include development of just one concept of the American family. However, the long-term costs—both financial and societal—of avoiding the difficult problems families face are becoming increasingly obvious. In light of not only soaring social welfare costs, but an awareness that something is happening to the very social fabric around which we order our lives, Option D is the most appropriate response.

1. b (Page 526) Option A is usually true about the birth of a child—but it need not be true, and it is not the determining factor here. It's the predictability that counts, the fact that such an event is common in the lives of most people—unlike, for example, having one's house demolished by a tornado. That is something few people experience and almost no one anticipates or plans for. Transitions do, by the way, cause disruption to everyday life (Option C).

2. a (Page 527)
3. b (Page 527)
4. c (Page 529–530)
5. d (Pages 526–529)
6. b (Pages 533–534)
7. a (Page 537)
8. a (Pages 541–542) Options B, C, and D are not helpful and are all potentially damaging—though B is a natural response that most people have at some point. It is necessary to get beyond denial, however, to realistic acceptance of the situation. Option A may sound like an attitude of helplessness, but in reality it is just a way of saying, "Look, no one is to blame here—let's just get on with things and do what we can." Thus, it's a first step toward constructive coping.
9. d (Box 16.1, page 528)
10. b (Pages 542–543) Option A, in fact, could be detrimental. It is true that how a family defines a crisis is important; but remember, that doesn't mean that denying feelings or minimizing another's fears or frustrations will be helpful. It's how people really feel that counts—not the face they show the world. Options C and D would both be harmful. Blame (Option C) is always destructive—both to the person blamed, and to the family as a whole. And crisis is a

**Lesson 20 – Turning Points**

time of change. Trying to keep everything the same is likely to produce only frustration. Riding with the change, and exploring new, promising alternatives is generally a better means of coping.

**Lesson 21 – The Strained Knot**

1. a (Pages 546–550)

2. c (Pages 546–550)

3. b (Pages 546–550) Psychologists do not recommend divorce as an inherently creative approach to solving problems. The point is that for some people, it is one way of reorganizing following a crisis. Whether it's the right approach is an individual decision that must be based on specific circumstances.

4. c (Pages 542–543 and entire lesson)

5. d (Page 546 and entire lesson) Option B may appear correct, but couldn't be more misleading. The last thing Arnie needs to do is compound his troubles by hiding his true feelings from his wife. Through open communication—admitting his fears, doubts, and guilt—he may find he's more capable of dealing with the problem than he thinks.

6. a (Page 546)

7. b (Page 546)

8. a (Page 546 and entire lesson) Adaptable families—who generally meet crises better than less adaptable families—allow democratic decision-making. If Holly feels she has a problem, then she has one. Ignoring it (Option D) certainly provides no kind of solution; it simply imposes someone else's definition of the problem on Holly. Options B and C are probably not as helpful as A since they take all responsibility for decision-making out of Holly's hands—and this can result in diminished self-concept for Holly, and blocked communication within the family.

9. b (Page 548) Many factors influence projections about kinship networks. On the one hand, needs for support—financial, emotional, child-care—are all increasing, at all levels of society. Thus, the kinship network is enjoying a kind of resurgence. On the other hand, the declining birth rate, high divorce rate, and general mobility of our society work against establishment of strong kinship networks, making it likely that in the future many families who wish to have kinship support will find it lacking.

10. c   (Pages 543–549 and entire lesson) No one escapes crisis totally, yet it is unrealistic to say that we're all embroiled in crisis all the time (Option D). Life is stressful, to be sure, but there is a distinction between everyday stress and true crisis.

1. a   (Page 450)

2. d   (Page 452)

3. c   (Page 451)

4. d   (Page 452)

5. b   (Page 454) There is a positive relationship between marital stability and income up to a certain level. Thus, Couple B is likely to be more stable than Couple C; however, once a certain point is reached, divorce becomes easier because *no* economic interdependence exists (Couple A). For Couple C, economic interdependence may well be a factor; however, it's likely to be overshadowed by the continuing stress of never having sufficient income. If each partner blames the other for this situation, they may very well divorce even if, in a practical sense, that move would be unwise.

6. c   (Page 454) Social scientists who've studied these data tend to agree that working outside the home does not increase the chances of divorce among women who are happily married. However, a woman who is already feeling trapped within an unhappy marriage may well consider divorce if a job provides her the potential for economic freedom.

7. d   (Page 455)

8. d   (Pages 456–457) The important factor seems to be expectations. A couple with very high or unrealistic expectations may be dissatisfied in a marriage that would seem quite fulfilling to a couple with more realistic expectations. In many cases, attitudes seem more significant than the nature of the situation itself in determining long-range stability and satisfaction.

9. a   (Page 458) The point here is that divorce, though sometimes a desirable alternative, is not likely to solve all problems or bring about happiness. Divorced or separated women report strong feelings of stress and depression, and often characterize their lives (for up to five years following divorce) as lone-

**Lesson 22 –
Irreconcilable
Differences**

ly, empty, and discouraging. Option B might be true if Fay were escaping a highly stressful situation—abuse or alcoholism, for example. But that seems not to be the case. Option C is partially correct, in that Fay's problem may not be totally related to the marriage itself. But Option A is still more likely.

10. d (Pages 466–467) Since the no-fault divorce laws, for example, women who have been married less than five years receive no alimony whatever. The movement toward equality has made it more difficult for divorced women to obtain alimony; unfortunately, because of continuing inequities in the workplace, women often require financial support—especially if they have children.

**Lesson 23 – Single, Head of Household**

1. b (Page 468) The figures are slightly higher for black children; but the overall percentage is about 60 percent.
2. d (Pages 471–472)
3. a (Pages 477–478) There is some truth in B, but it is inaccurate to say that lowered self-esteem is inevitable. It *is* likely without the strong, consistent support of both parents. Many children do feel guilty, depressed, or angry (though OptionC exaggerates), but most adjust well in the long term if parents cooperate during and after the divorce, and if the child has the opportunity to retain contact with the noncustodial parent. Option D might be true in some cases, but would be the exception.
4. d (Pages 468–470)
5. d (Pages 464–466) Divorce may be costly enough to precipitate a true financial crisis for a family; and this factor should be carefully considered before a couple decides to go through with a divorce. No-fault divorce (Option B) has little to do with the financial costs of divorce.
6. a (Page 486) Two factors are important: whether the parents divorce, and whether they approve or disapprove of divorce (apart from their own actions). Both factors are highly influential.
7. b (Pages 478–479) This is a complex issue, and one where generalities are difficult to apply. The trend is to award custody to the father in a growing number of cases, but usually this occurs with the mother's

consent. Mothers still receive custody in about 90 percent of all cases. Still, fathers who fight for custody are granted custody in about a third of all such cases; and that's different from what we've witnessed in previous decades.

8.  c  (Pages 479–480) It's the closeness of the relationship that counts here, not the economic or employment status of the parent (Option D). Research indicates that children who do not maintain a closeness with the noncustodial parent may suffer setbacks in achieving lasting emotional adjustment.

9.  d  (Pages 462–464)

10. a  (Pages 462–464) In fact, psychologists advise against Options B, C, and D—all are potentially harmful because they tend to bind the divorced person to the past instead of clearing the way to the future. Option B is alright once the period of initial grief and mourning is over, but suppression of feelings, even through work, is unhealthy emotionally.


1.  b  (Page 494)

2.  a  (Page 502)

3.  c  (Pages 495–496)

4.  d  (Page 495) Remarriage rates are higher for divorced women than for widowed women. Further, about 64 percent of white women remarry following divorce, while fewer than 46 percent of black women and 55 percent of Hispanic women remarry.

5.  a  (Pages 500–501) Betty's education is likely to be a plus, as isher professional status. However, two big factors work against her here: her age (women over 30 have a very difficult time finding a remarriage partner) and the fact she has children—many men do not want the emotional or financial responsibility of raising someone else's children.

6.  d  (Pages 501–502) In fact, this tendency toward heterogamous marriage is thought by some social psychologists to be one factor contributing to the relative instability of second marriages.

7.  c  (Pages 502–505) While Option D raises an interesting issue, it is generally safe to conclude that most second marriages tend to be less stable than first marriages—for a number of reasons. Second marriages can be better, though, if experience matures

## Lesson 24 – The Second Time Around

the partners so that they are more realistic in their expectations, tend to assess what they can bring to a marriage (not just what they can get out of it), and base their compatibility on significant factors such as common values rather than on more superficial likes and dislikes (e.g., cats, sports). There is little evidence of a mature attitude on Greg's part, nor of a desire to be highly supportive of his new wife.

8.  a  (Page 499)
9.  a  (Page 510)
10.  b  (Page 521)

**Lesson 25 – Yours, Mine, and Ours**

1.  b  (Page 511)
2.  a  (Pages 513–514)
3.  c  (Page 512)
4.  b  (Pages 513–516)
5.  d  (Page 514)
6.  a  (Pages 514–515) Stepparents feel that they are expected to love stepchildren in much the same way they would love their biological children—and often, they simply do not. Stepchildren, by the way, feel the same pressures and conflicts. In short, Ed's feelings are not at all unusual.
7.  a  (Page 515)
8.  d  (Page 516–517)
9.  b  (Page 517) Options A, C, and D could all be true, of course, but none is as likely as Option B. This is a common experience for stepfathers, who go through a period of difficult adjustment, and who—because of the stress and persistent role conflicts—may wonder whether they're really doing a good job. For the stepfather who lacks a strong emotional bond with his stepchildren, such feelings are likely to be intensified, perhaps by guilt.
10.  c  (Pages 5181–519) Options A, B, and D are likely to cause more troubles than they'll resolve. In fact, most social psychologists recommend seeing partners in a variety of circumstances and observing their interactions with one's children (Option A), not to mention the importance of helping future stepchildren get to know one another. Similarly, motives for marriage (Option B) should be fully and carefully explored to avoid misunderstandings later. Option D isn't realistic, either. Doubts and frustrations are part of enter-

ing a second marriage, especially one that involves stepchildren. Acknowledging them makes them easier to deal with. Psychologists recommend accepting such doubts as normal, and being patient with ourselves in dealing with them.

1. b   ("Vintage Years," page 395)
2. a   ("Vintage Years," page 397)
3. d   ("Vintage Years," pages 380–381; "Families," page 372) Options A, B, and C are all myths that recent research generally debunks.
4. c   ("Families," pages 372–373) Option D would be an exaggeration. Old age does take its toll; but Options A and B overstate the case dramatically. The majority of older persons in Warren's age group are able to carry out most everyday activities with only minimal support or assistance—despite some increase in illness or disability.
5. d   ("Families," pages 373–374) Option C is incorrect; formal care facilities, though important, have in no way supplanted the family as primary caregivers.
6. b   ("Families," pages 376–378) Options C and D have no basis in research. In fact, research indicates that families do care for their older members, and that older persons prefer the care provided by families to what they might obtain from a social service—which is often viewed as a last resort, even when staffed by caring, qualified professionals. Option A is true to a degree for some families, but is not the typical problem. Many older people have sufficient income to more than offset any financial burden; the bigger problem by far is simply finding the time and energy to provide the care required—especially when grown children are caring for young children of their own, holding down jobs, or traveling long distances to provide needed care.
7. b   ("Never Too Late," page 383) Options A, C, and D are all false. Option D raises an important point. Seniors do typically care a great deal about companionship; that doesn't mean, however, that they lose interest in sex. Of particular importance is the physical closeness with another human being mentioned in Option B. This can also be acquired through other relationships—with grandchildren, for instance—

**Lesson 26 – The Later Years**

but is definitely an important factor in giving sexual intimacy the value it has for older daters.

8. d ("Never Too Late," page 382)

9. a ("PARENT/Grandparent," page 387) Option D may be part of the picture, too; however, not every child who grows up with a hired caregiver has lost all touch with grandparents. Some grandparents may be physically unable to care for children (especially in the children's very early years), but may still be important figures in their lives.

10. c ("PARENT/Grandparent," pages 388–389)